BY

by LIZ PRINCE

ZEST BOOKS
San Francisco

ZEST BOOKS

FOR YOUNG ADULTS OF ALL AGES.

35 Stillman Street, Suite 121
San Francisco, CA 94107
www.zestbooks.net

CONNECT WITH ZEST!

zestbooks.net/blog
zestbooks.net/contests
twitter.com/zestbooks
facebook.com/zestbook
facebook.com/BooksWithATwist
pinterest.com/zestbooks

Nonfiction / Biography & Autobiography / Art
Library of Congress data available
ISBN: 978-1-936976-55-3

Design by Liz Prince and Adam Grano

Manufactured in the U.S.A.
DOC 10 9 8 7 6 5 4
4500512520

This book is dedicated to these strong women:

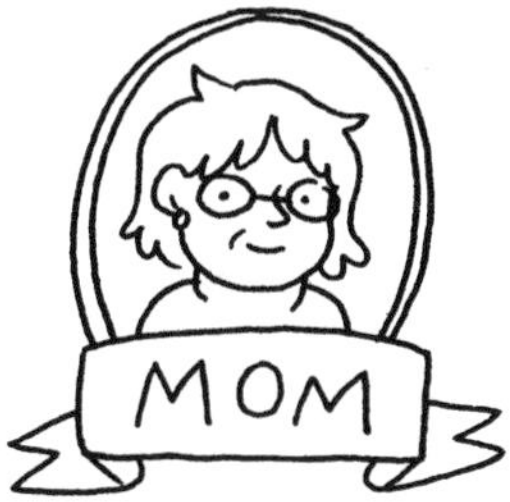
MOM

My mom, Linda Prince, who raised three strong-willed kids and treated us all with support, understanding, and respect.

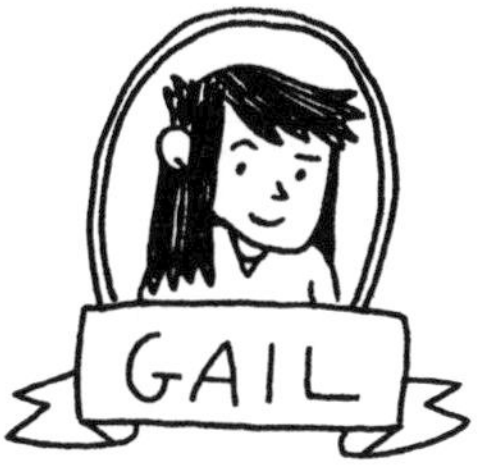
GAIL

Gail Snyder, who taught me to look more closely at the hard things in life: they're trying to tell you something if you'll listen.

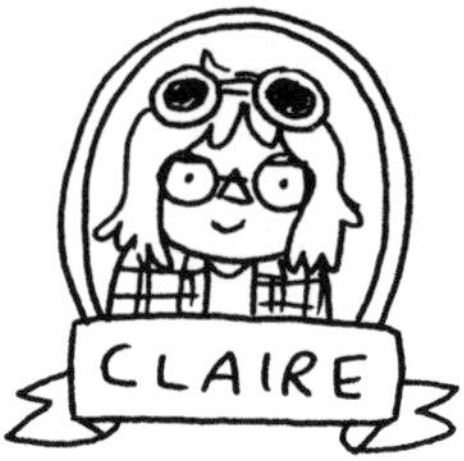
CLAIRE

Claire Sanders, who faced cancer with sass and humor, and continues to laugh her way through what life throws at her.

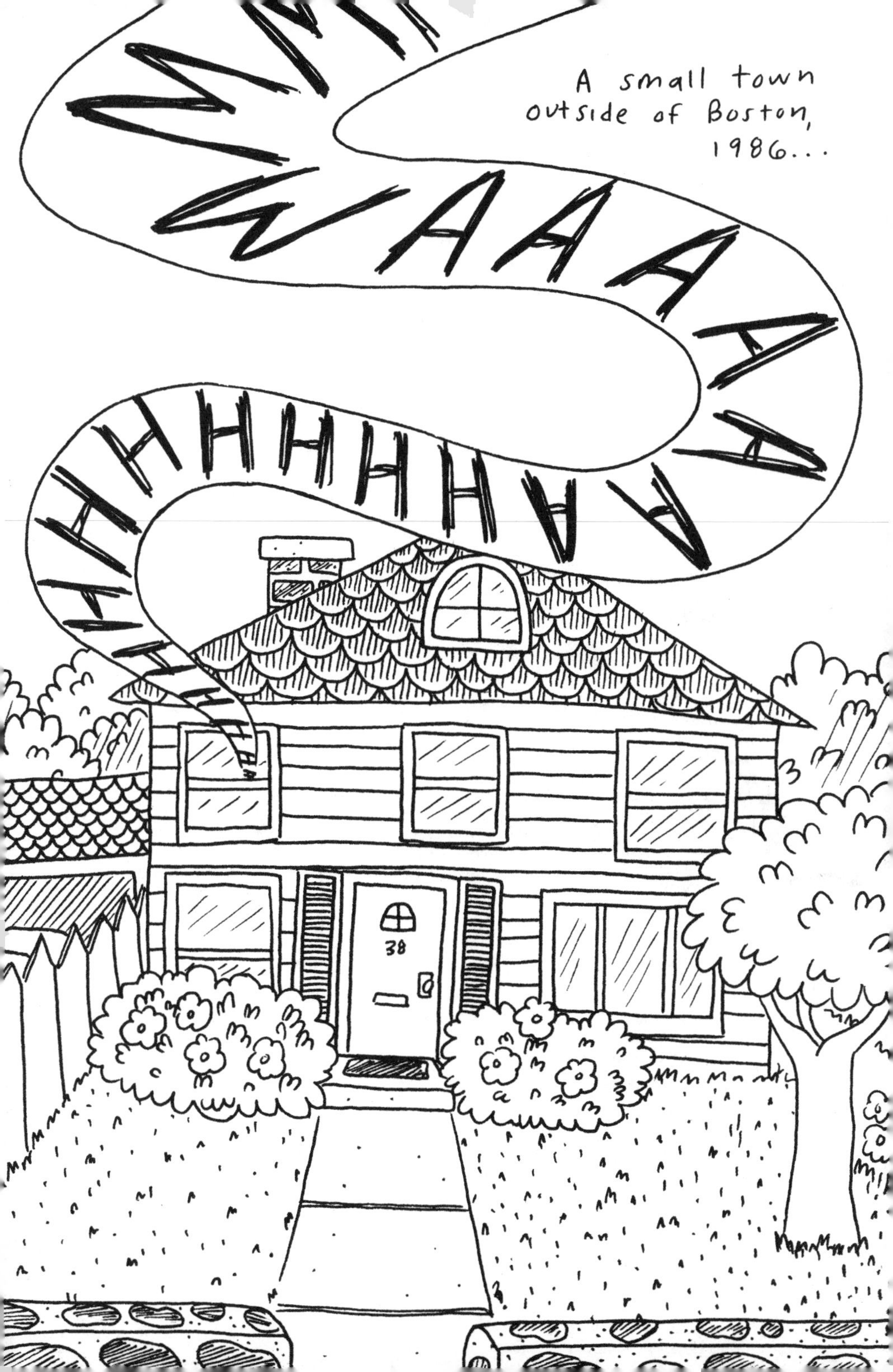
WWWWAAAAAAHHHHHHHHHHHHH
A small town outside of Boston, 1986...
38

CHAPTER 1

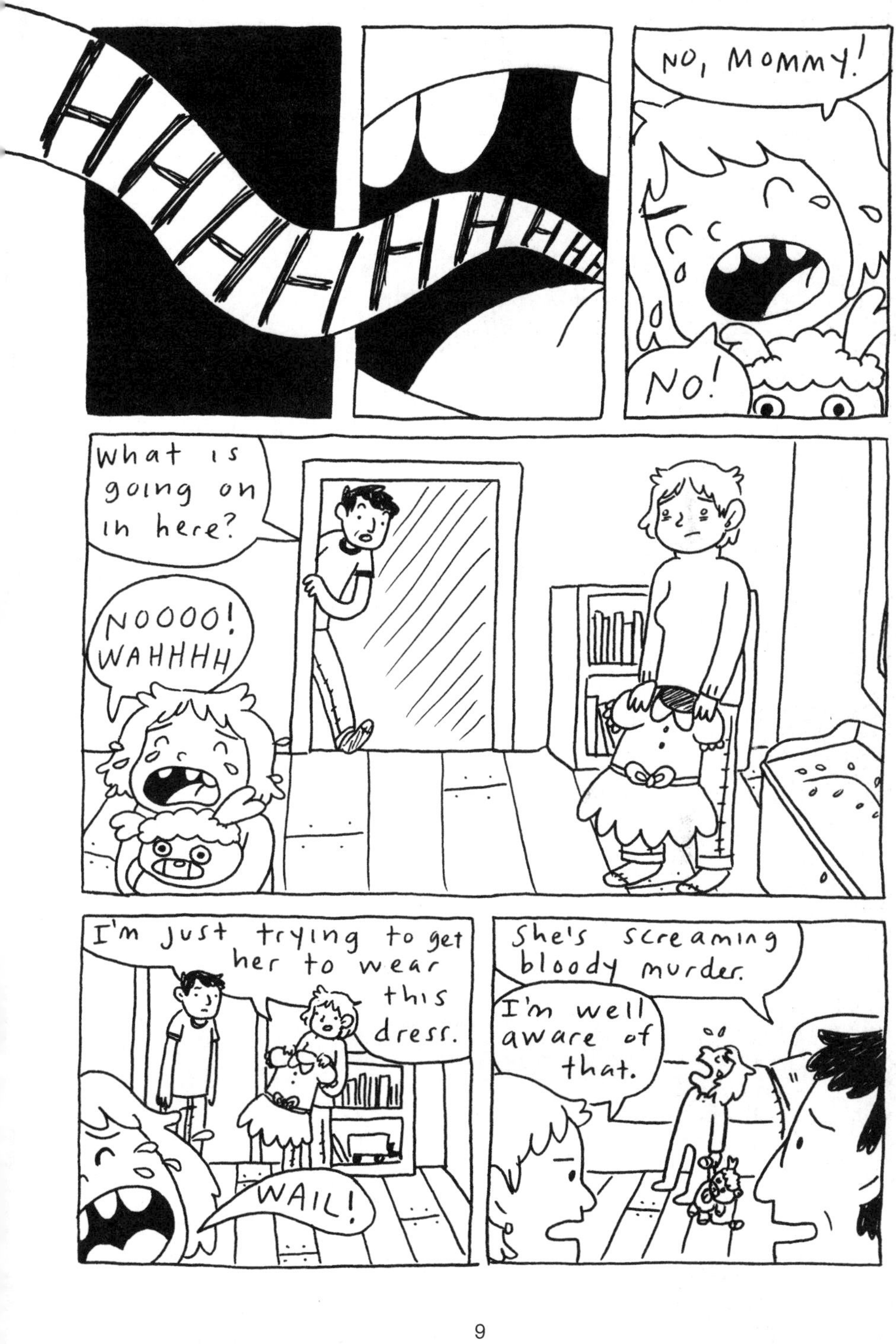
HHHHHHHHHHHHHH
NO, MOMMY!
NO!
What is going on in here?
NOOOO! WAHHHH
I'm just trying to get her to wear this dress.
WAIL!
She's screaming bloody murder.
I'm well aware of that.

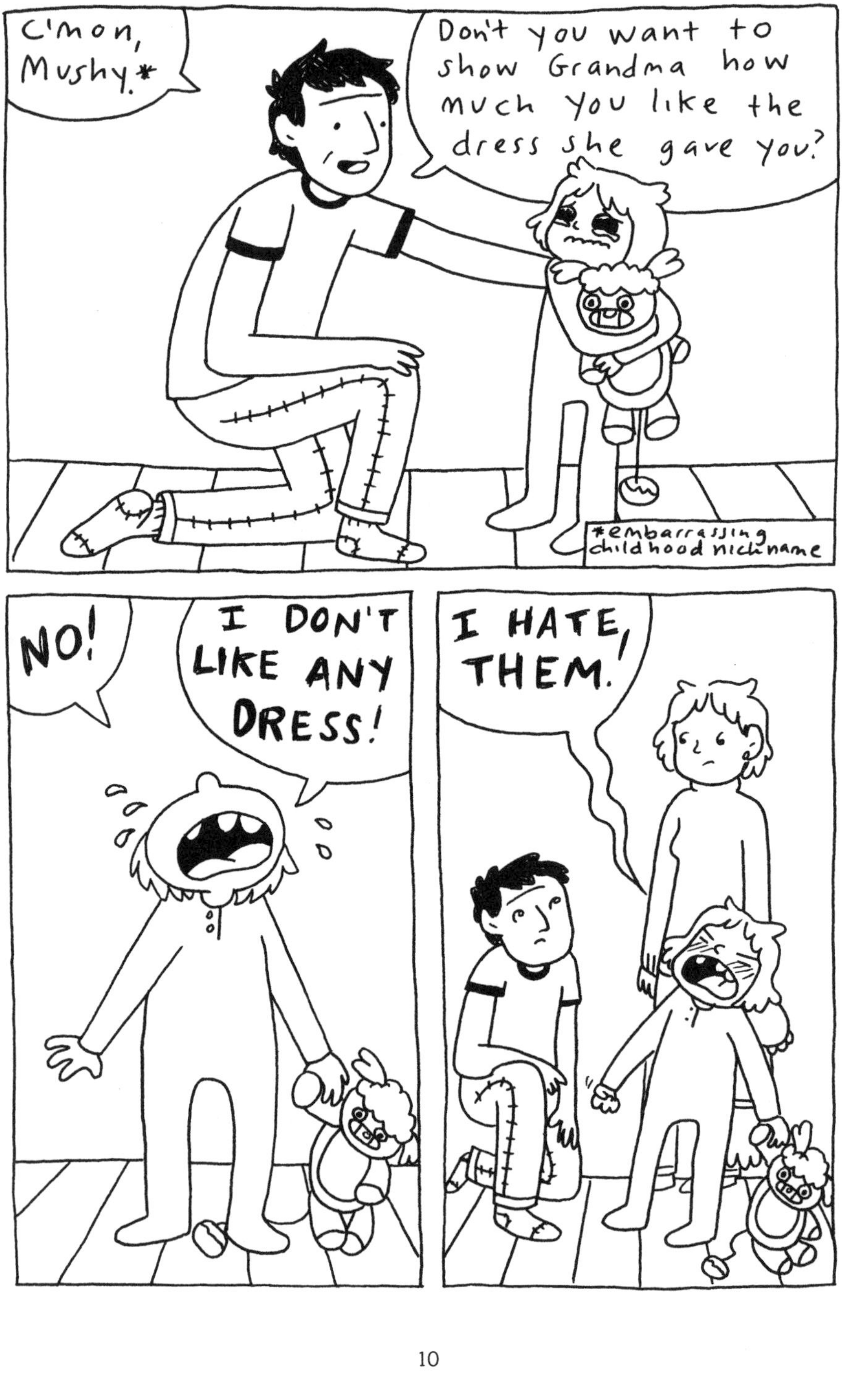
C'mon, Mushy.*
Don't you want to show Grandma how much you like the dress she gave you?
*embarrassing childhood nickname
NO!
I DON'T LIKE ANY DRESS!
I HATE THEM!

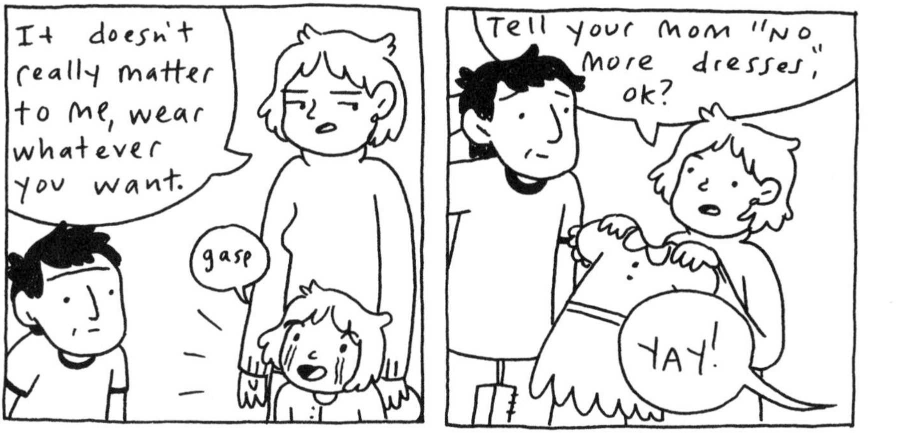
It doesn't really matter to me, wear whatever you want.
gasp
Tell your mom "No more dresses," ok?
YAY!

LIZ PRINCE, TOMBOY, AGE 4

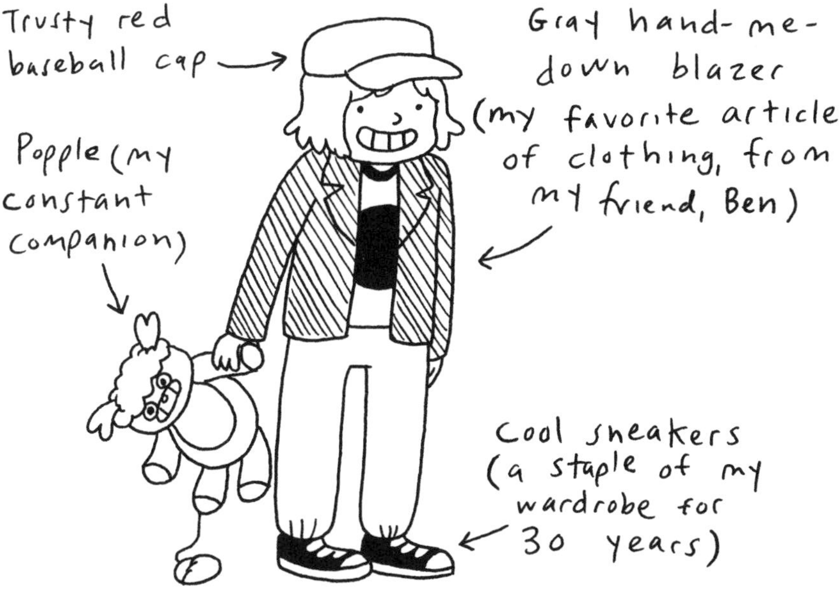
Trusty red baseball cap
Gray hand-me-down blazer (my favorite article of clothing, from my friend, Ben)
Popple (my constant companion)
Cool sneakers (a staple of my wardrobe for 30 years)

General demeanor: totally happy as long as I don't have to wear a dress.

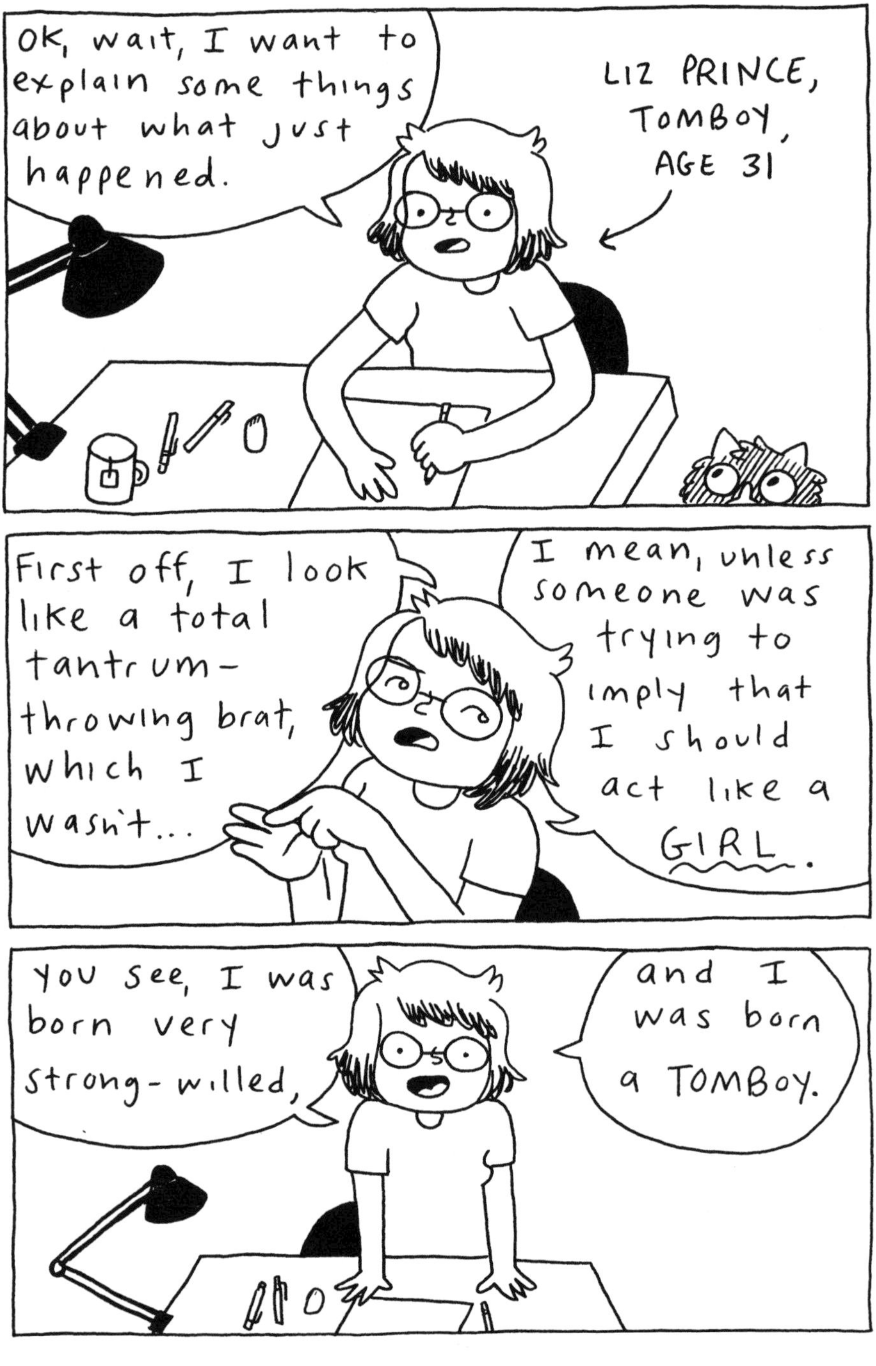
Ok, wait, I want to explain some things about what just happened.
LIZ PRINCE, TOMBOY, AGE 31
First off, I look like a total tantrum-throwing brat, which I wasn't...
I mean, unless someone was trying to imply that I should act like a GIRL.
You see, I was born very strong-willed,
and I was born a TOMBOY.

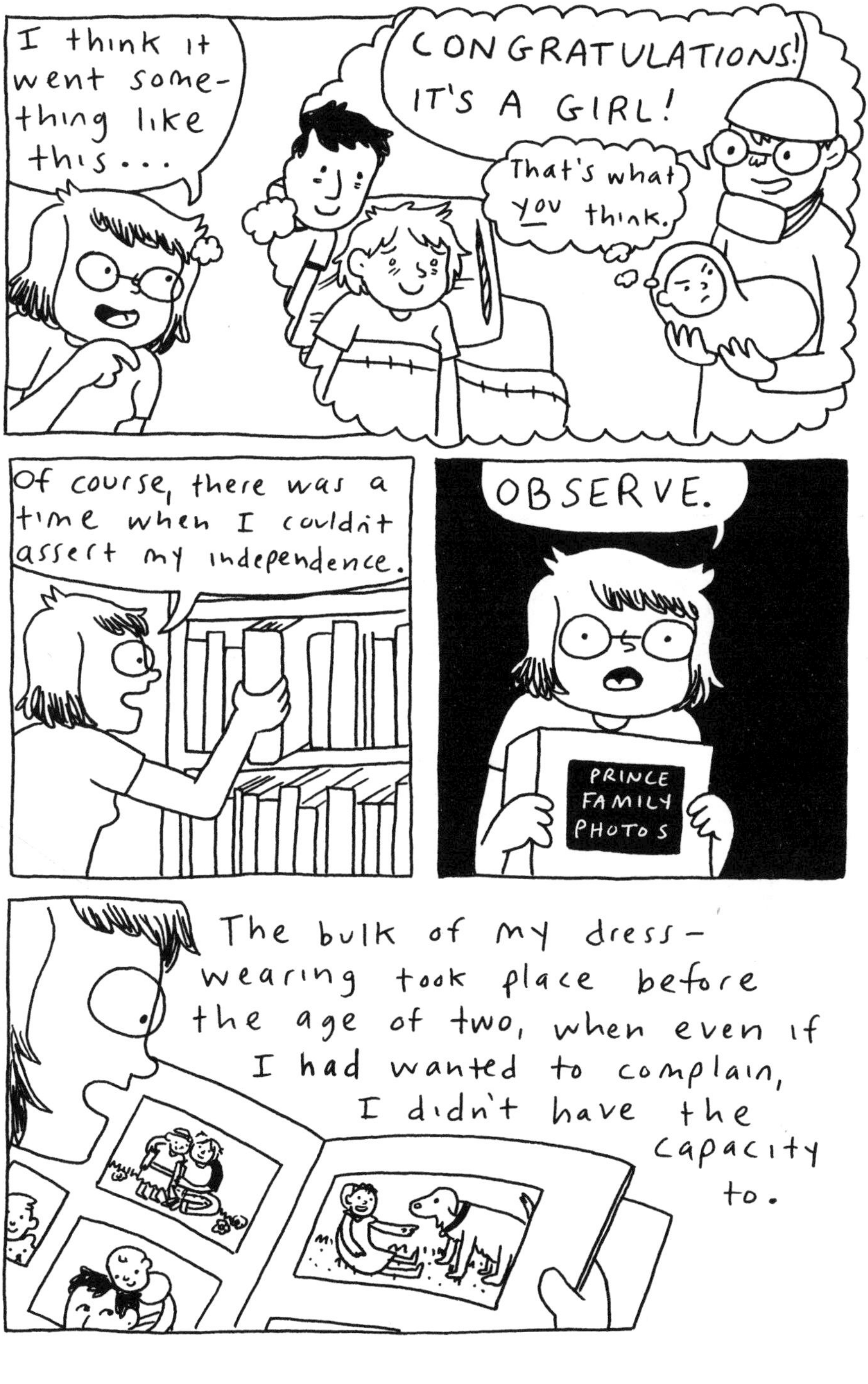
I think it went something like this...
CONGRATULATIONS! IT'S A GIRL!
That's what you think.
Of course, there was a time when I couldn't assert my independence.
OBSERVE.
PRINCE FAMILY PHOTOS
The bulk of my dress-wearing took place before the age of two, when even if I had wanted to complain, I didn't have the capacity to.

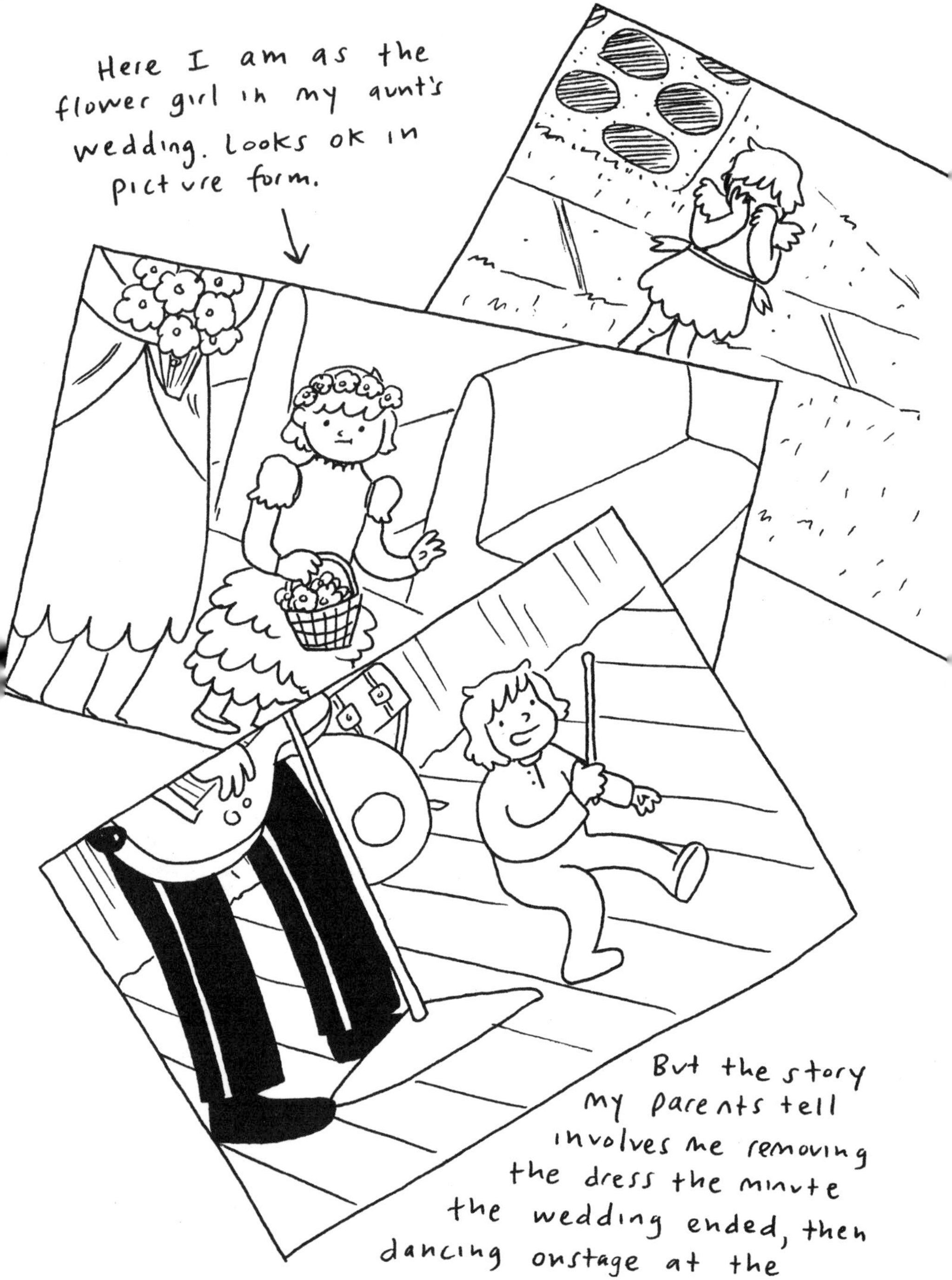
Here I am as the flower girl in my aunt's wedding. Looks ok in picture form.
But the story my parents tell involves me removing the dress the minute the wedding ended, then dancing onstage at the reception in my footy pajamas.

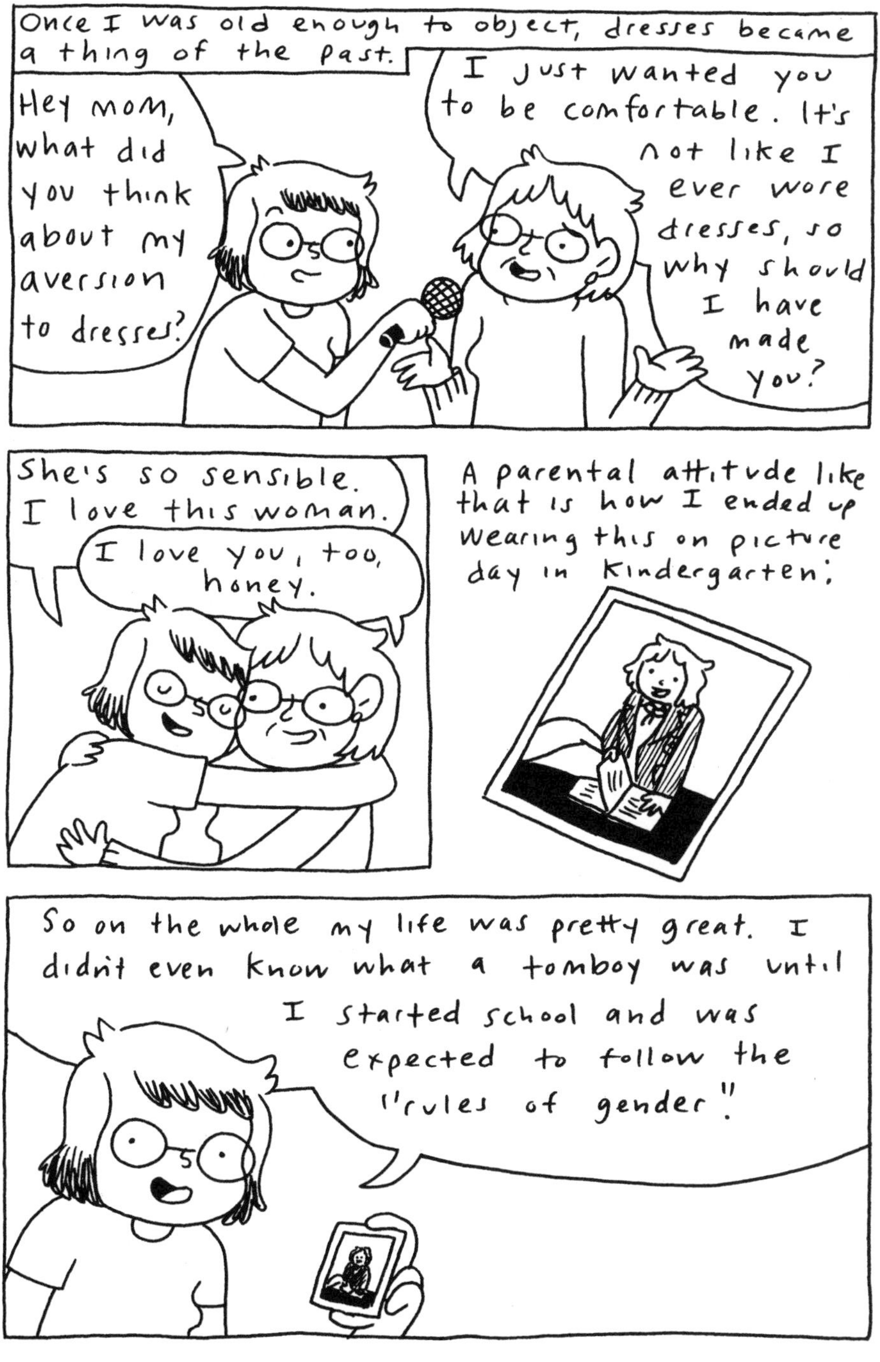
Once I was old enough to object, dresses became a thing of the past.
Hey mom, what did you think about my aversion to dresses?
I just wanted you to be comfortable. It's not like I ever wore dresses, so why should I have made you?
She's so sensible. I love this woman.
I love you, too, honey.
A parental attitude like that is how I ended up wearing this on picture day in kindergarten:
So on the whole my life was pretty great. I didn't even know what a tomboy was until I started school and was expected to follow the "rules of gender."

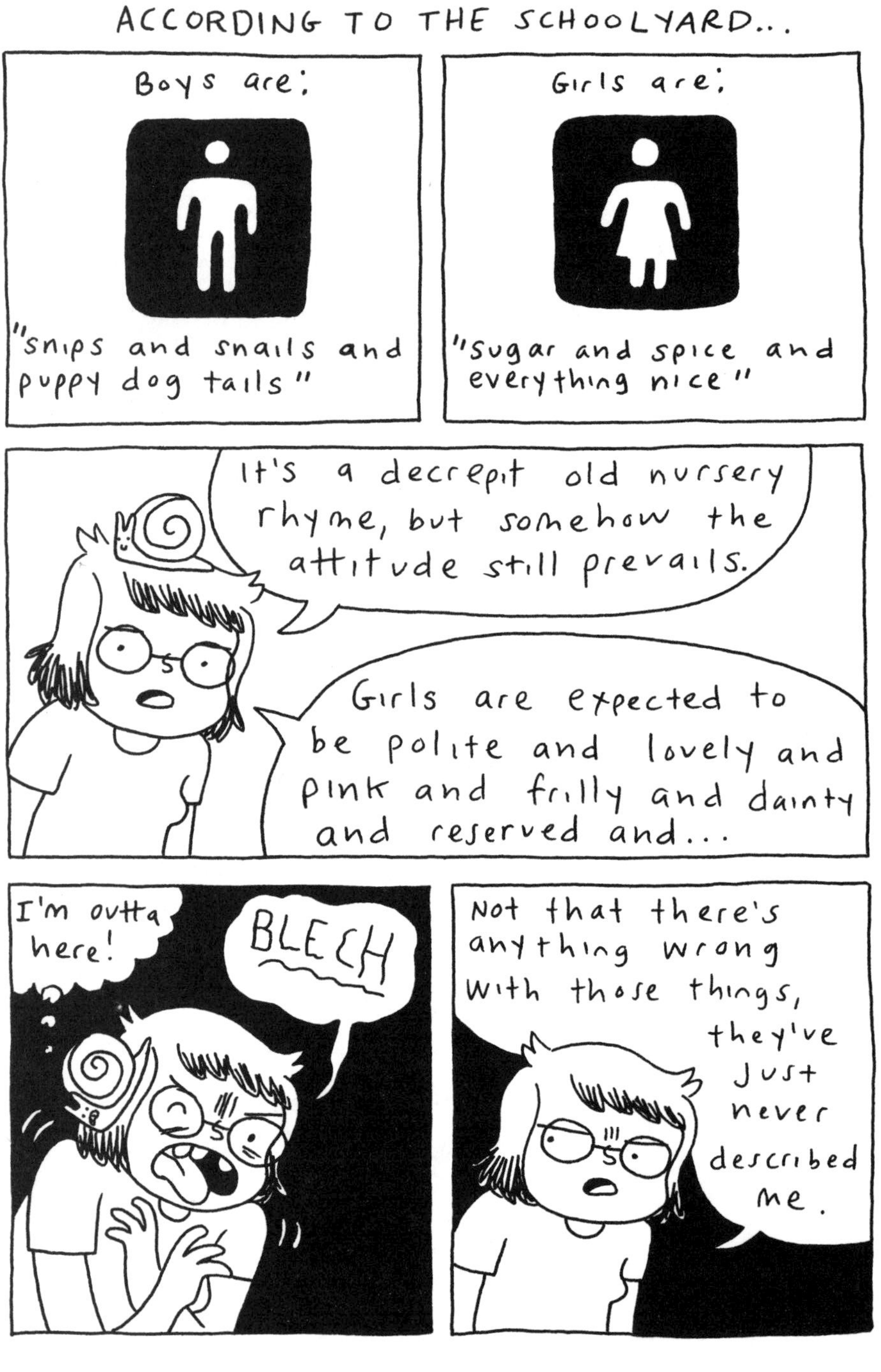
ACCORDING TO THE SCHOOLYARD...
Boys are:
"snips and snails and puppy dog tails"
Girls are:
"sugar and spice and everything nice"
It's a decrepit old nursery rhyme, but somehow the attitude still prevails.
Girls are expected to be polite and lovely and pink and frilly and dainty and reserved and...
I'm outta here!
BLECH
Not that there's anything wrong with those things,
they've just never described me.

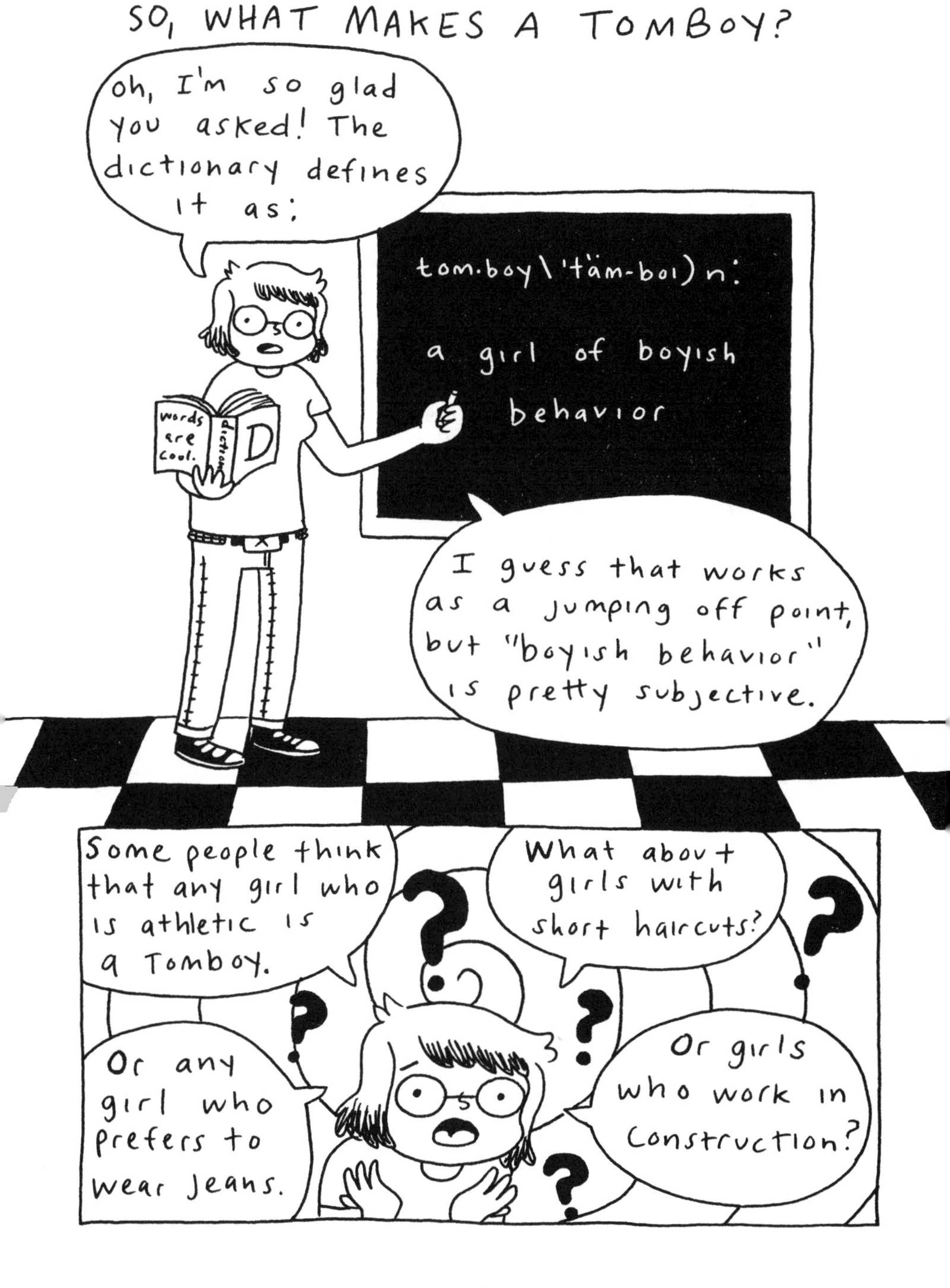
SO, WHAT MAKES A TOMBOY?
Oh, I'm so glad you asked! The dictionary defines it as:
tom.boy \ 'täm-boi) n:
a girl of boyish behavior
words are cool.
dictionary
D
I guess that works as a jumping off point, but "boyish behavior" is pretty subjective.
Some people think that any girl who is athletic is a Tomboy.
What about girls with short haircuts?
Or any girl who prefers to wear jeans.
Or girls who work in construction?

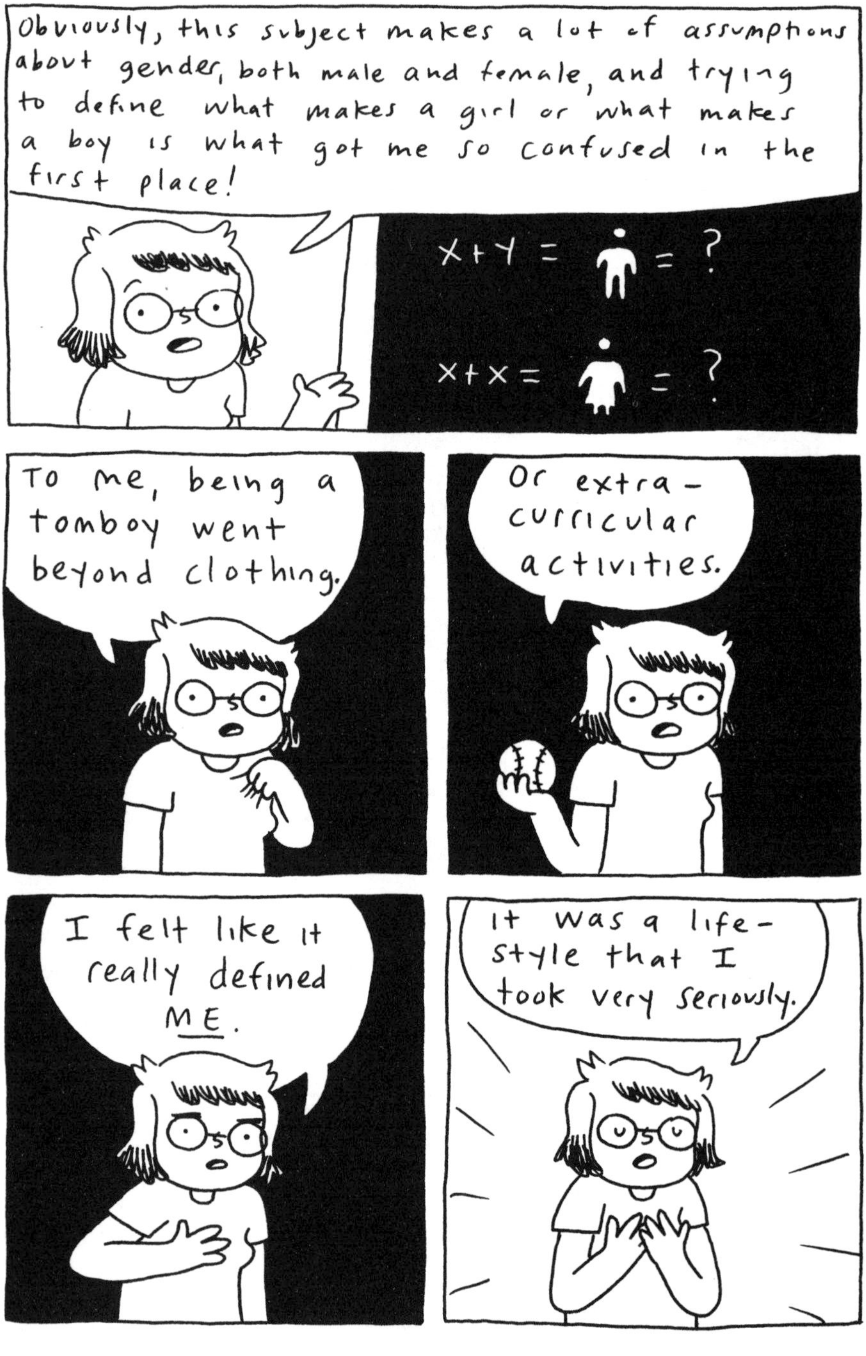
Obviously, this subject makes a lot of assumptions about gender, both male and female, and trying to define what makes a girl or what makes a boy is what got me so confused in the first place!
X+Y = = ?
X+X = = ?
To me, being a tomboy went beyond clothing.
Or extra-curricular activities.
I felt like it really defined ME.
It was a life-style that I took very seriously.

And I felt like I needed to defend it.

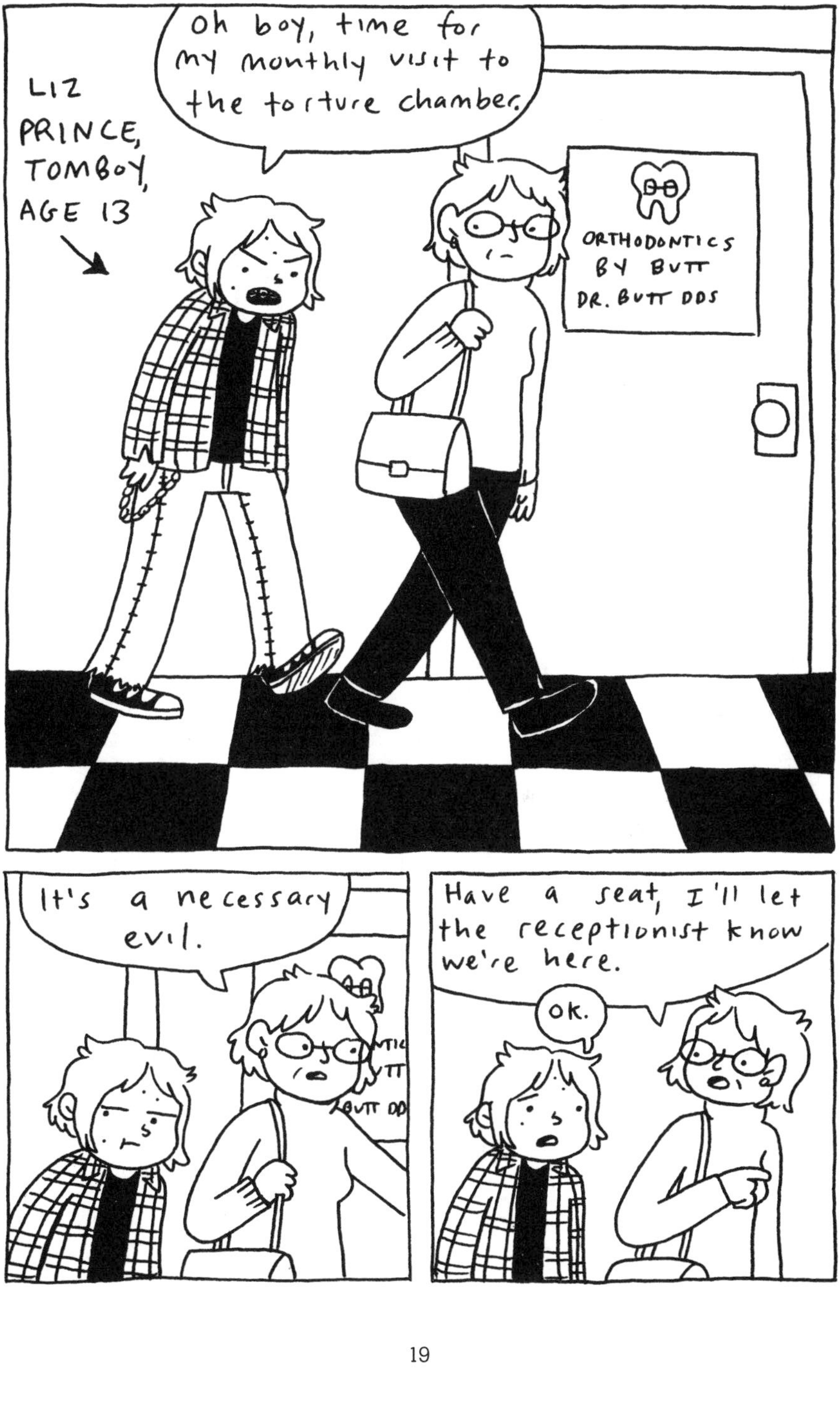
Oh boy, time for my monthly visit to the torture chamber.
LIZ PRINCE, TOMBOY, AGE 13
ORTHODONTICS BY BUTT
DR. BUTT DDS
It's a necessary evil.
Have a seat, I'll let the receptionist know we're here.
OK.

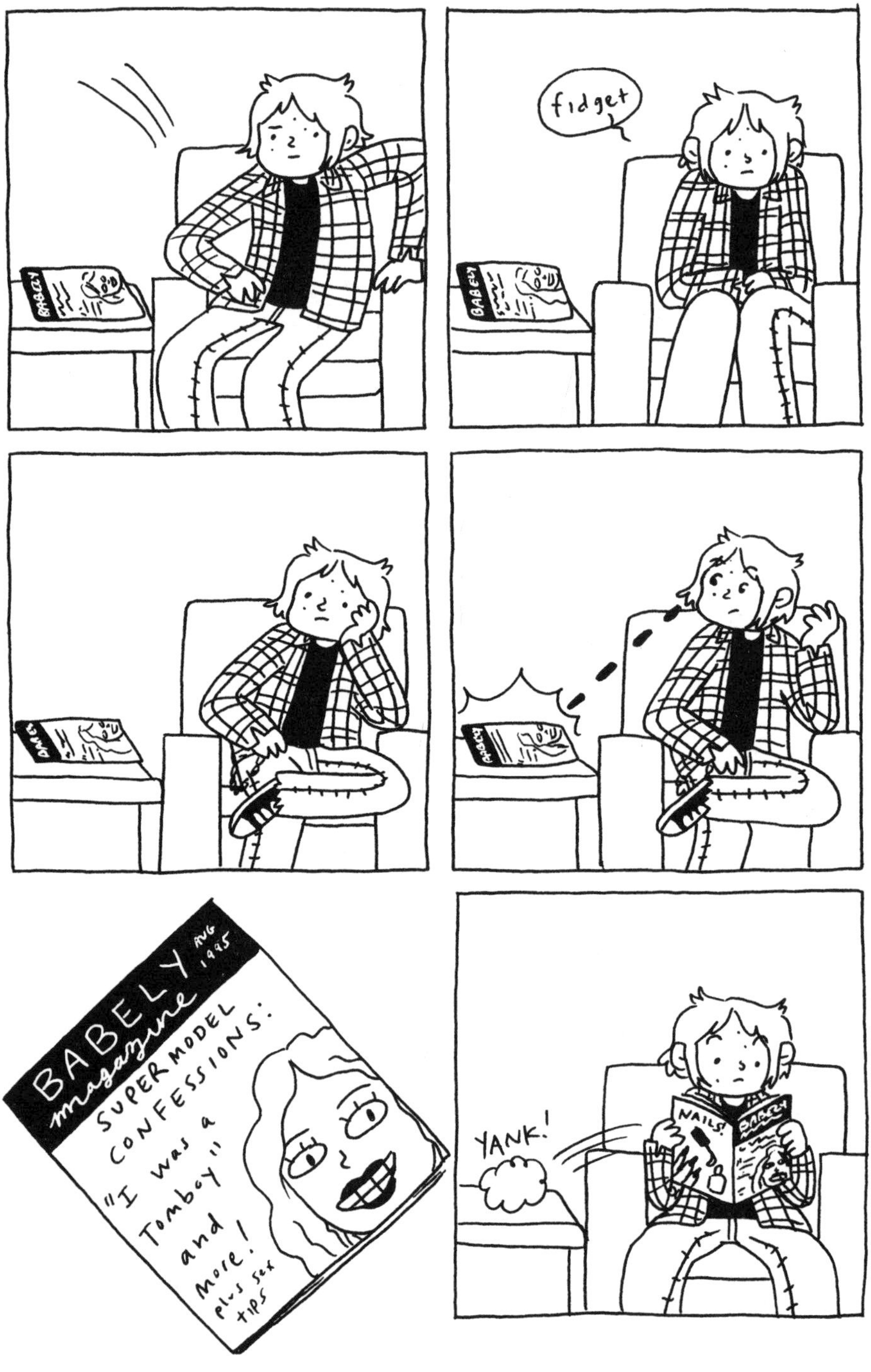
fidget
BABELY magazine
AUG 1995
SUPERMODEL CONFESSIONS:
"I was a Tomboy" and more!
plus sex tips
YANK!
NAILS!

"I was such a tomboy in elementary school! I played soccer, and was even friends with boys! In fact, I was invited to the cutest boy in school's birthday party. I was so excited to wear my favorite purple dress, and my mom did my hair in two long braids. We painted my nails to match! It was so much fun getting dressed up; that was how I discovered my passion for modeling. The boy lived close to me, so I walked to his house, but on the way a bird pooped on my shoulder and ruined my outfit! I ran home and cried and I was so upset that even though I could have worn a different dress, I decided not to go to the party."

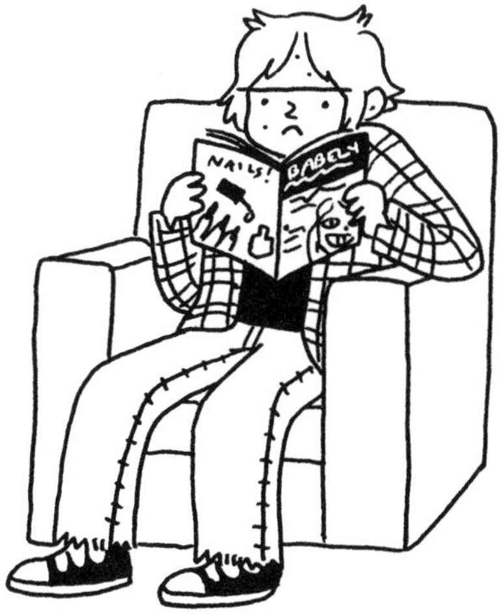
NAILS!
BABELY

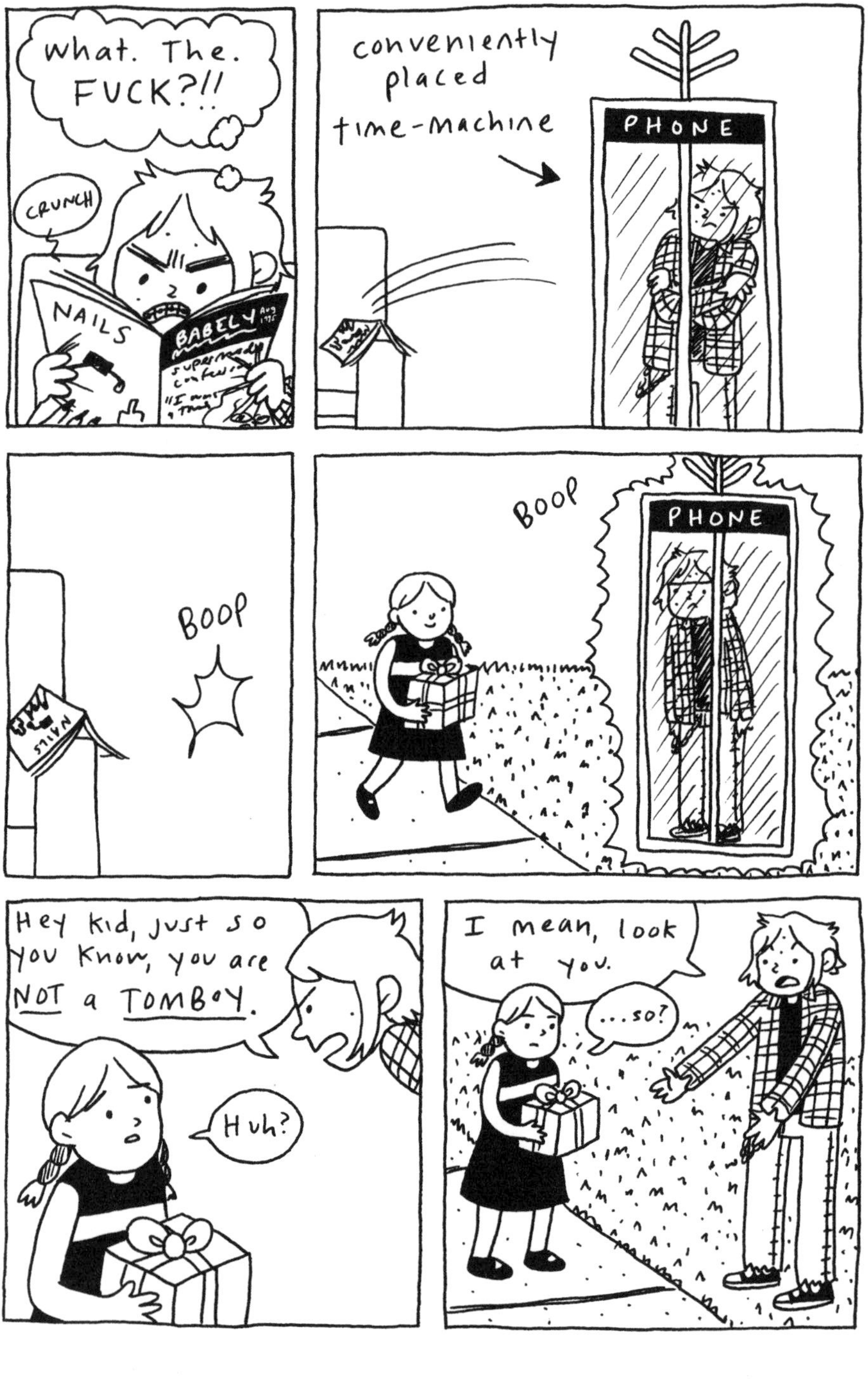

What. The. FUCK?!!
CRUNCH
NAILS
BABELY
conveniently placed time-machine
PHONE
BOOP
BOOP
PHONE
Hey kid, just so you know, you are NOT a TOMBOY.
Huh?
I mean, look at you.
...so?

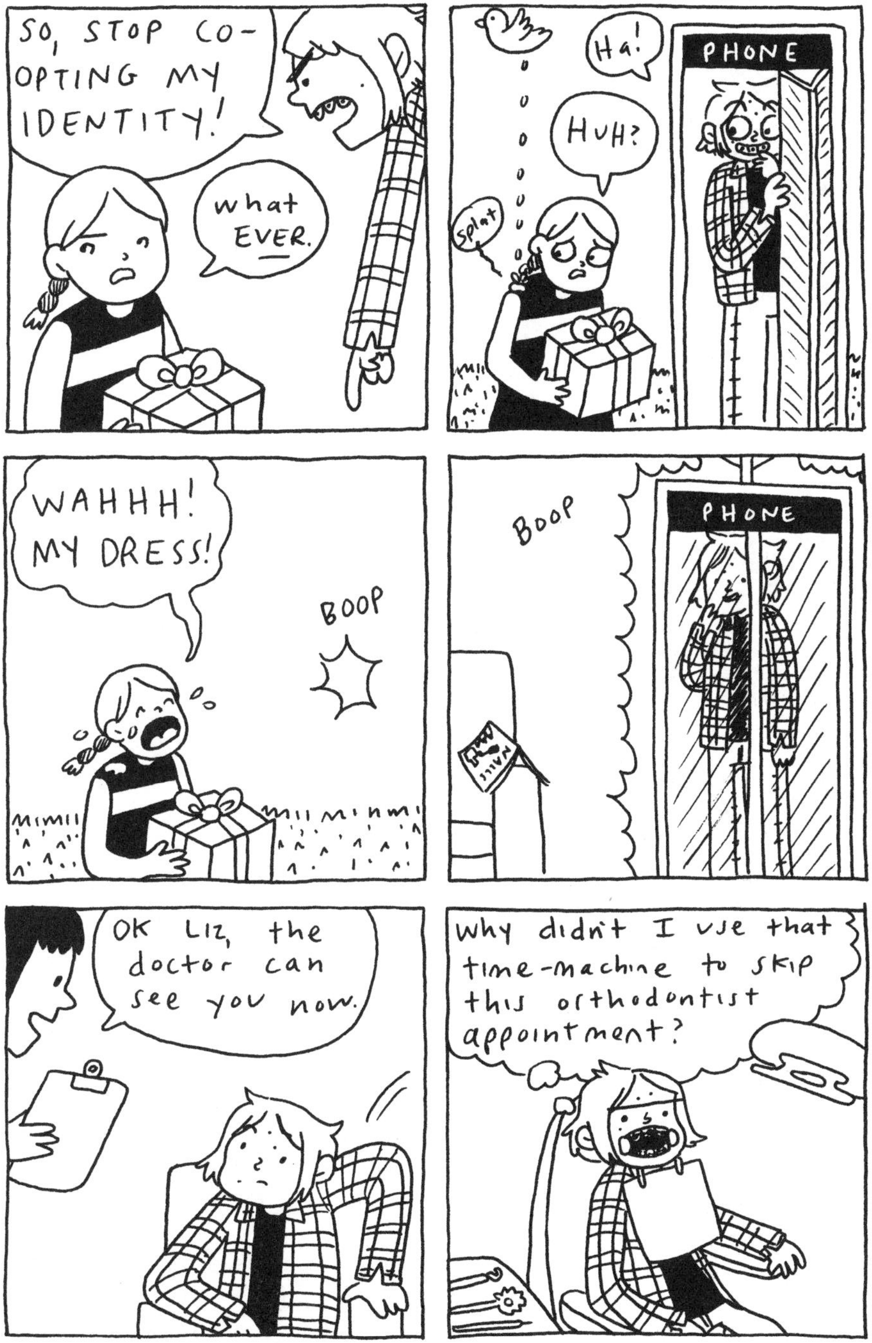
SO, STOP CO-OPTING MY IDENTITY!
what EVER.
Ha!
HUH?
splat
PHONE
WAHHH! MY DRESS!
BOOP
BOOP
PHONE
OK Liz, the doctor can see you now.
Why didn't I use that time-machine to skip this orthodontist appointment?

CHAPTER 2

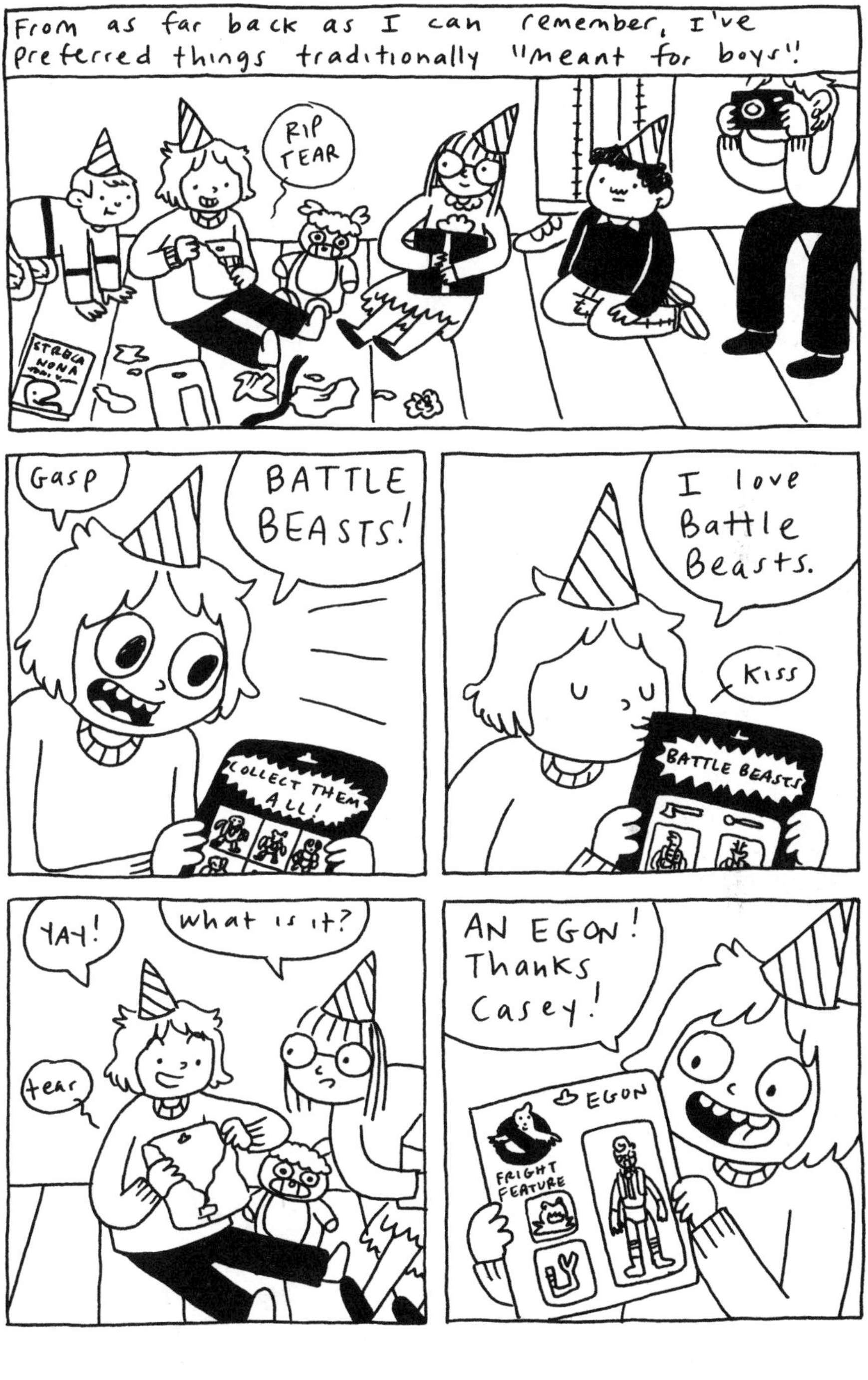
From as far back as I can remember, I've preferred things traditionally "meant for boys"!
RIP TEAR
STREGA NONA
Gasp
BATTLE BEASTS!
COLLECT THEM ALL!
I love Battle Beasts.
KISS
BATTLE BEASTS
YAY!
What is it?
tear
AN EGON! Thanks Casey!
EGON
FRIGHT FEATURE

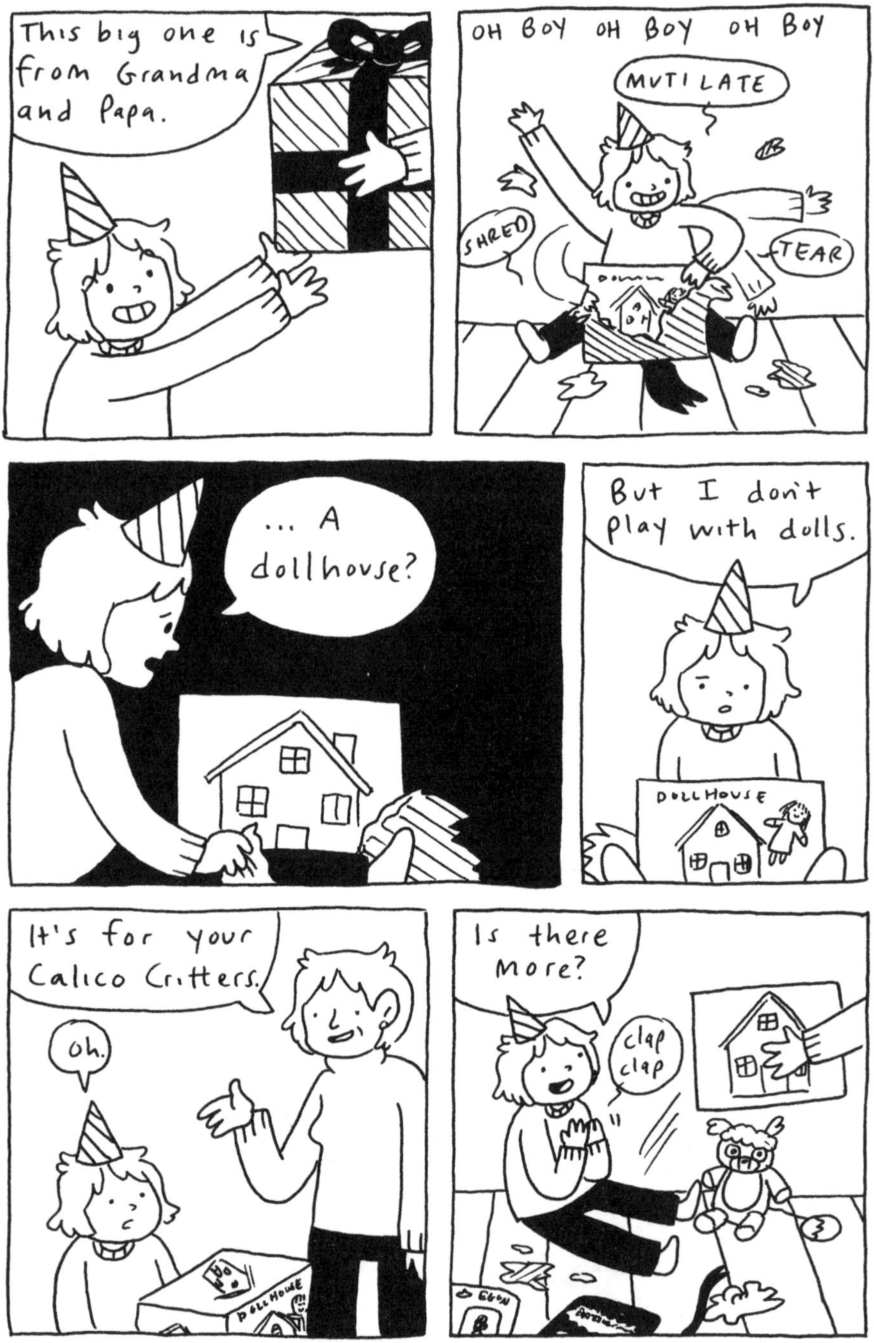
This big one is from Grandma and Papa.
OH BOY OH BOY OH BOY
MUTILATE
SHRED
TEAR
... A dollhouse?
But I don't play with dolls.
DOLLHOUSE
It's for your Calico Critters.
Oh.
DOLLHOUSE
Is there more?
clap clap

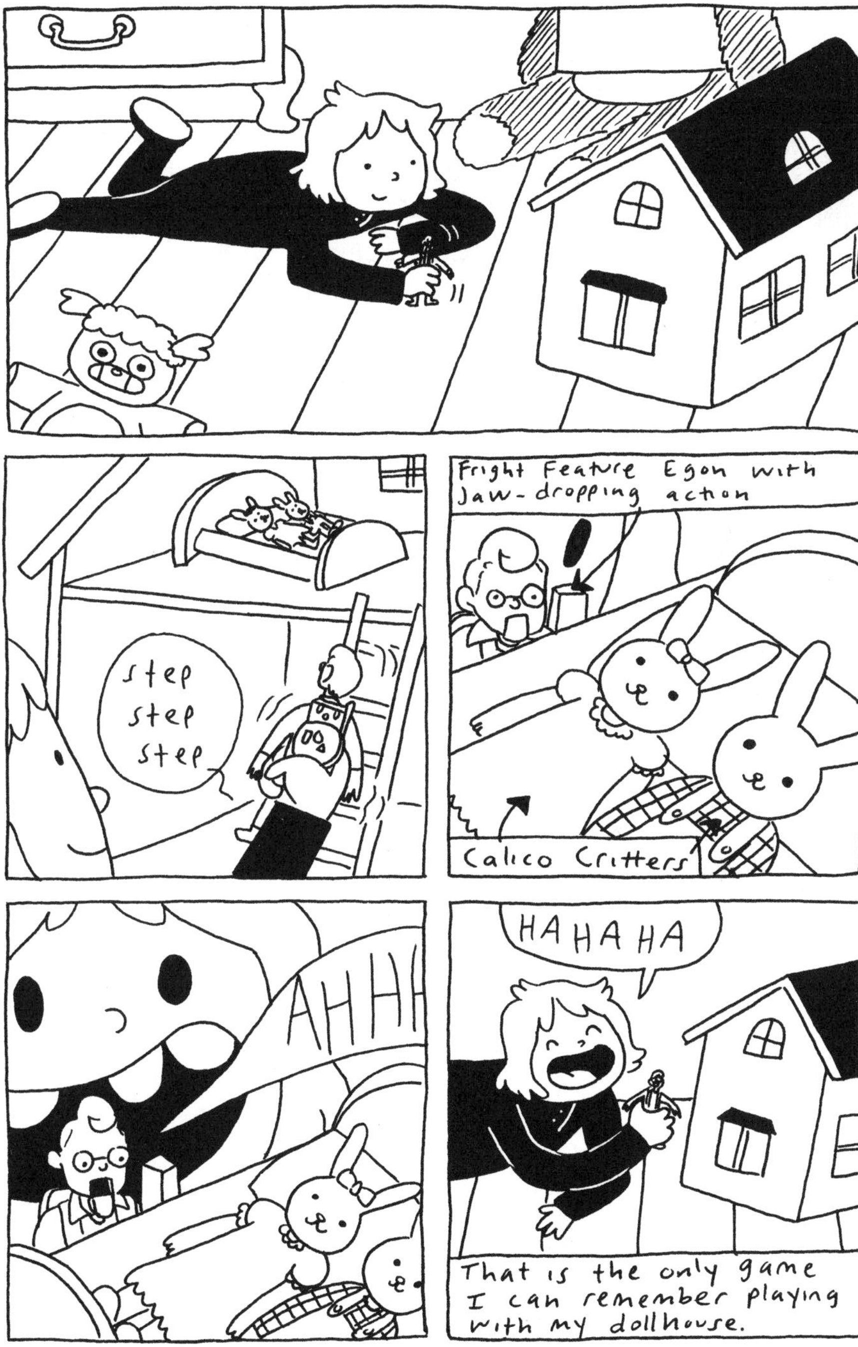
step
step
step
Fright Feature Egon with Jaw-dropping action
Calico Critters
AHHH
HAHAHA
That is the only game I can remember playing with my dollhouse.

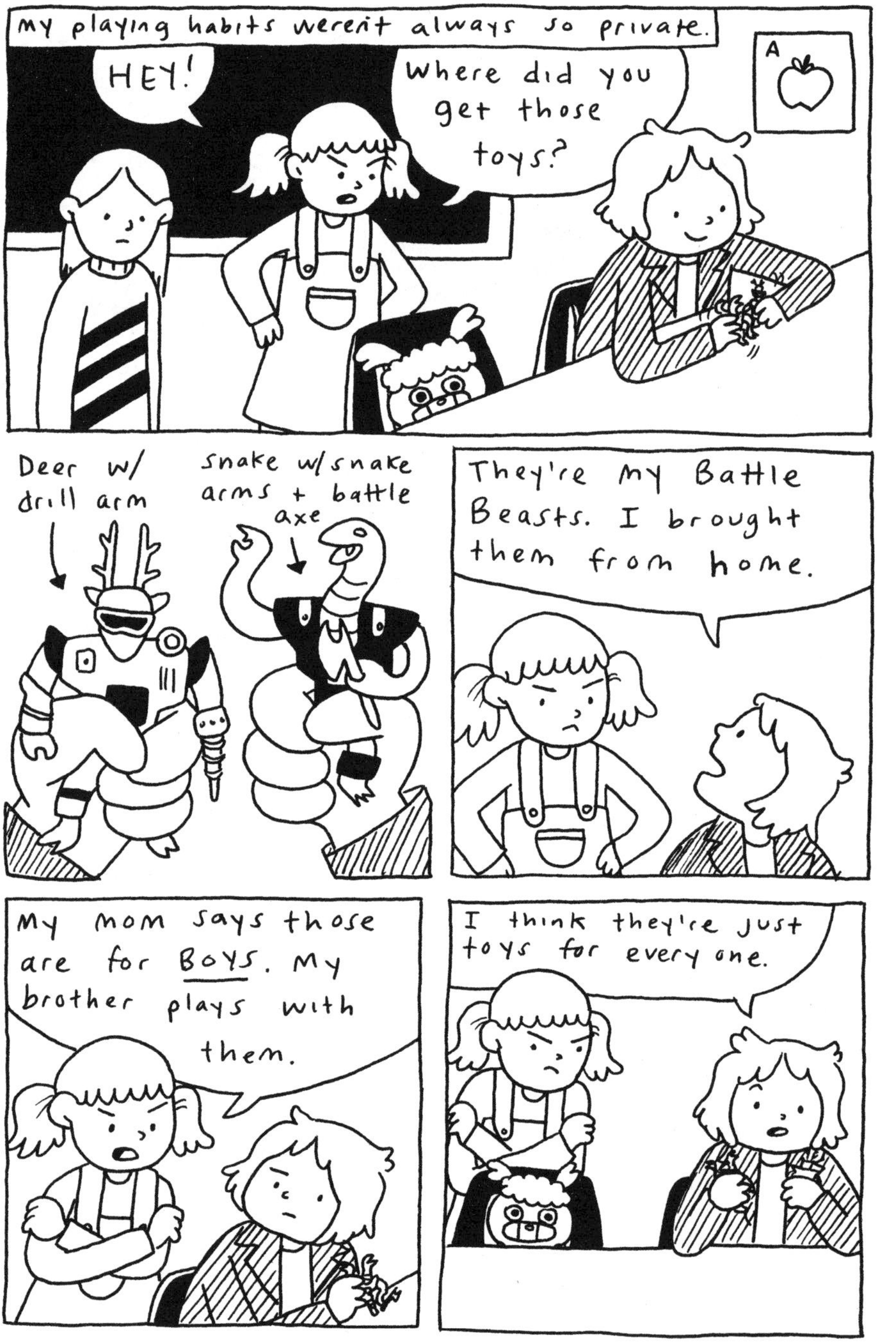
my playing habits weren't always so private.
HEY!
Where did you get those toys?
Deer w/ drill arm
snake w/snake arms + battle axe
They're my Battle Beasts. I brought them from home.
My mom says those are for BOYS. My brother plays with them.
I think they're just toys for every one.

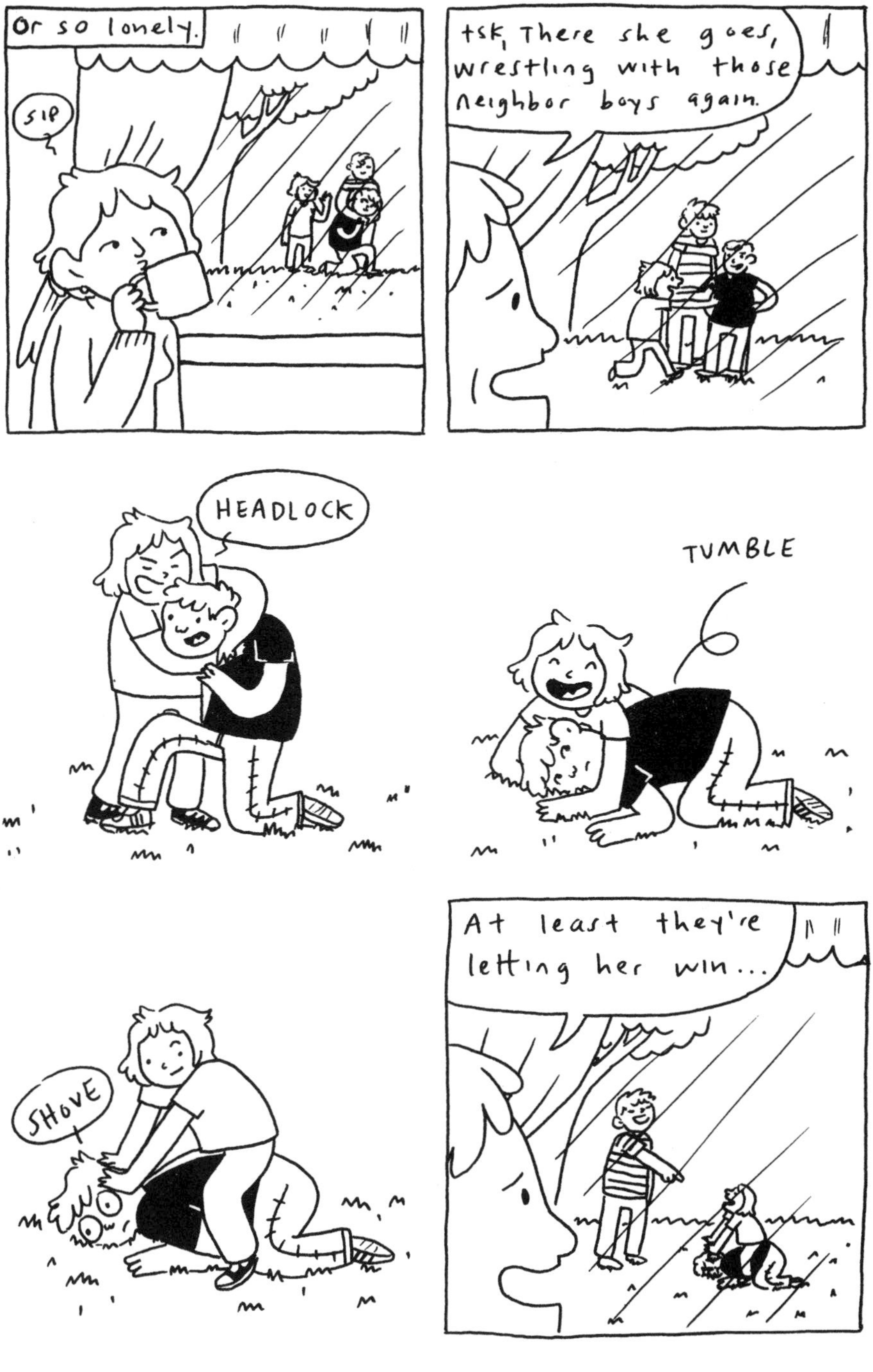
Or so lonely.
SIP
tsk, There she goes, wrestling with those neighbor boys again.
HEADLOCK
TUMBLE
SHOVE
At least they're letting her win...

My cousin Luke was only a year younger than me and we became best friends through our mutual obsession with the REAL GHOSTBUSTERS cartoon.

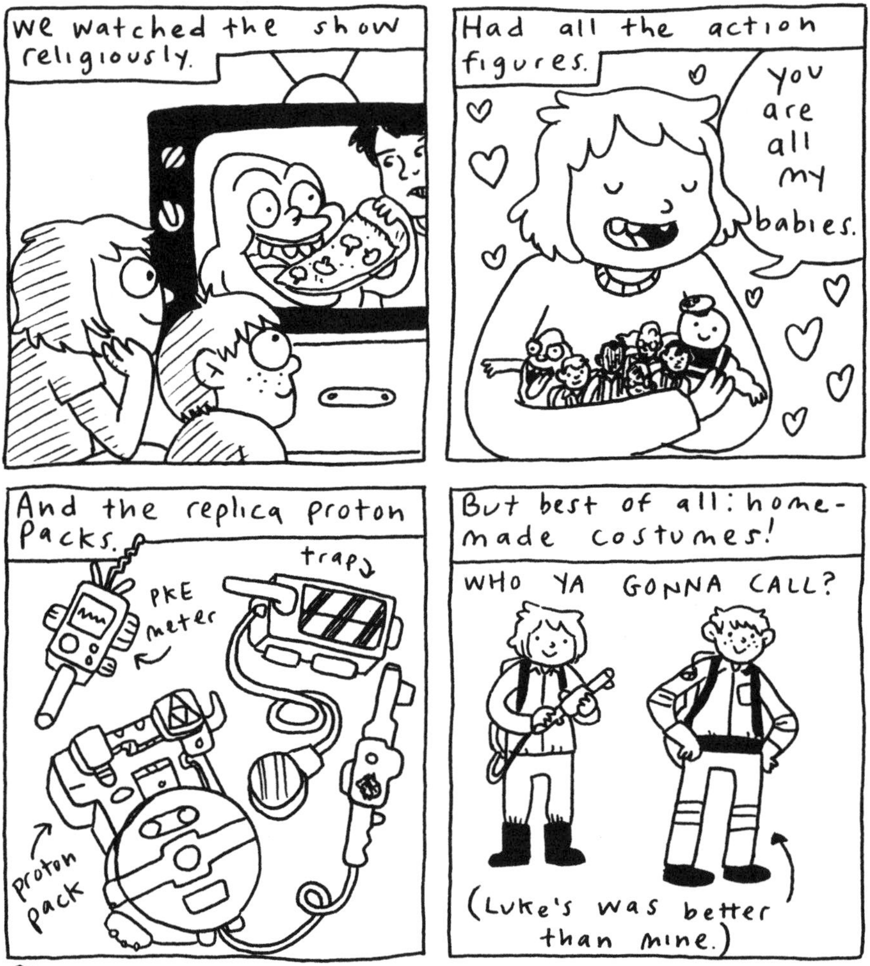
We watched the show religiously.
Had all the action figures.
You are all my babies.
And the replica proton packs.
trap
PKE meter
proton pack
But best of all: home-made costumes!
WHO YA GONNA CALL?
(Luke's was better than mine.)

Playing dress-up was really important to me, but not in the typical girl-tries-on-her-mother's-heels-and-prances-around-in-a-tiara kind of way.

When I admired someone, I wanted to BE them. This resulted in a mile-long list of embarrassing imitations that must have been very trying for my parents.

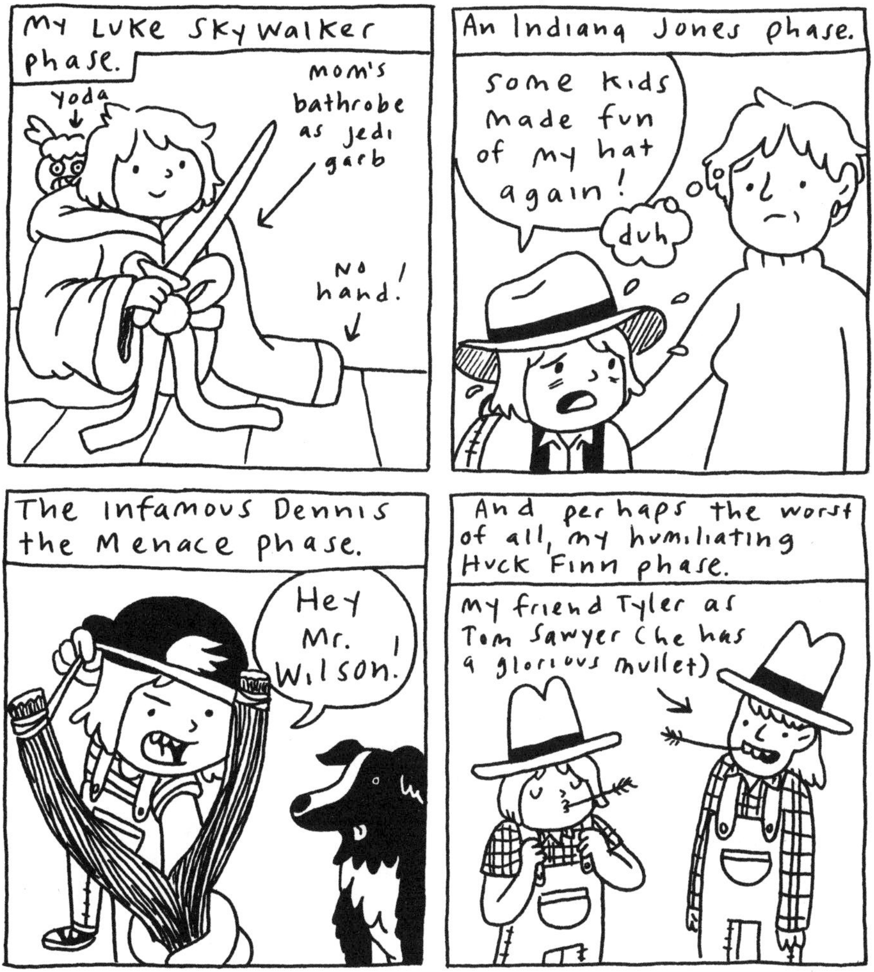
My Luke Skywalker phase.
Yoda
Mom's bathrobe as jedi garb
No hand!
An Indiana Jones phase.
Some kids made fun of my hat again!
duh
The infamous Dennis the Menace phase.
Hey Mr. Wilson!
And perhaps the worst of all, my humiliating Huck Finn phase.
My friend Tyler as Tom Sawyer (he has a glorious mullet)

Besides the fact that my fashion statements were ill-advised, what stands out the most is that all of my role models were boys.

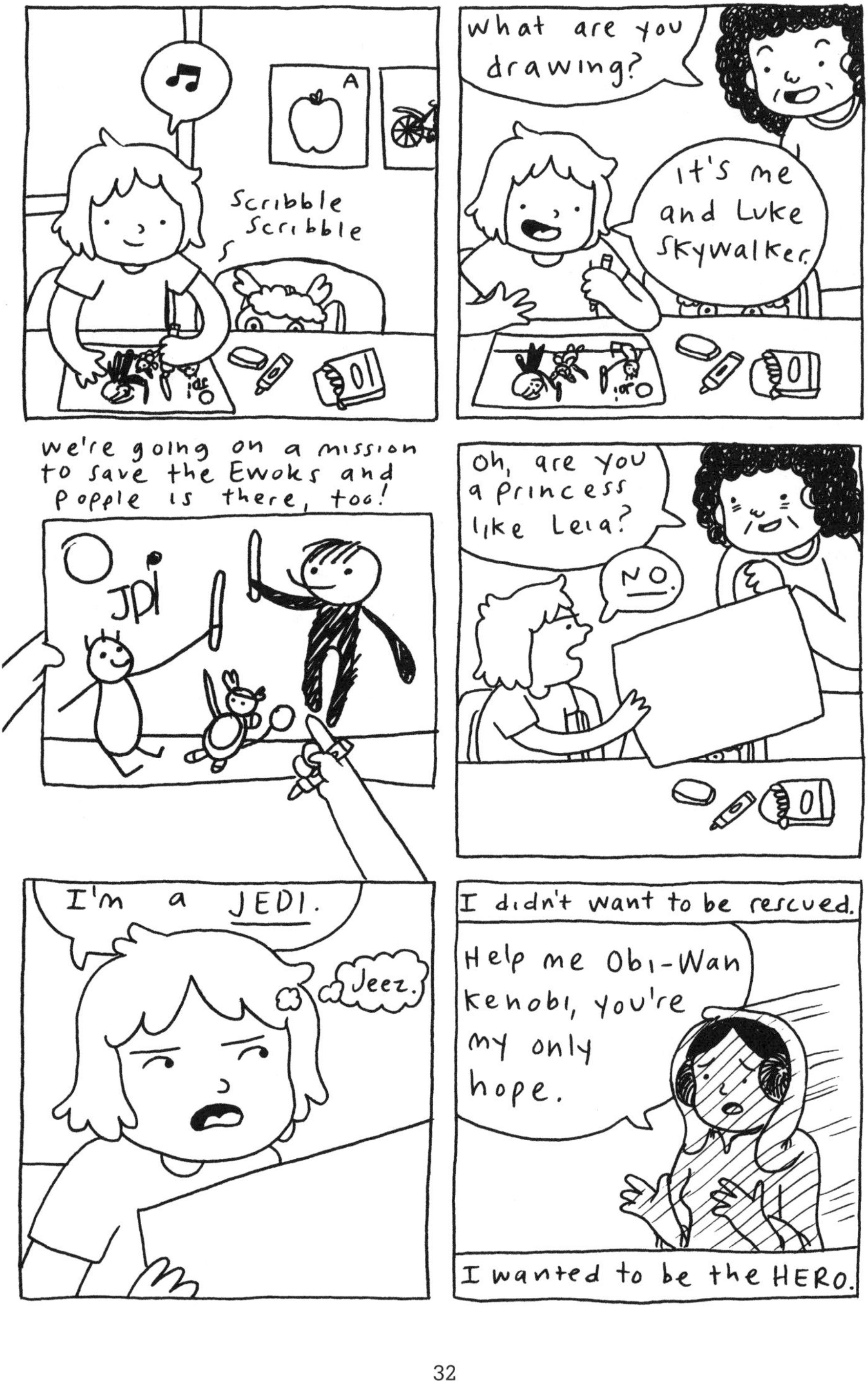
Scribble
Scribble
A
what are you drawing?
It's me and Luke Skywalker.
we're going on a mission to save the Ewoks and popple is there, too!
JDI
Oh, are you a princess like Leia?
NO.
I'm a JEDI.
Jeez.
I didn't want to be rescued.
Help me Obi-Wan kenobi, you're my only hope.
I wanted to be the HERO.

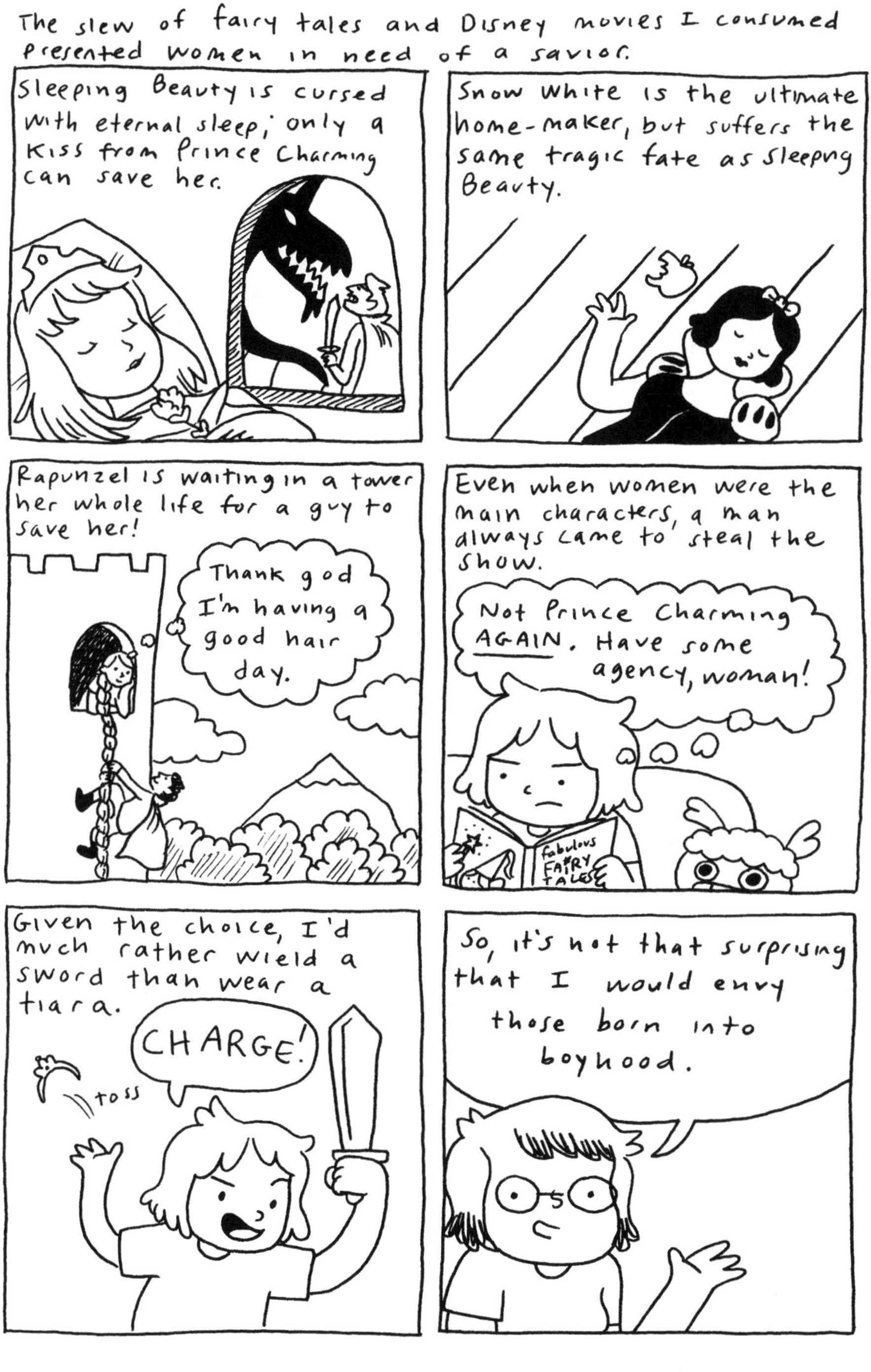
The slew of fairy tales and Disney movies I consumed presented women in need of a savior.
Sleeping Beauty is cursed with eternal sleep; only a kiss from Prince Charming can save her.
Snow White is the ultimate home-maker, but suffers the same tragic fate as Sleeping Beauty.
Rapunzel is waiting in a tower her whole life for a guy to save her!
Thank god I'm having a good hair day.
Even when women were the main characters, a man always came to steal the show.
Not Prince Charming AGAIN. Have some agency, woman!
fabulous FAIRY TALES
Given the choice, I'd much rather wield a sword than wear a tiara.
CHARGE!
toss
So, it's not that surprising that I would envy those born into boyhood.

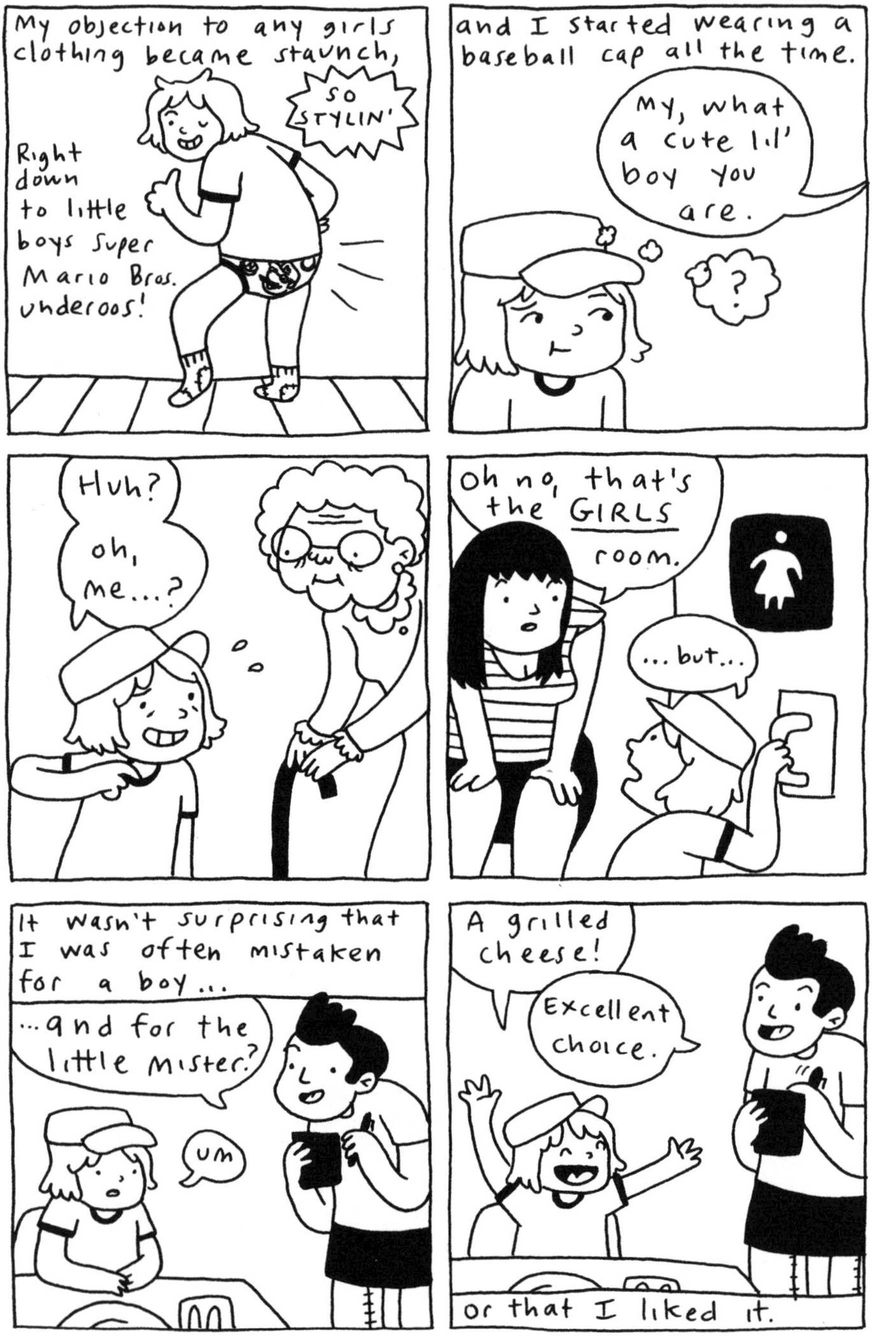
My objection to any girls clothing became staunch,
SO STYLIN'
Right down to little boys Super Mario Bros. underoos!
and I started wearing a baseball cap all the time.
My, what a cute lil' boy you are.
?
Huh?
oh, me...?
Oh no, that's the GIRLS room.
...but...
It wasn't surprising that I was often mistaken for a boy...
...and for the little mister?
um
A grilled cheese!
Excellent choice.
or that I liked it.

CHAPTER 3

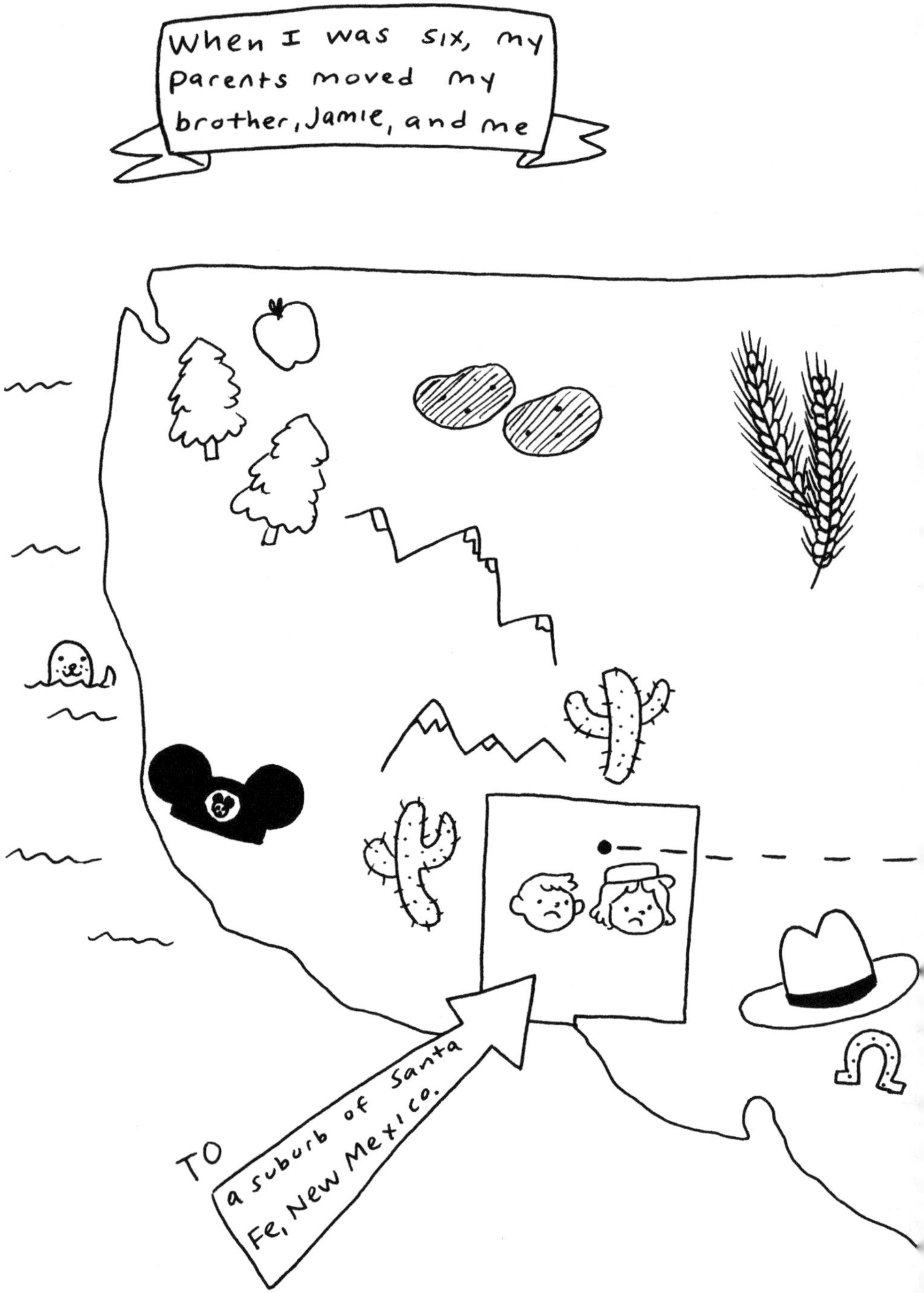
When I was six, my parents moved my brother, Jamie, and me
TO
a suburb of Santa Fe, New Mexico.

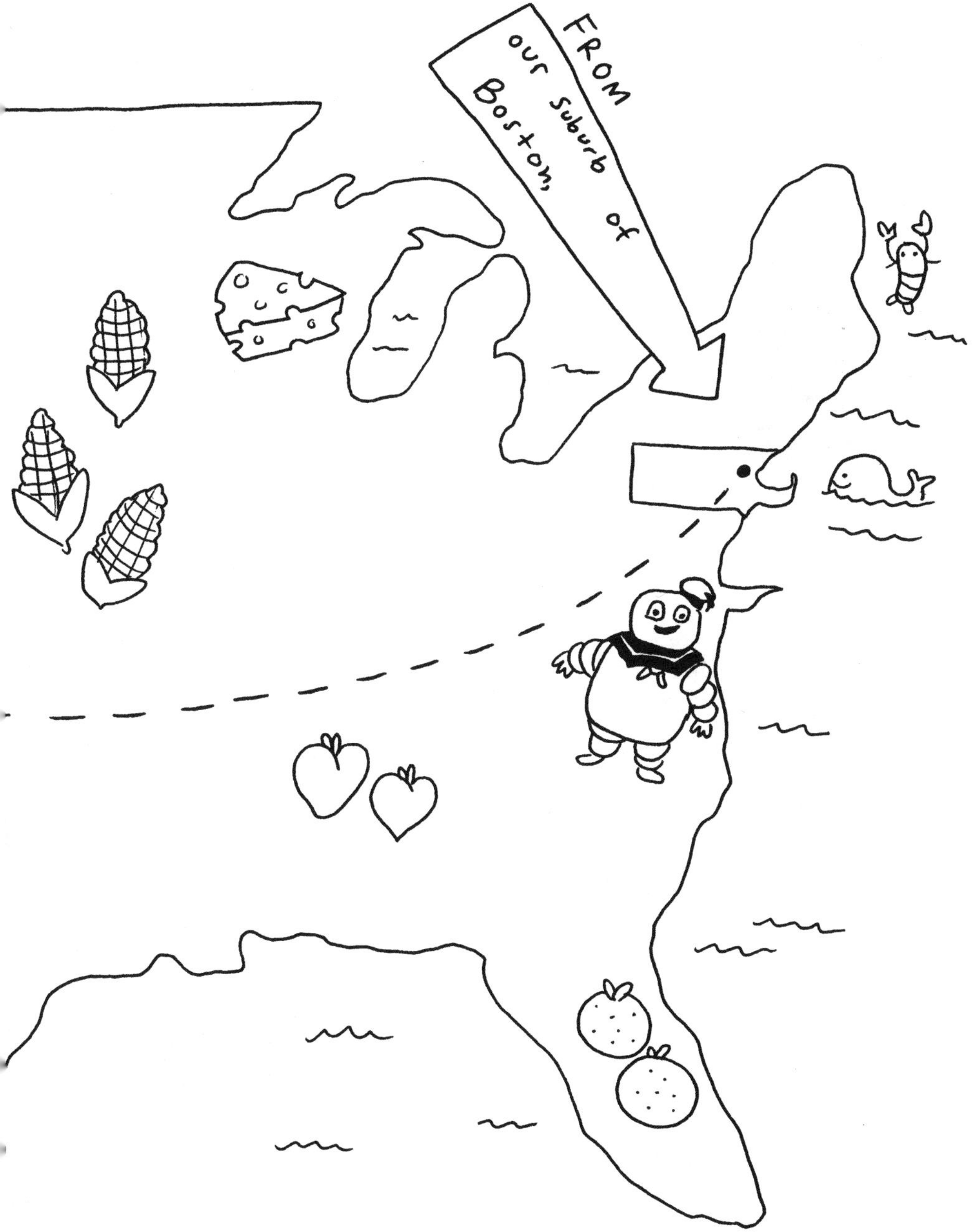
FROM
our suburb of
Boston,

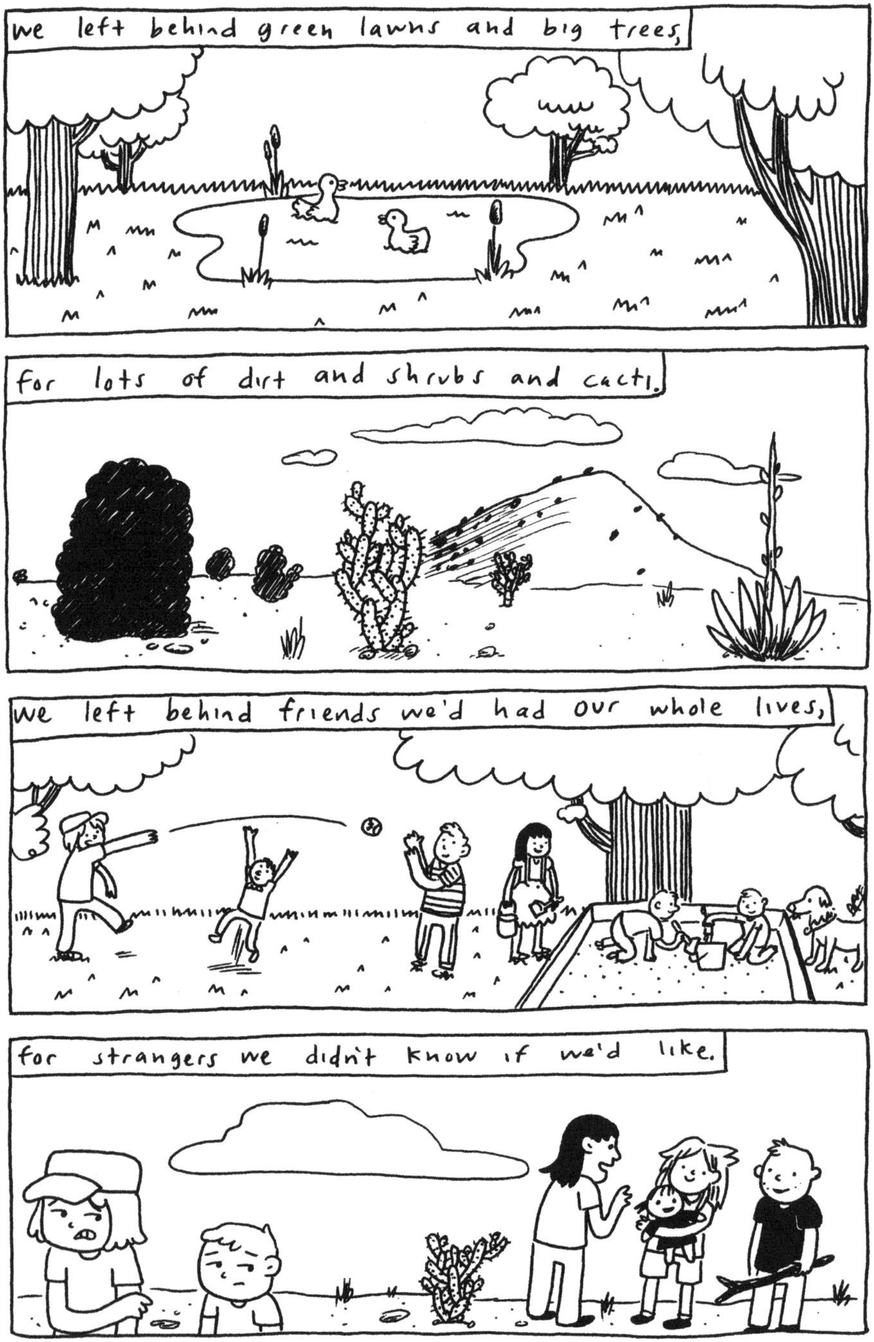
we left behind green lawns and big trees,
for lots of dirt and shrubs and cacti.
we left behind friends we'd had our whole lives,
for strangers we didn't know if we'd like.

The desert made us uncomfortable. We were scared of things we'd never seen before.

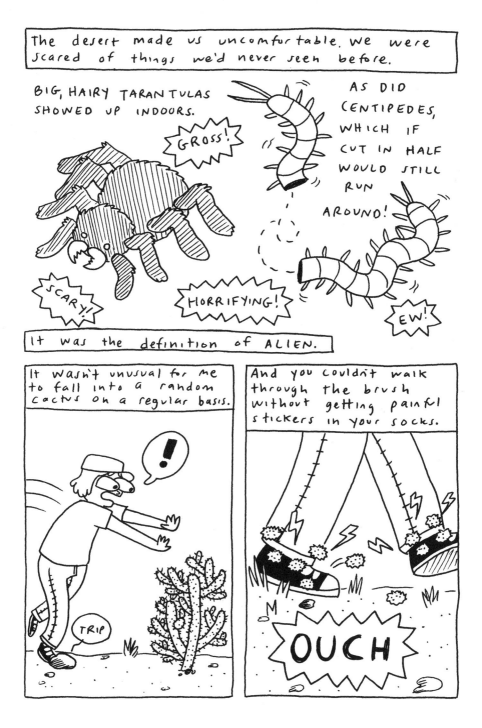

BIG, HAIRY TARANTULAS SHOWED UP INDOORS.

GROSS!

AS DID CENTIPEDES, WHICH IF CUT IN HALF WOULD STILL RUN AROUND!

SCARY!

HORRIFYING!

EW!

It was the definition of ALIEN.

It wasn't unusual for me to fall into a random cactus on a regular basis.

!

TRIP

And you couldn't walk through the brush without getting painful stickers in your socks.

OUCH

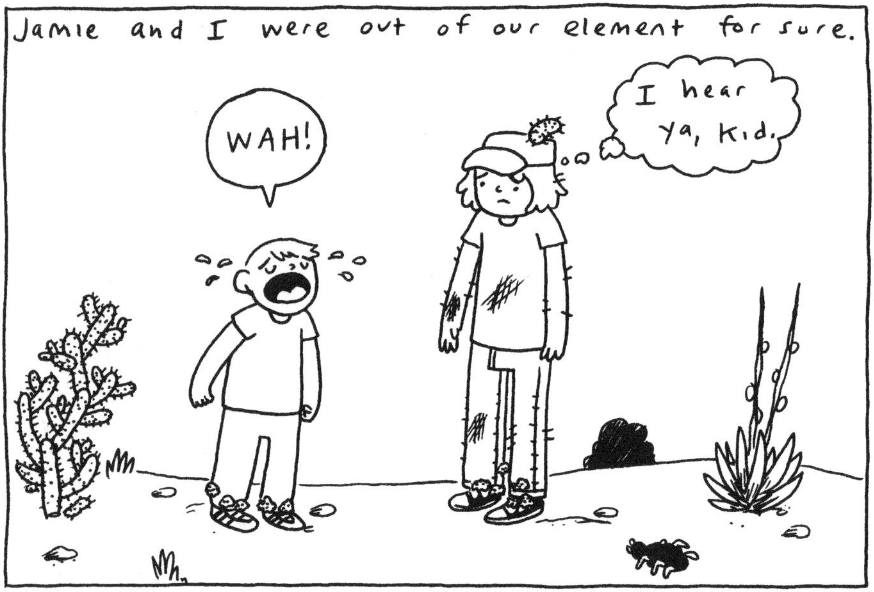
Jamie and I were out of our element for sure.
WAH!
I hear ya, kid.

I was eager for school to start so I could make new friends in first grade.

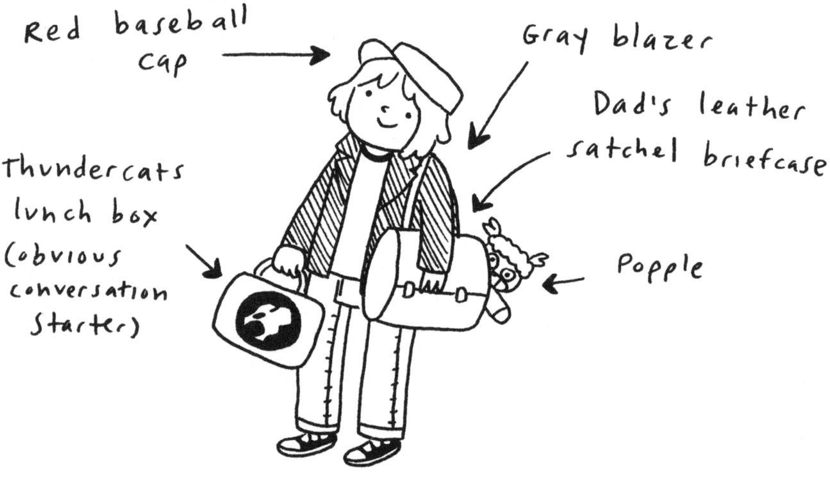
Red baseball cap
Gray blazer
Dad's leather satchel briefcase
Thundercats lunch box (obvious conversation starter)
Popple

In retrospect, maybe it wasn't the best idea to have quite so many quirky accessories.

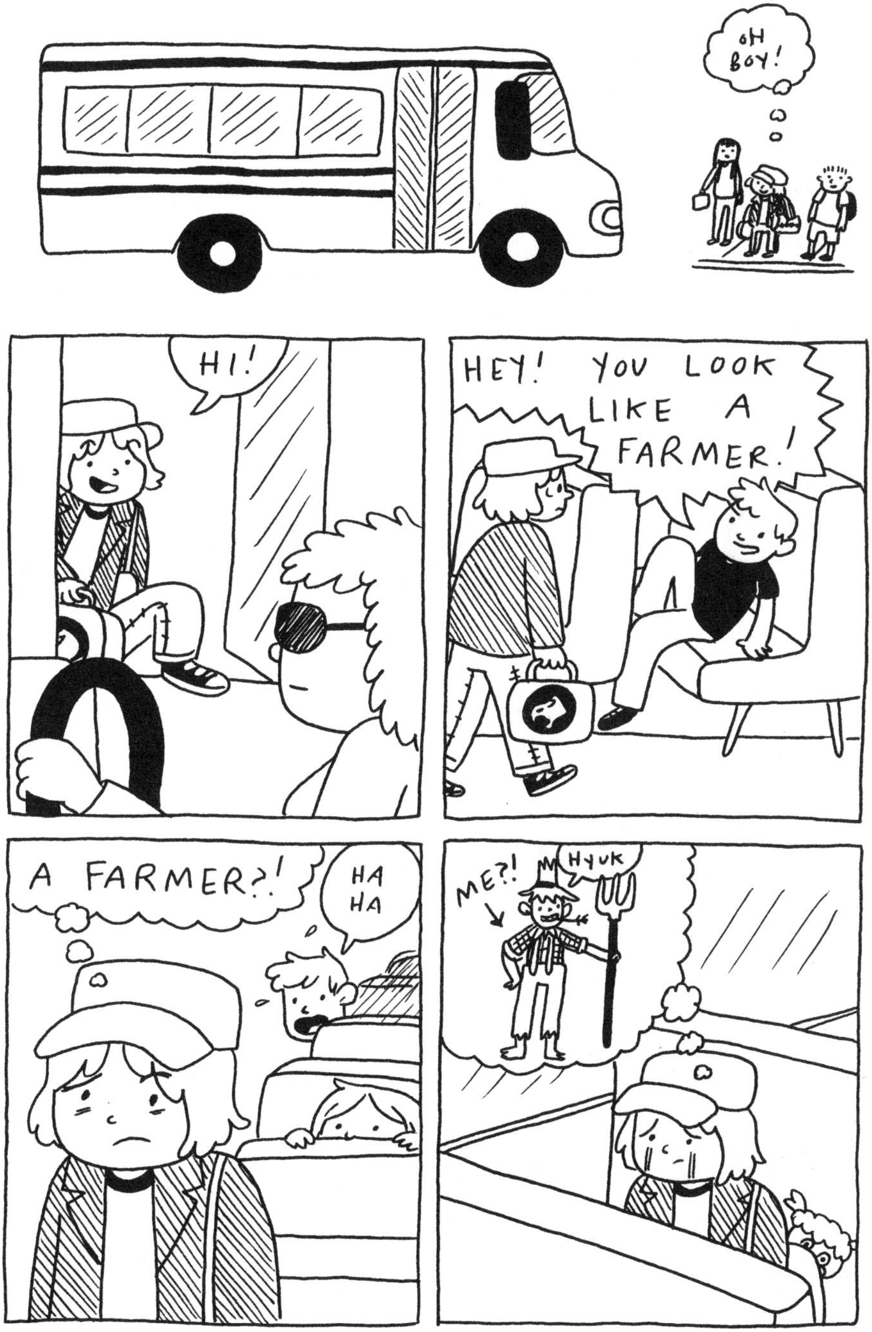
OH BOY!
HI!
HEY! YOU LOOK LIKE A FARMER!
A FARMER?!
HA HA
ME?!
HYUK

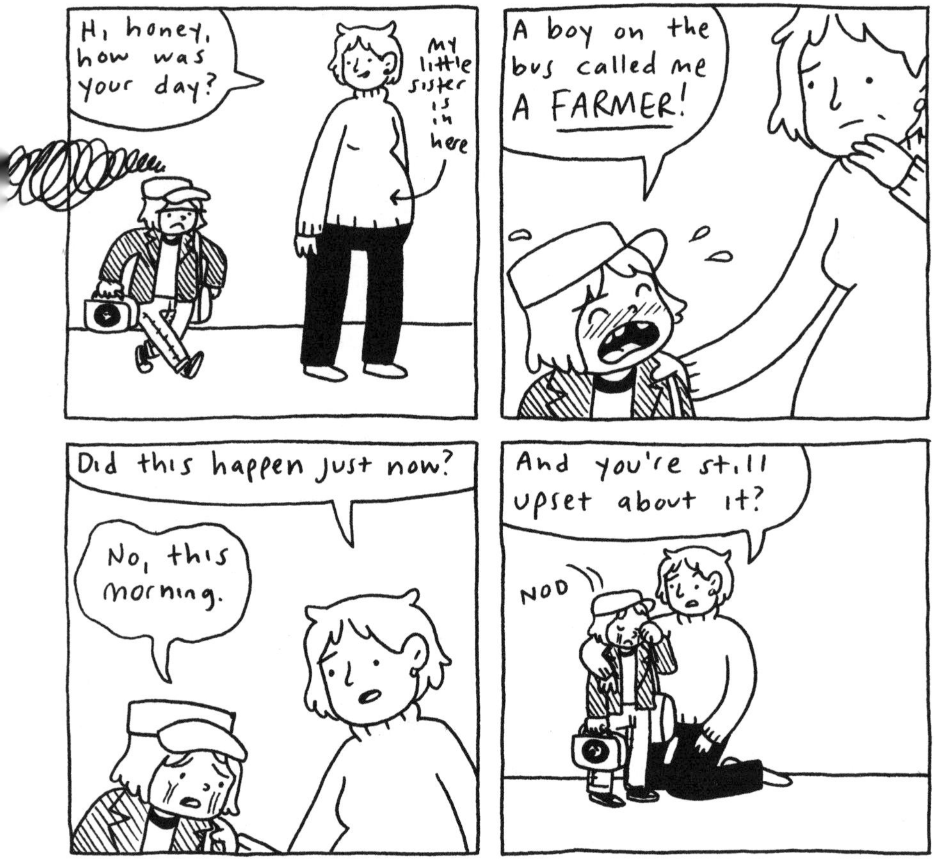
Hi, honey, how was your day?
My little sister is in here
A boy on the bus called me A FARMER!
Did this happen just now?
No, this morning.
And you're still upset about it?
NOD

It turns out that the kid called me a farmer because he'd never seen a girl in a baseball cap before.

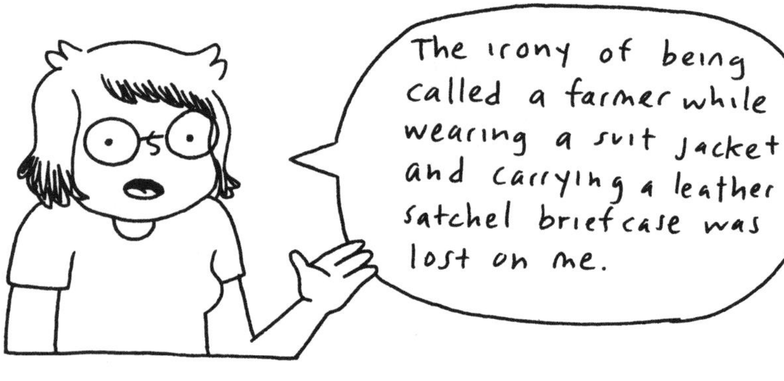
The irony of being called a farmer while wearing a suit jacket and carrying a leather satchel briefcase was lost on me.

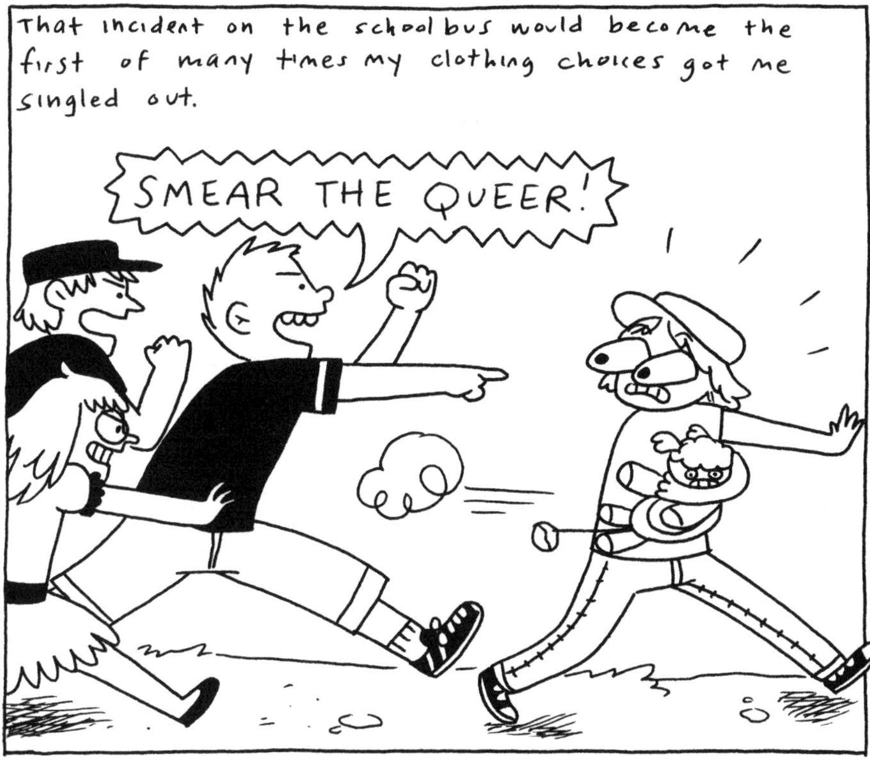
That incident on the schoolbus would become the first of many times my clothing choices got me singled out.
SMEAR THE QUEER!

But it wasn't all bad. We moved into a neighborhood with a lot of boys my age and I made some friends.

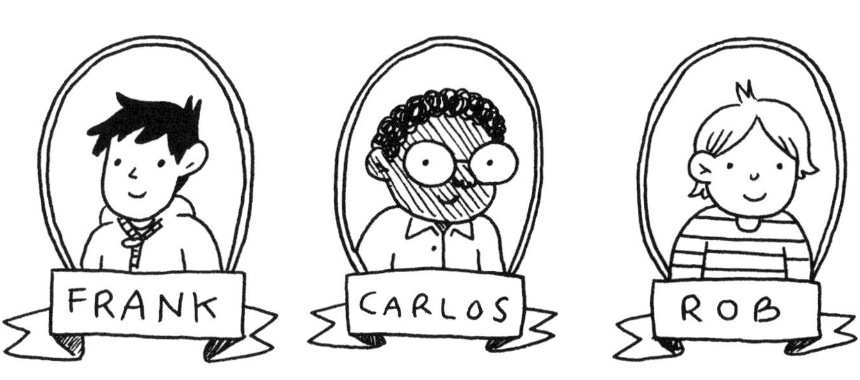
FRANK
CARLOS
ROB

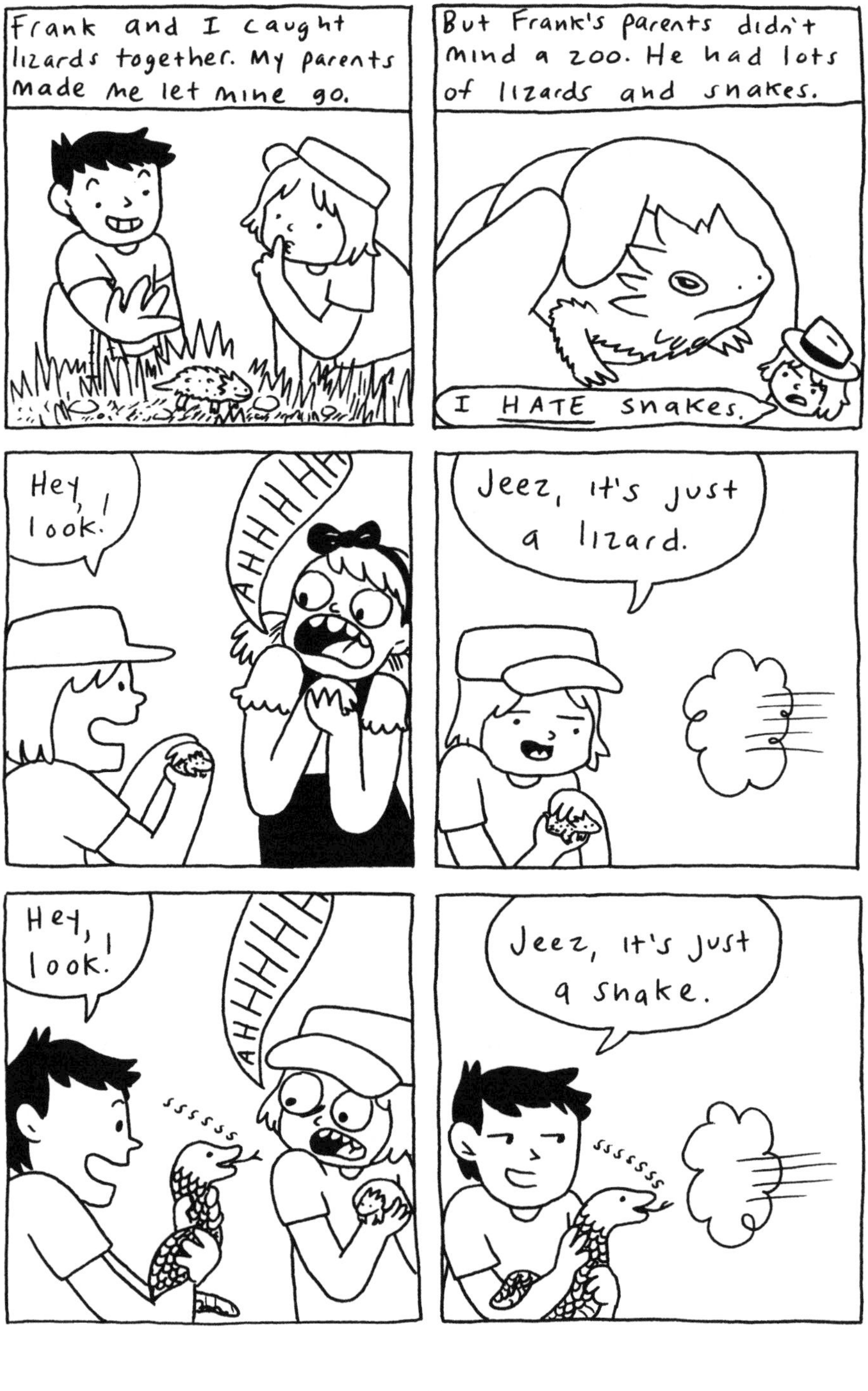
Frank and I caught lizards together. My parents made me let mine go.
But Frank's parents didn't mind a zoo. He had lots of lizards and snakes.
I HATE snakes.
Hey, look!
AHHHHH
Jeez, it's just a lizard.
Hey, look!
AHHHHHH
SSSSSS
Jeez, it's just a snake.
SSSSSSS

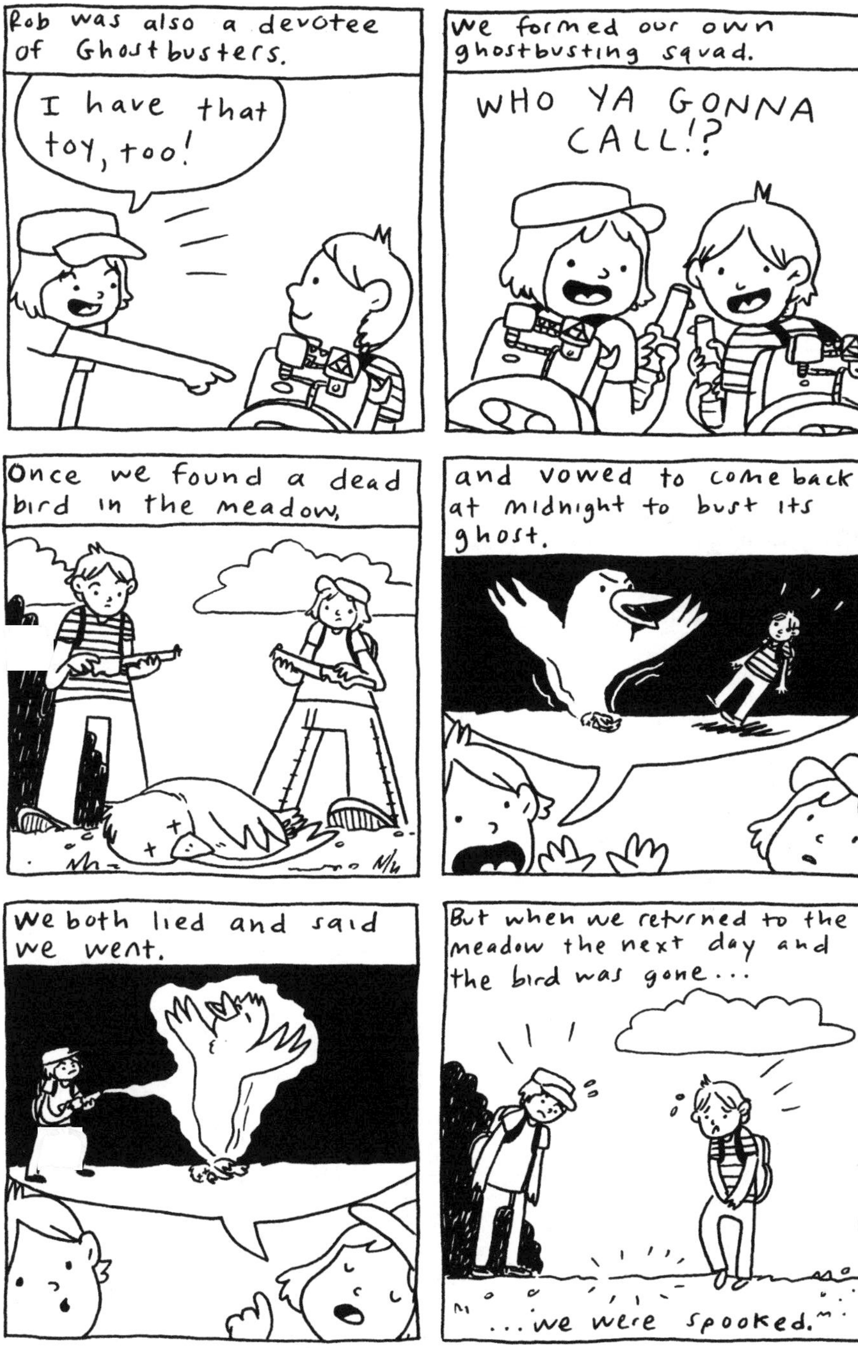
Rob was also a devotee of Ghostbusters.
I have that toy, too!
We formed our own ghostbusting squad.
WHO YA GONNA CALL!?
Once we found a dead bird in the meadow,
and vowed to come back at midnight to bust its ghost.
We both lied and said we went.
But when we returned to the meadow the next day and the bird was gone...
...we were spooked.

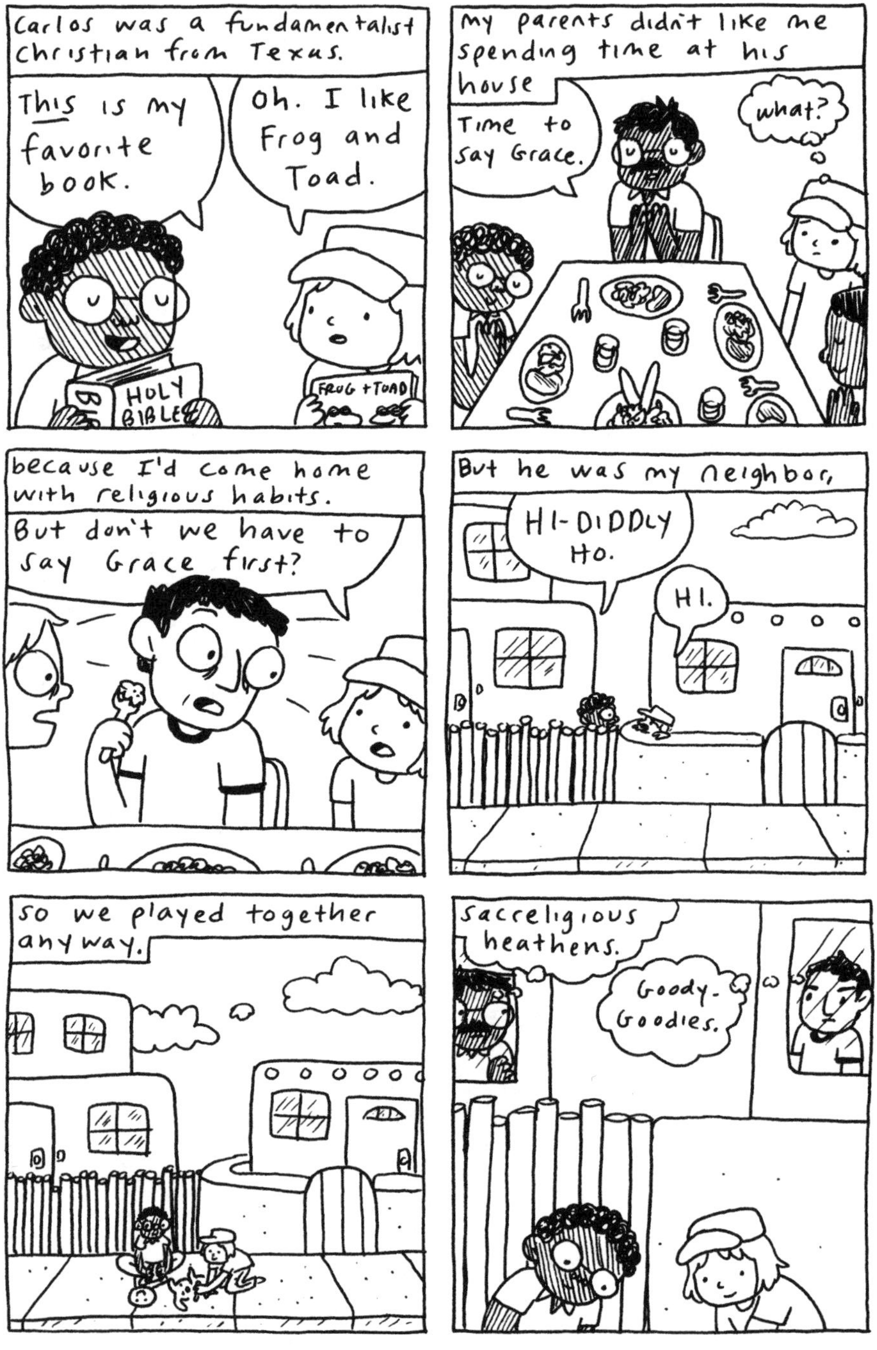

Carlos was a fundamentalist Christian from Texas.
This is my favorite book.
Oh. I like Frog and Toad.
HOLY BIBLE
FROG + TOAD
My parents didn't like me spending time at his house
Time to say Grace.
what?
because I'd come home with religious habits.
But don't we have to say Grace first?
But he was my neighbor,
HI-DIDDLY HO.
HI.
so we played together anyway.
Sacreligious heathens.
Goody-Goodies.

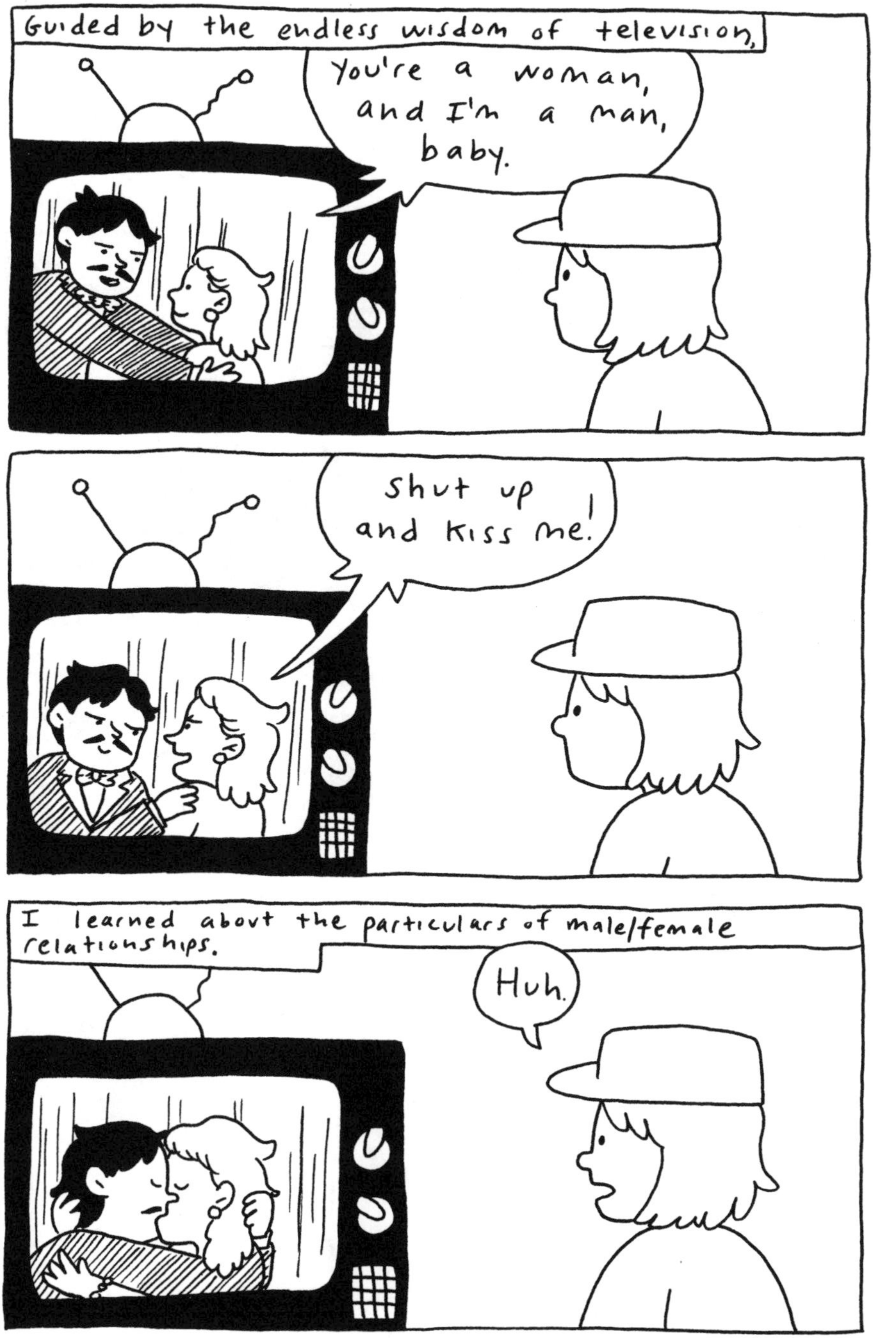
Guided by the endless wisdom of television,
You're a woman, and I'm a man, baby.
Shut up and kiss me!
I learned about the particulars of male/female relationships.
Huh.

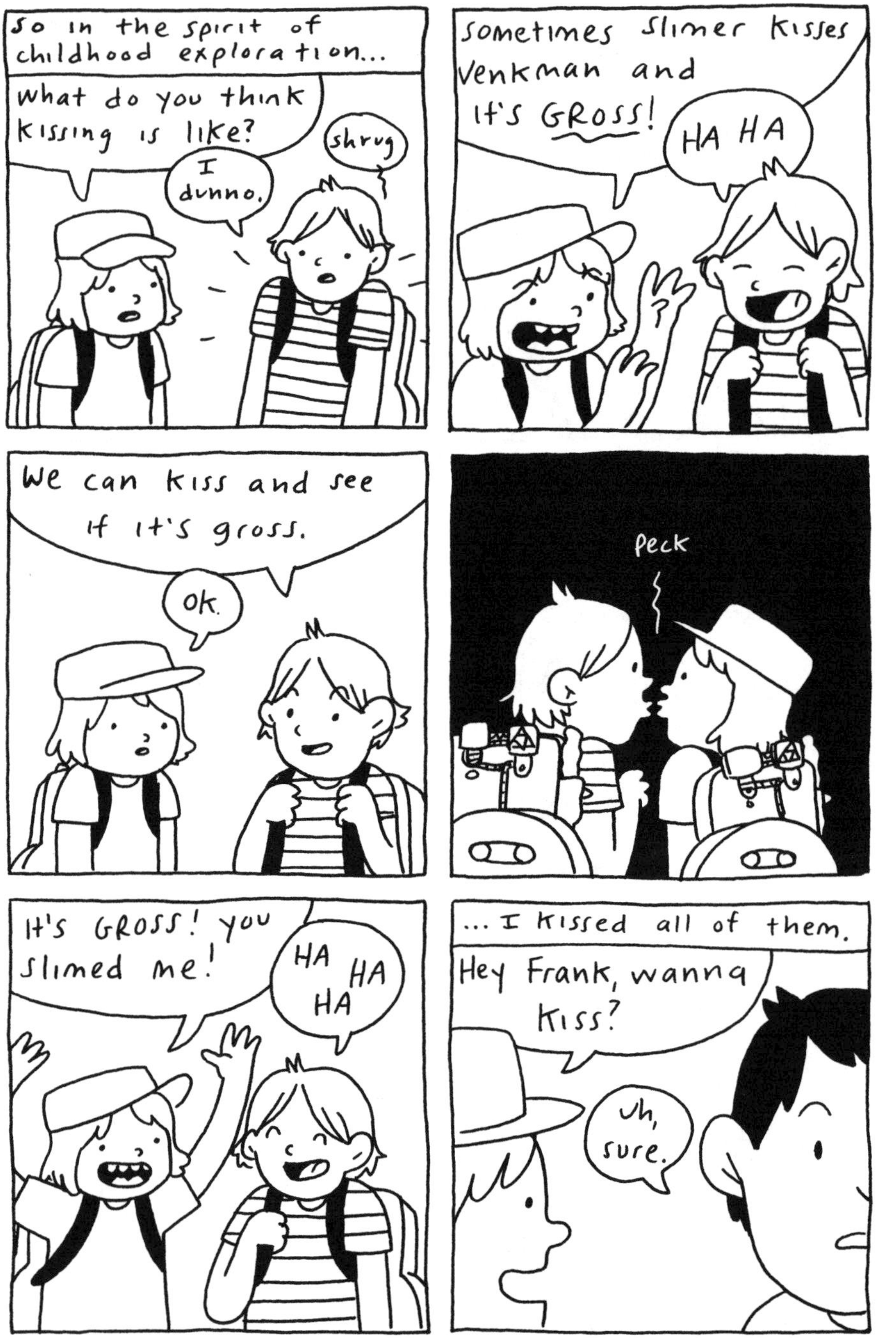
So in the spirit of childhood exploration...
What do you think kissing is like?
I dunno.
shrug
Sometimes Slimer kisses Venkman and it's GROSS!
HA HA
We can kiss and see if it's gross.
Ok.
peck
It's GROSS! you slimed me!
HA HA HA
... I kissed all of them.
Hey Frank, wanna kiss?
uh, sure.

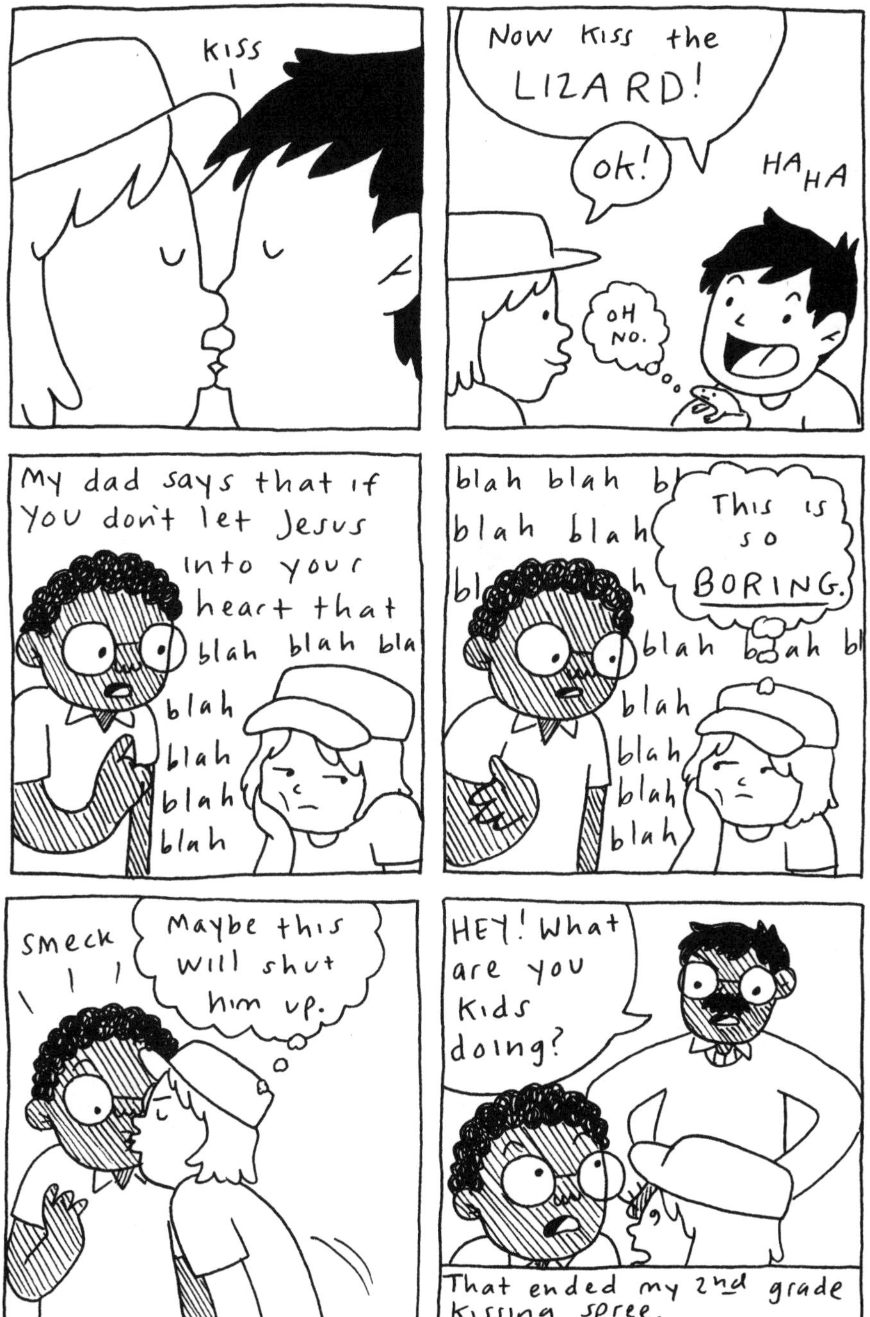
KISS
Now kiss the LIZARD!
Ok!
HA HA
OH NO.
My dad says that if you don't let Jesus into your heart that blah blah bla
blah
blah
blah
blah
blah blah bl
blah blah
bl h
This is so BORING.
blah blah bl
blah
blah
blah
blah
SMECK
Maybe this will shut him up.
HEY! What are you kids doing?
That ended my 2nd grade kissing spree.

Not that I minded. Kissing wasn't nearly as interesting as TV made it seem.

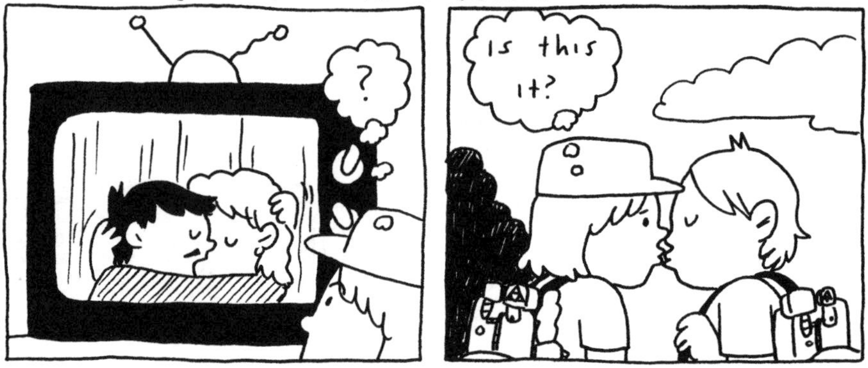
?
Is this it?

Still, when girls chased boys on the playground to kiss them, I had a strange sense of satisfaction.

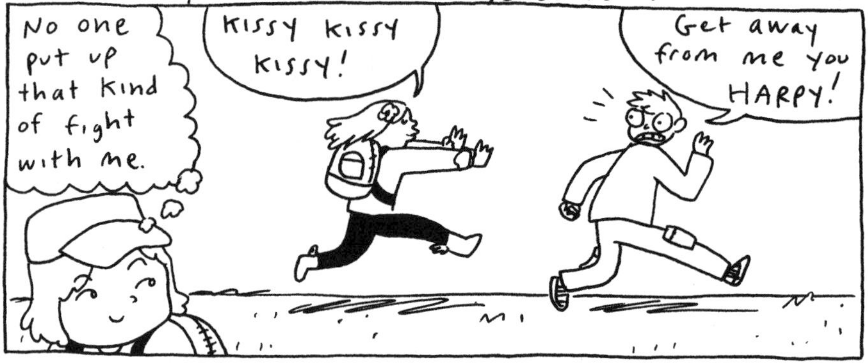
No one put up that kind of fight with me.
KISSY KISSY KISSY!
Get away from me you HARPY!

I had a different problem: Despite having kissed me, those same boys wouldn't admit to being friends with me at school.

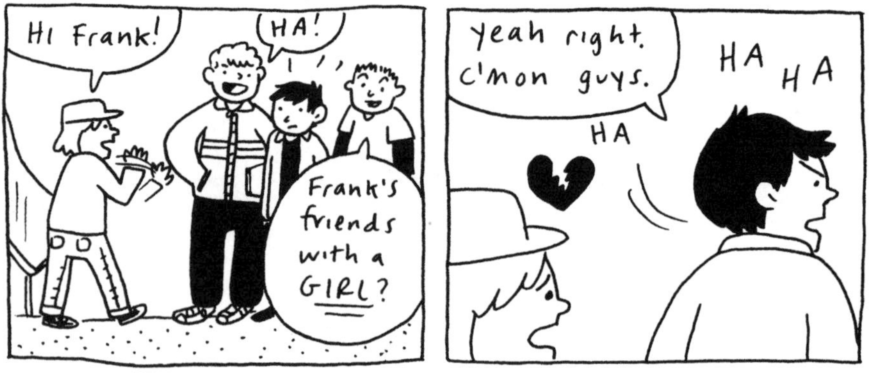
Hi Frank!
HA!
Frank's friends with a GIRL?
Yeah right. C'mon guys.
HA
HA
HA

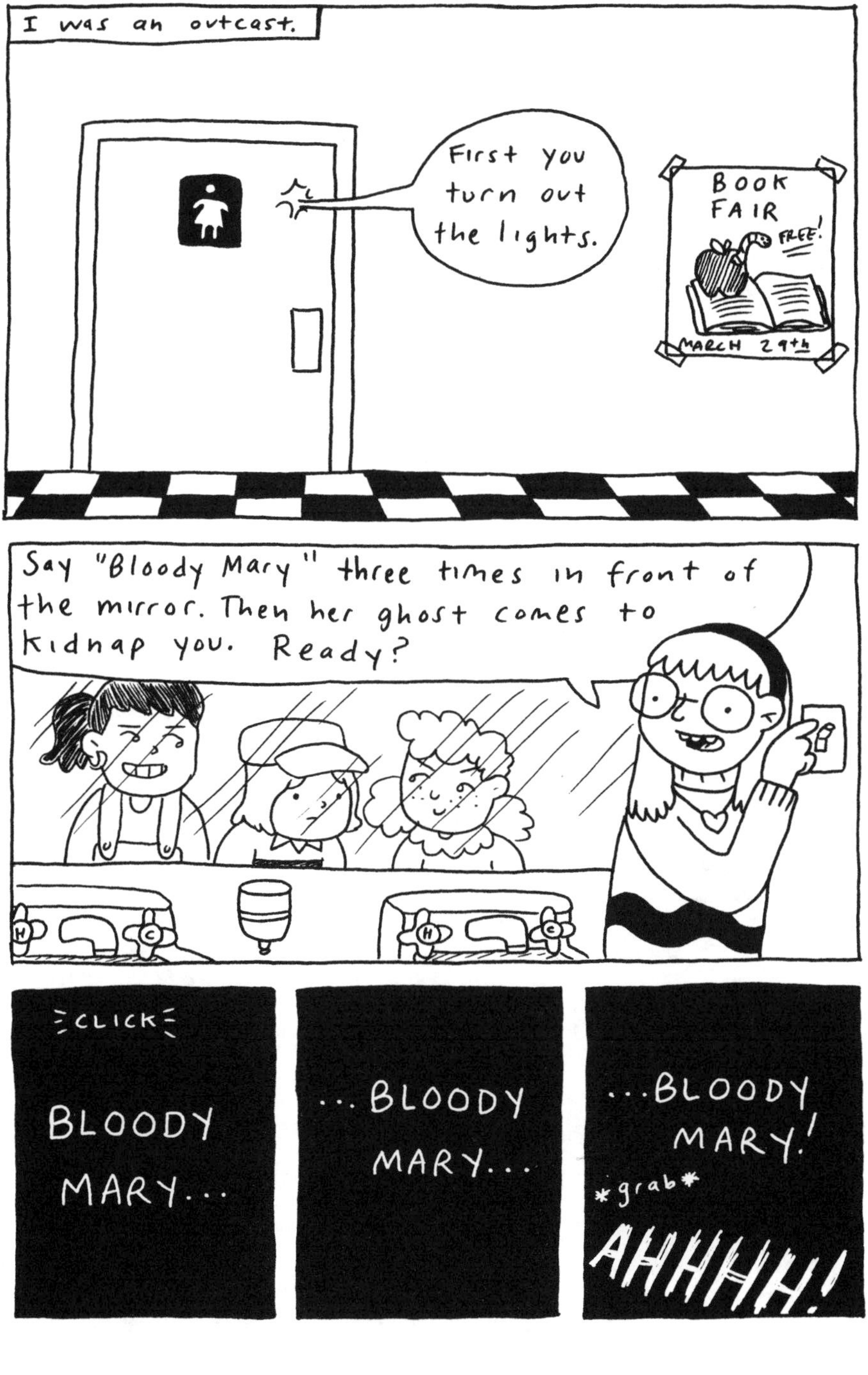
I was an outcast.
First you turn out the lights.
BOOK FAIR
FREE!
MARCH 29th
Say "Bloody Mary" three times in front of the mirror. Then her ghost comes to kidnap you. Ready?
H
C
H
C
CLICK
BLOODY MARY...
...BLOODY MARY...
...BLOODY MARY!
grab
AHHHH!

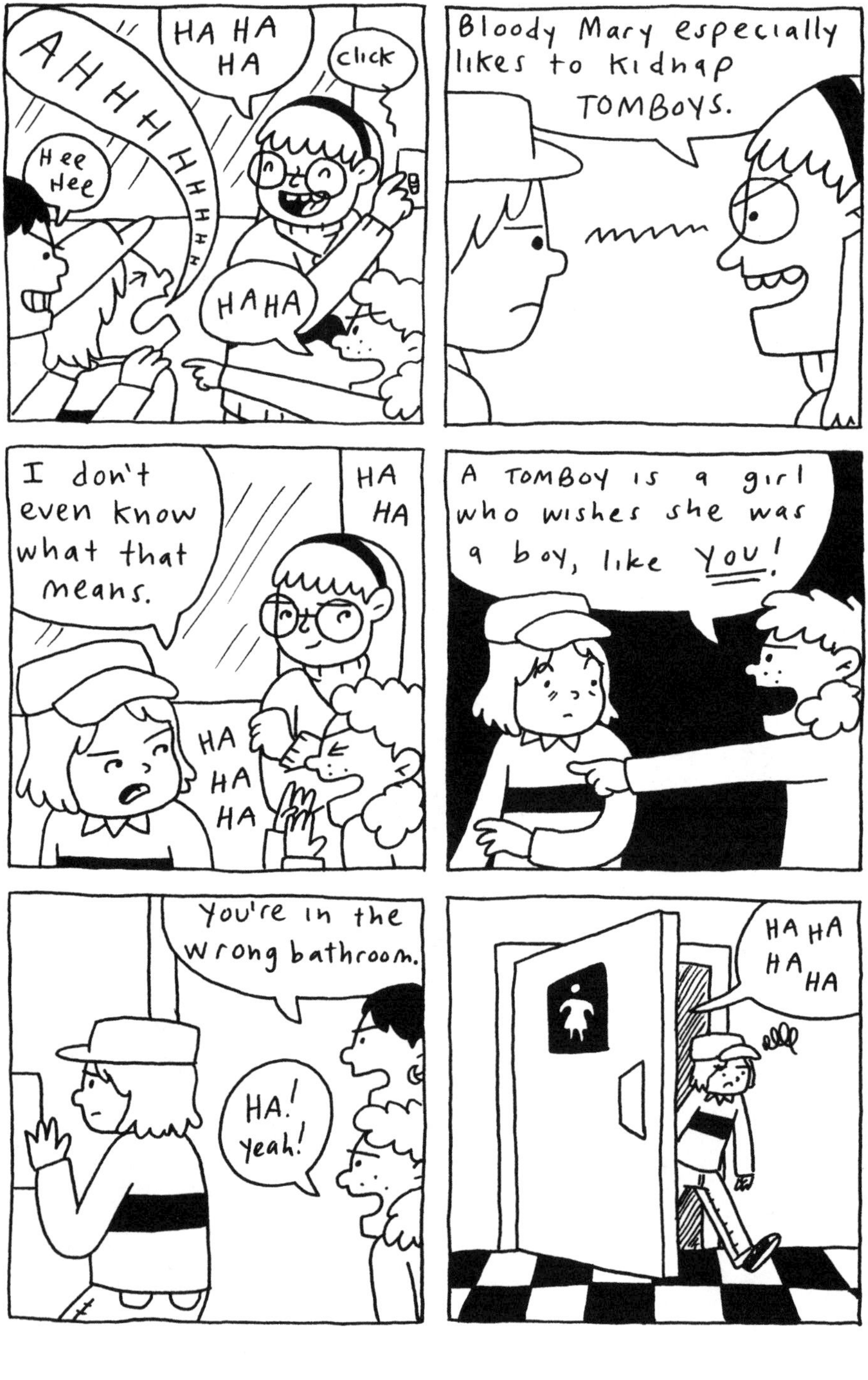
AHHHHHHHHHH
HA HA HA
click
Hee Hee
HAHA
Bloody Mary especially likes to kidnap TOMBOYS.
I don't even know what that means.
HA HA
HA HA HA
A TOMBOY is a girl who wishes she was a boy, like YOU!
You're in the wrong bathroom.
HA! yeah!
HA HA HA HA

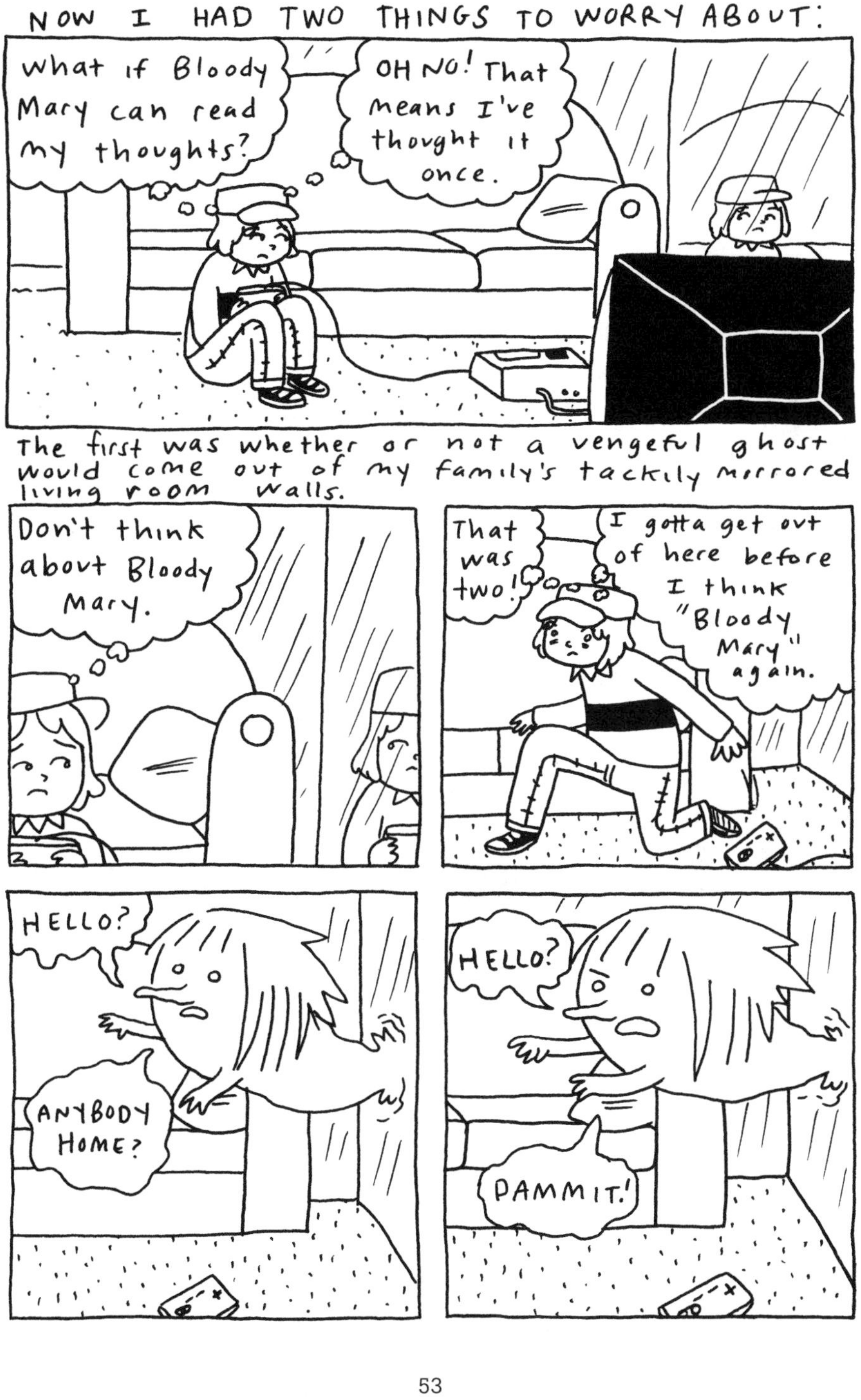
NOW I HAD TWO THINGS TO WORRY ABOUT:
What if Bloody Mary can read my thoughts?
OH NO! That means I've thought it once.
The first was whether or not a vengeful ghost would come out of my family's tackily mirrored living room walls.
Don't think about Bloody Mary.
That was two!
I gotta get out of here before I think "Bloody Mary" again.
HELLO?
ANYBODY HOME?
HELLO?
DAMMIT!

The second was whether or not those girls were right: maybe I DID want to be a boy. Why else would He-Man be my hero?

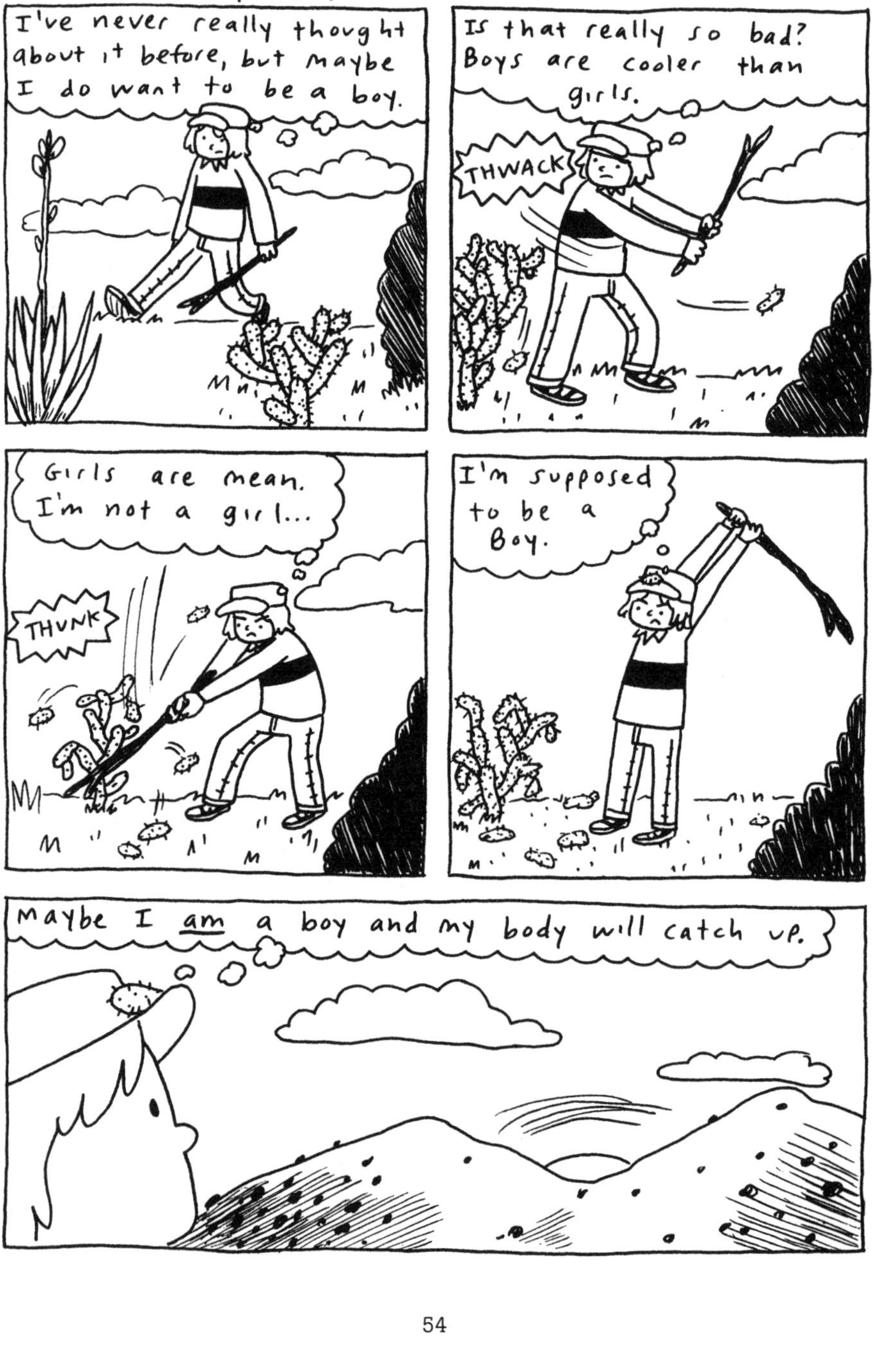
I've never really thought about it before, but maybe I do want to be a boy.
Is that really so bad? Boys are cooler than girls.
THWACK
Girls are mean. I'm not a girl...
THUNK
I'm supposed to be a Boy.
Maybe I am a boy and my body will catch up.

Obviously my grasp of biology wasn't so great in second grade, but I was no stranger to unrealistic expectations.

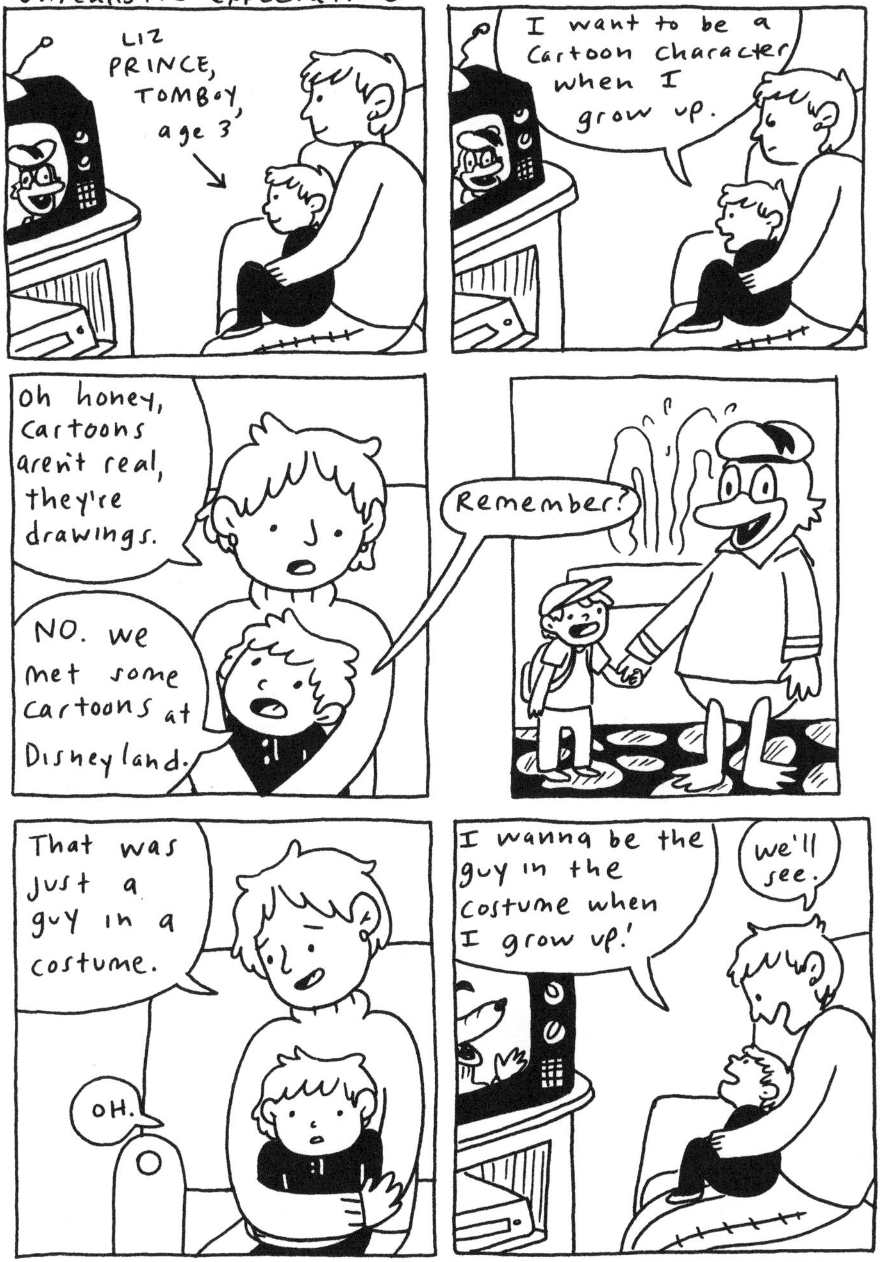
LIZ PRINCE, TOMBOY, age 3
I want to be a cartoon character when I grow up.
Oh honey, cartoons aren't real, they're drawings.
NO. We met some cartoons at Disneyland.
Remember?
That was just a guy in a costume.
OH.
I wanna be the guy in the costume when I grow up!
We'll see.

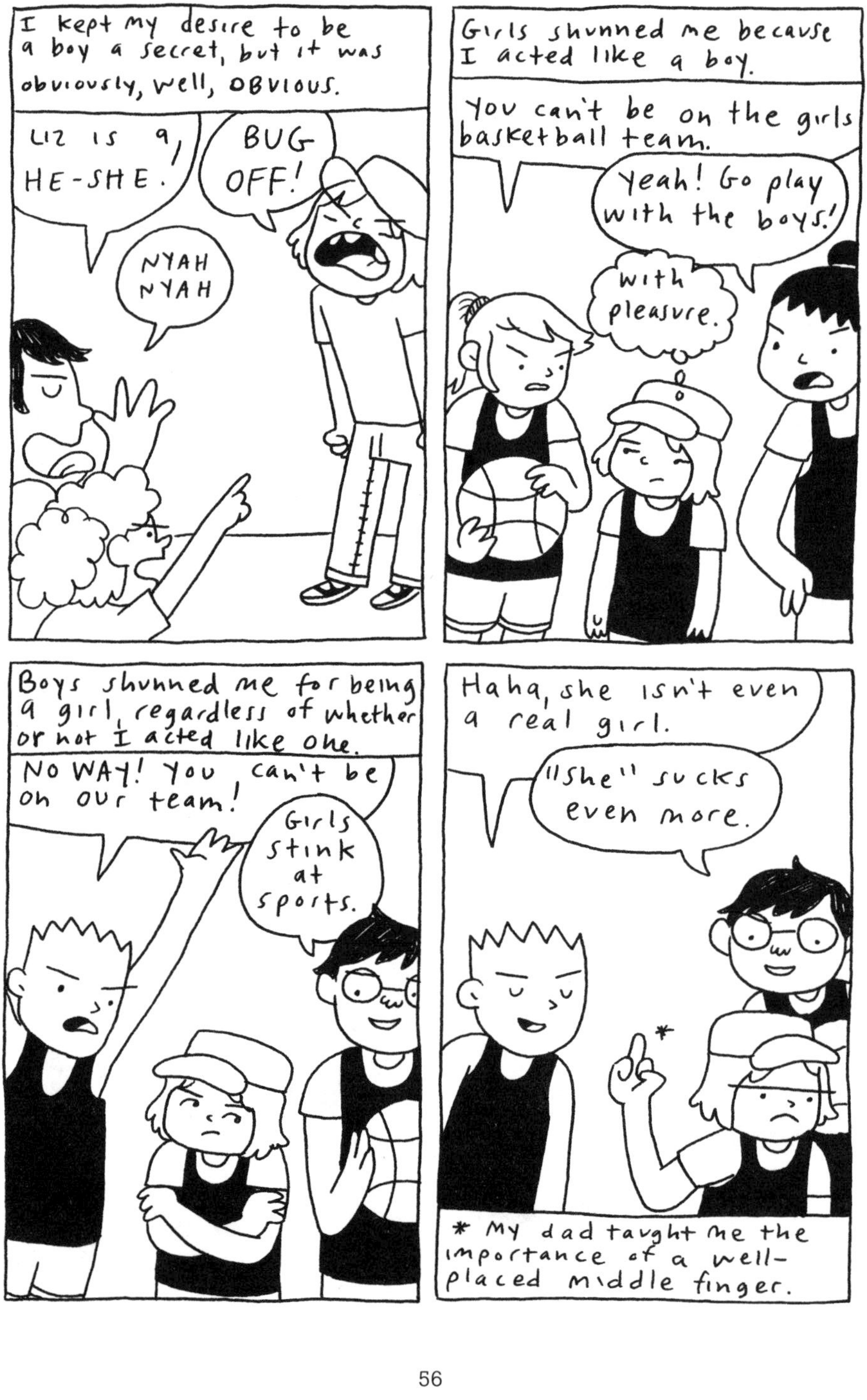
I kept my desire to be a boy a secret, but it was obviously, well, OBVIOUS.
LIZ IS a HE-SHE.
BUG OFF!
NYAH NYAH
Girls shunned me because I acted like a boy.
You can't be on the girls basketball team.
Yeah! Go play with the boys!
with pleasure.
Boys shunned me for being a girl, regardless of whether or not I acted like one.
NO WAY! You can't be on our team!
Girls stink at sports.
Haha, she isn't even a real girl.
"She" sucks even more.
*
* My dad taught me the importance of a well-placed middle finger.

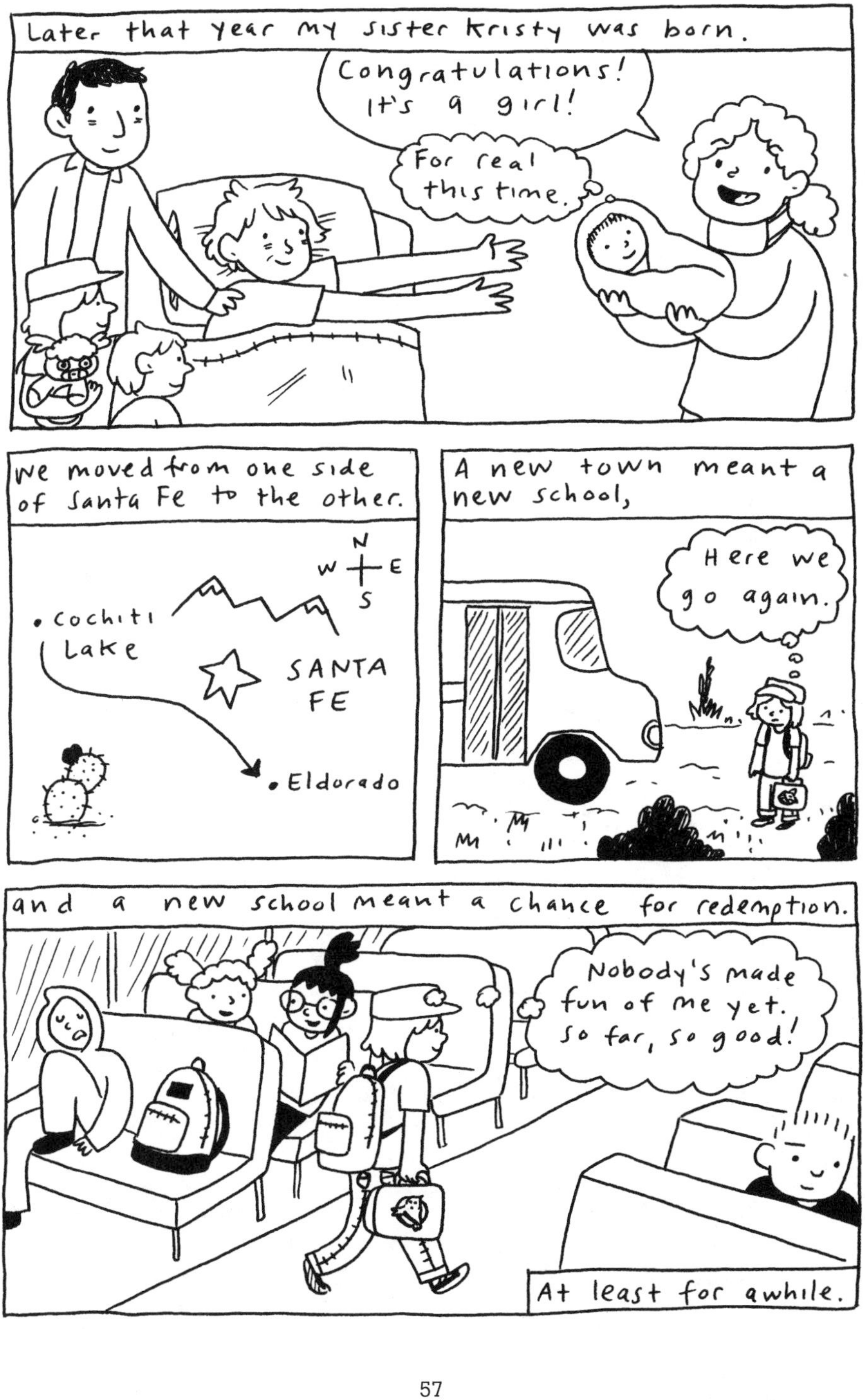

Later that year my sister Kristy was born.
Congratulations! It's a girl!
For real this time.
We moved from one side of Santa Fe to the other.
N
W
E
S
Cochiti Lake
SANTA FE
Eldorado
A new town meant a new school,
Here we go again.
and a new school meant a chance for redemption.
Nobody's made fun of me yet. So far, so good!
At least for awhile.

CHAPTER 4

For the first time ever, I met other Tomboys.

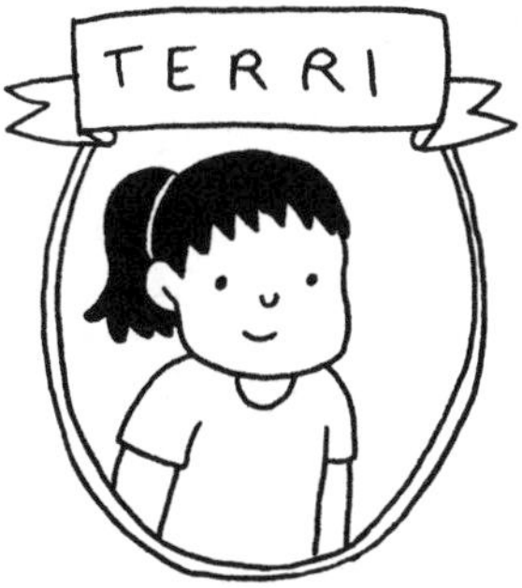
TERRI

and

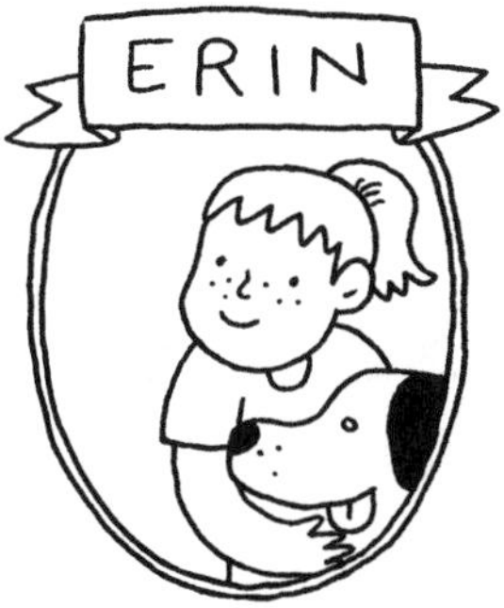
ERIN

* Is in my class.
* Likes science and cartoons.
* Wants a bat as a pet.
* Likes to watch baseball.
* Has a ponytail.

* Is best friends with Terri.
* Likes Queen and The Police.
* Has a dog that will steal food off your plate.
* Has a ponytail.

I fit in really well with them, even though I didn't have a ponytail.

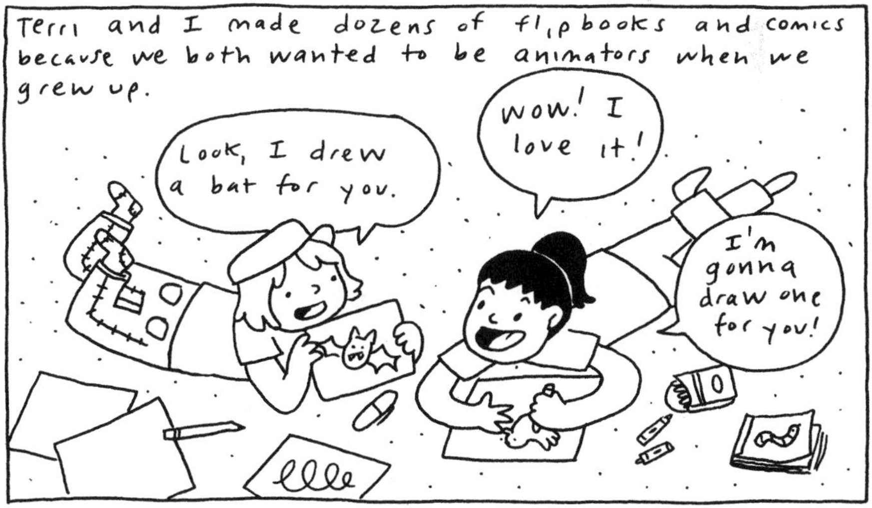
Terri and I made dozens of flipbooks and comics because we both wanted to be animators when we grew up.
Look, I drew a bat for you.
Wow! I love it!
I'm gonna draw one for you!

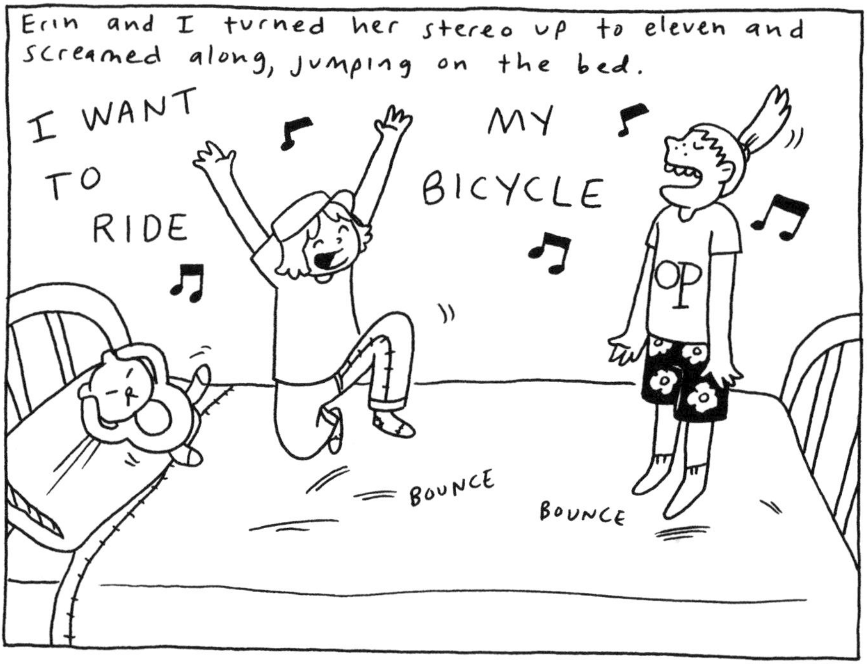
Erin and I turned her stereo up to eleven and screamed along, jumping on the bed.
I WANT TO RIDE
MY BICYCLE
OP
BOUNCE
BOUNCE

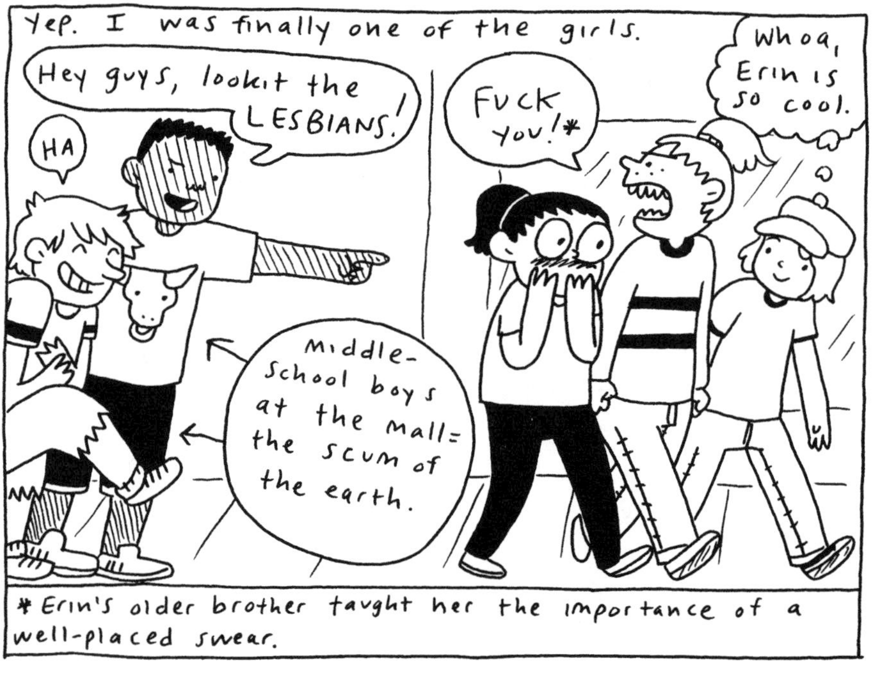
Yep. I was finally one of the girls.
Hey guys, lookit the LESBIANS!
HA
Middle-School boys at the mall= the scum of the earth.
FUCK YOU!*
Whoa, Erin is so cool.
* Erin's older brother taught her the importance of a well-placed swear.

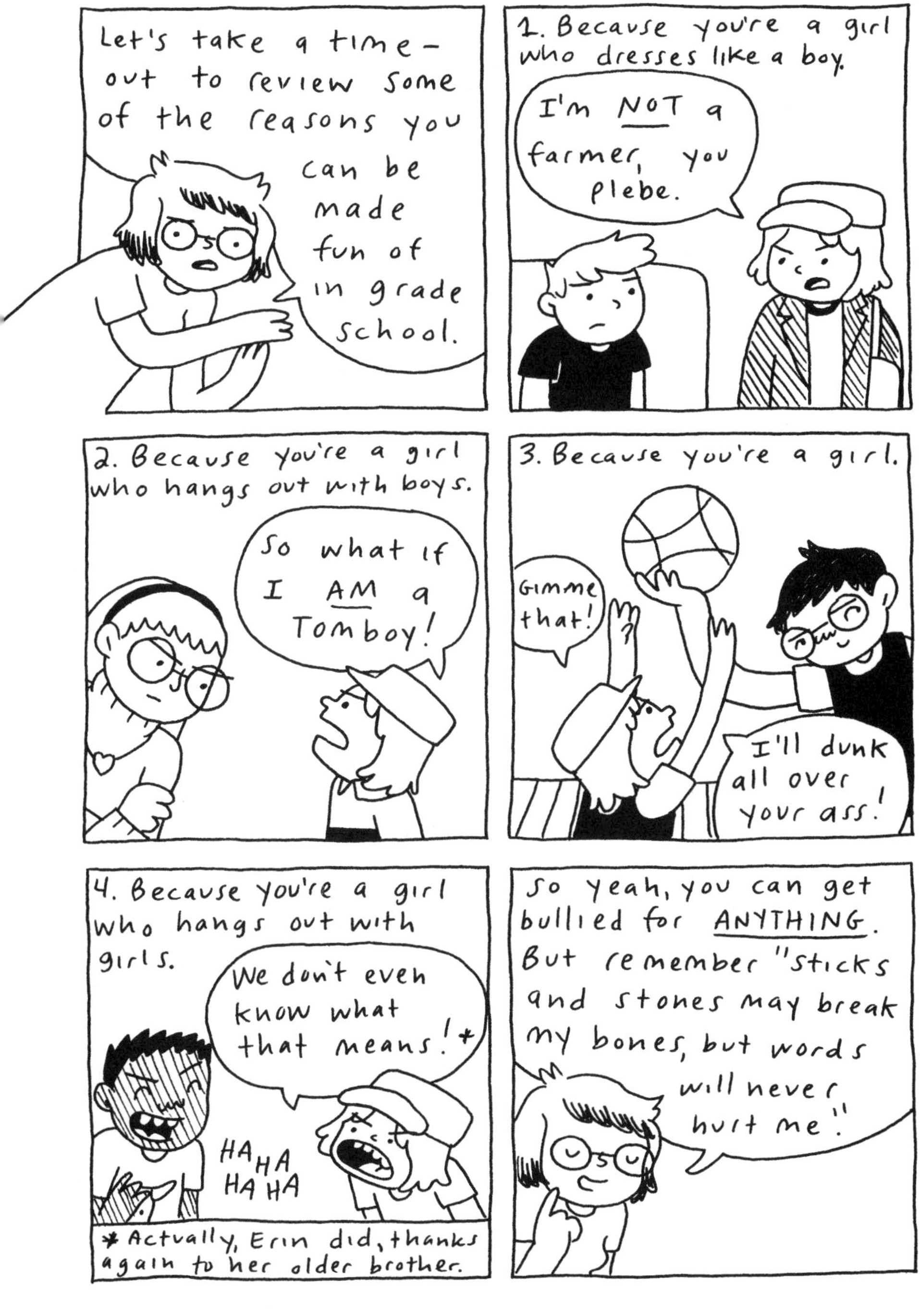
Let's take a time-out to review some of the reasons you
can be made fun of in grade school.
1. Because you're a girl who dresses like a boy.
I'm NOT a farmer, you plebe.
2. Because you're a girl who hangs out with boys.
So what if I AM a Tomboy!
3. Because you're a girl.
Gimme that!
?
I'll dunk all over your ass!
4. Because you're a girl who hangs out with girls.
We don't even know what that means!*
HA HA HA HA
* Actually, Erin did, thanks again to her older brother.
So yeah, you can get bullied for ANYTHING. But remember "sticks and stones may break my bones, but words
will never hurt me"!

Which, unfortunately for me, was an invitation for my bullies to try even harder...

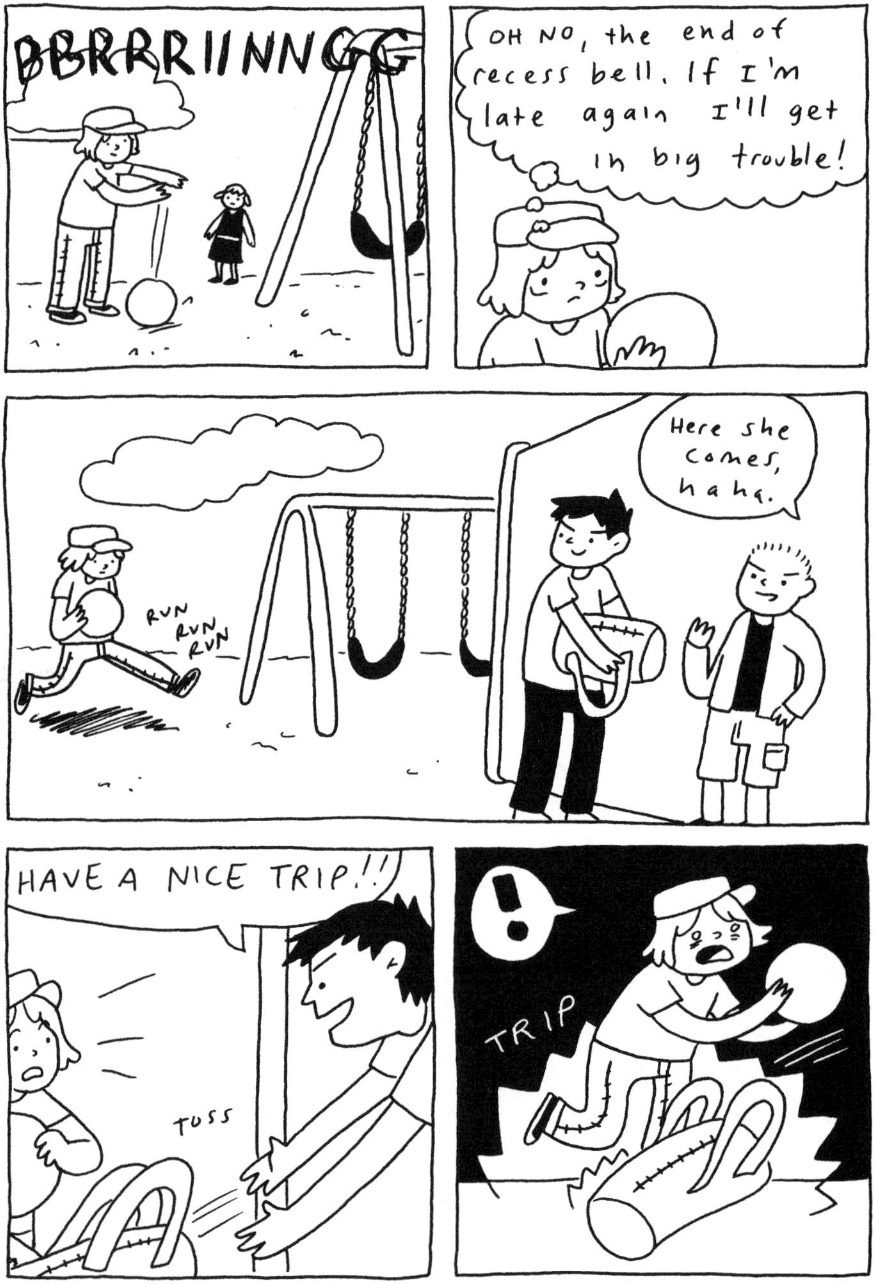
BBRRRRIINNGG
OH NO, the end of recess bell. If I'm late again I'll get in big trouble!
RUN RUN RUN
Here she comes, haha.
HAVE A NICE TRIP!!
TOSS
!
TRIP

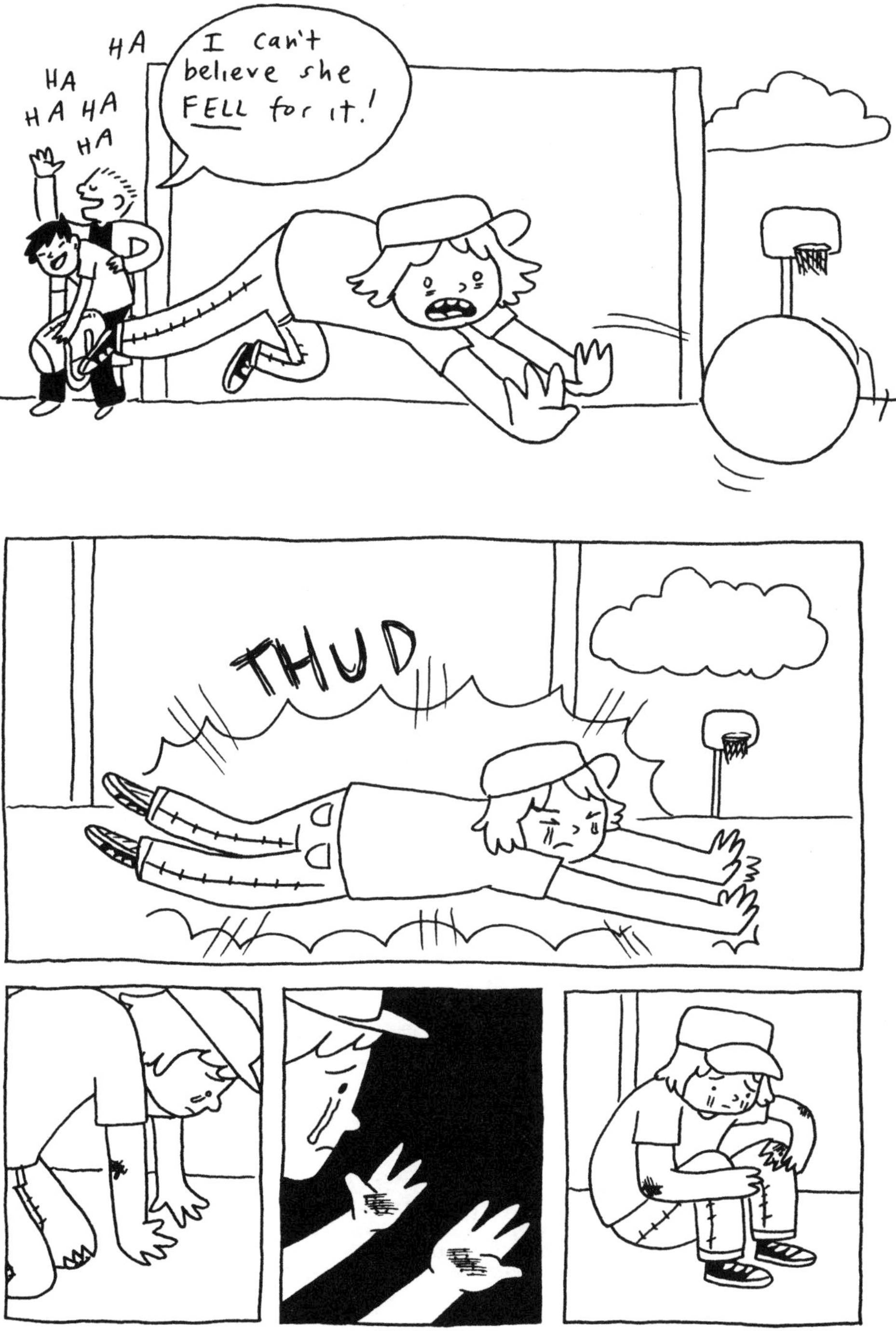
HA
HA
HA HA
HA
I can't believe she FELL for it!
THUD

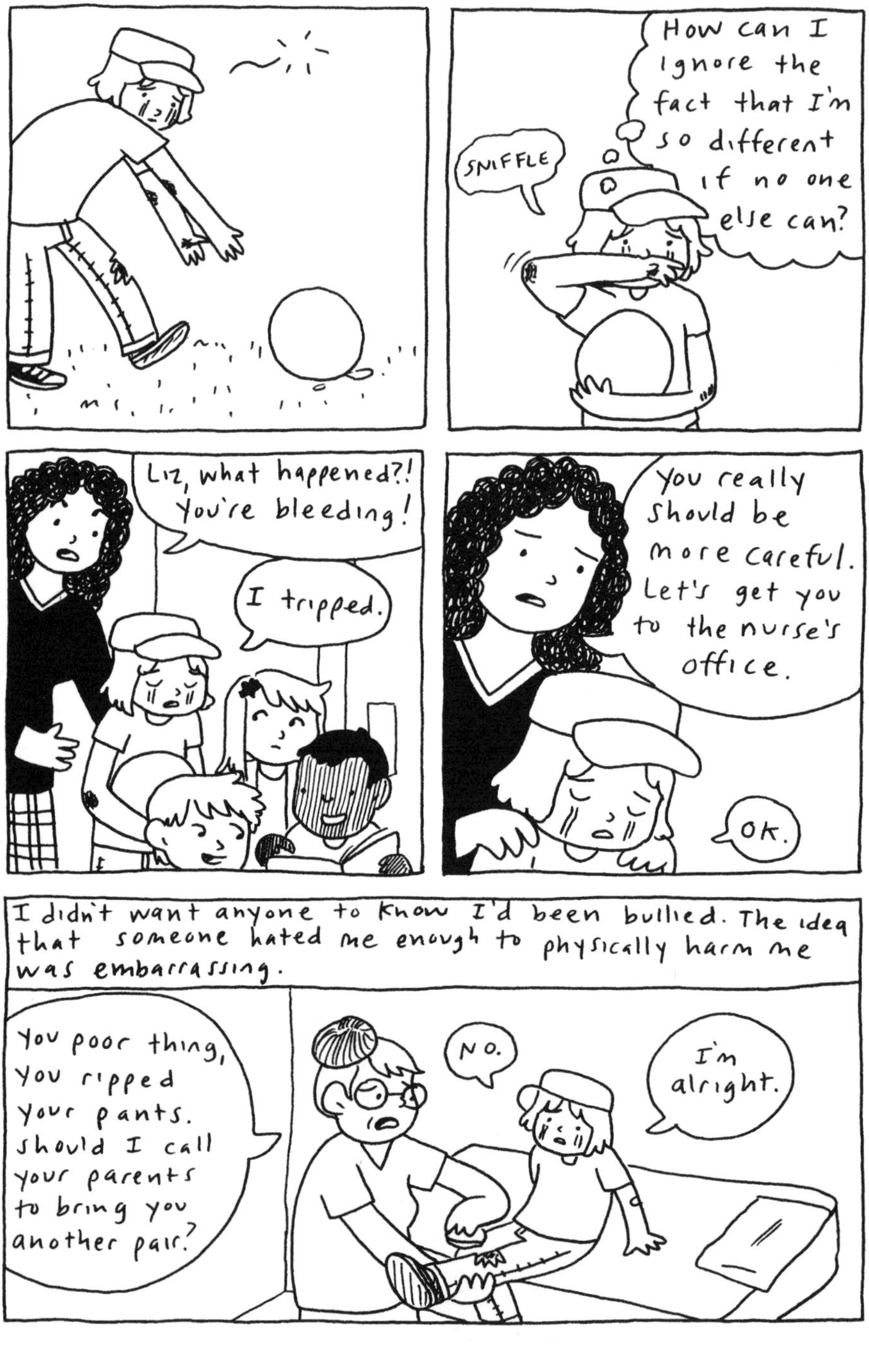
How can I ignore the fact that I'm so different if no one else can?
SNIFFLE
Liz, what happened?! You're bleeding!
I tripped.
You really should be more careful. Let's get you to the nurse's office.
OK.
I didn't want anyone to know I'd been bullied. The idea that someone hated me enough to physically harm me was embarrassing.
You poor thing, you ripped your pants. Should I call your parents to bring you another pair?
No.
I'm alright.

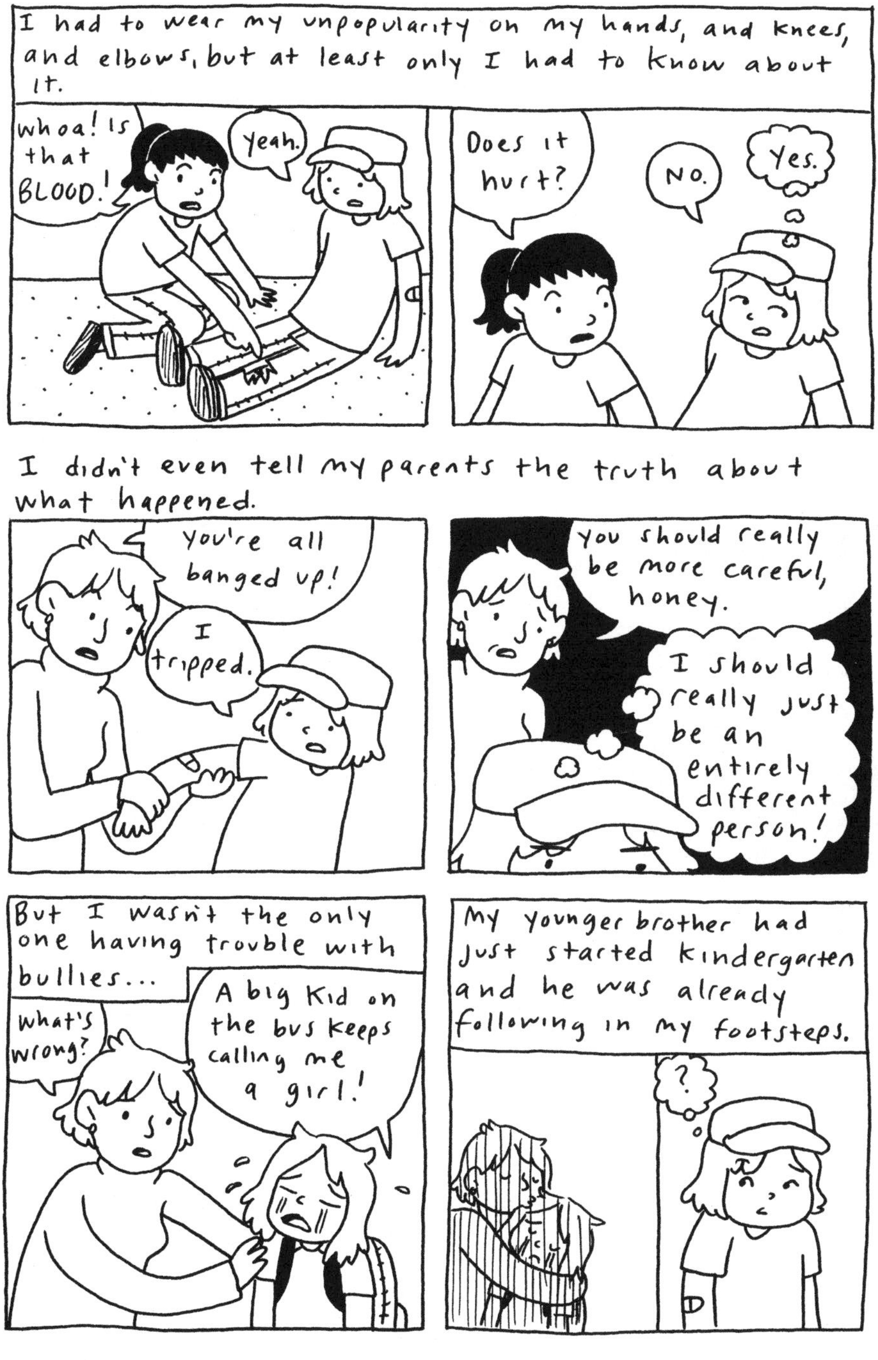
I had to wear my unpopularity on my hands, and knees, and elbows, but at least only I had to know about it.
whoa! Is that BLOOD!
yeah.
Does it hurt?
No.
Yes.
I didn't even tell my parents the truth about what happened.
you're all banged up!
I tripped.
You should really be more careful, honey.
I should really just be an entirely different person!
But I wasn't the only one having trouble with bullies...
what's wrong?
A big kid on the bus keeps calling me a girl!
My younger brother had just started kindergarten and he was already following in my footsteps.
?

In my brother's case, his only offense was having long hair, which became a trend a few years later when grunge got big, so Jamie was just ahead of his time. An unappreciated fashion guru, perhaps.

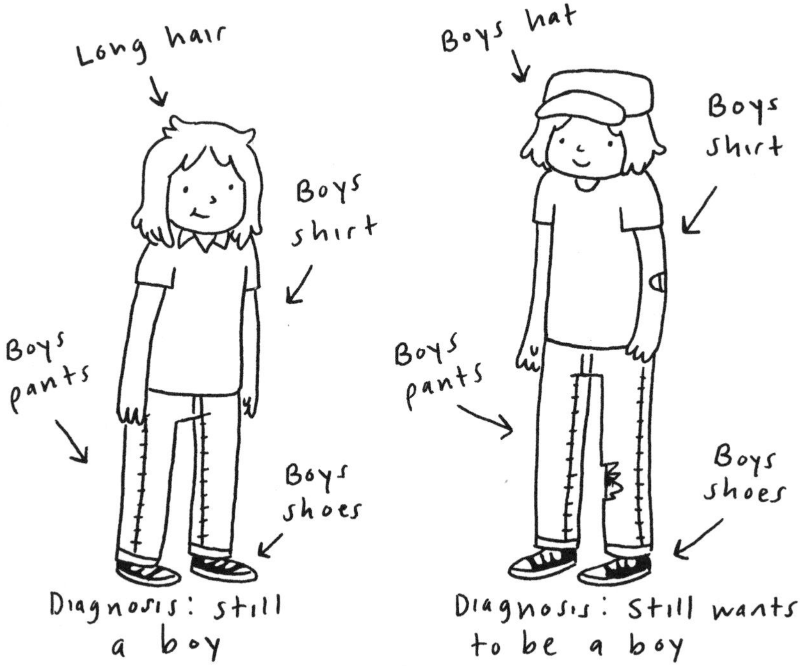
Long hair
Boys shirt
Boys pants
Boys shoes
Diagnosis: still a boy
Boys hat
Boys shirt
Boys pants
Boys shoes
Diagnosis: still wants to be a boy

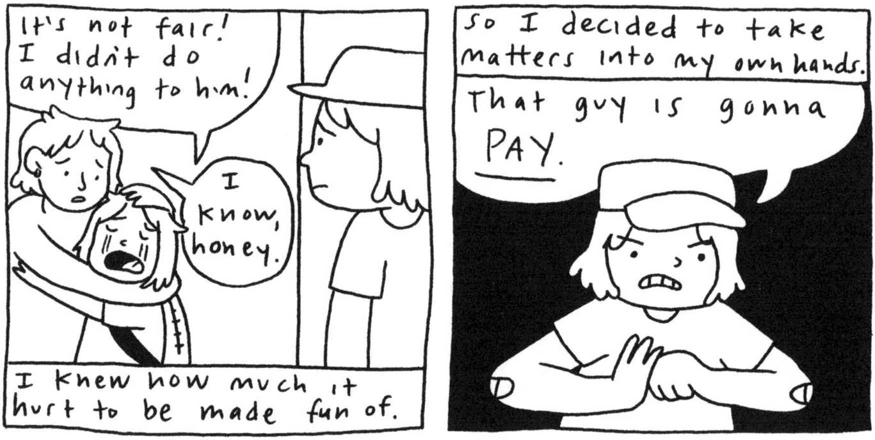
It's not fair! I didn't do anything to him!
I know, honey.
I knew how much it hurt to be made fun of.
So I decided to take matters into my own hands.
That guy is gonna PAY.

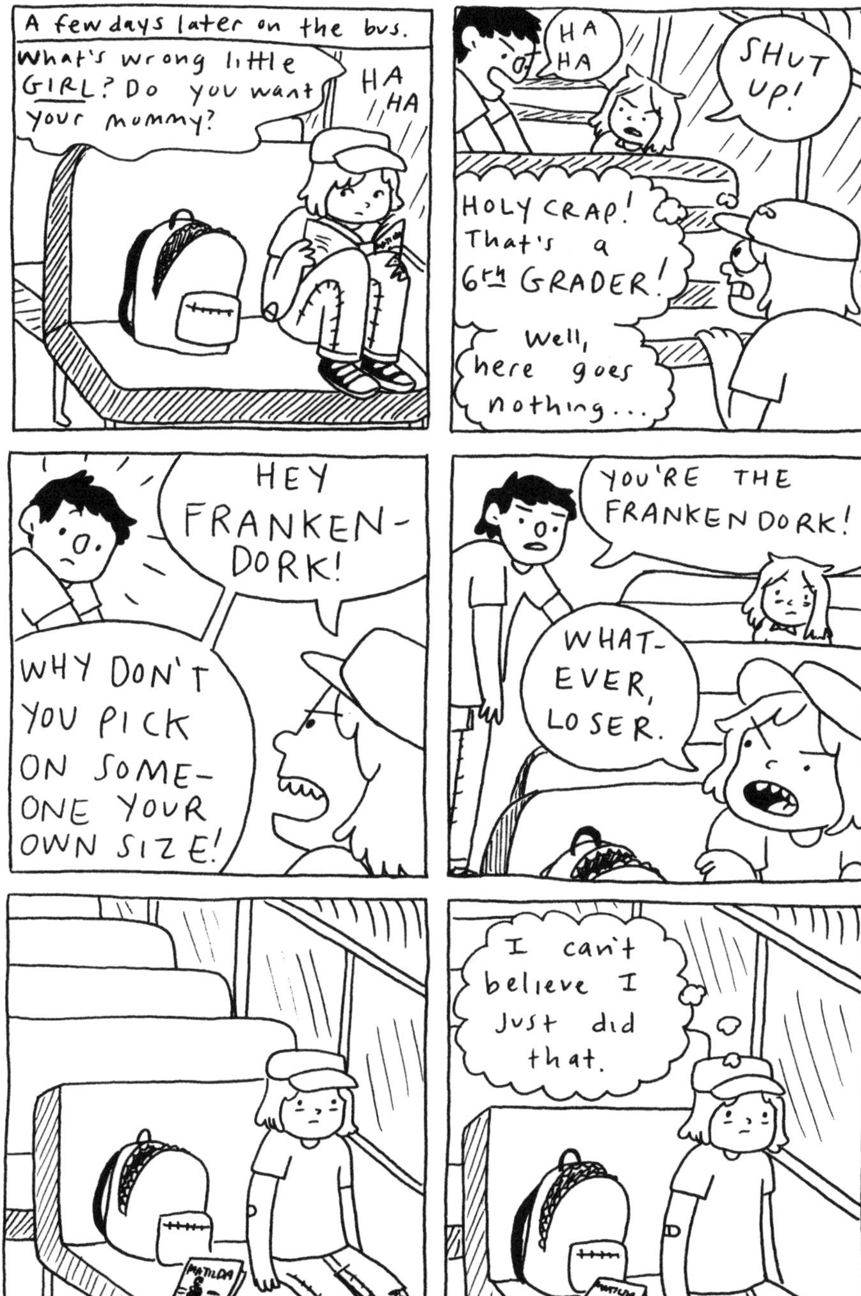

A few days later on the bus.
What's wrong little GIRL? Do you want your mommy?
HA HA
HA HA
SHUT UP!
HOLY CRAP! That's a 6th GRADER!
Well, here goes nothing...
HEY FRANKEN-DORK!
WHY DON'T YOU PICK ON SOME-ONE YOUR OWN SIZE!
YOU'RE THE FRANKENDORK!
WHAT-EVER, LOSER.
MATILDA
I can't believe I just did that.
MATILDA

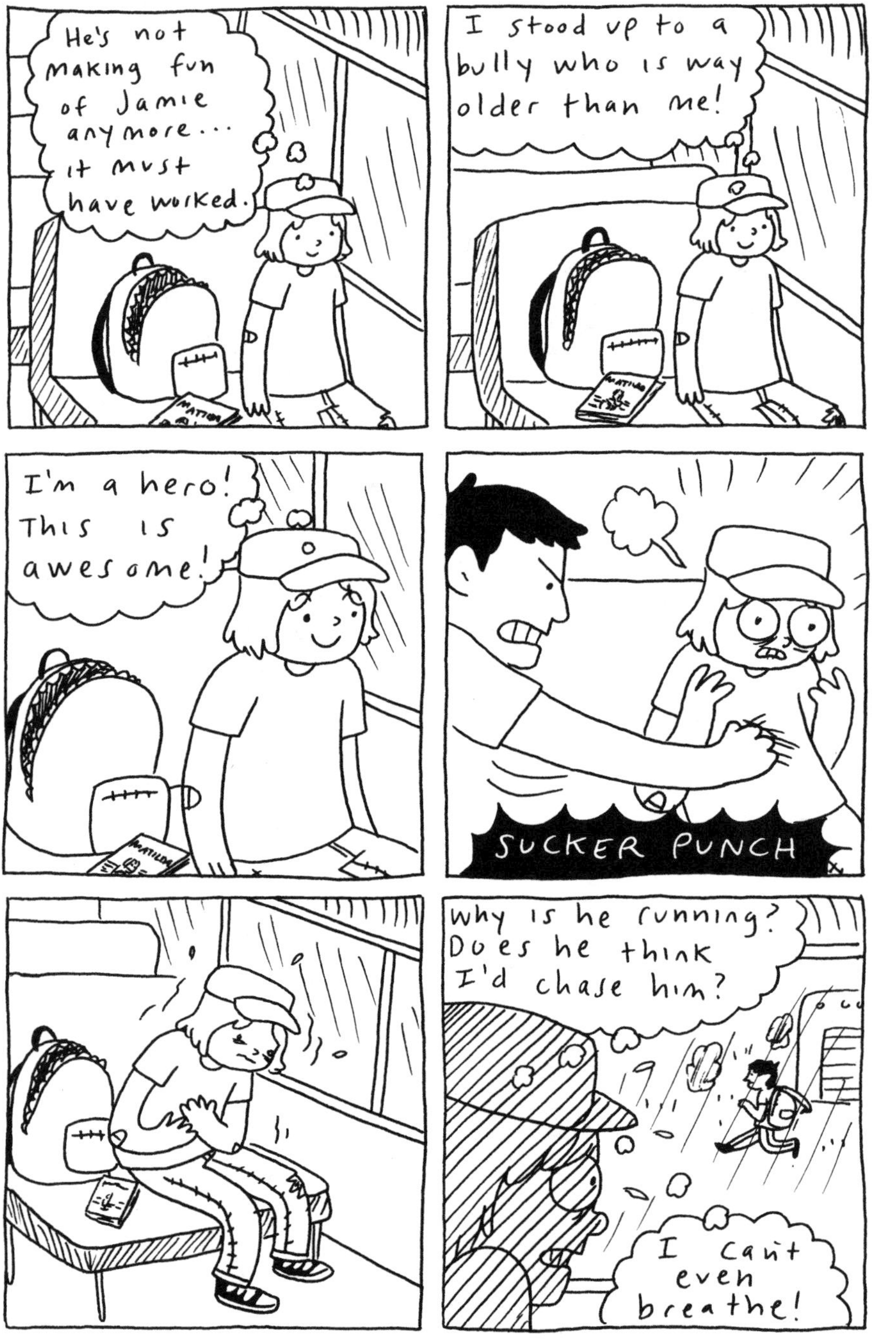
He's not making fun of Jamie anymore... it must have worked.
I stood up to a bully who is way older than me!
I'm a hero! This is awesome!
SUCKER PUNCH
Why is he running? Does he think I'd chase him?
I can't even breathe!

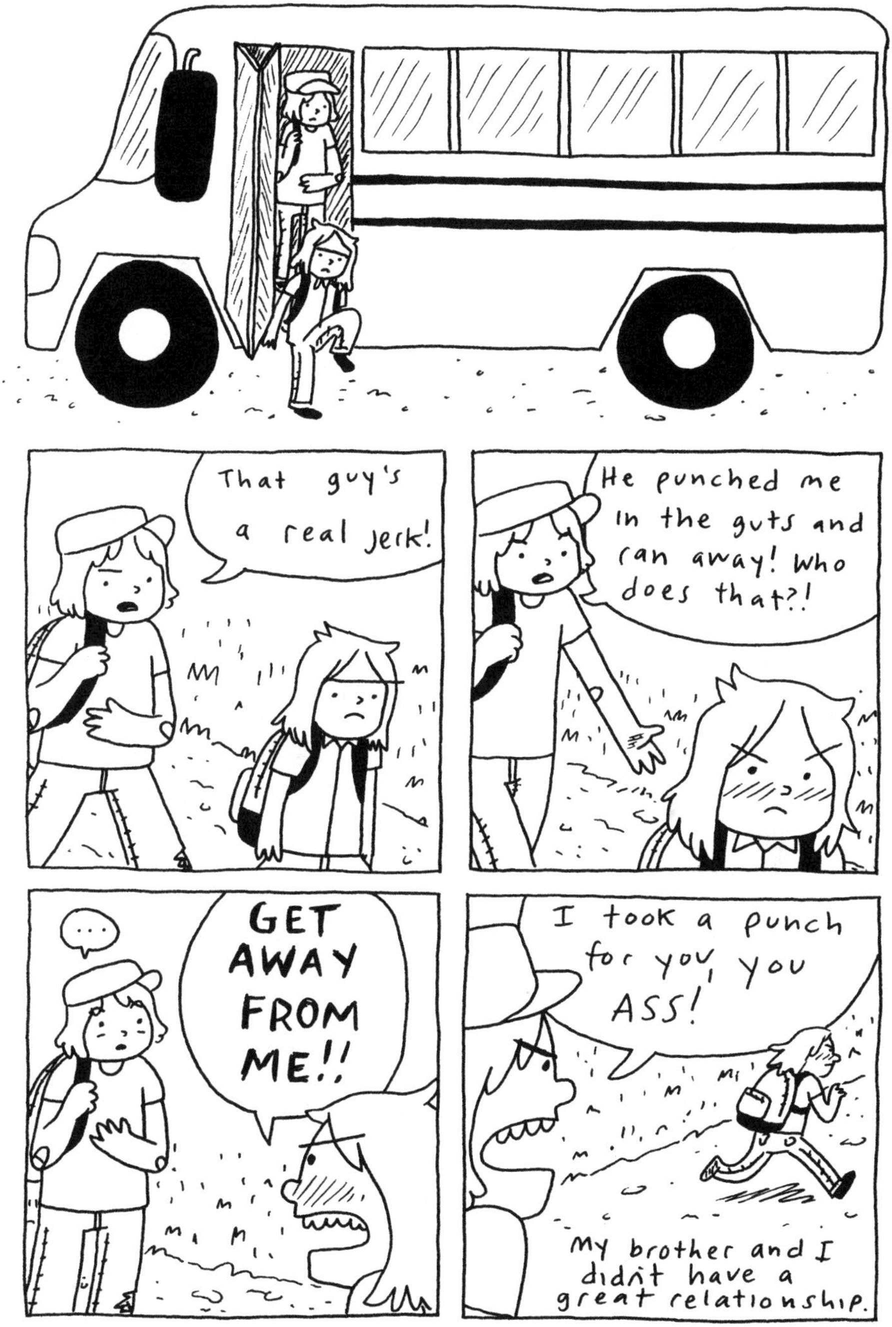
That guy's a real jerk!
He punched me in the guts and ran away! Who does that?!
...
GET AWAY FROM ME!!
I took a punch for you, you ASS!
My brother and I didn't have a great relationship.

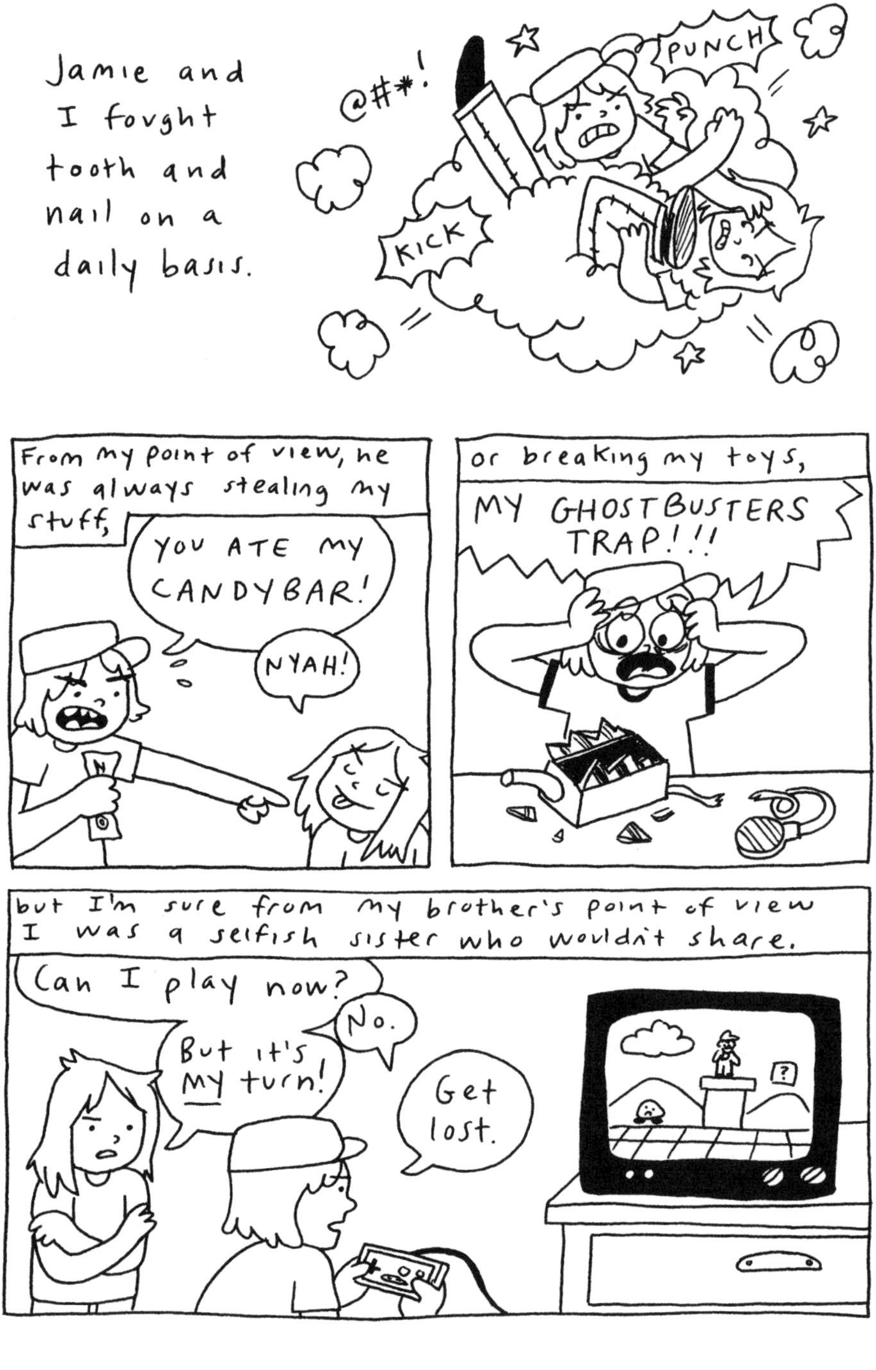
Jamie and I fought tooth and nail on a daily basis.
@#*!
PUNCH
KICK
From my point of view, he was always stealing my stuff,
YOU ATE MY CANDYBAR!
NYAH!
or breaking my toys,
MY GHOSTBUSTERS TRAP!!!
but I'm sure from my brother's point of view I was a selfish sister who wouldn't share.
Can I play now?
No.
But it's MY turn!
Get lost.

I felt my chivalrous act made up for our prior differences. I mean, I got sucker-punched by a boy who was at least two years older than me!

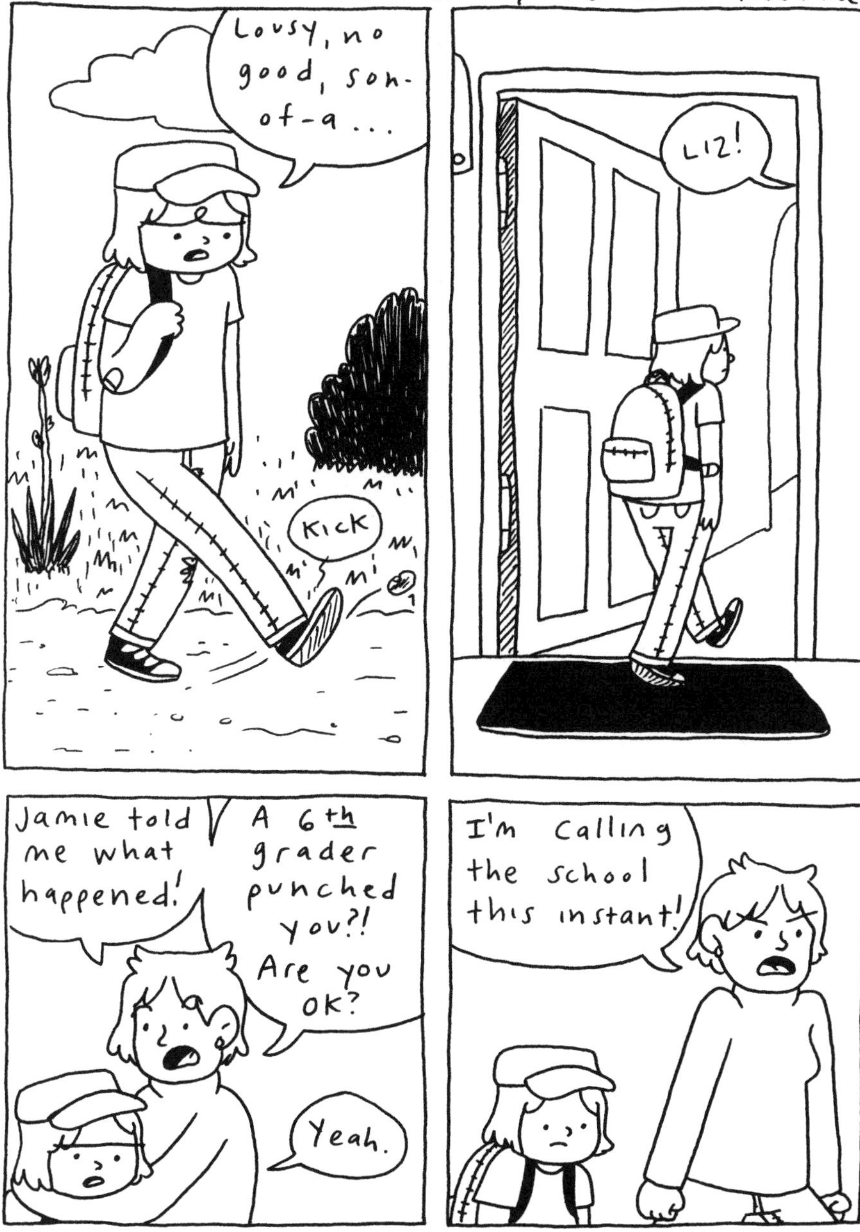
Lousy, no good, son-of-a...
KICK
LIZ!
Jamie told me what happened!
A 6th grader punched you?! Are you OK?
Yeah.
I'm calling the school this instant!

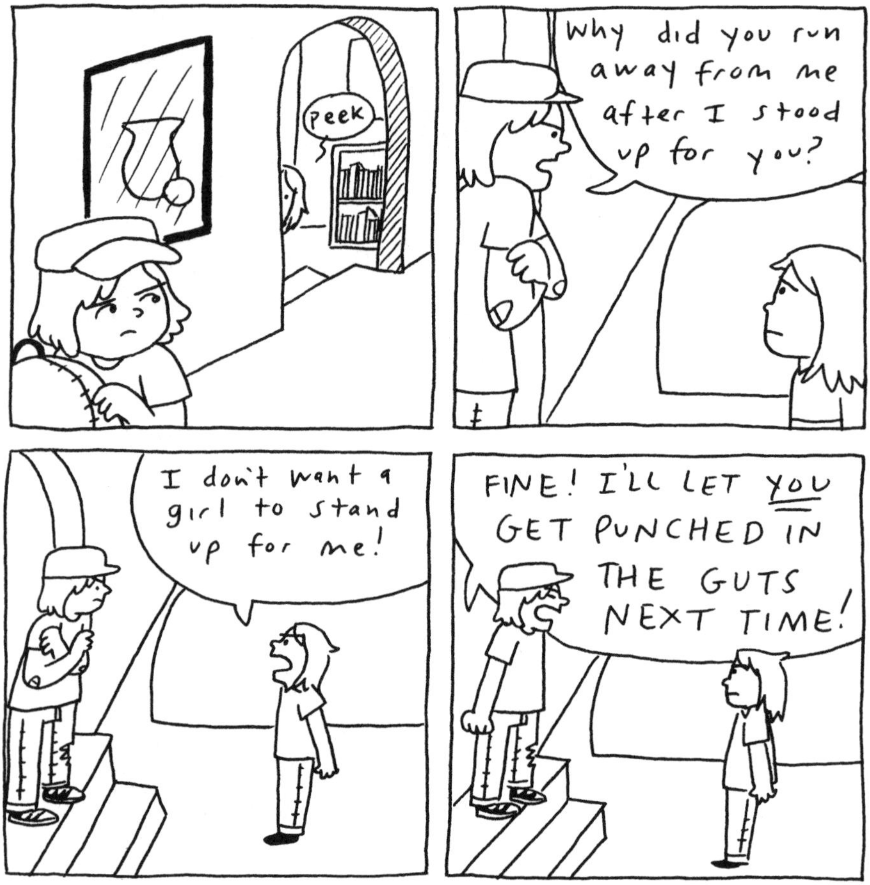
peek
Why did you run away from me after I stood up for you?
I don't want a girl to stand up for me!
FINE! I'LL LET YOU GET PUNCHED IN THE GUTS NEXT TIME!

Apparently this had happened while I was too busy riding the high of my victory to notice:

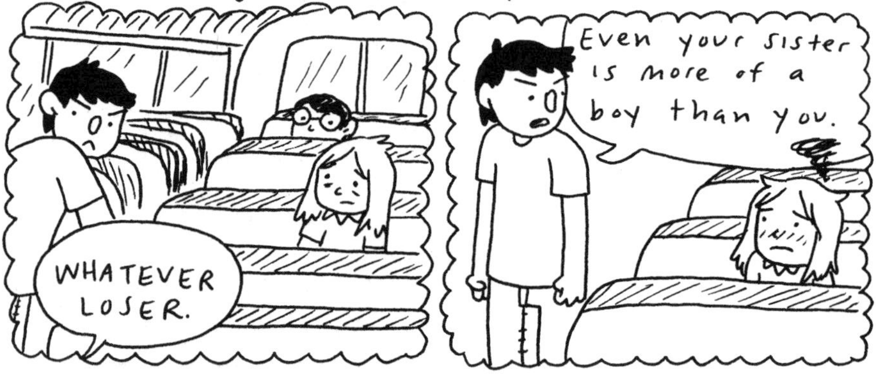
WHATEVER LOSER.
Even your sister is more of a boy than you.

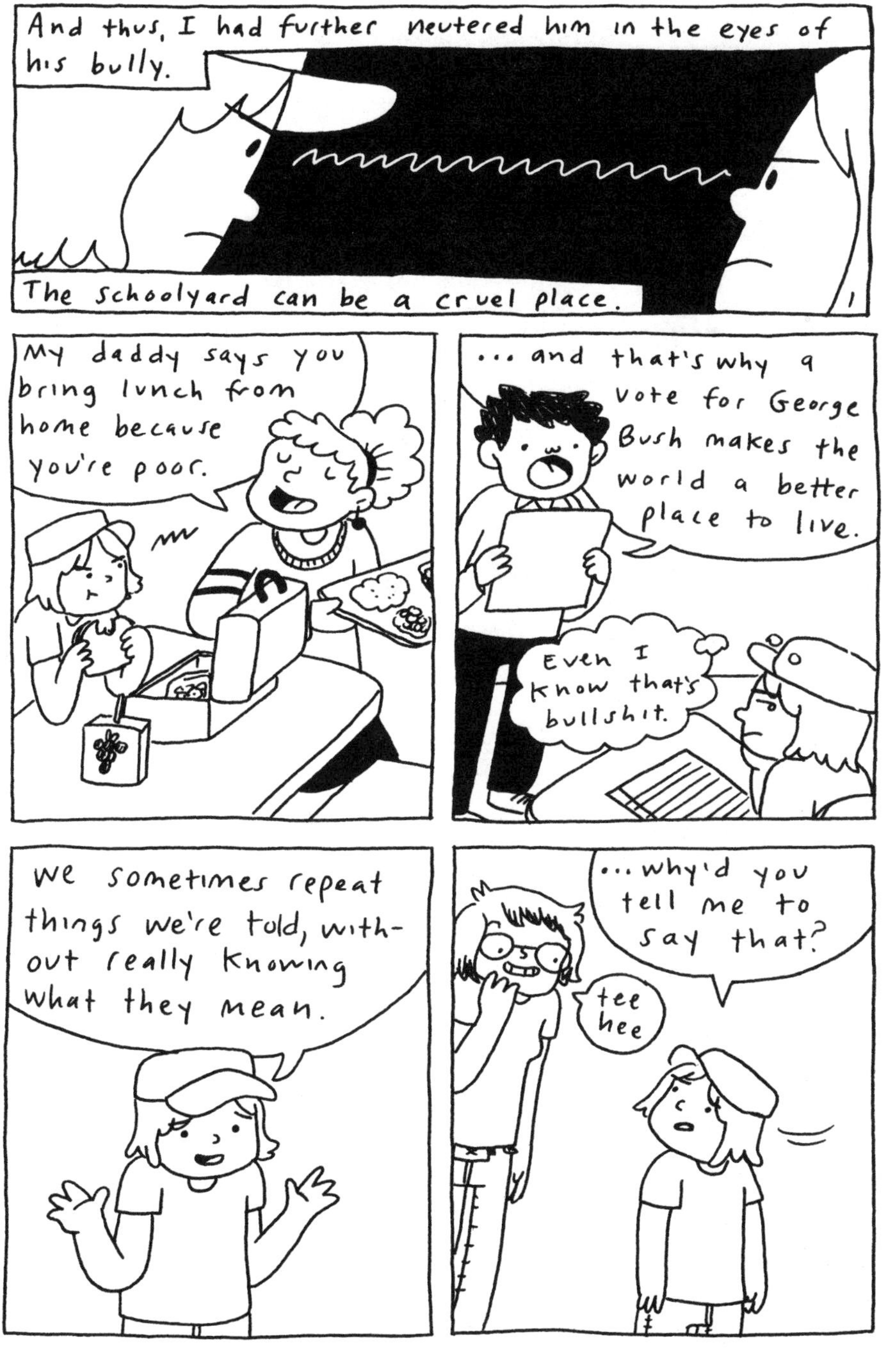
And thus, I had further neutered him in the eyes of his bully.
The schoolyard can be a cruel place.
My daddy says you bring lunch from home because you're poor.
... and that's why a vote for George Bush makes the world a better place to live.
Even I know that's bullshit.
We sometimes repeat things we're told, without really knowing what they mean.
...why'd you tell me to say that?
tee hee

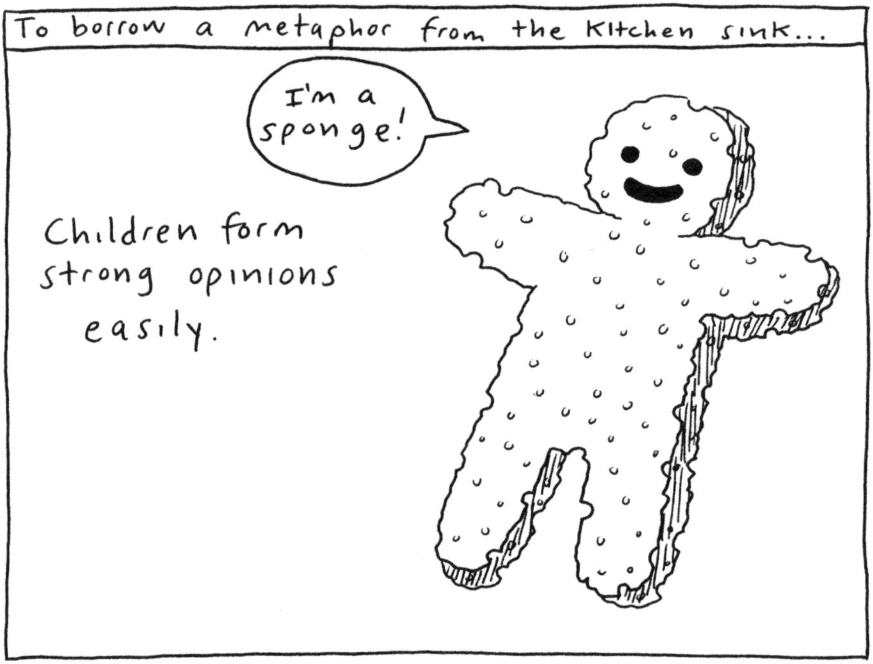
To borrow a metaphor from the kitchen sink...
I'm a sponge!
Children form strong opinions easily.

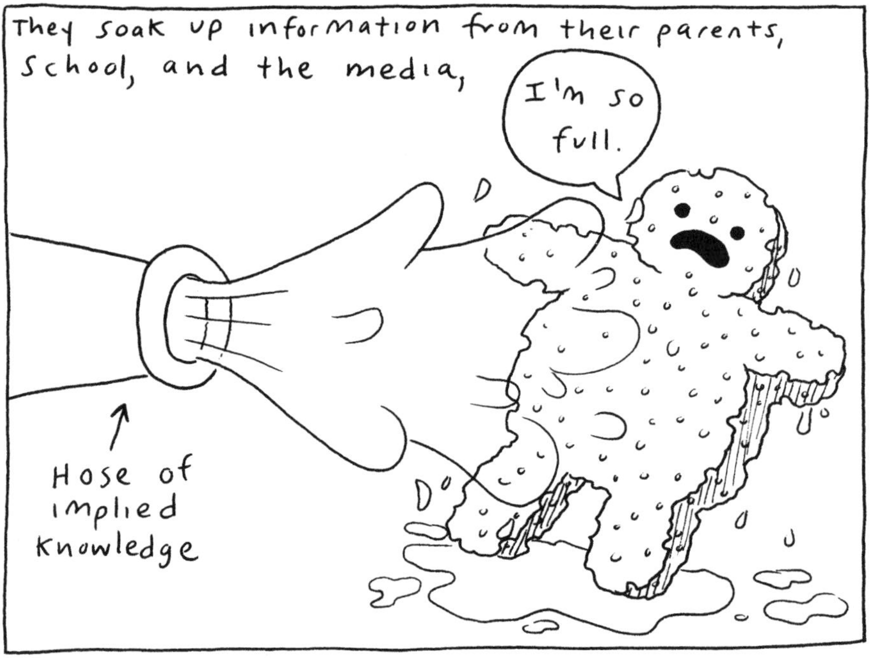
They soak up information from their parents, school, and the media,
I'm so full.
Hose of implied knowledge

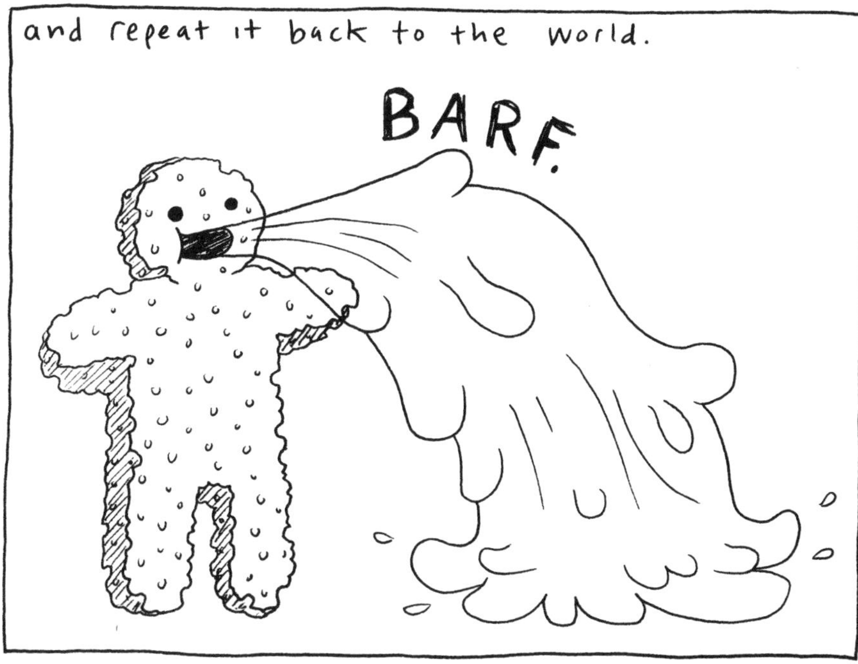
and repeat it back to the world.
BARF.

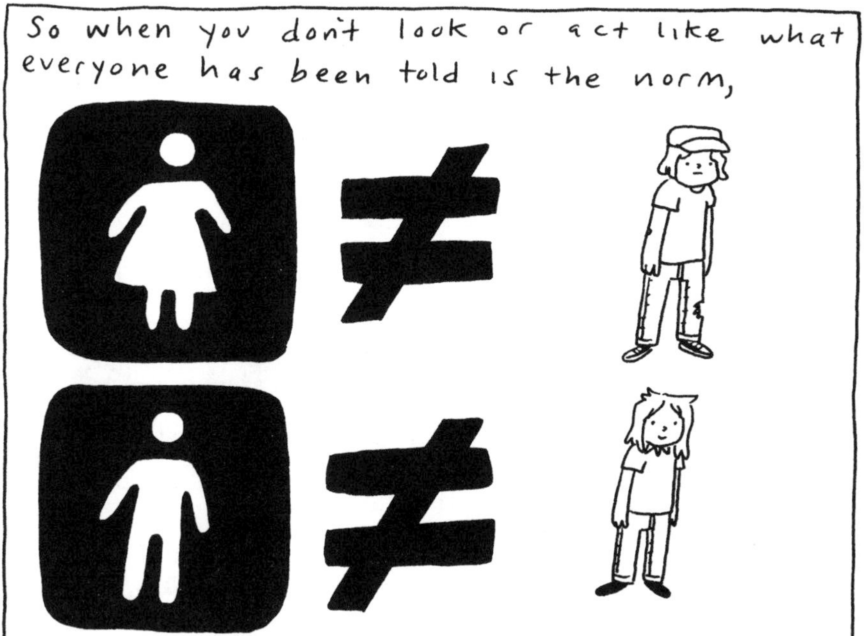
So when you don't look or act like what everyone has been told is the norm,

you get proverbially barfed on a lot.

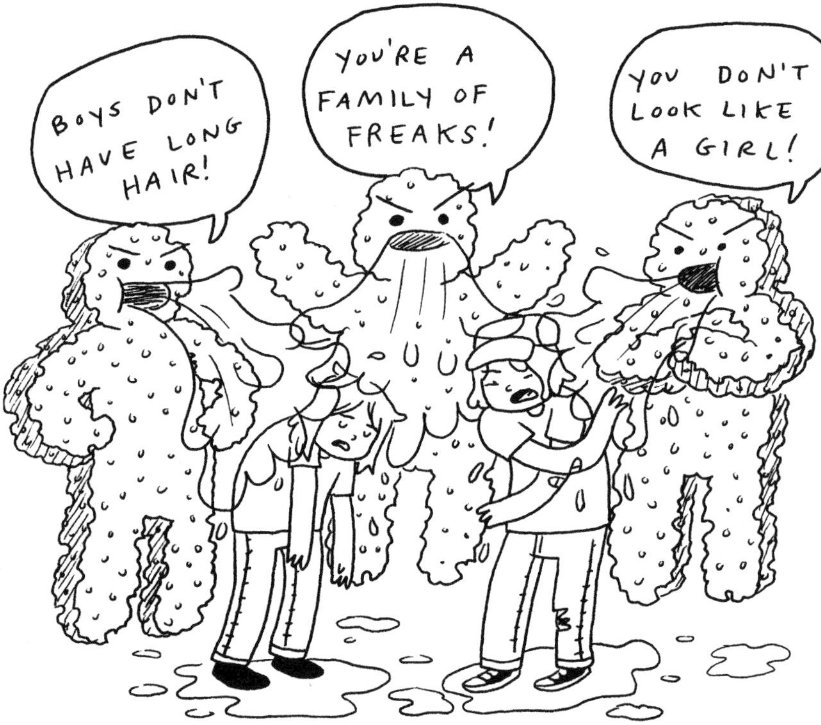
BOYS DON'T HAVE LONG HAIR!
YOU'RE A FAMILY OF FREAKS!
YOU DON'T LOOK LIKE A GIRL!

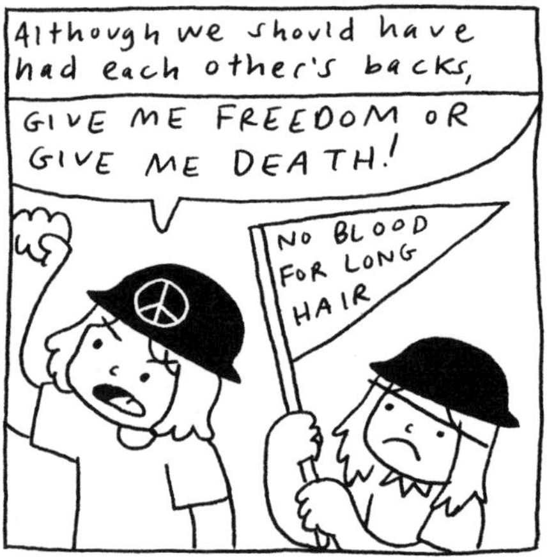
Although we should have had each other's backs,
GIVE ME FREEDOM OR GIVE ME DEATH!
NO BLOOD FOR LONG HAIR

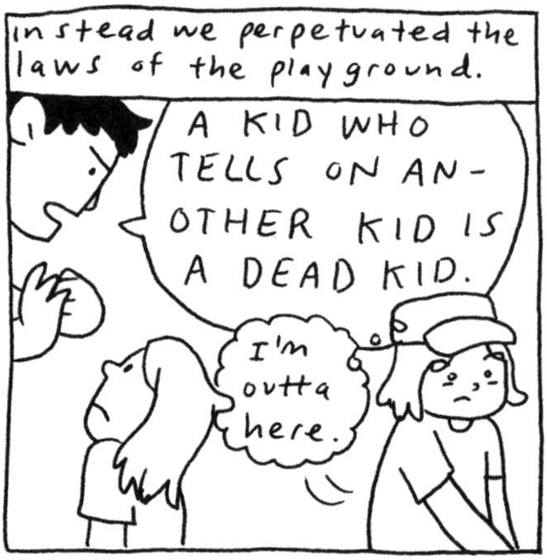
instead we perpetuated the laws of the playground.
A KID WHO TELLS ON ANOTHER KID IS A DEAD KID.
I'm outta here.

CHAPTER 5

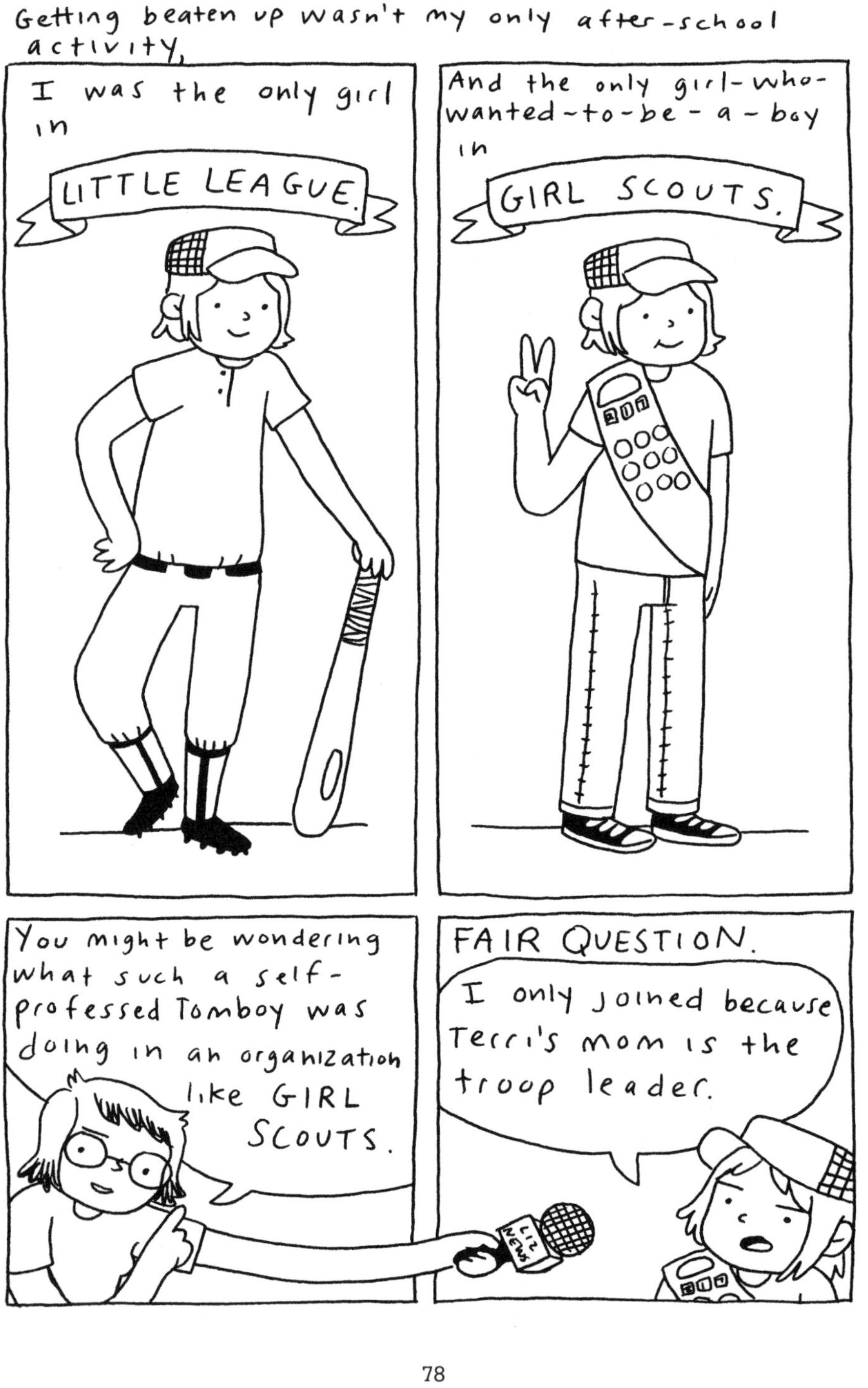
Getting beaten up wasn't my only after-school activity,
I was the only girl in
LITTLE LEAGUE.
And the only girl-who-wanted-to-be-a-boy in
GIRL SCOUTS.
You might be wondering what such a self-professed Tomboy was doing in an organization like GIRL SCOUTS.
LIZ NEWS
FAIR QUESTION.
I only joined because Terri's mom is the troop leader.

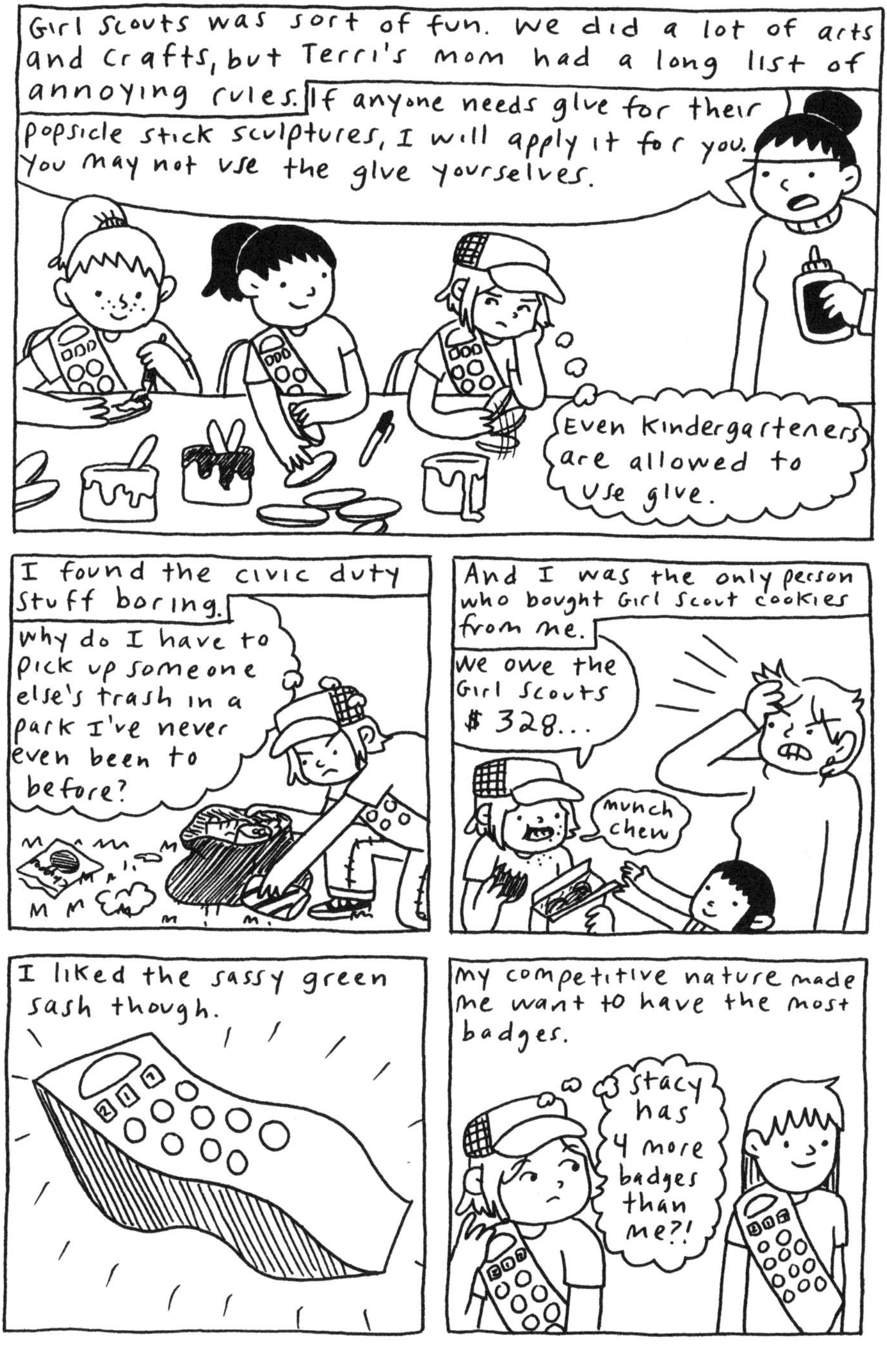

Girl Scouts was sort of fun. We did a lot of arts and crafts, but Terri's mom had a long list of annoying rules.
If anyone needs glue for their popsicle stick sculptures, I will apply it for you. You may not use the glue yourselves.
Even kindergarteners are allowed to use glue.
I found the civic duty stuff boring.
Why do I have to pick up someone else's trash in a park I've never even been to before?
And I was the only person who bought Girl Scout cookies from me.
We owe the Girl Scouts $328...
munch chew
I liked the sassy green sash though.
My competitive nature made me want to have the most badges.
Stacy has 4 more badges than me?!

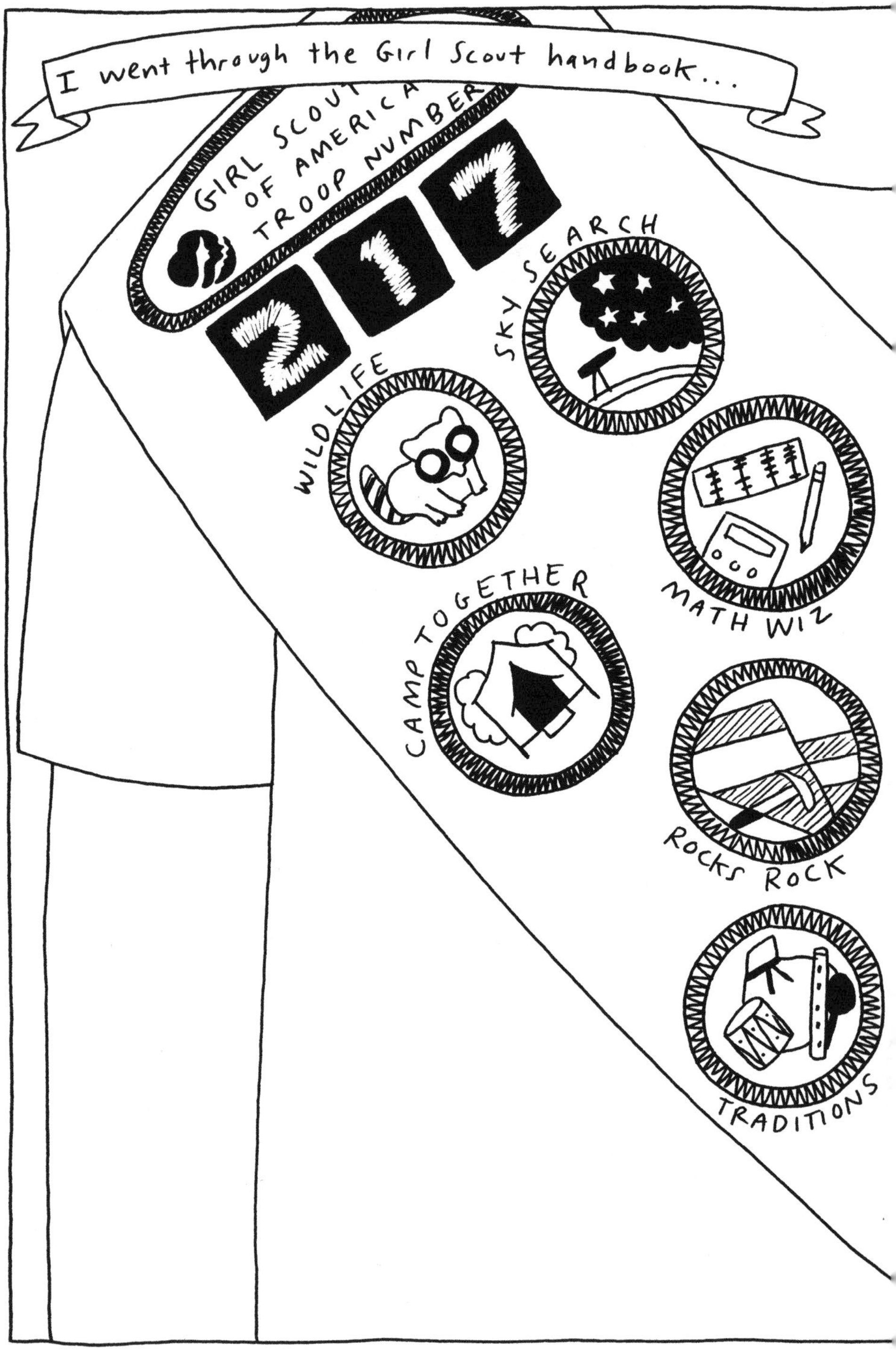
I went through the Girl Scout handbook...
GIRL SCOUTS OF AMERICA TROOP NUMBER
217
SKY SEARCH
WILDLIFE
MATH WIZ
CAMP TOGETHER
ROCKS ROCK
TRADITIONS

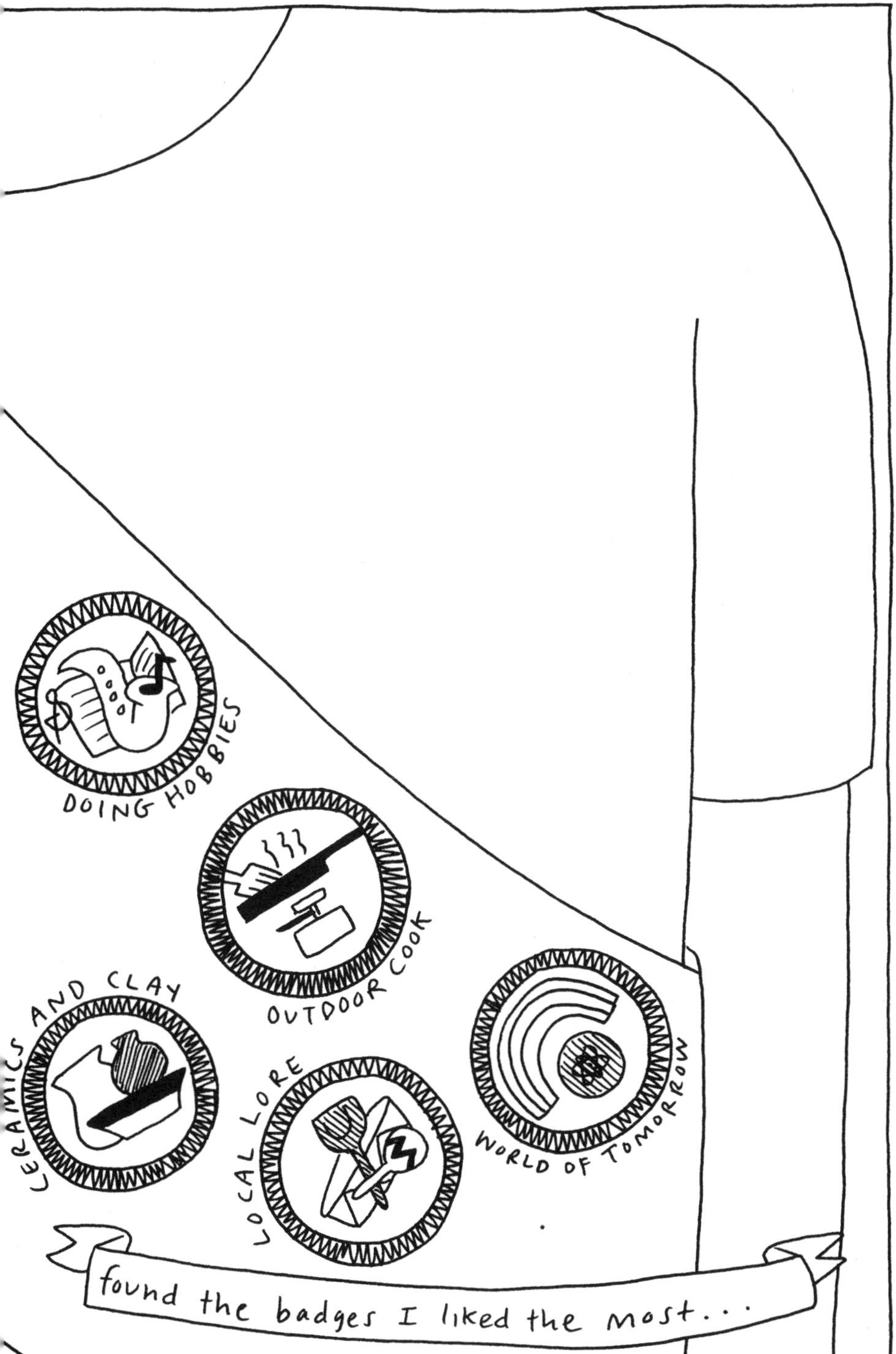
DOING HOBBIES
OUTDOOR COOK
CERAMICS AND CLAY
LOCAL LORE
WORLD OF TOMORROW
found the badges I liked the most...

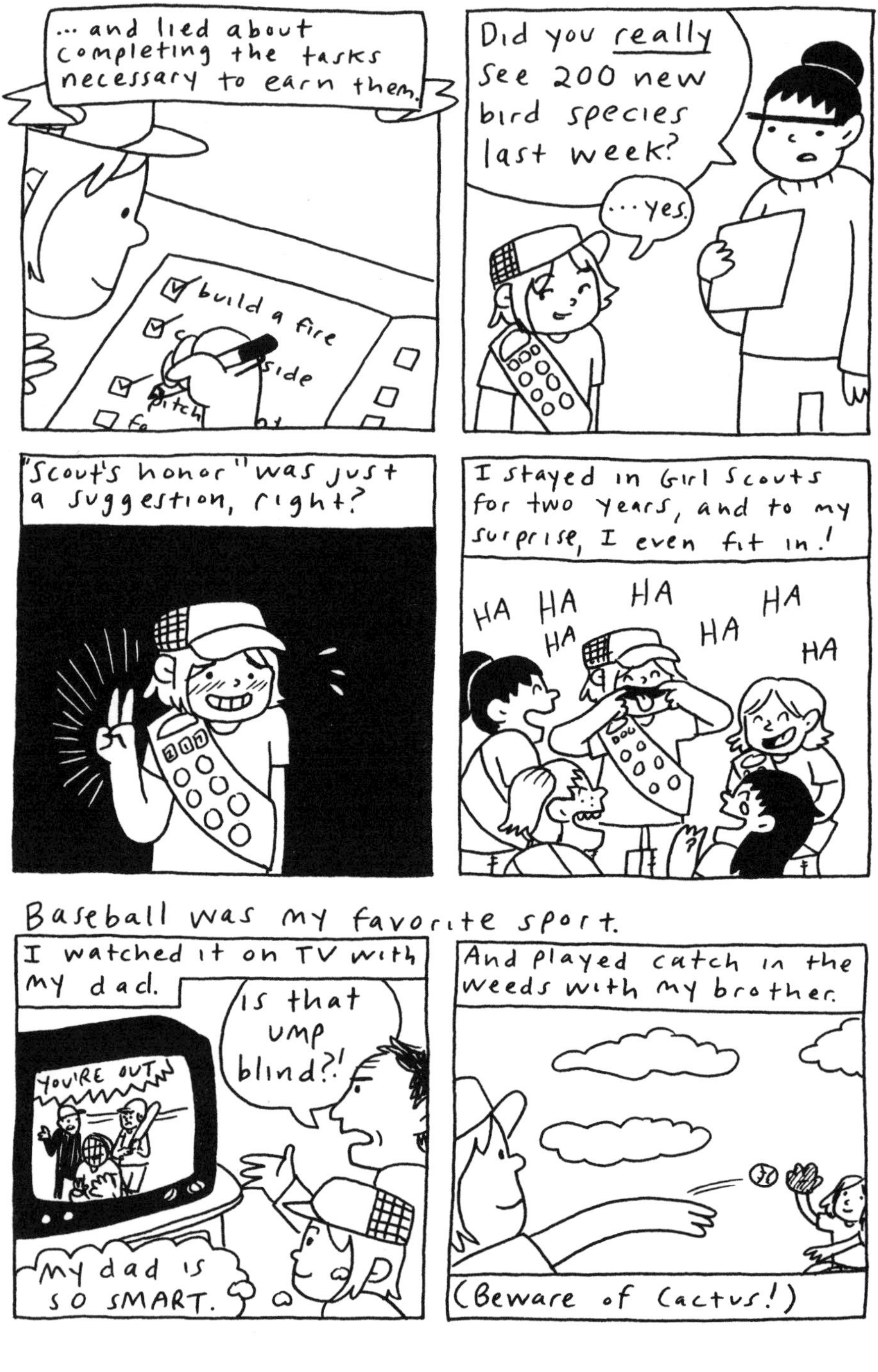
...and lied about completing the tasks necessary to earn them.
build a fire
Did you really see 200 new bird species last week?
...yes.
"Scout's honor" was just a suggestion, right?
I stayed in Girl Scouts for two years, and to my surprise, I even fit in!
HA HA HA HA HA HA HA
Baseball was my favorite sport.
I watched it on TV with my dad.
YOU'RE OUT
Is that ump blind?!
My dad is so smart.
And played catch in the weeds with my brother.
(Beware of Cactus!)

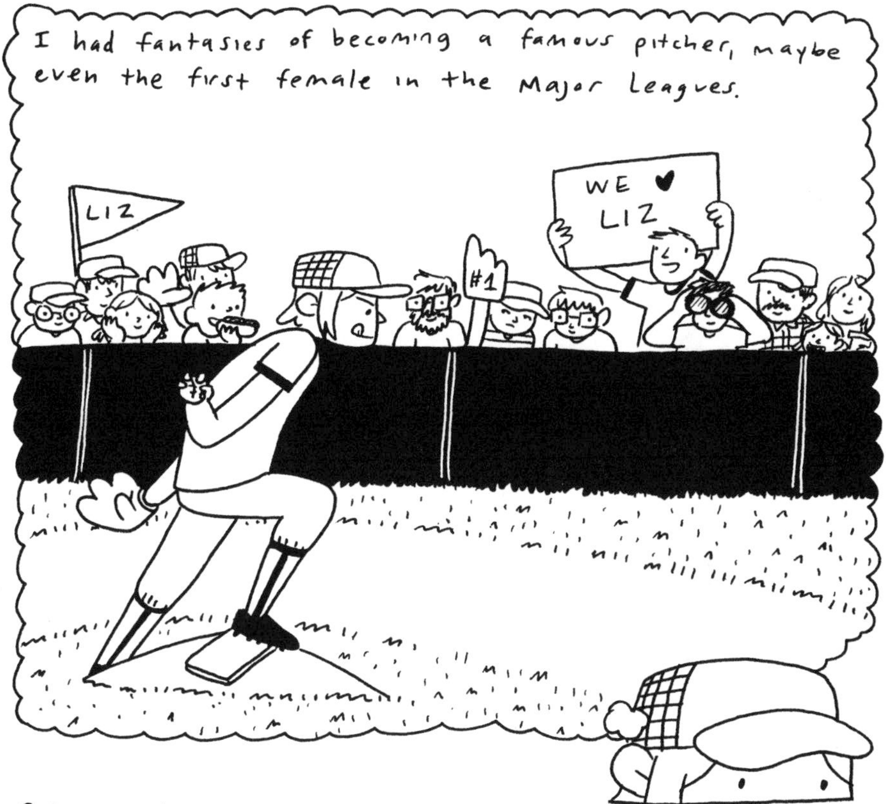
I had fantasies of becoming a famous pitcher, maybe even the first female in the Major Leagues.
LIZ
WE ♥ LIZ
#1

But in order to gain any confidence in your athletic ability, you'd need a coach or teammates who cheered you on and turned your passion into talent.

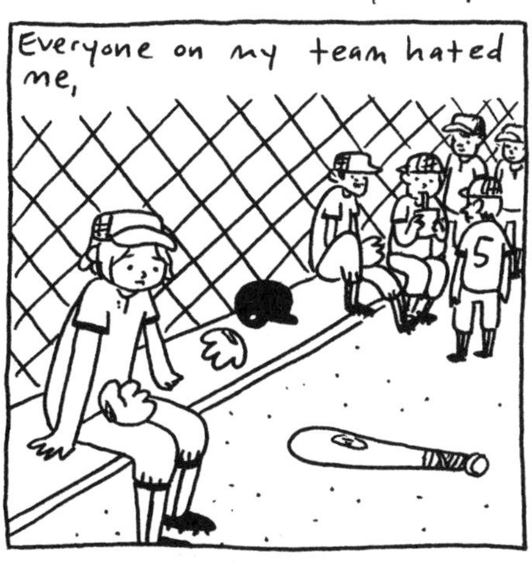
Everyone on my team hated me,
5

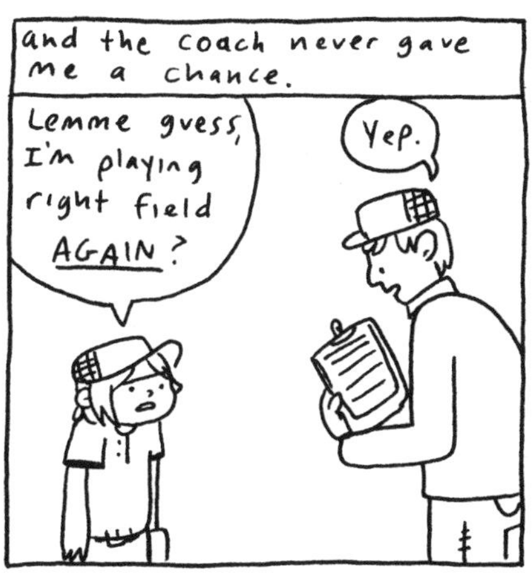
and the coach never gave me a chance.
Lemme guess, I'm playing right field AGAIN?
Yep.

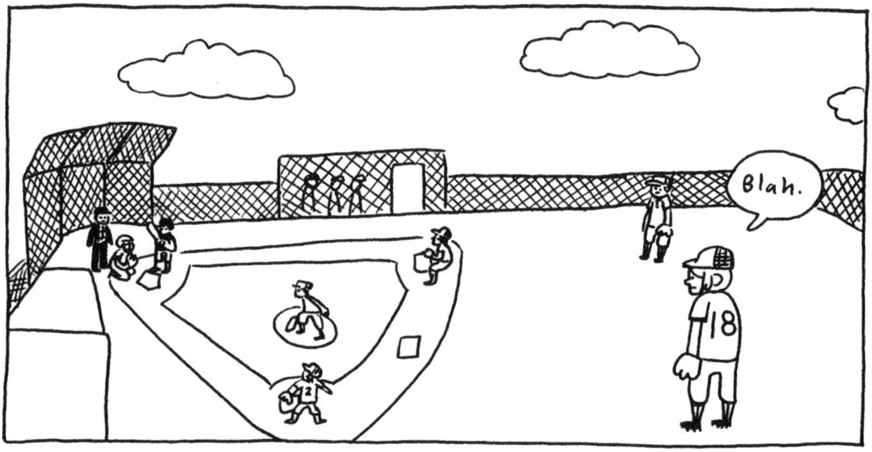
Blah.

I would spend my exile in the outfield daydreaming.

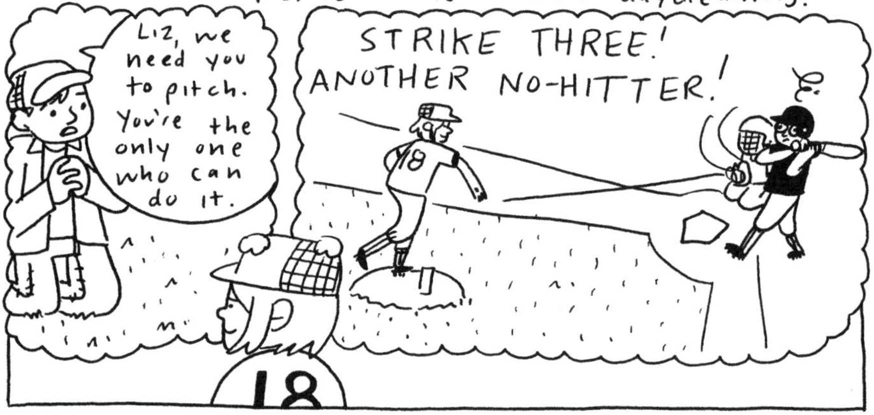
Liz, we need you to pitch. You're the only one who can do it.
STRIKE THREE! ANOTHER NO-HITTER!
18

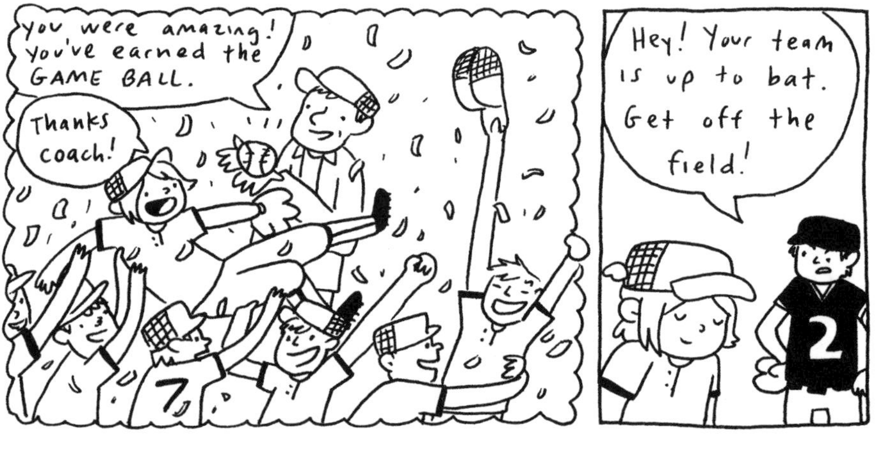
You were amazing! You've earned the GAME BALL.
Thanks coach!
Hey! Your team is up to bat. Get off the field!

I was perplexed as to why all the boys on my team shunned me. Wouldn't they think a girl who played baseball was cooler than one who didn't?

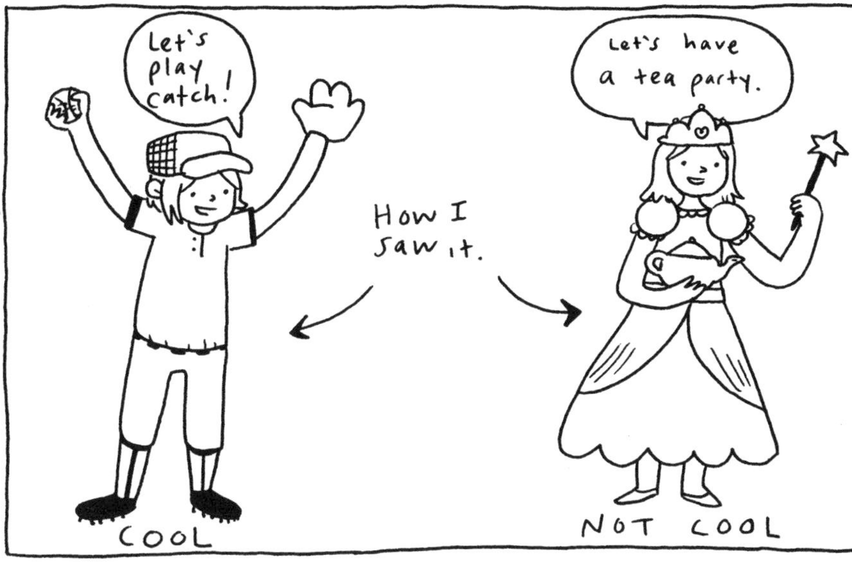
Let's play catch!
Let's have a tea party.
How I saw it.
COOL
NOT COOL

In hindsight, it was probably less that they disliked me and more that they saw having a girl on their team as a weakness.

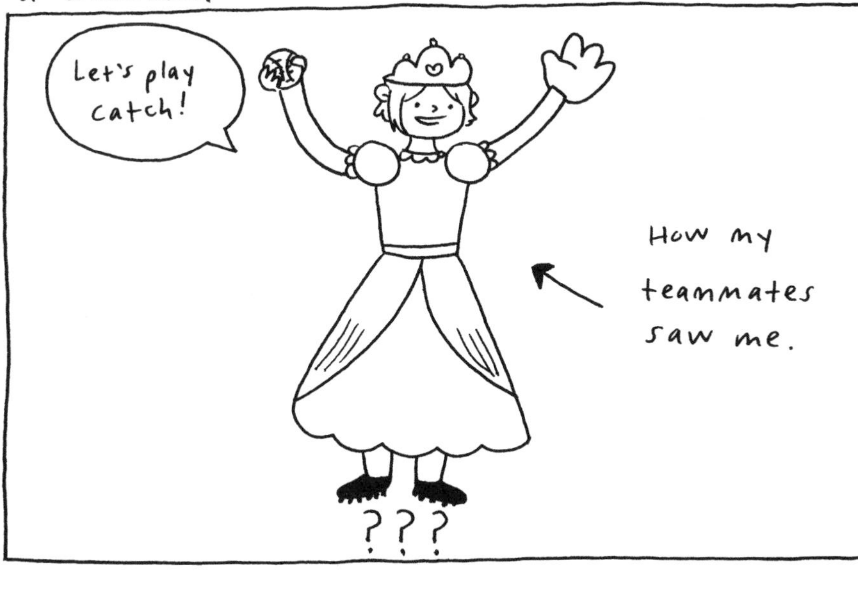
Let's play catch!
How my teammates saw me.
???

And why shouldn't they percieve me as a weakness? I saw other girls as being weak, too.

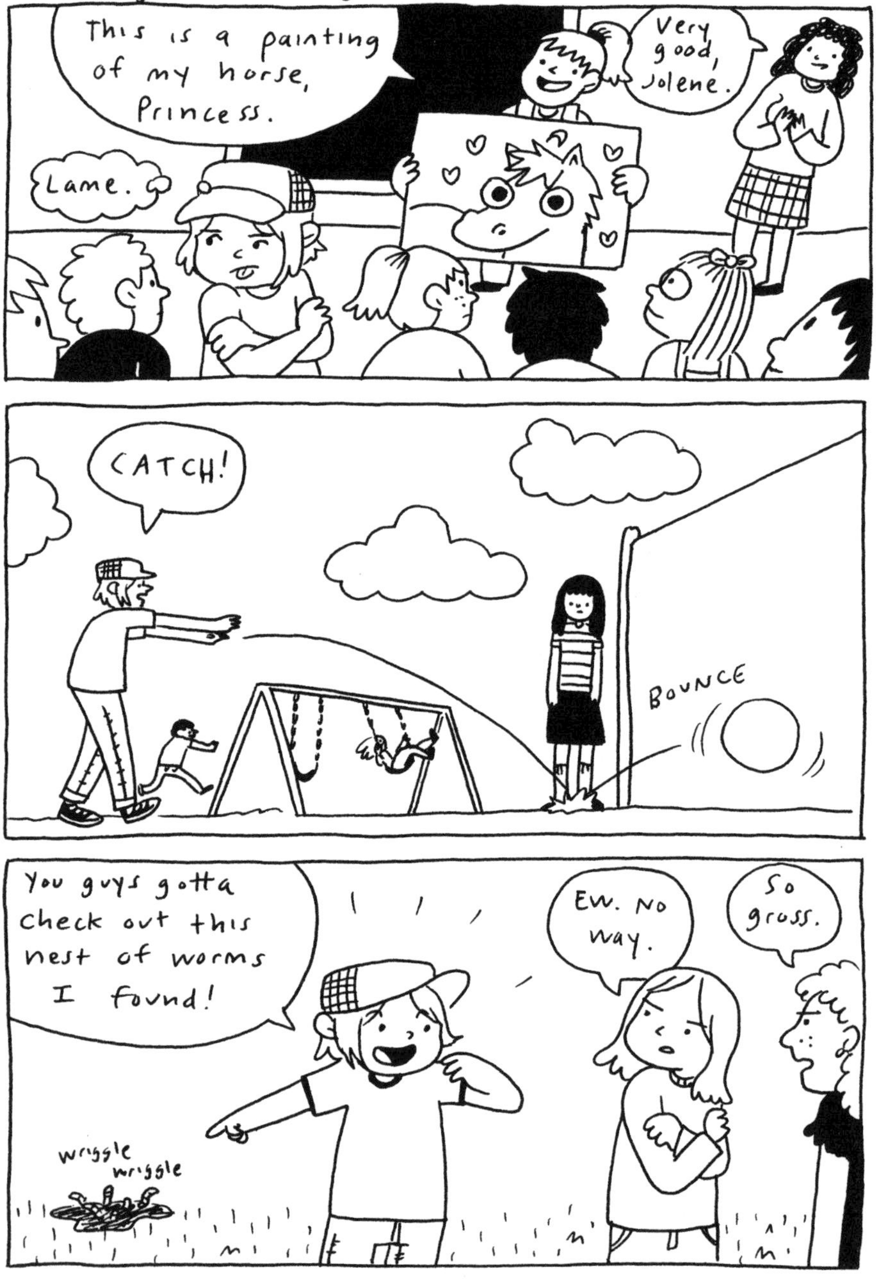
This is a painting of my horse, Princess.
Very good, Jolene.
Lame.
CATCH!
BOUNCE
You guys gotta check out this nest of worms I found!
Ew. No way.
So gross.
wriggle wriggle

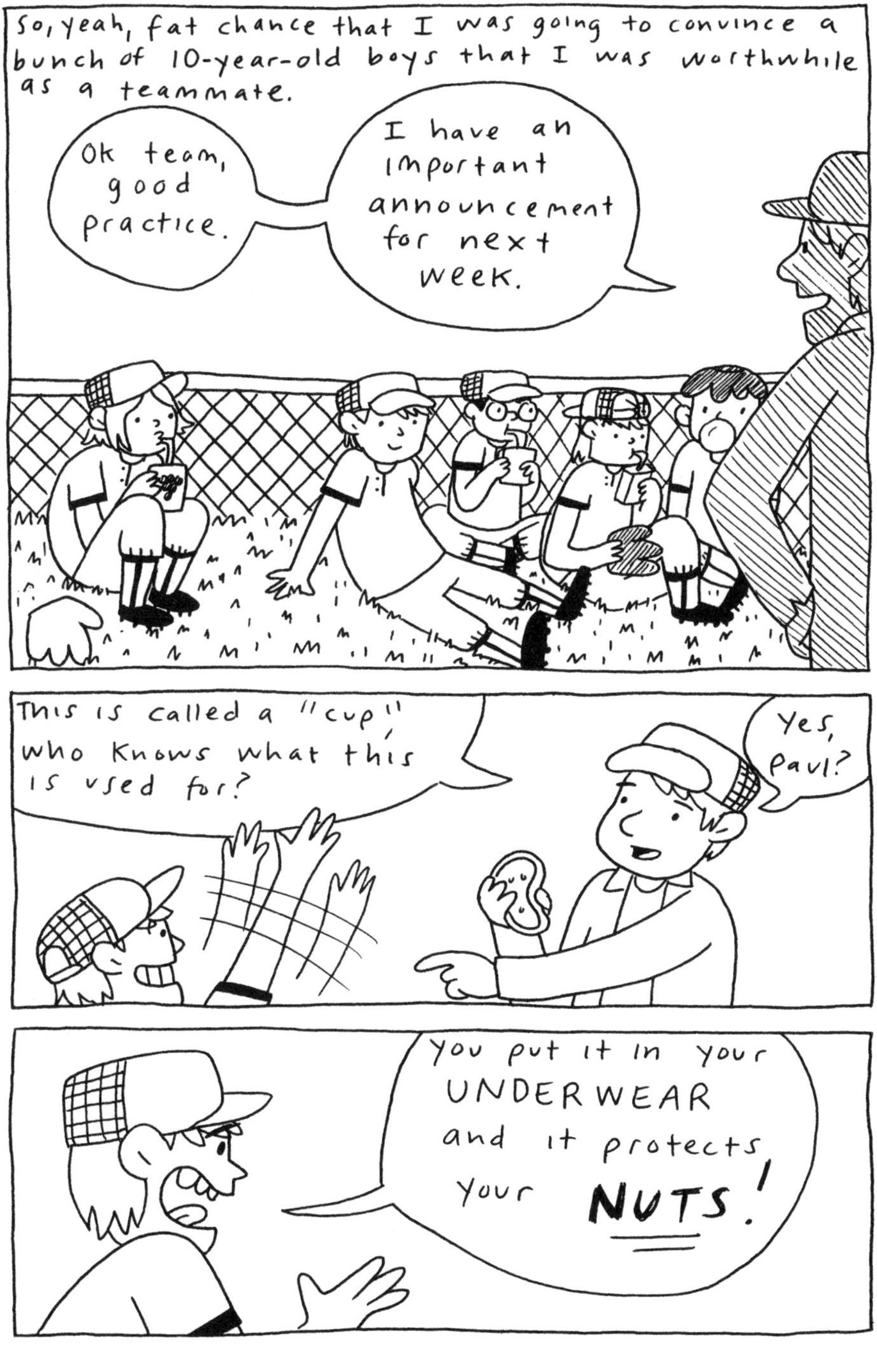
So, yeah, fat chance that I was going to convince a bunch of 10-year-old boys that I was worthwhile as a teammate.
Ok team, good practice.
I have an important announcement for next week.
This is called a "cup", who knows what this is used for?
Yes, Paul?
You put it in your UNDERWEAR and it protects your NUTS!

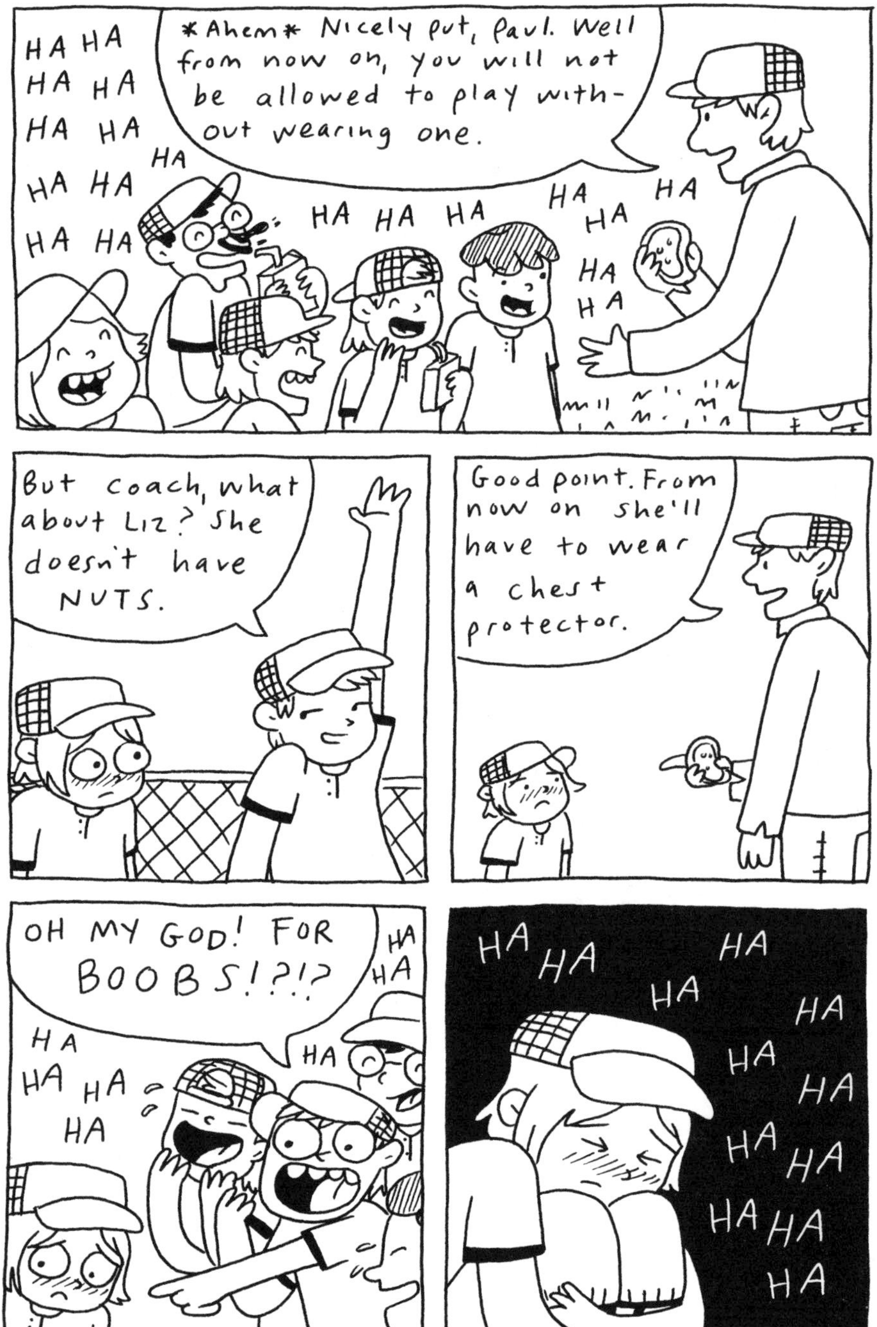

HA HA HA HA HA HA HA HA HA HA HA
Ahem Nicely put, Paul. Well from now on, you will not be allowed to play without wearing one.
HA HA HA HA HA HA HA HA HA
But coach, what about Liz? She doesn't have NUTS.
Good point. From now on she'll have to wear a chest protector.
OH MY GOD! FOR BOOBS!?!?
HA HA HA HA HA HA HA HA
HA HA HA HA HA HA HA HA HA HA HA HA HA

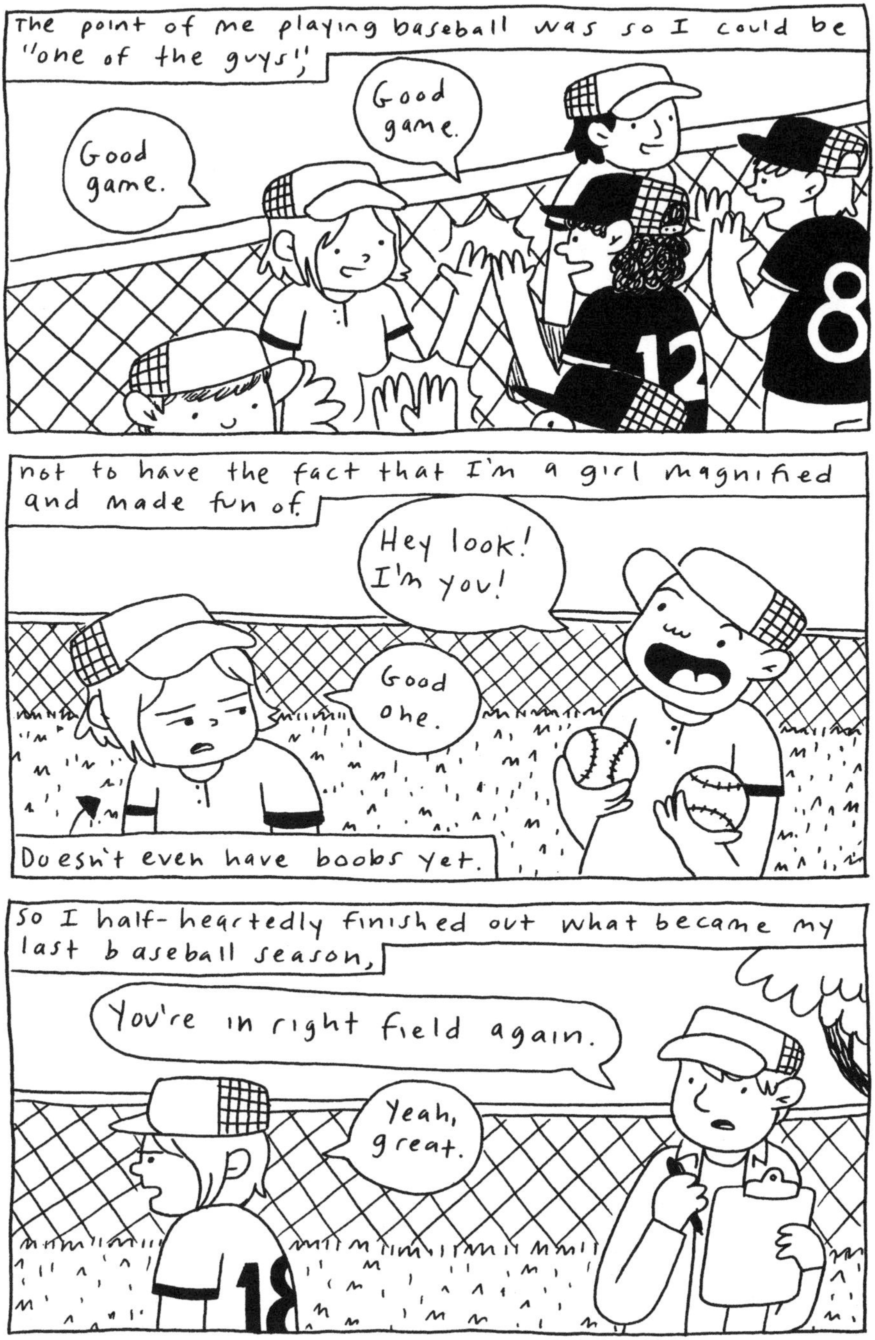
The point of me playing baseball was so I could be "one of the guys!",
Good game.
Good game.
8
12
not to have the fact that I'm a girl magnified and made fun of.
Hey look! I'm you!
Good one.
Doesn't even have boobs yet.
So I half-heartedly finished out what became my last baseball season,
You're in right field again.
Yeah, great.
18

in favor of a place where I thought my boy-ishness would stand out. A place called

GIRL SCOUT CAMP

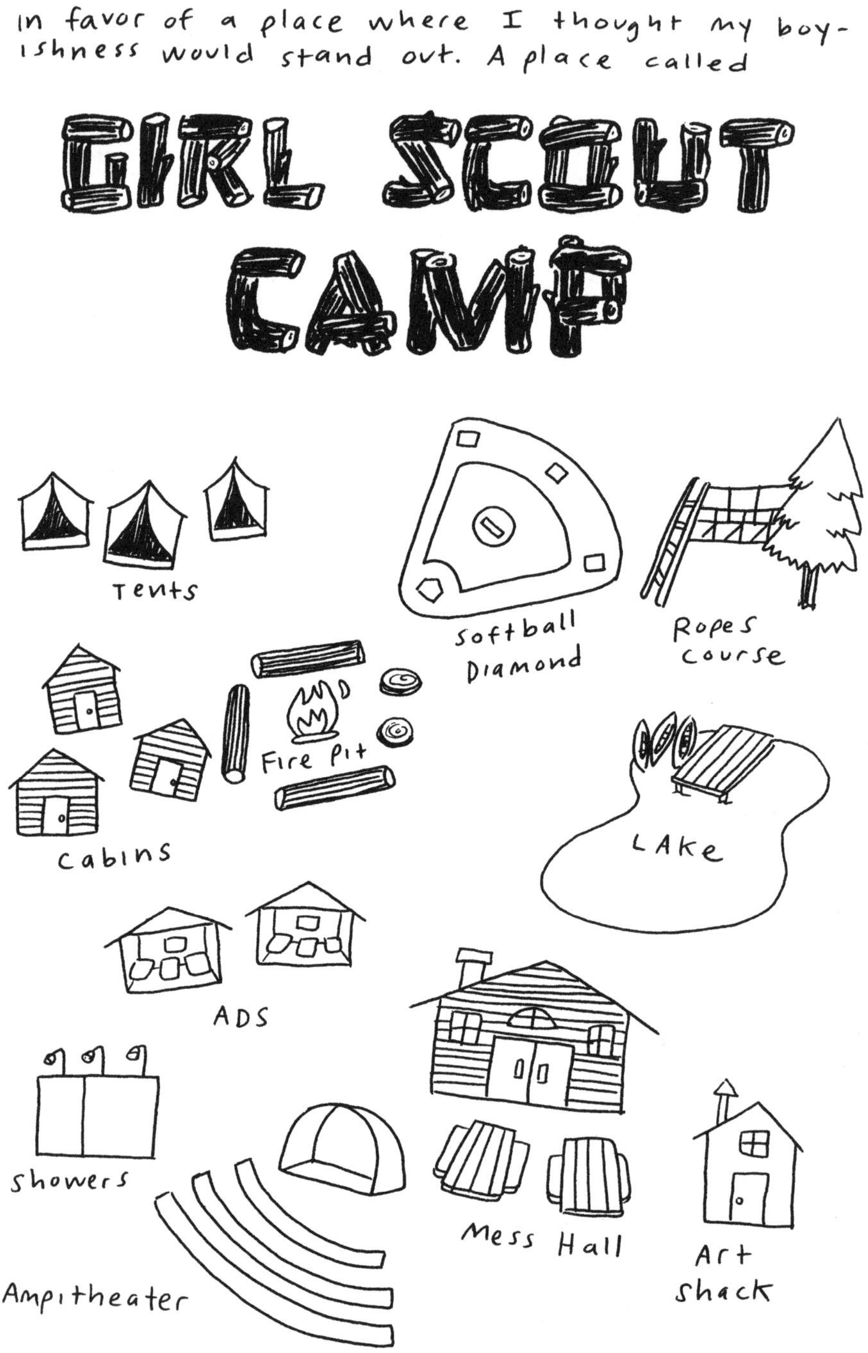
Tents
Softball Diamond
Ropes course
cabins
Fire Pit
LAke
ADS
showers
Ampitheater
Mess Hall
Art shack

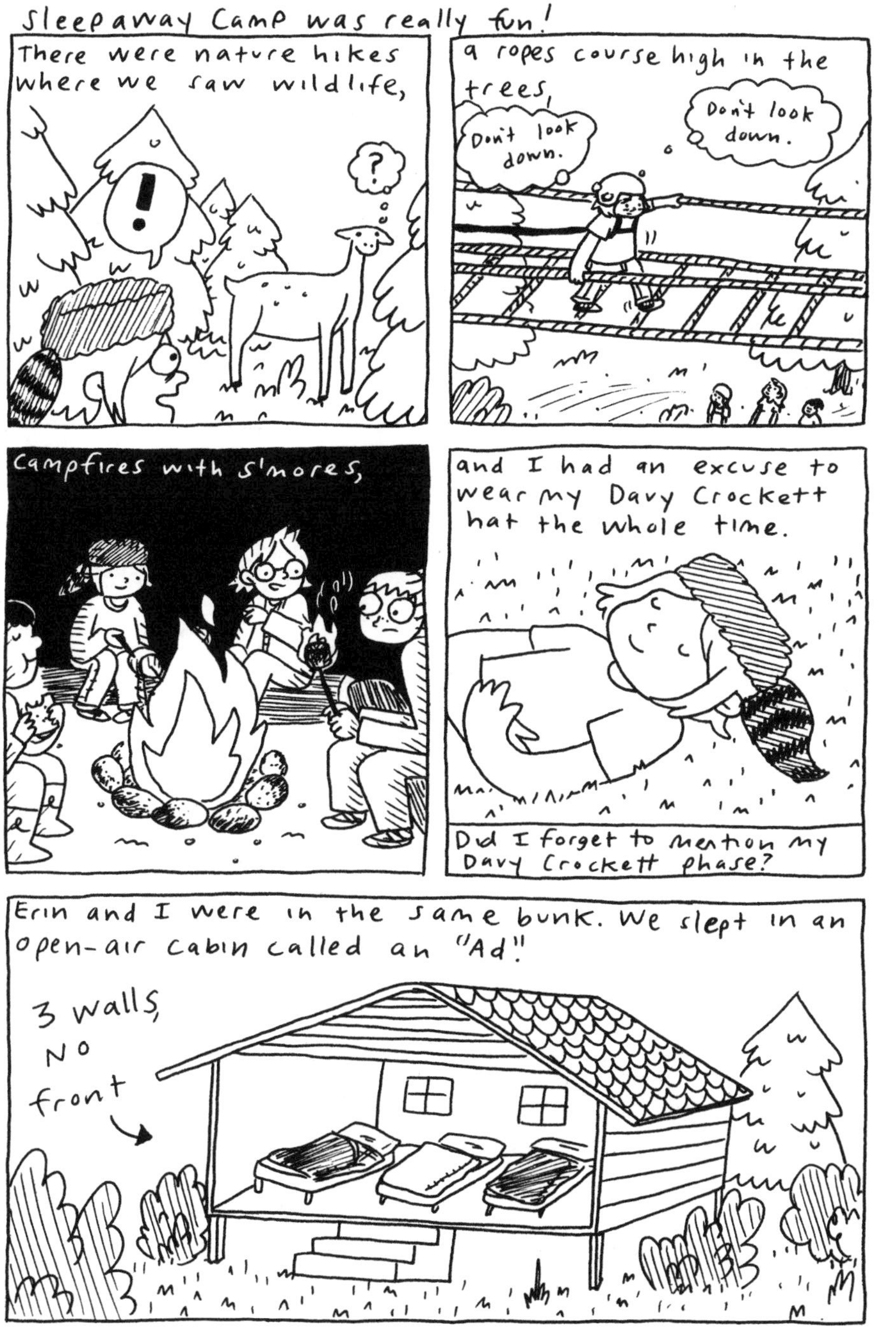
Sleepaway Camp was really fun!
There were nature hikes where we saw wildlife,
!
?
a ropes course high in the trees,
Don't look down.
Don't look down.
campfires with s'mores,
and I had an excuse to wear my Davy Crockett hat the whole time.
Did I forget to mention my Davy Crockett phase?
Erin and I were in the same bunk. We slept in an open-air cabin called an "Ad"!
3 walls, NO front

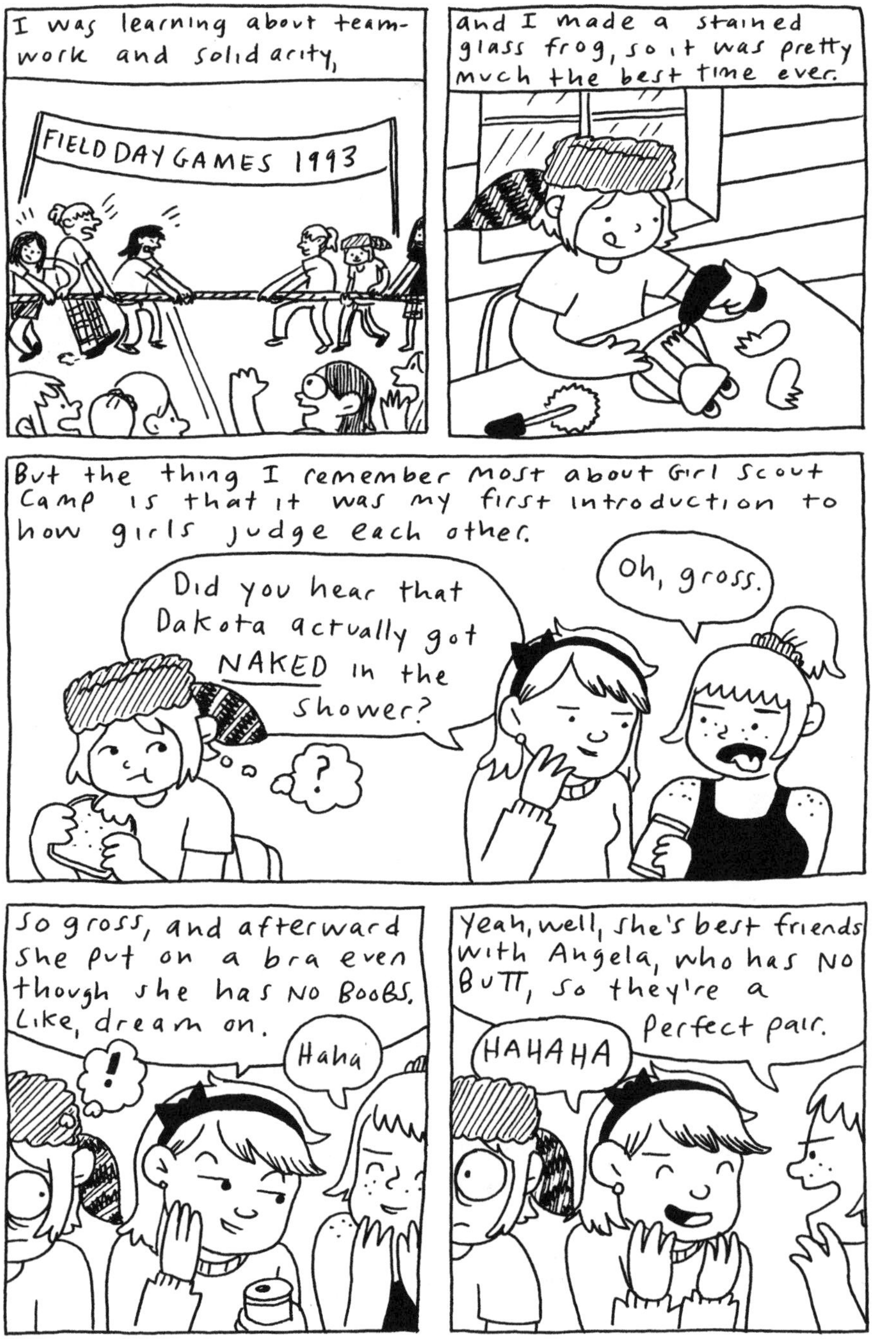
I was learning about team-work and solidarity,
FIELD DAY GAMES 1993
and I made a stained glass frog, so it was pretty much the best time ever.
But the thing I remember most about Girl Scout Camp is that it was my first introduction to how girls judge each other.
Did you hear that Dakota actually got NAKED in the shower?
Oh, gross.
?
So gross, and afterward she put on a bra even though she has NO BOOBS. Like, dream on.
Haha
!
Yeah, well, she's best friends with Angela, who has NO BUTT, so they're a perfect pair.
HAHAHA

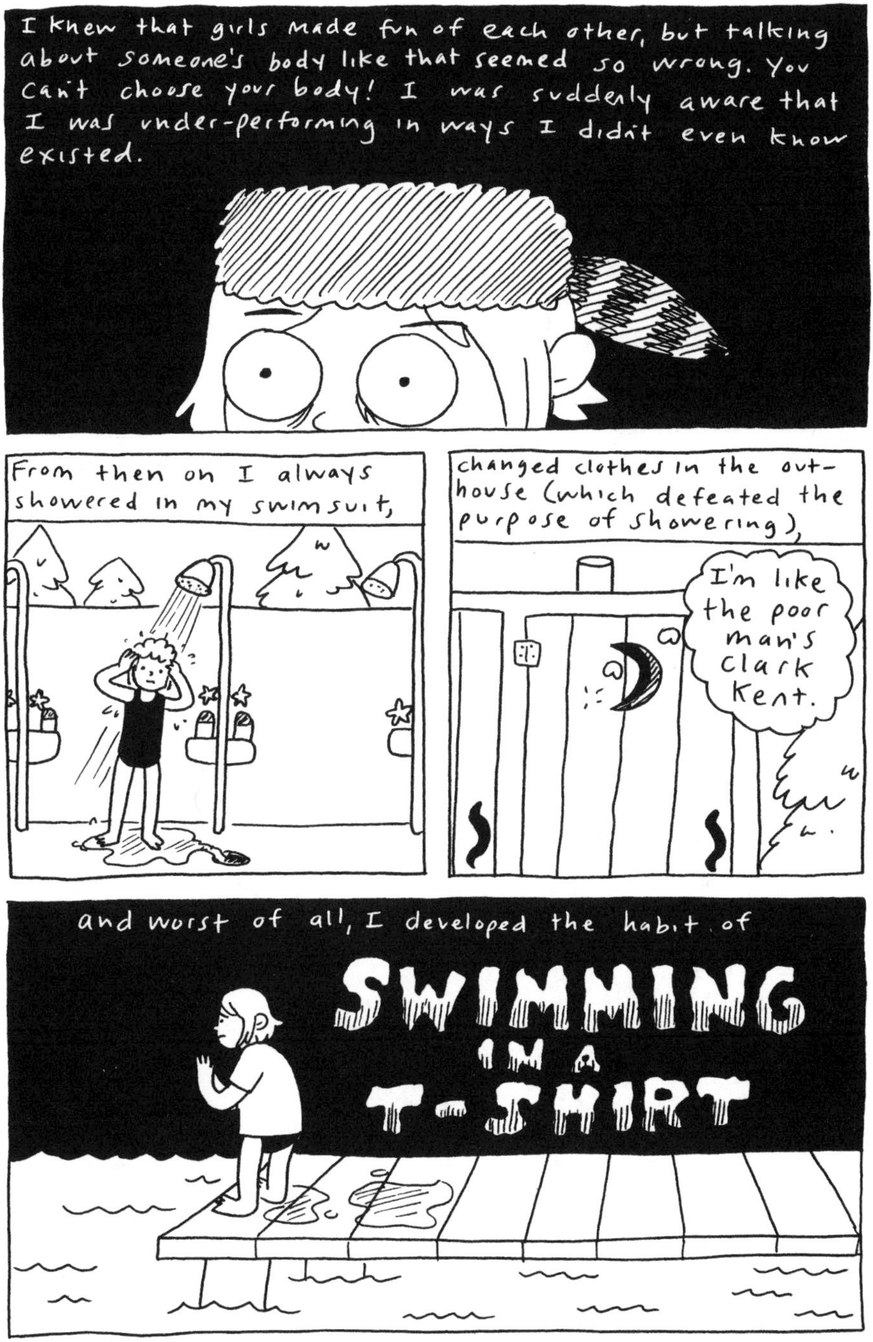
I knew that girls made fun of each other, but talking about someone's body like that seemed so wrong. You can't choose your body! I was suddenly aware that I was under-performing in ways I didn't even know existed.
From then on I always showered in my swimsuit,
changed clothes in the out-house (which defeated the purpose of showering),
I'm like the poor man's Clark Kent.
and worst of all, I developed the habit of
SWIMMING IN A T-SHIRT

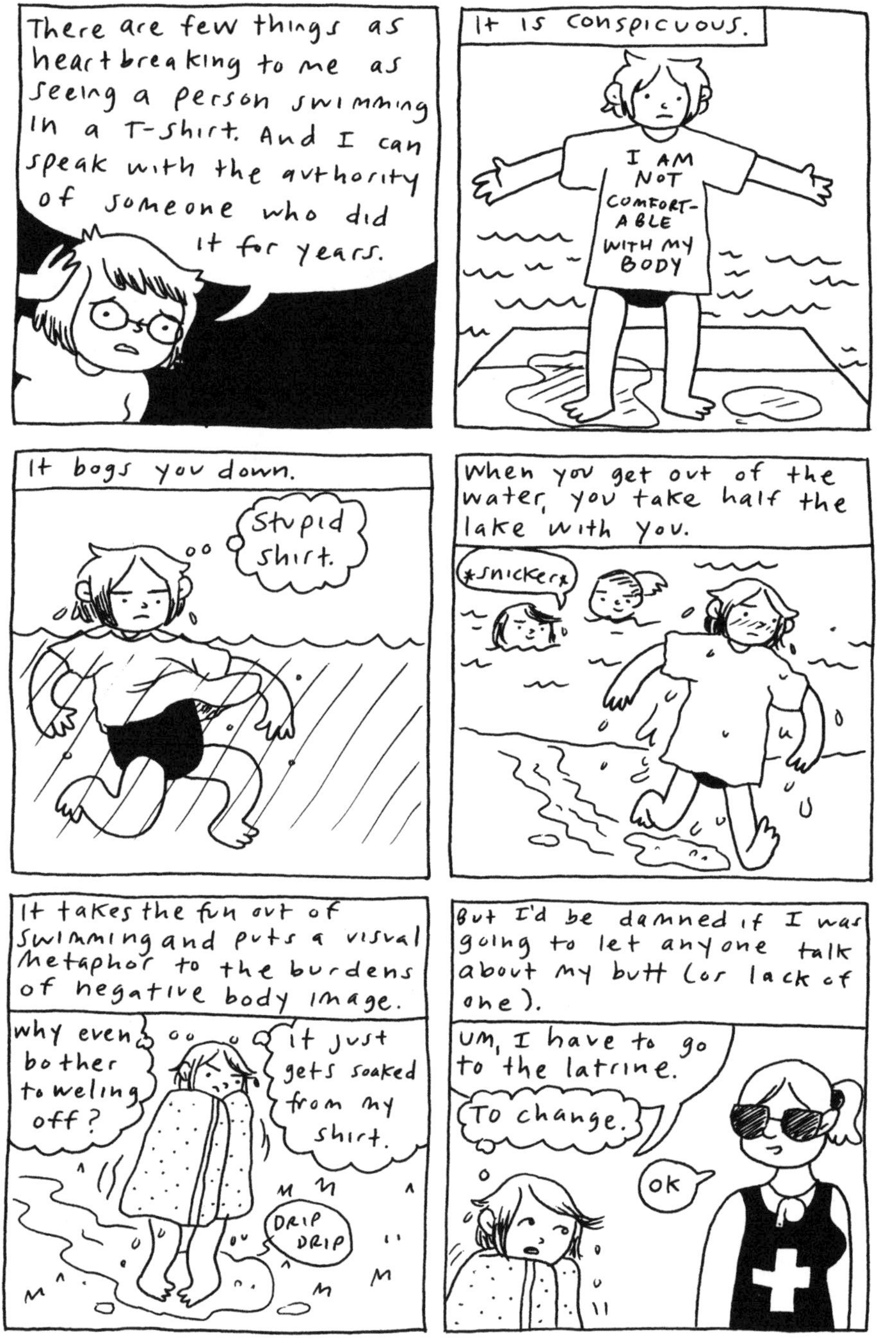
There are few things as heartbreaking to me as seeing a person swimming in a T-shirt. And I can speak with the authority of someone who did it for years.
It is conspicuous.
I AM NOT COMFORTABLE WITH MY BODY
It bogs you down.
Stupid shirt.
When you get out of the water, you take half the lake with you.
snicker
It takes the fun out of swimming and puts a visual metaphor to the burdens of negative body image.
Why even bother toweling off?
It just gets soaked from my shirt.
DRIP DRIP
But I'd be damned if I was going to let anyone talk about my butt (or lack of one).
Um, I have to go to the latrine.
To change.
OK

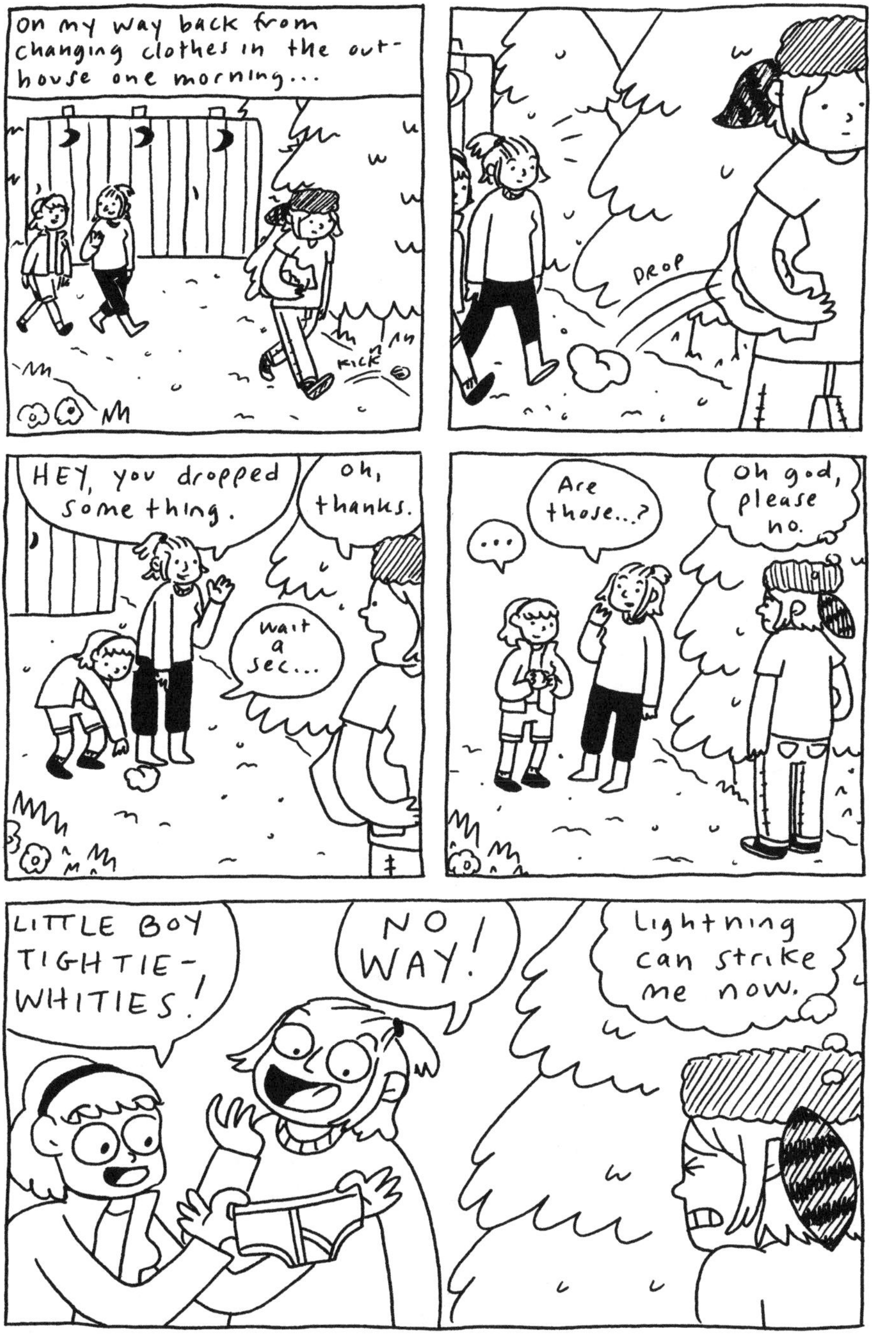
On my way back from changing clothes in the out-house one morning...
KICK
DROP
HEY, you dropped something.
oh, thanks.
wait a sec...
...
Are those...?
Oh god, please no.
LITTLE BOY TIGHTIE-WHITIES!
NO WAY!
Lightning can strike me now.

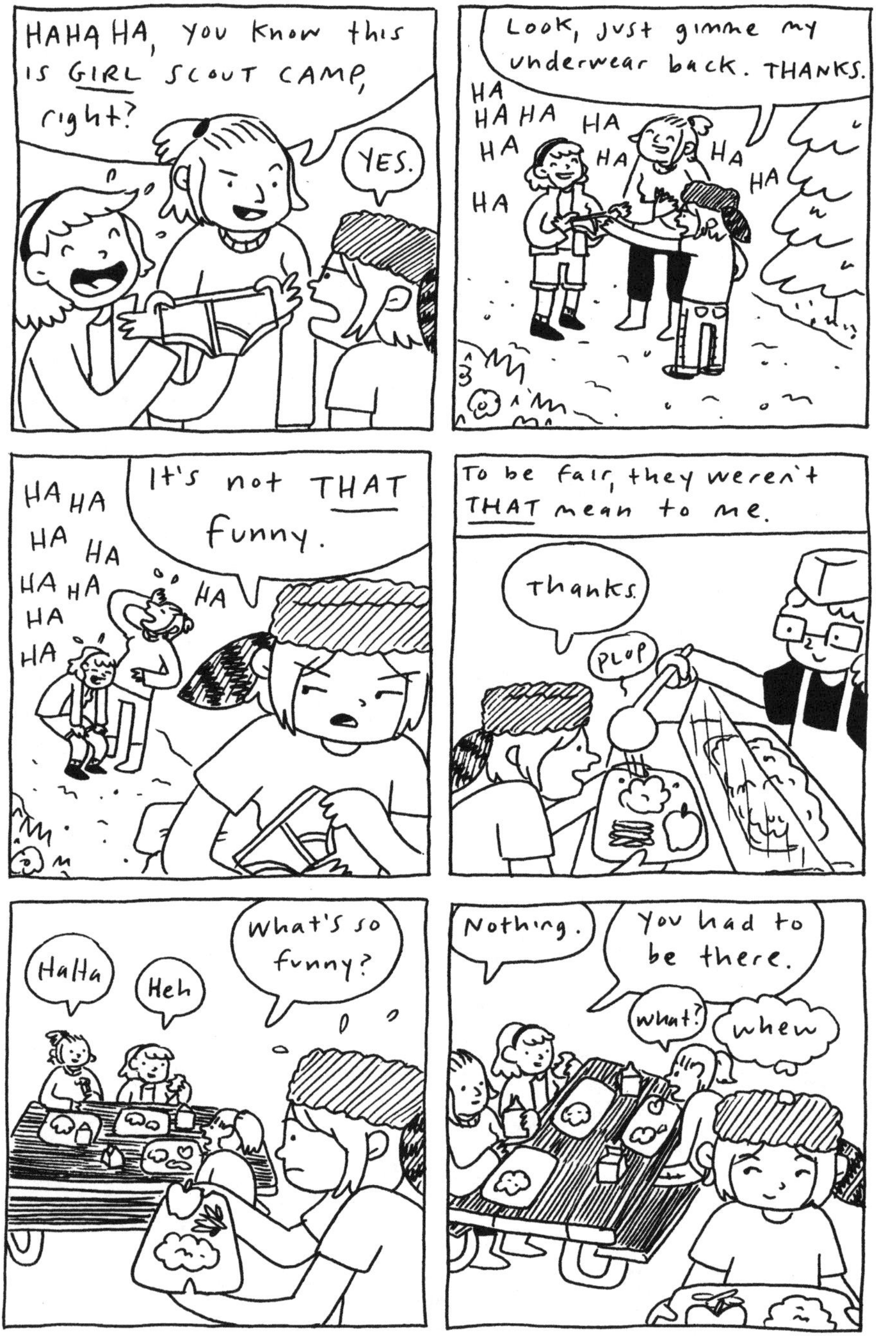
HAHAHA, you know this is GIRL SCOUT CAMP, right?
YES.
Look, just gimme my underwear back. THANKS.
HA HAHA HA HA HA HA HA HA HA
HAHA HA HA HAHA HA HA HA
It's not THAT funny.
To be fair, they weren't THAT mean to me.
thanks.
PLOP
HaHa
Heh
What's so funny?
Nothing.
You had to be there.
what?
whew

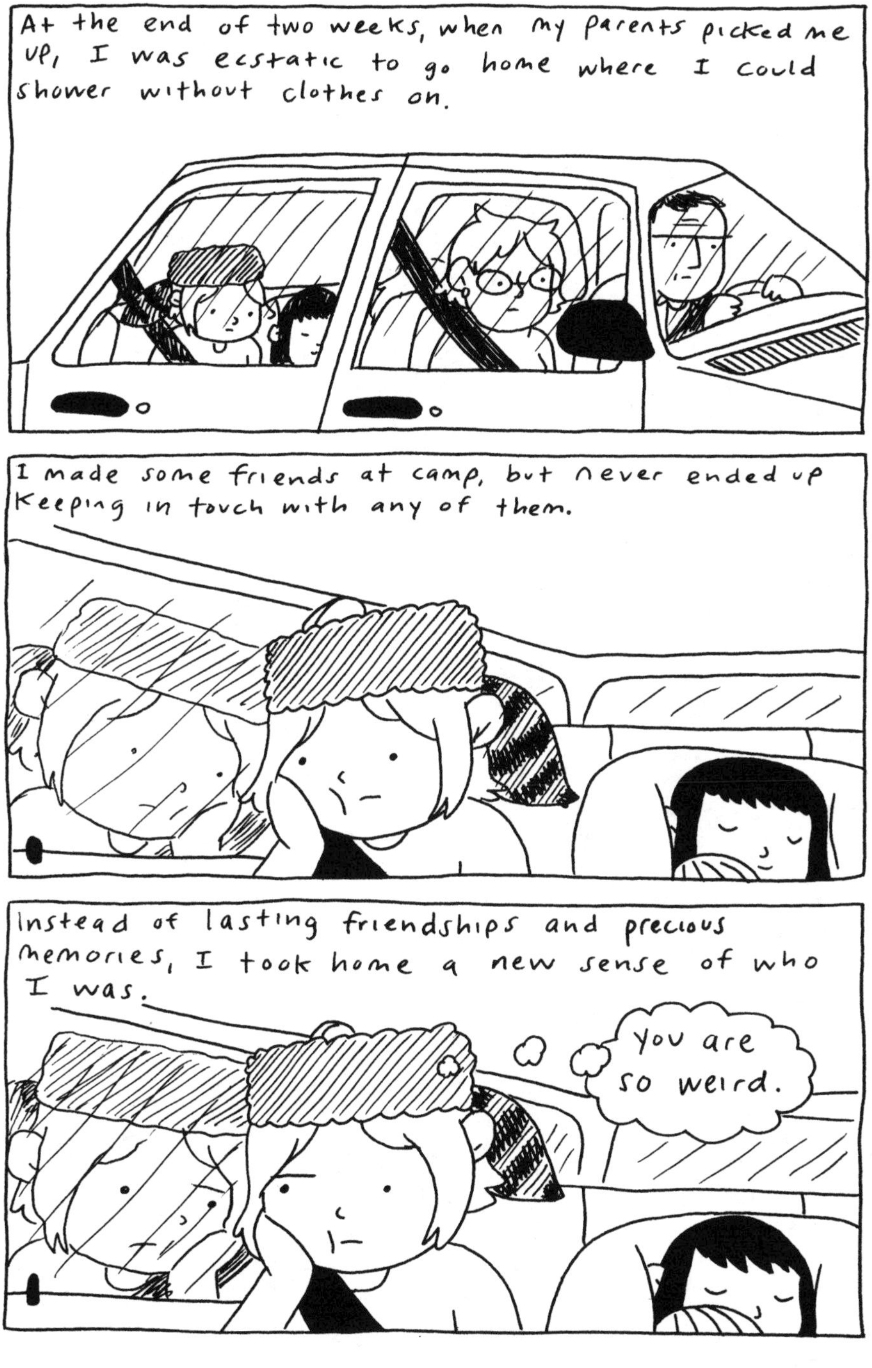
At the end of two weeks, when my parents picked me up, I was ecstatic to go home where I could shower without clothes on.
I made some friends at camp, but never ended up keeping in touch with any of them.
Instead of lasting friendships and precious memories, I took home a new sense of who I was.
You are so weird.

CHAPTER 6

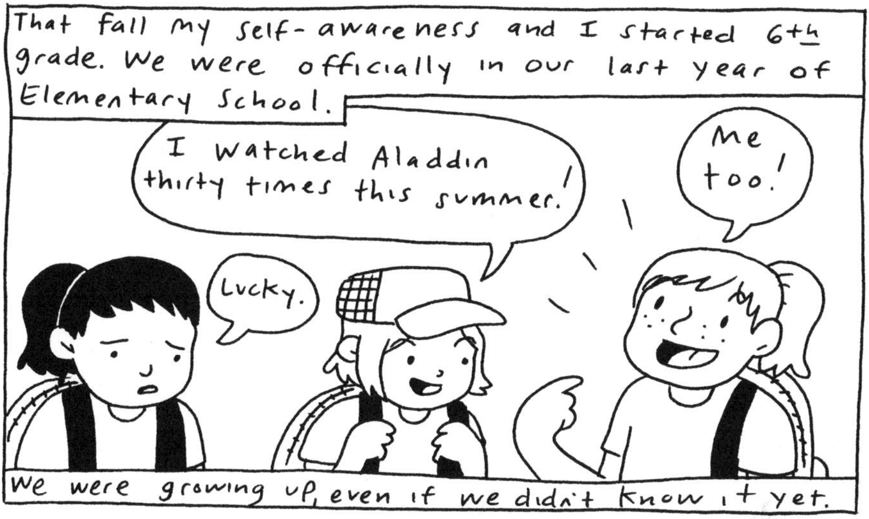
That fall my self-awareness and I started 6th grade. We were officially in our last year of Elementary School.
I watched Aladdin thirty times this summer!
Me too!
Lucky.
We were growing up, even if we didn't know it yet.

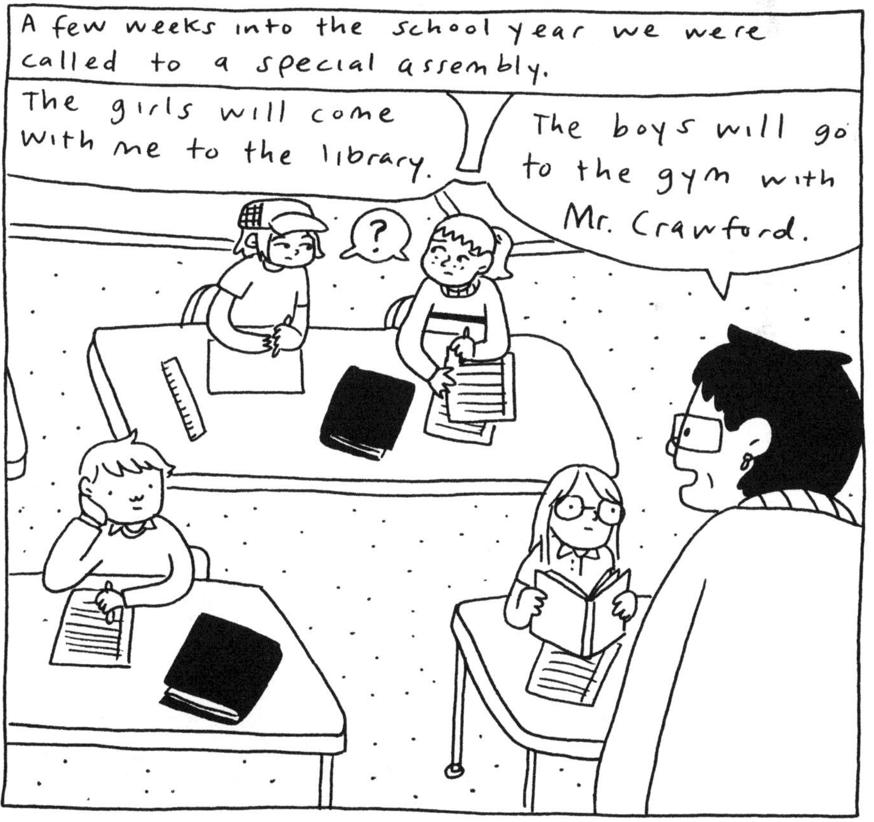
A few weeks into the school year we were called to a special assembly.
The girls will come with me to the library.
The boys will go to the gym with Mr. Crawford.
?

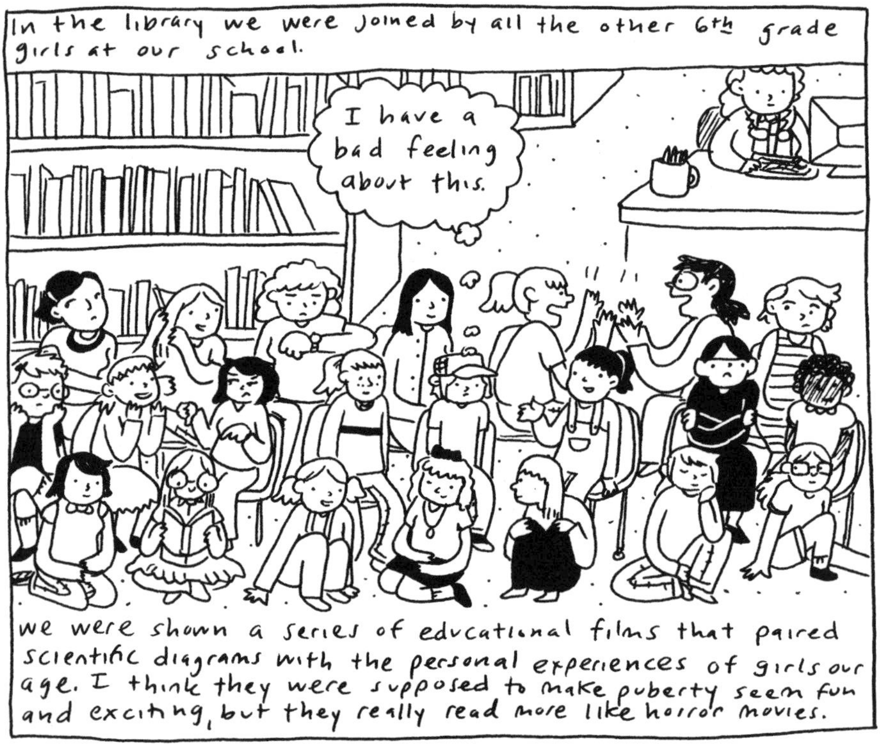
In the library we were joined by all the other 6th grade girls at our school.
I have a bad feeling about this.
We were shown a series of educational films that paired scientific diagrams with the personal experiences of girls our age. I think they were supposed to make puberty seem fun and exciting, but they really read more like horror movies.

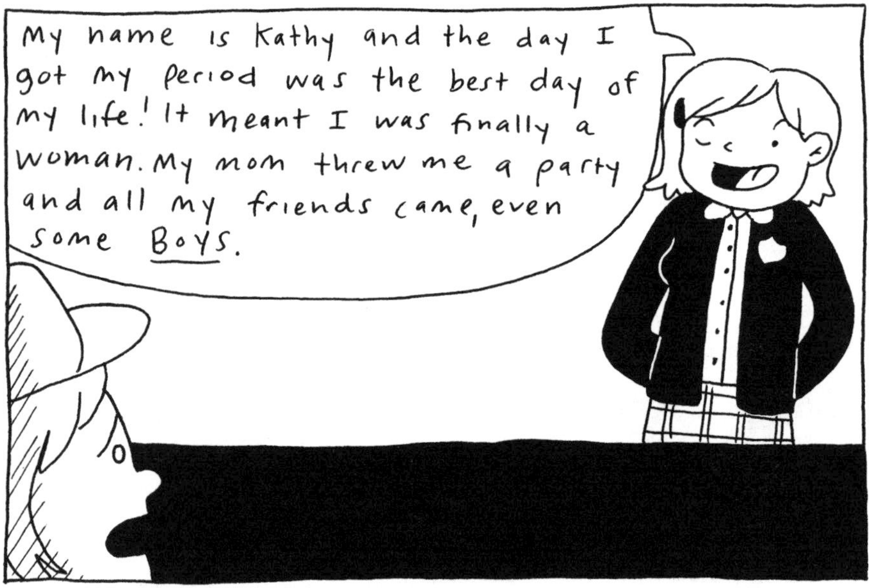
My name is Kathy and the day I got my period was the best day of my life! It meant I was finally a woman. My mom threw me a party and all my friends came, even some BOYS.

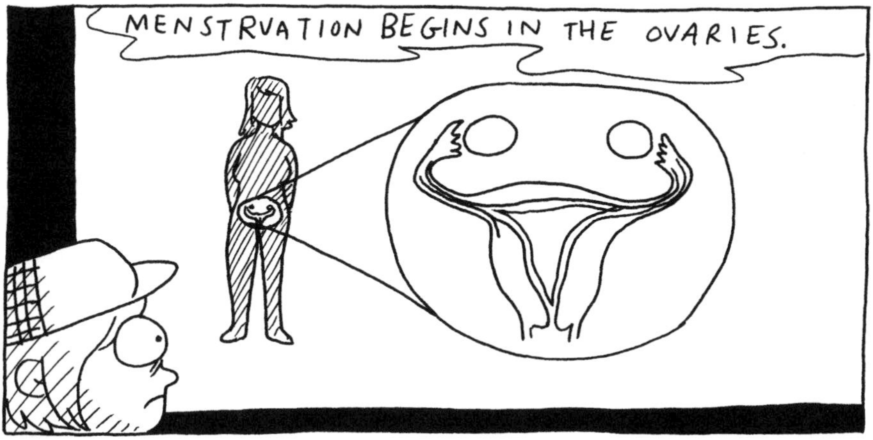
MENSTRUATION BEGINS IN THE OVARIES.

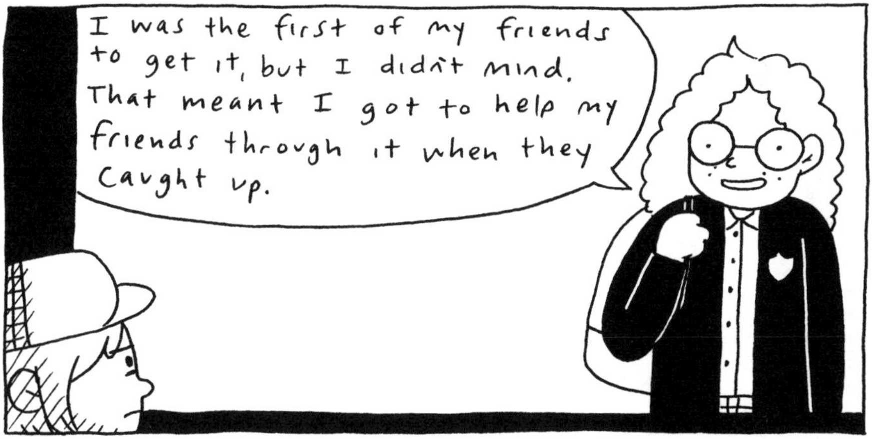
I was the first of my friends to get it, but I didn't mind. That meant I got to help my friends through it when they caught up.

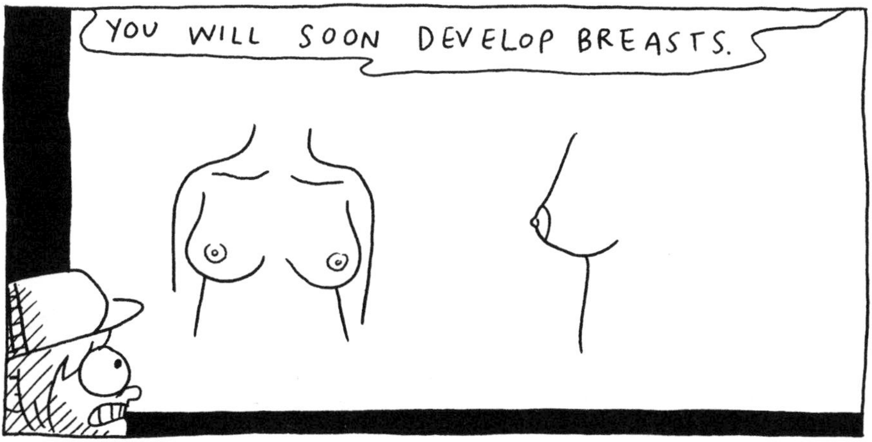
YOU WILL SOON DEVELOP BREASTS.

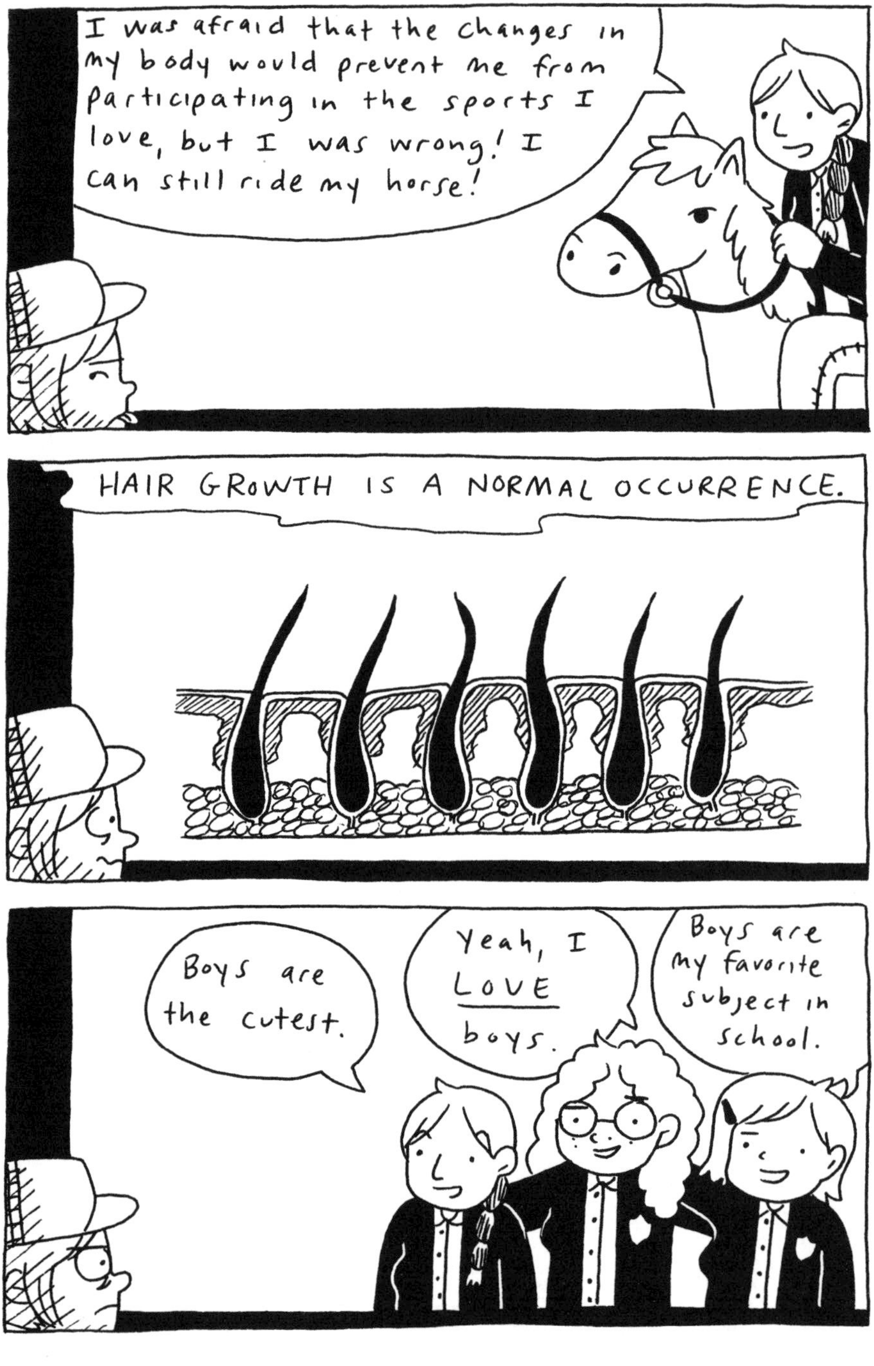
I was afraid that the changes in my body would prevent me from participating in the sports I love, but I was wrong! I can still ride my horse!
HAIR GROWTH IS A NORMAL OCCURRENCE.
Boys are the cutest.
Yeah, I LOVE boys.
Boys are my favorite subject in school.

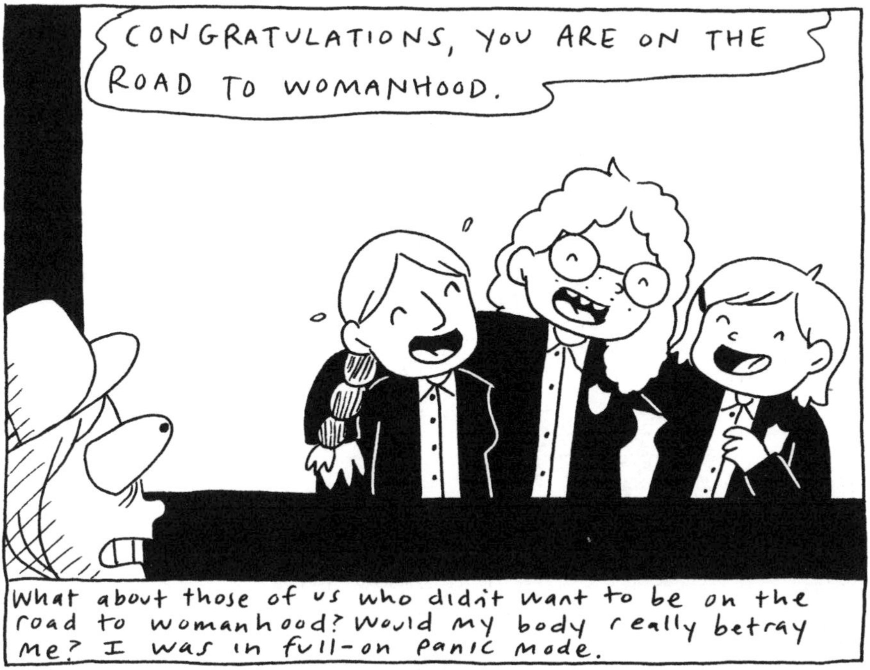
CONGRATULATIONS, YOU ARE ON THE ROAD TO WOMANHOOD.
What about those of us who didn't want to be on the road to womanhood? Would my body really betray me? I was in full-on panic mode.

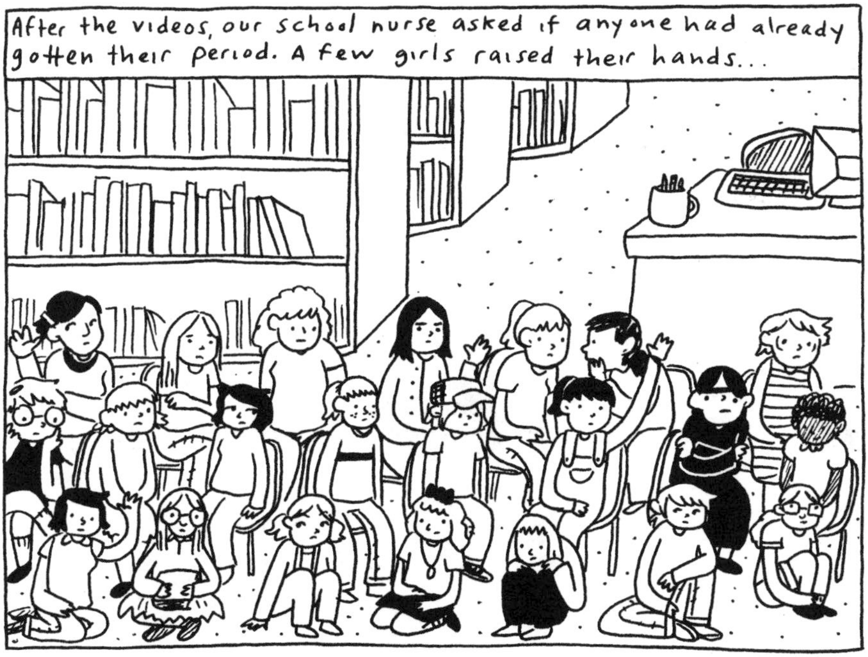
After the videos, our school nurse asked if anyone had already gotten their period. A few girls raised their hands...

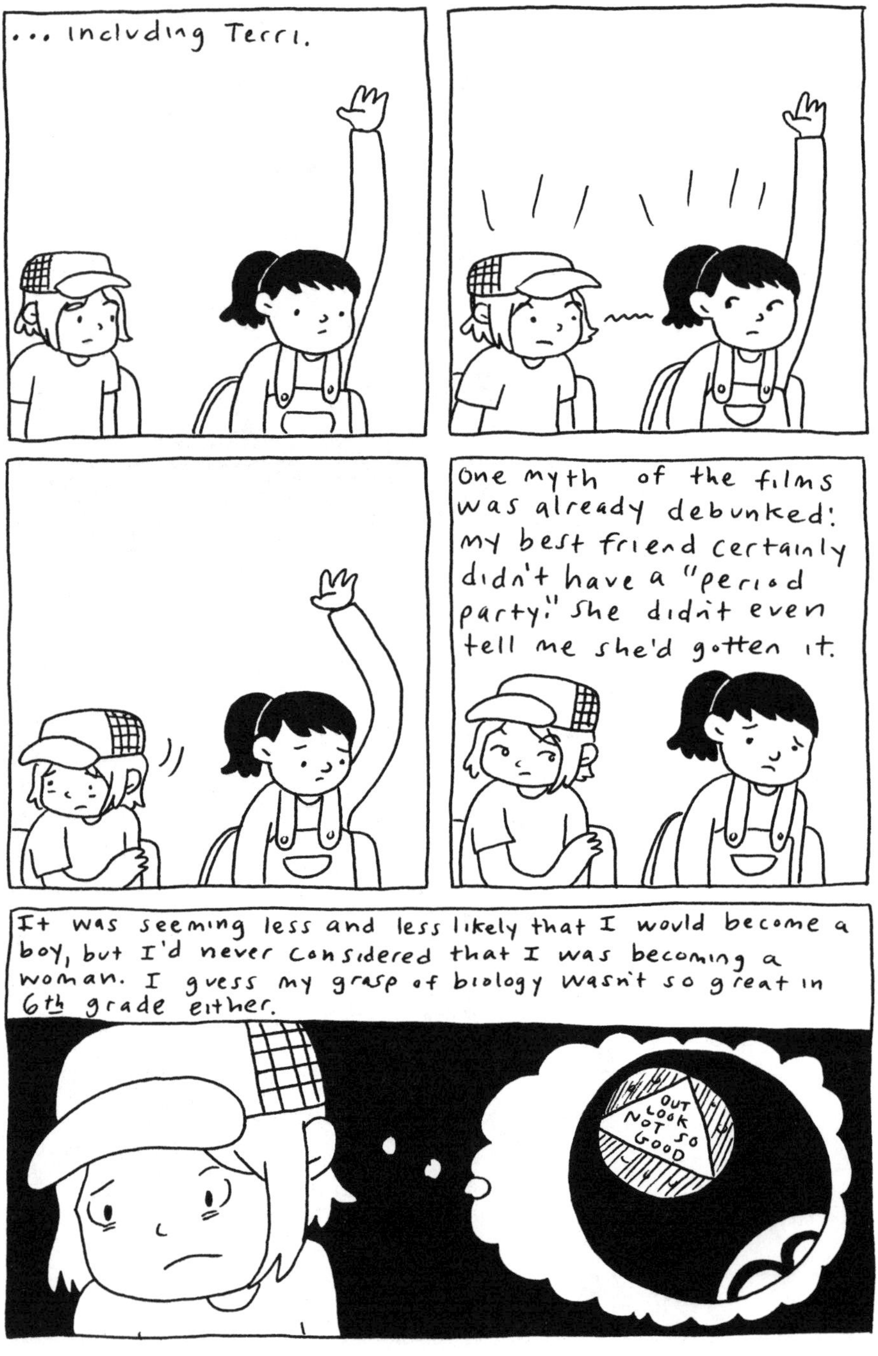
... including Terri.
One myth of the films was already debunked: my best friend certainly didn't have a "period party." She didn't even tell me she'd gotten it.
It was seeming less and less likely that I would become a boy, but I'd never considered that I was becoming a woman. I guess my grasp of biology wasn't so great in 6th grade either.
OUTLOOK NOT SO GOOD

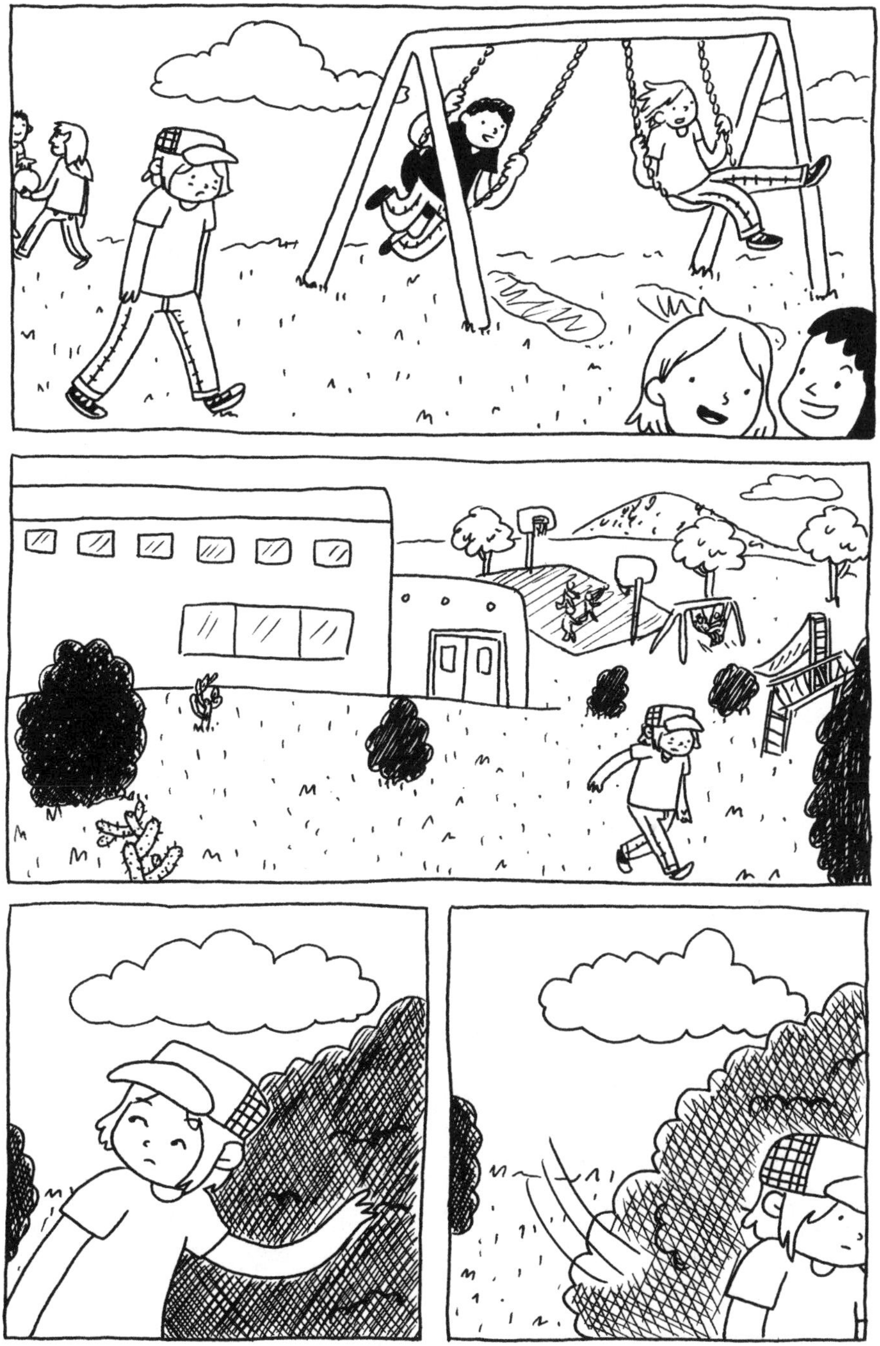

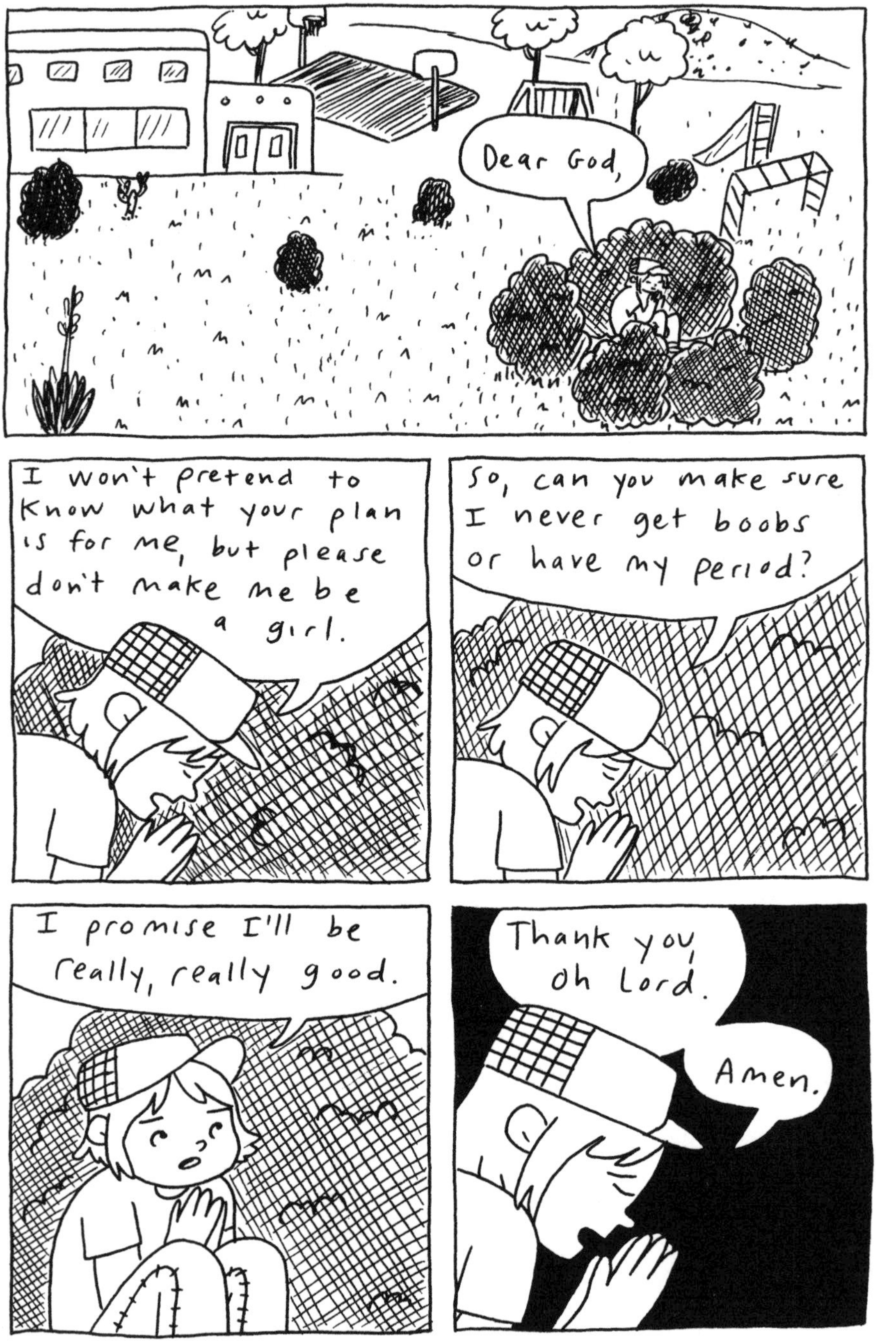
Dear God,
I won't pretend to know what your plan is for me, but please don't make me be a girl.
So, can you make sure I never get boobs or have my period?
I promise I'll be really, really good.
Thank you, oh Lord.
Amen.

My prayers usually read more like a shopping list than an appeal for spiritual aid.

Dear God, please let me get a Popple for my birthday.

Dear God, Luke has a proton pack, and I need one, too.

Dear God, have you seen the new Battle Beasts? You know what to do.

I was more accurately praying to Santa Claus, but this time was different, this was about the outcome of my LIFE, and I felt I needed divine intervention more than ever.

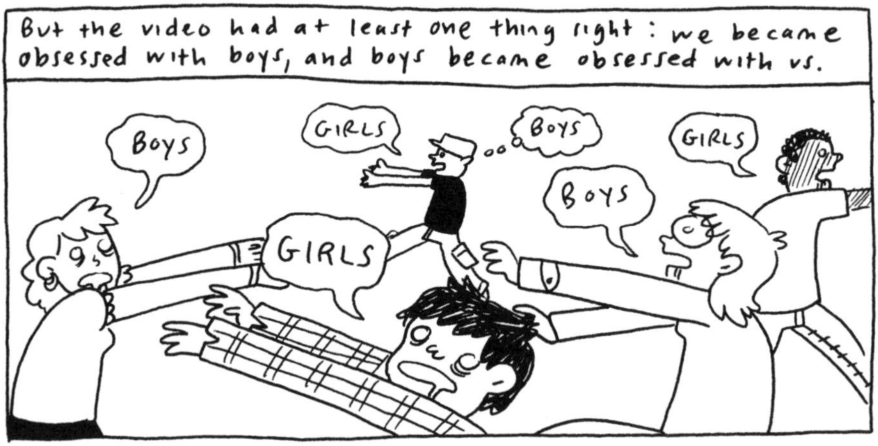
But the video had at least one thing right: we became obsessed with boys, and boys became obsessed with us.
Boys
GIRLS
BOYS
GIRLS
BOYS
GIRLS

I was not immune to this rampant lovesickness.

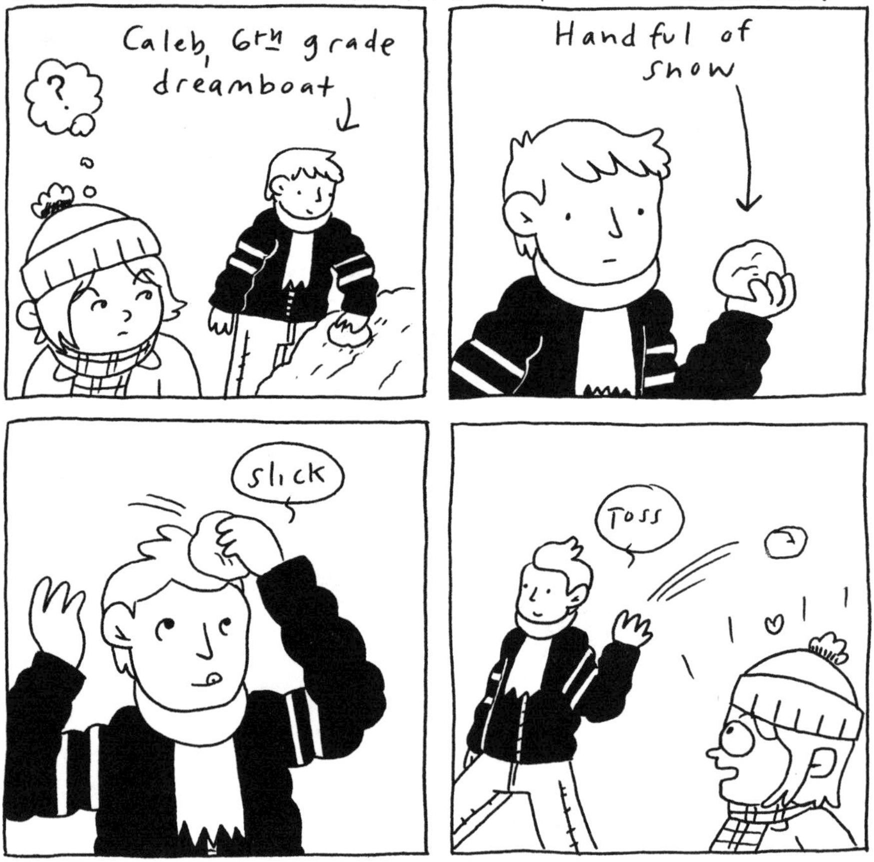
?
Caleb, 6th grade dreamboat
Handful of snow
slick
TOSS

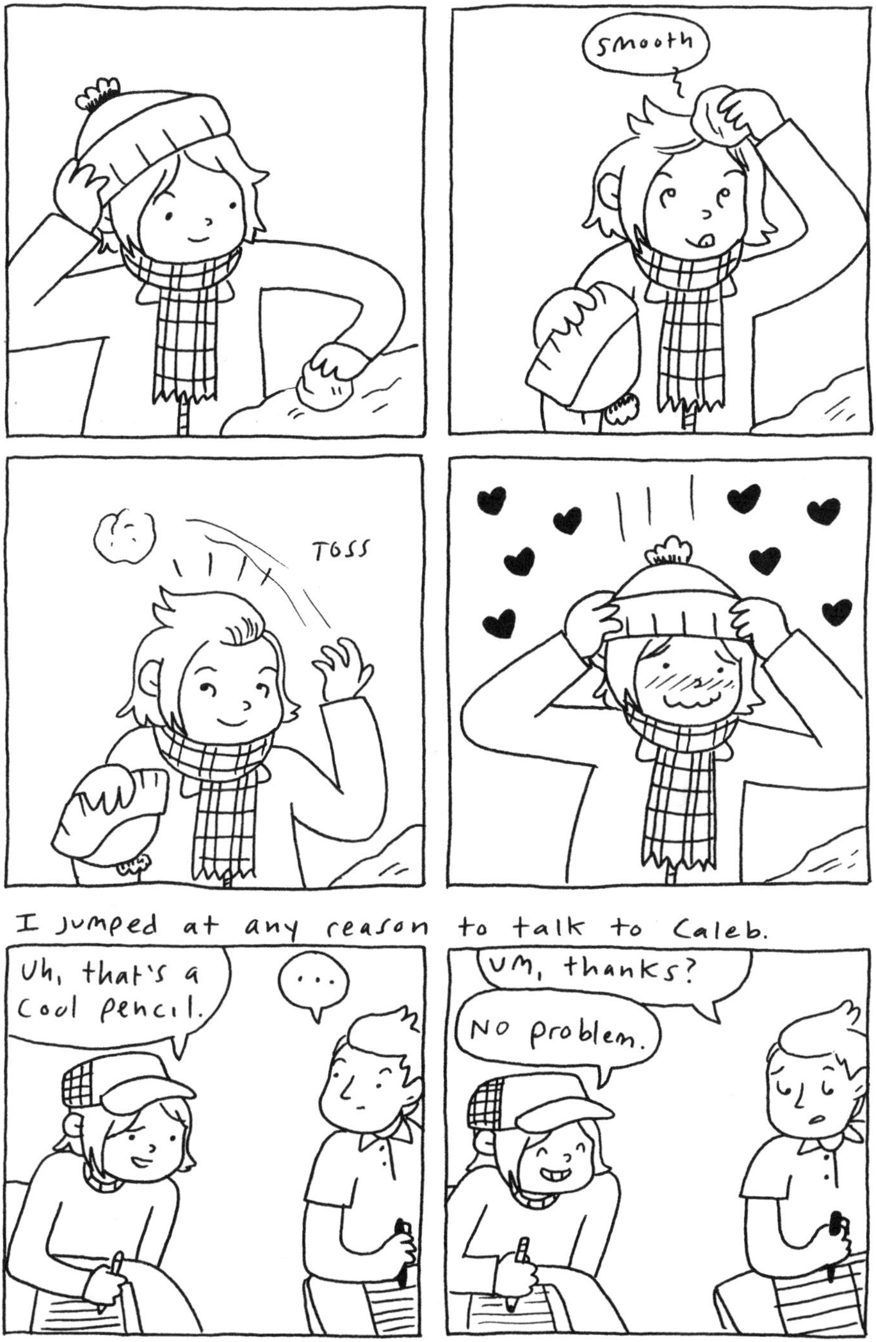
smooth
TOSS
I jumped at any reason to talk to Caleb.
Uh, that's a cool pencil.
...
Um, thanks?
No problem.

And routinely stalked out his place on the playground to position myself strategically for interaction.

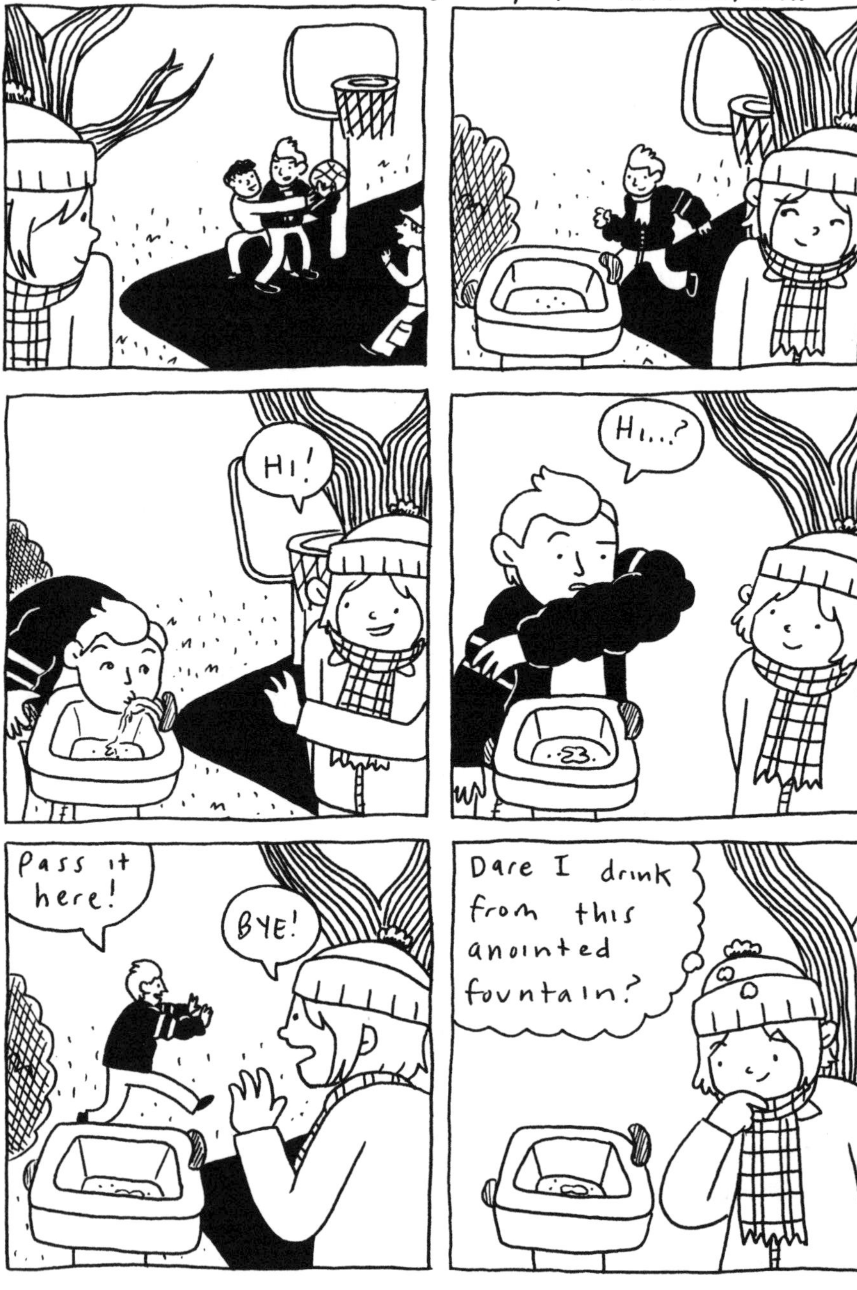
HI!
HI...?
Pass it here!
BYE!
Dare I drink from this anointed fountain?

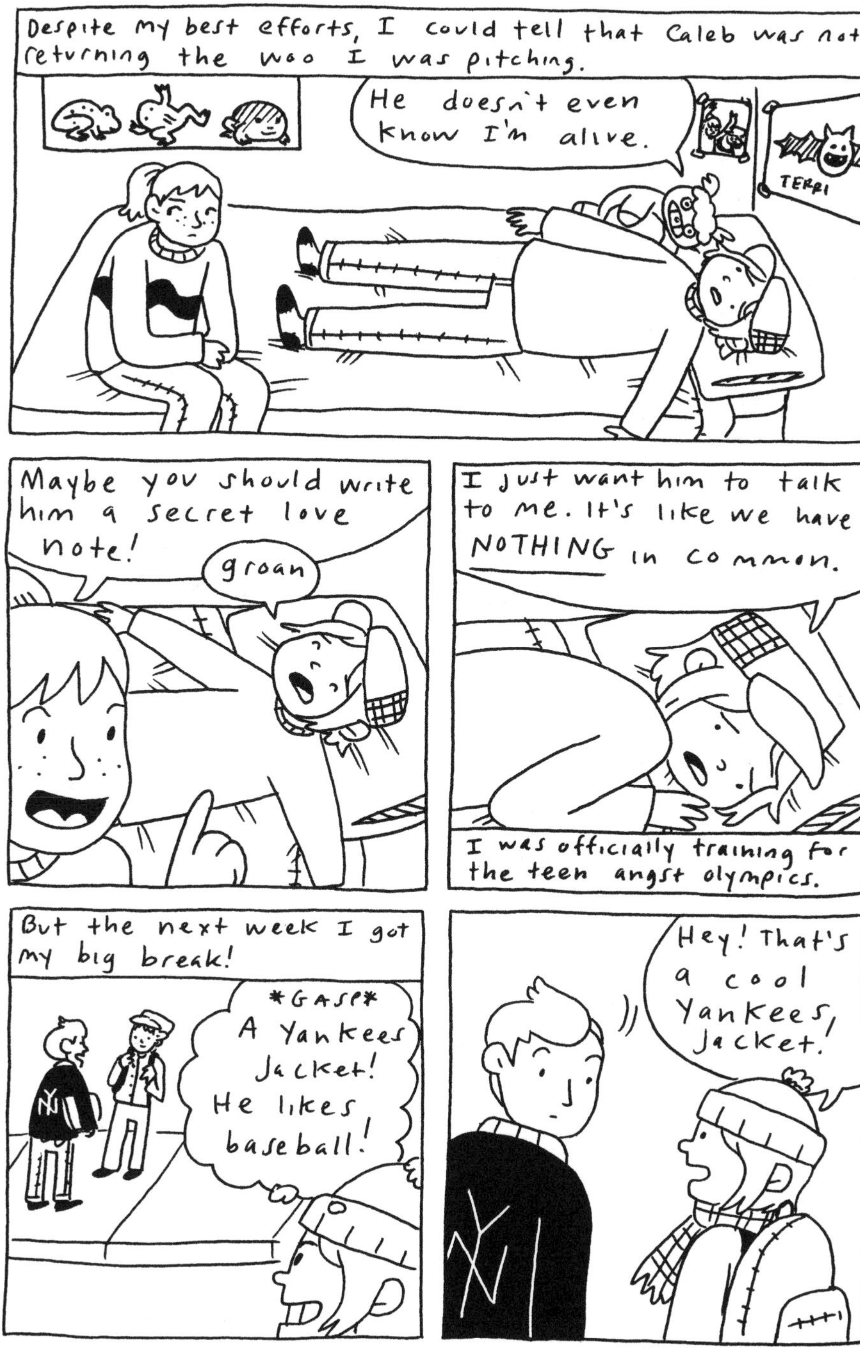
Despite my best efforts, I could tell that Caleb was not returning the woo I was pitching.
He doesn't even know I'm alive.
TERRI
Maybe you should write him a secret love note!
groan
I just want him to talk to me. It's like we have NOTHING in common.
I was officially training for the teen angst olympics.
But the next week I got my big break!
GASP A Yankees Jacket! He likes baseball!
Hey! That's a cool Yankees Jacket!

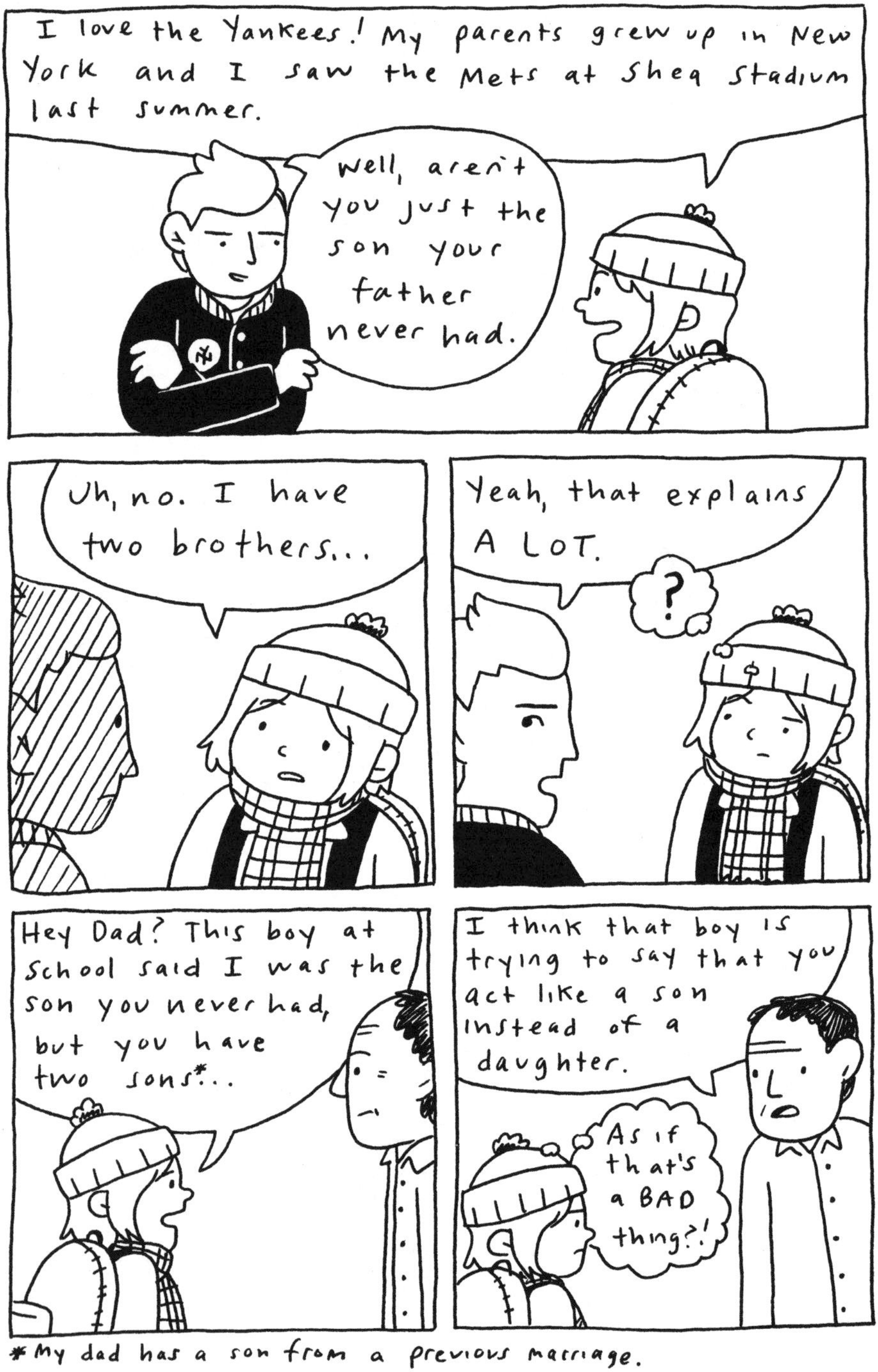
I love the Yankees! My parents grew up in New York and I saw the Mets at Shea Stadium last summer.
Well, aren't you just the son your father never had.
Uh, no. I have two brothers...
Yeah, that explains A LOT.
?
Hey Dad? This boy at school said I was the son you never had, but you have two sons*...
I think that boy is trying to say that you act like a son instead of a daughter.
As if that's a BAD thing?!

* My dad has a son from a previous marriage.

So Caleb made fun of me for being a Tomboy. I was a tad bummed, but there were other fish in the sea.

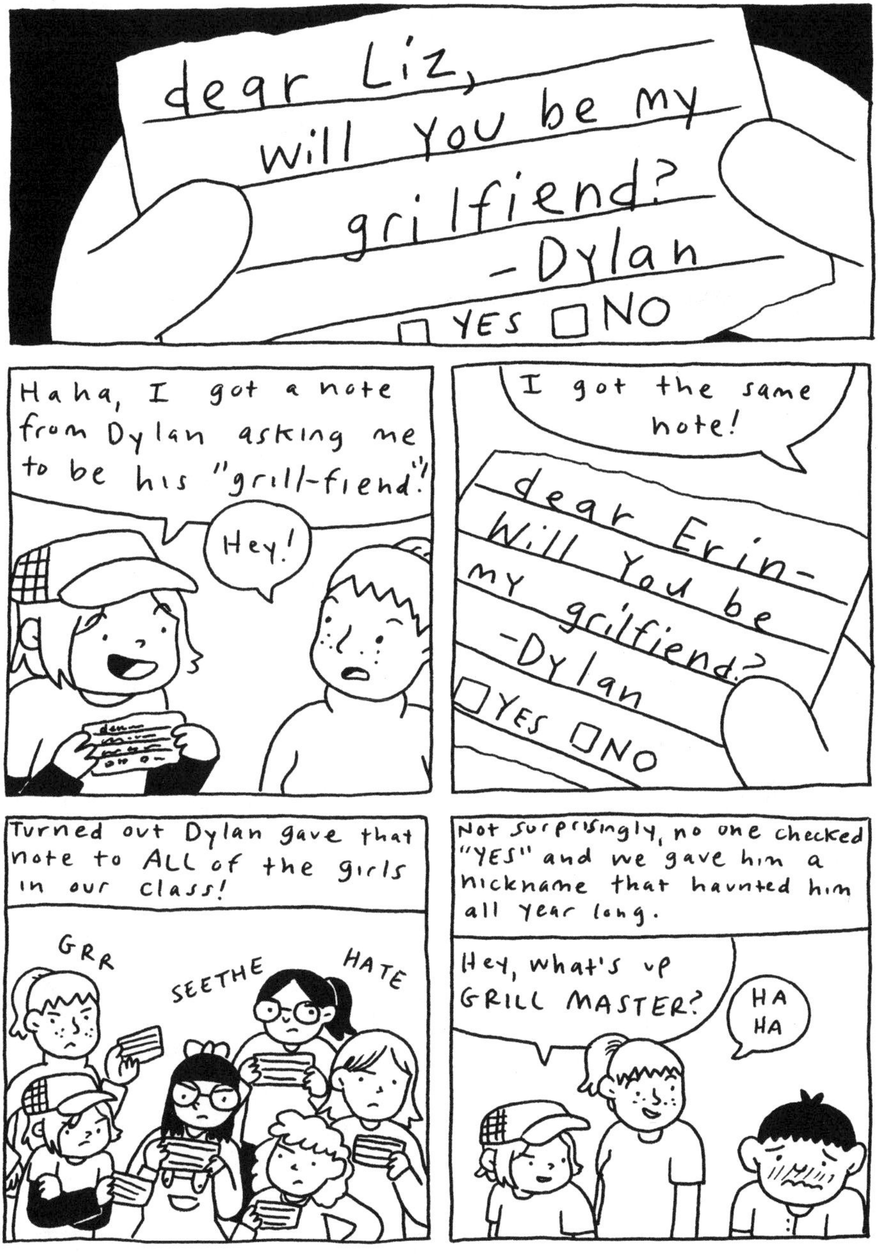

dear Liz,
will You be my grilfiend?
-Dylan
YES NO
Haha, I got a note from Dylan asking me to be his "grill-fiend"!
Hey!
I got the same note!
dear Erin-
Will You be MY grilfiend?
-Dylan
YES NO
Turned out Dylan gave that note to ALL of the girls in our class!
GRR
SEETHE
HATE
Not surprisingly, no one checked "YES" and we gave him a nickname that haunted him all year long.
Hey, what's up GRILL MASTER?
HA HA

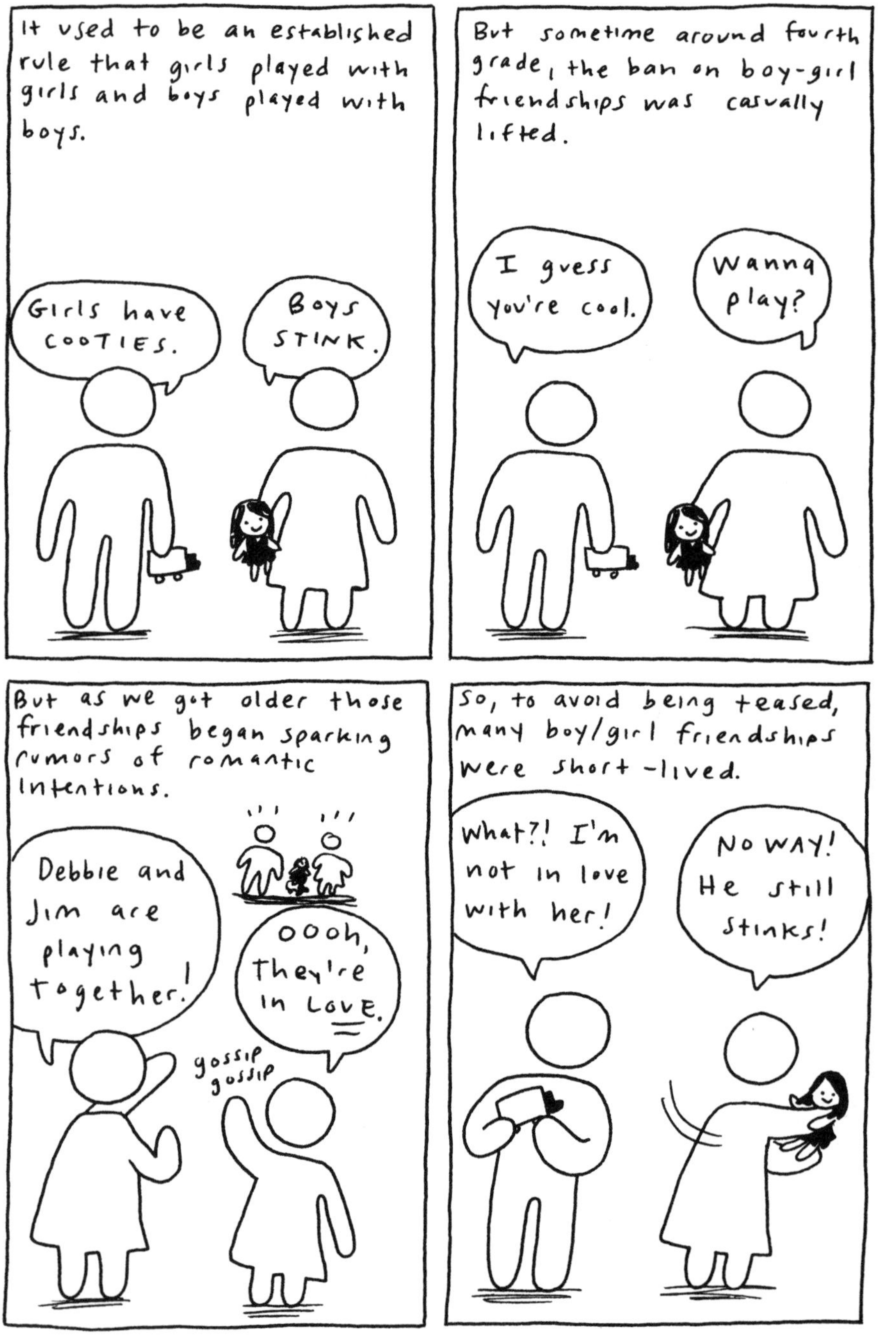
It used to be an established rule that girls played with girls and boys played with boys.
Girls have COOTIES.
Boys STINK.
But sometime around fourth grade, the ban on boy-girl friendships was casually lifted.
I guess you're cool.
Wanna play?
But as we got older those friendships began sparking rumors of romantic intentions.
Debbie and Jim are playing together!
Oooh, They're in LOVE.
gossip gossip
So, to avoid being teased, many boy/girl friendships were short-lived.
What?! I'm not in love with her!
NO WAY! He still stinks!

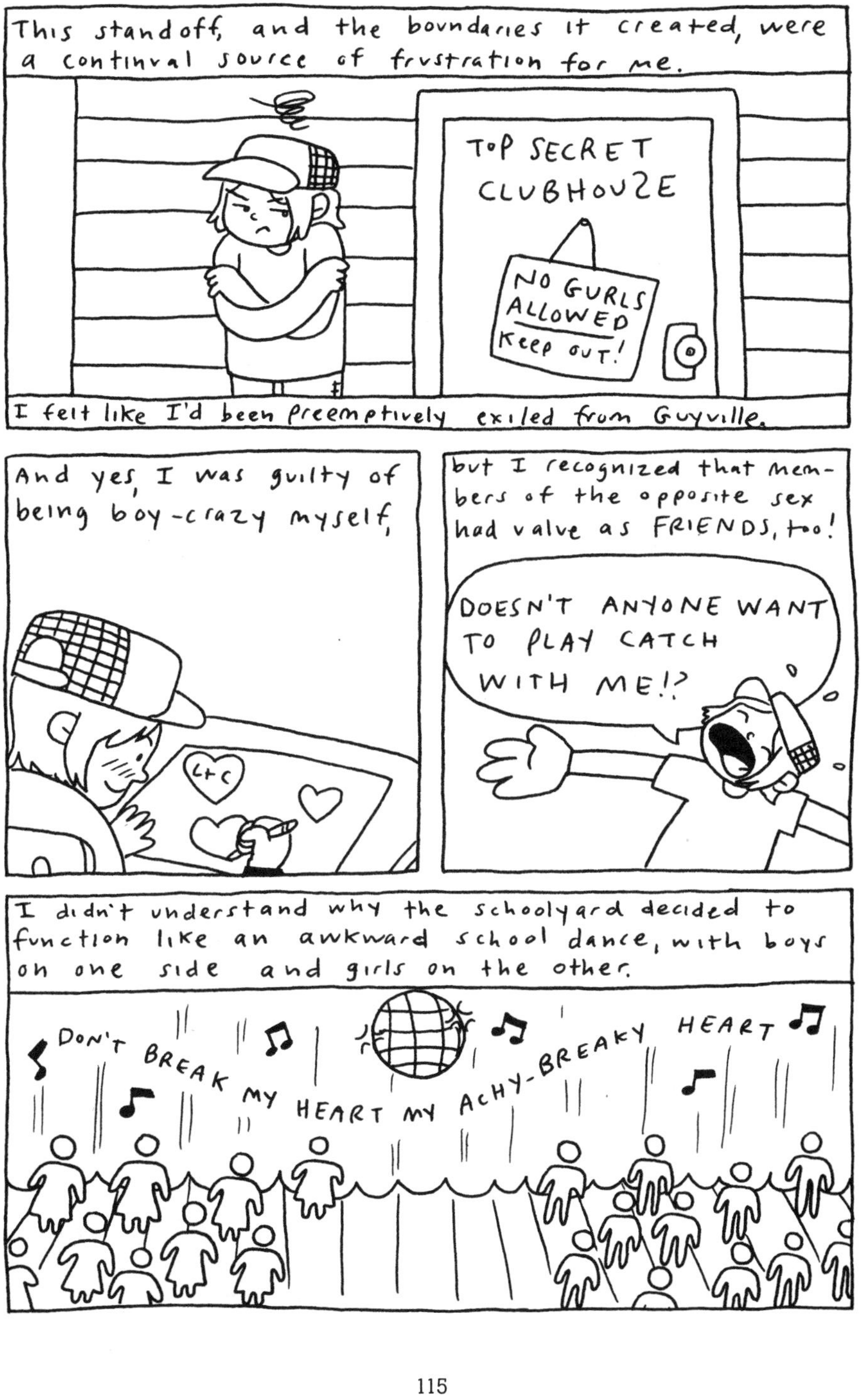
This standoff, and the boundaries it created, were a continual source of frustration for me.
TOP SECRET CLUBHOUSE
NO GURLS ALLOWED Keep out!
I felt like I'd been preemptively exiled from Guyville.
And yes, I was guilty of being boy-crazy myself,
L+C
but I recognized that members of the opposite sex had value as FRIENDS, too!
DOESN'T ANYONE WANT TO PLAY CATCH WITH ME!?
I didn't understand why the schoolyard decided to function like an awkward school dance, with boys on one side and girls on the other.
DON'T BREAK MY HEART MY ACHY-BREAKY HEART

That's why I treasured my friendship with Tyler so much. He was my friend after School AND during.

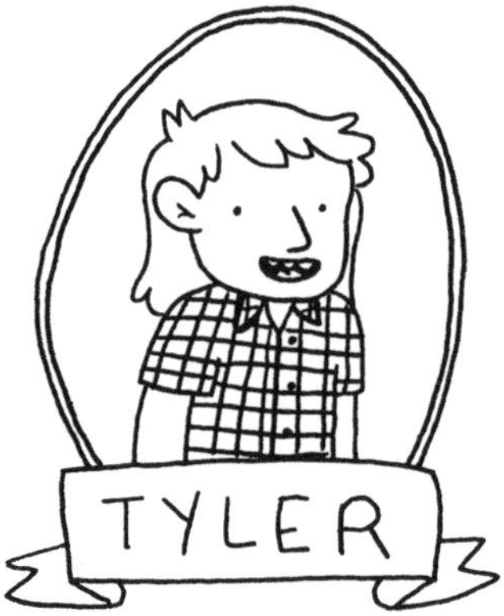
TYLER

* Loves drawing the Genie from Aladdin.
* Went through my Huck Finn phase with me (as Tom Sawyer.)
* Is in my combination 4th, 5th, and 6th grade class, but is a grade below me.
* Has a younger brother named Evan, who is best friends with my younger brother, Jamie.

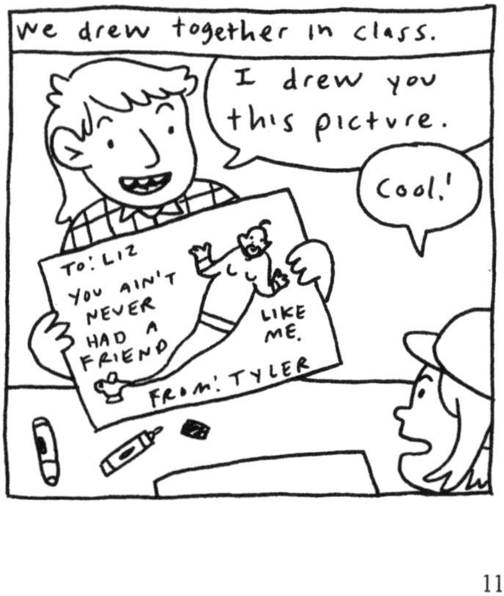
We drew together in class.
I drew you this picture.
Cool!
To: LIZ
YOU AIN'T NEVER HAD A FRIEND LIKE ME.
FROM: TYLER

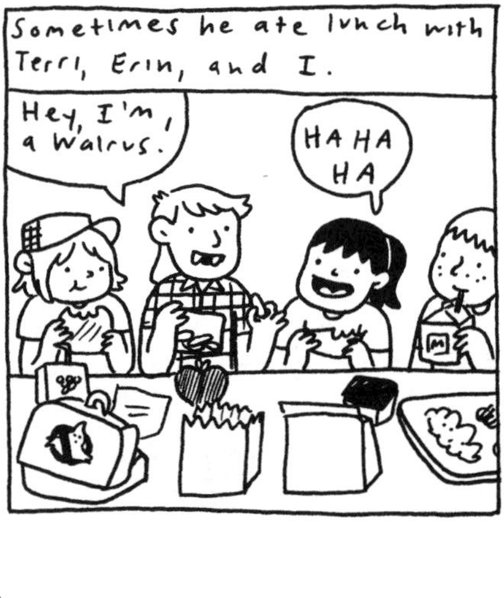
Sometimes he ate lunch with Terri, Erin, and I.
Hey, I'm a Walrus.
HA HA HA

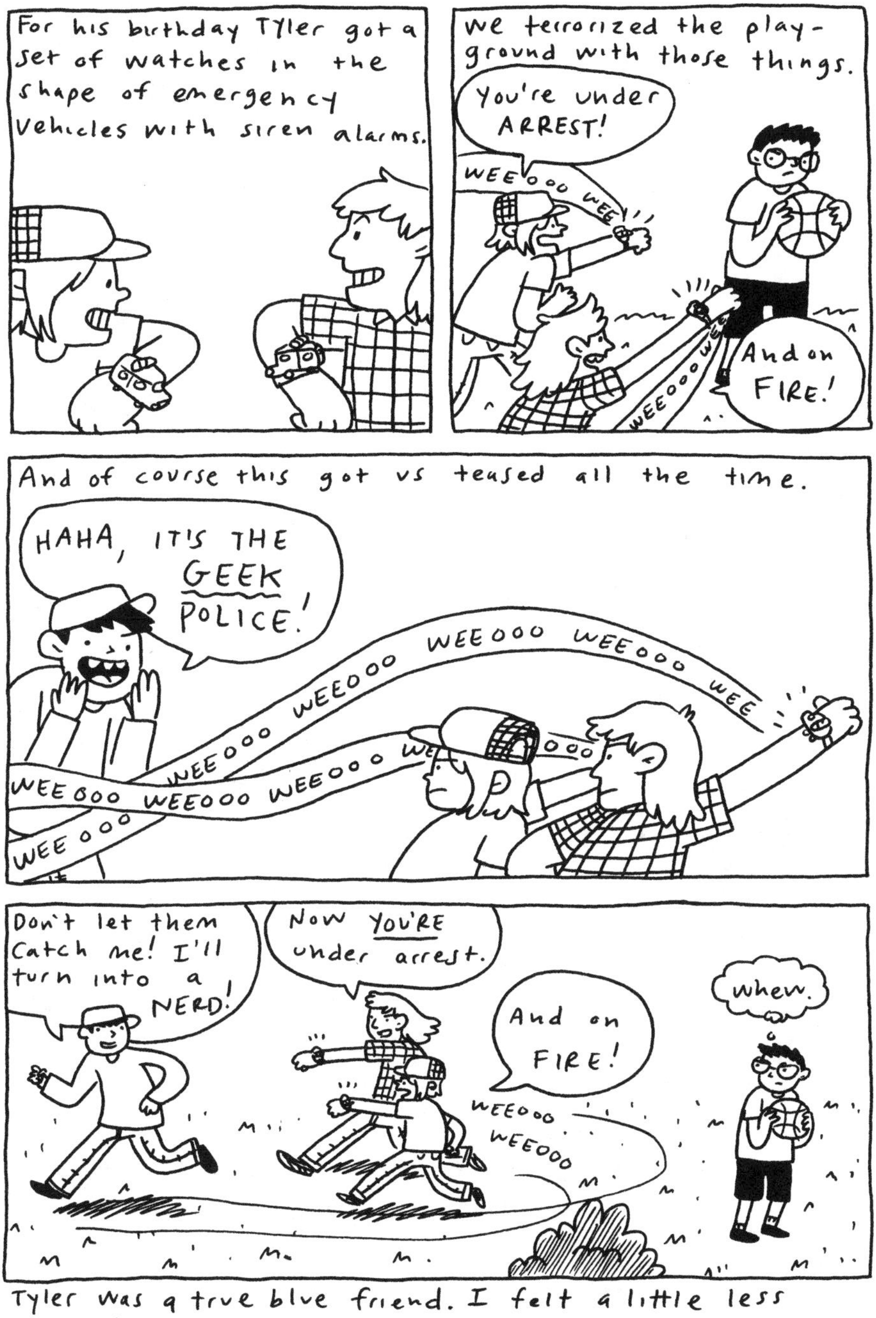
For his birthday Tyler got a set of watches in the shape of emergency vehicles with siren alarms.
We terrorized the playground with those things.
You're under ARREST!
WEE OOO WEE
WEEOOO WEE
And on FIRE!
And of course this got us teased all the time.
HAHA, IT'S THE GEEK POLICE!
WEE OOO WEE OOO WEE OOO WEE OOO WEE OOO WEE
WEE OOO WEE OOO WEE OOO WEE OOO
Don't let them catch me! I'll turn into a NERD!
Now YOU'RE under arrest.
And on FIRE!
whew.
WEEOOO WEEOOO

Tyler was a true blue friend. I felt a little less exiled when he was around.

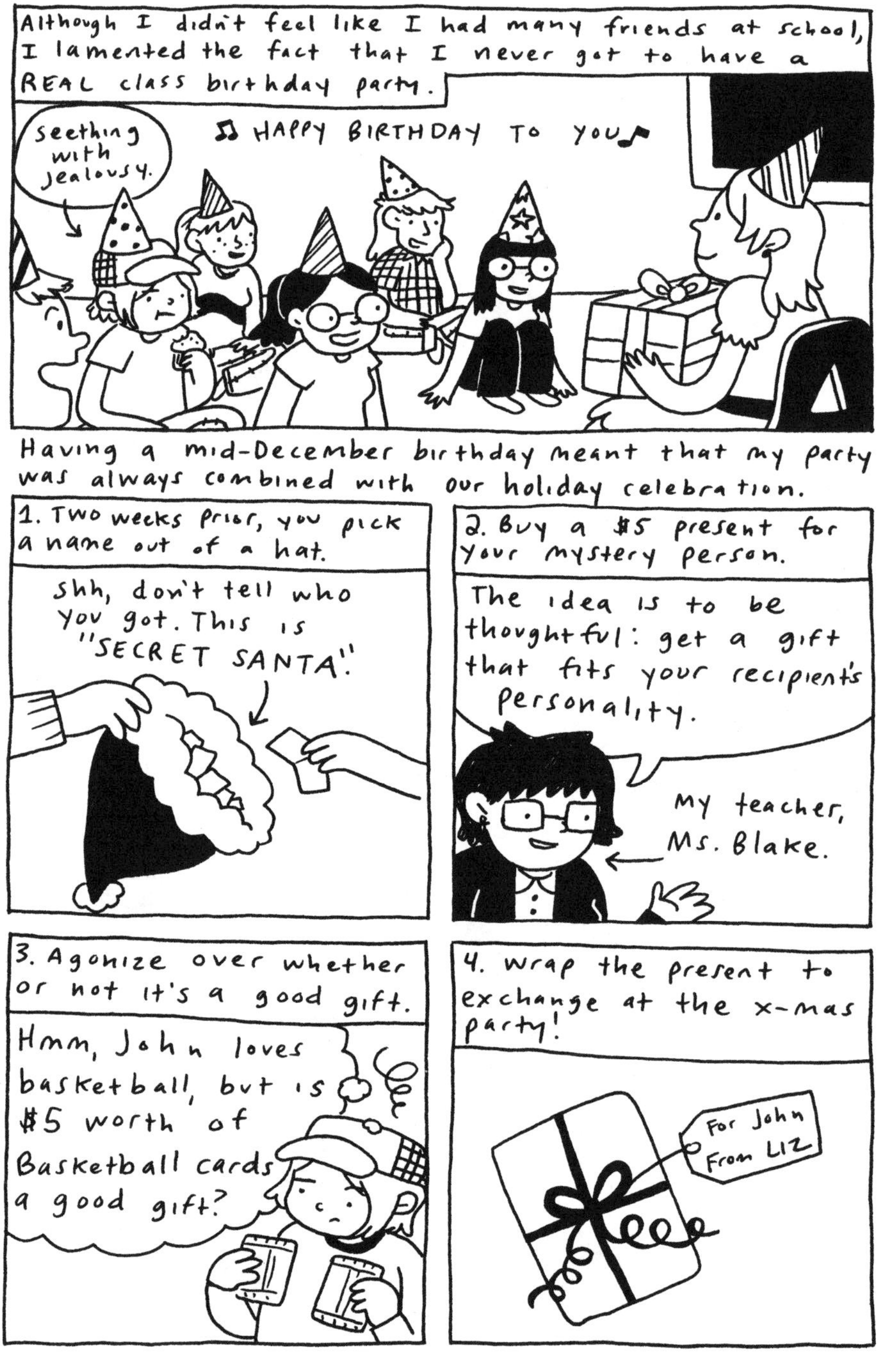
Although I didn't feel like I had many friends at school, I lamented the fact that I never got to have a REAL class birthday party.
seething with jealousy.
♫ HAPPY BIRTHDAY TO YOU ♪
Having a mid-December birthday meant that my party was always combined with our holiday celebration.
1. Two weeks prior, you pick a name out of a hat.
Shh, don't tell who you got. This is "SECRET SANTA".
2. Buy a $5 present for your mystery person.
The idea is to be thoughtful: get a gift that fits your recipient's personality.
My teacher, Ms. Blake.
3. Agonize over whether or not it's a good gift.
Hmm, John loves basketball, but is $5 worth of Basketball cards a good gift?
4. Wrap the present to exchange at the x-mas party!
For John From LIZ

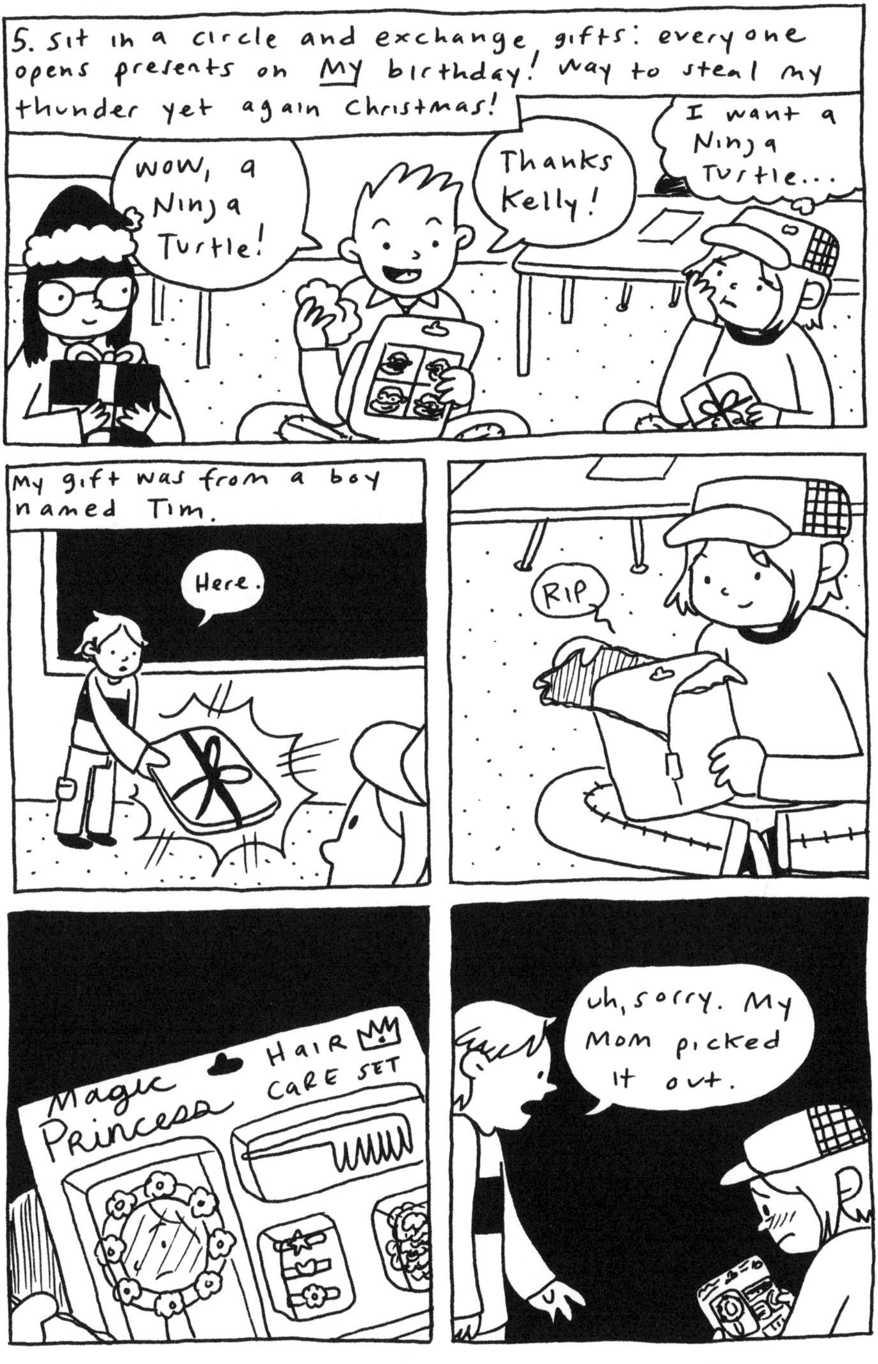

5. Sit in a circle and exchange gifts: everyone opens presents on MY birthday! Way to steal my thunder yet again Christmas!
Wow, a Ninja Turtle!
Thanks Kelly!
I want a Ninja Turtle...
My gift was from a boy named Tim.
Here.
RIP
Magic Princess Hair Care Set
uh, sorry. My Mom picked it out.

Fortunately, my real birthday party that weekend more than made up for it.

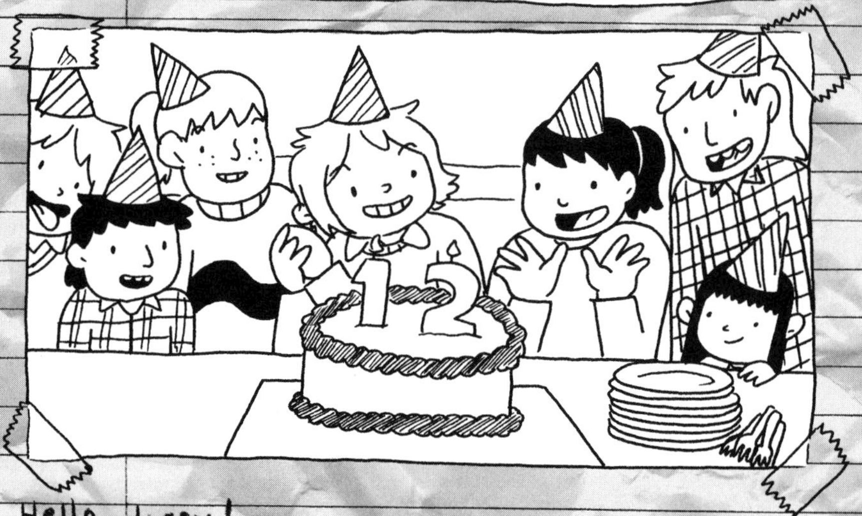

Hello diary!

Today was my birthday party! Terri, Erin, and Tyler came (with Evan to play with my brother, thank god). I got lots of good presents.

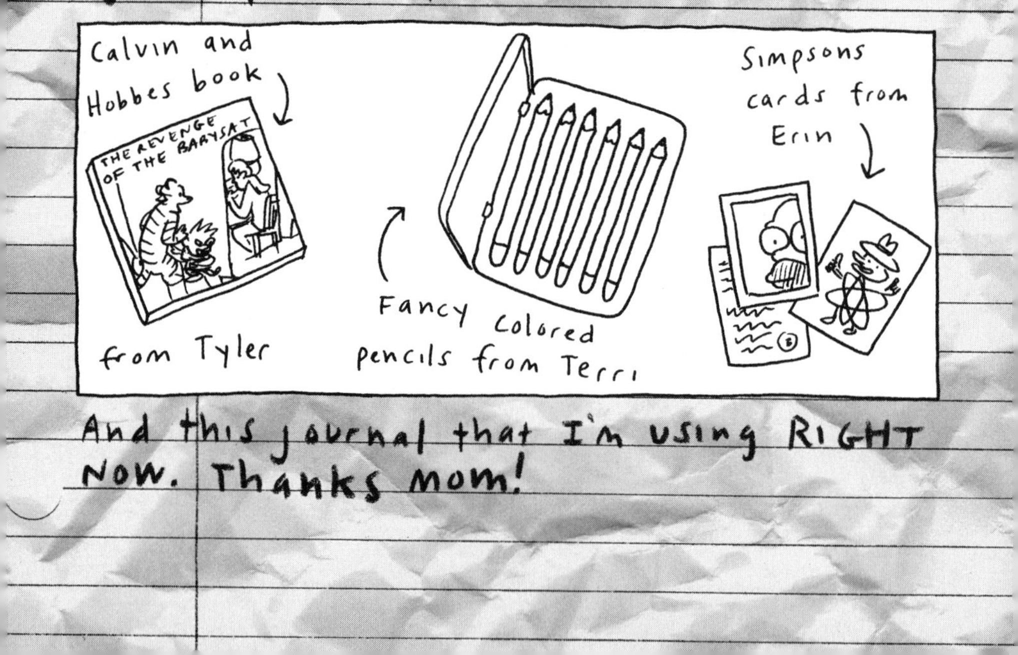
Calvin and Hobbes book
THE REVENGE OF THE BABYSAT
from Tyler
Fancy colored pencils from Terri
Simpsons cards from Erin

And this journal that I'm using RIGHT NOW. Thanks mom!

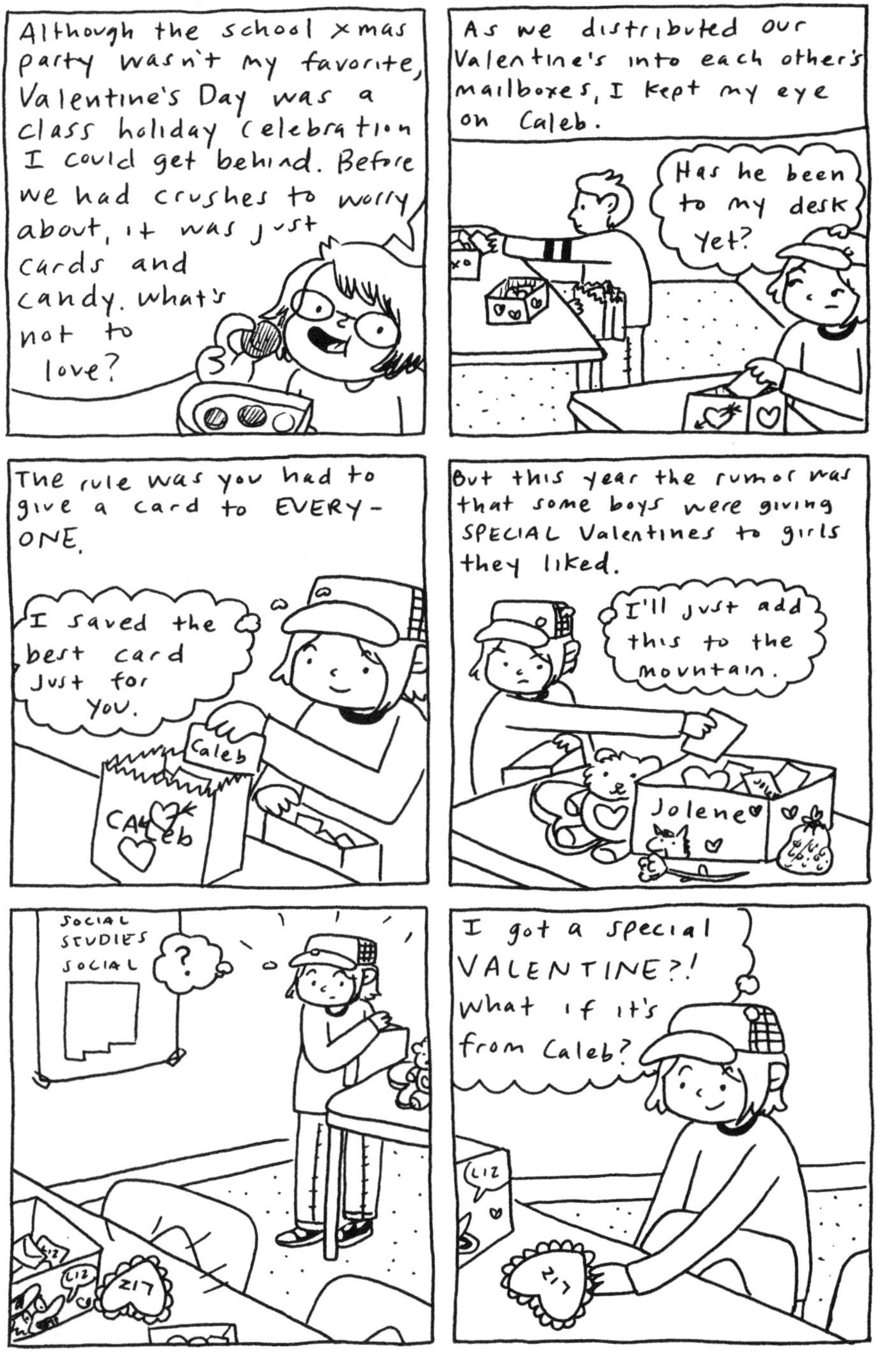
Although the school xmas party wasn't my favorite, Valentine's Day was a class holiday celebration I could get behind. Before we had crushes to worry about, it was just cards and candy. What's not to love?
As we distributed our Valentine's into each other's mailboxes, I kept my eye on Caleb.
Has he been to my desk yet?
XO
The rule was you had to give a card to EVERY-ONE.
I saved the best card just for you.
Caleb
CALeb
But this year the rumor was that some boys were giving SPECIAL Valentines to girls they liked.
I'll just add this to the mountain.
Jolene
SOCIAL STUDIES SOCIAL
?
LIZ
LIZ
LIZ
I got a special VALENTINE?! What if it's from Caleb?
LIZ
LIZ

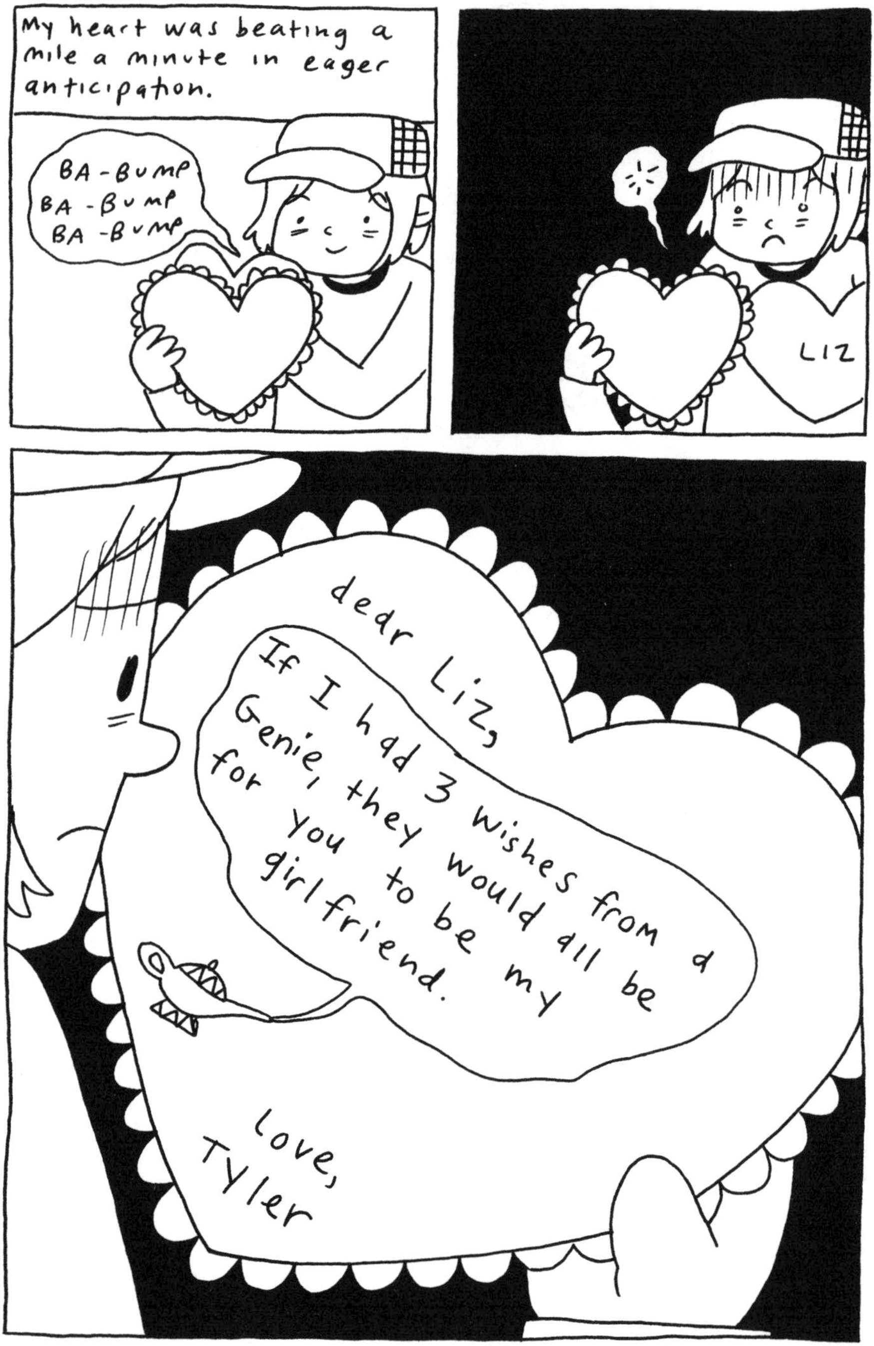
My heart was beating a mile a minute in eager anticipation.
BA-BUMP BA-BUMP BA-BUMP
LIZ
dear LiZ,
If I had 3 wishes from a Genie, they would all be for you to be my girlfriend.
Love, Tyler

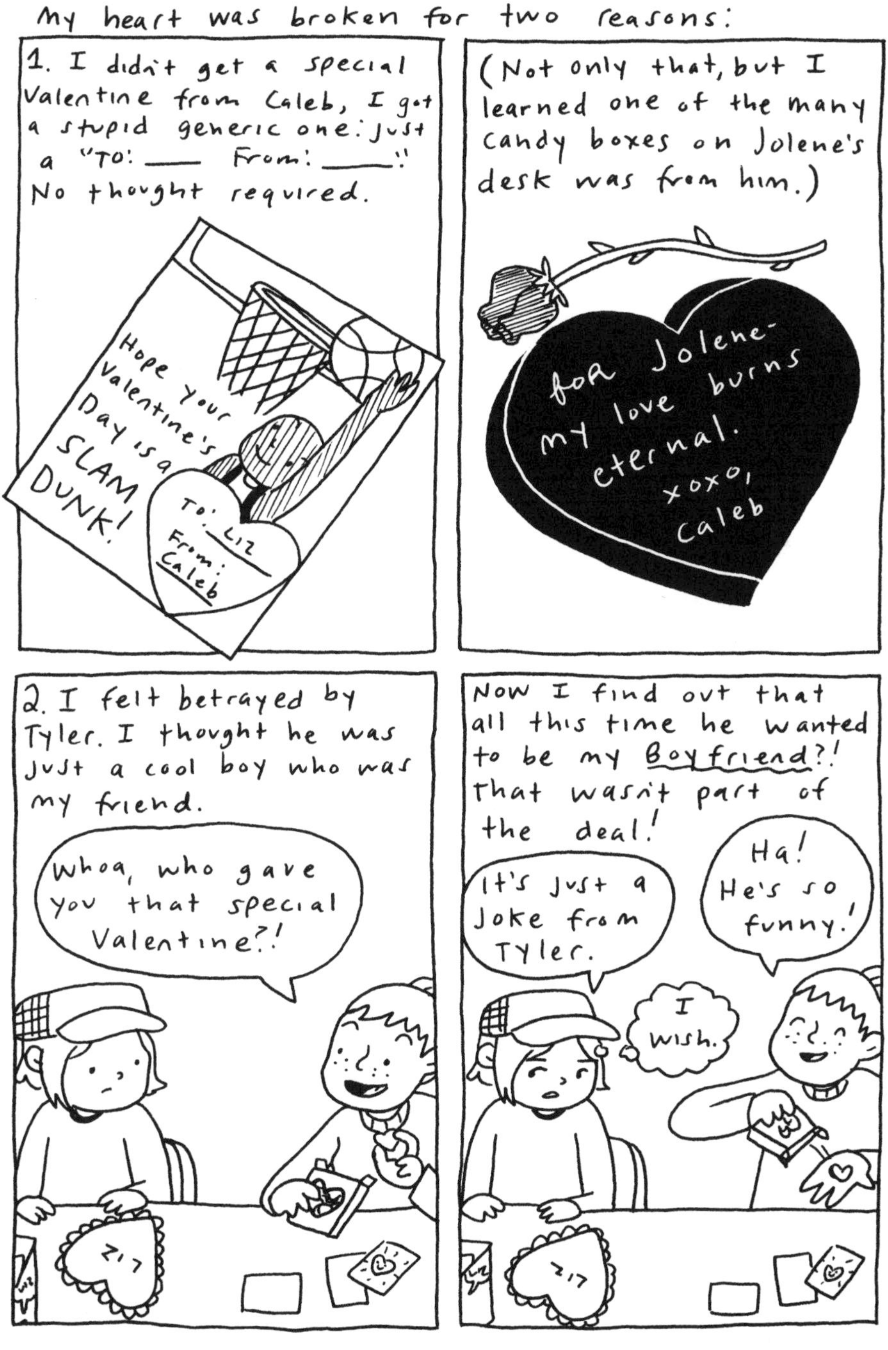
My heart was broken for two reasons:
1. I didn't get a special Valentine from Caleb, I got a stupid generic one: just a "To: ___ From: ___" No thought required.
Hope your Valentine's Day is a SLAM DUNK!
To: Liz From: Caleb
(Not only that, but I learned one of the many candy boxes on Jolene's desk was from him.)
for Jolene- my love burns eternal. xoxo, Caleb
2. I felt betrayed by Tyler. I thought he was just a cool boy who was my friend.
Whoa, who gave you that special Valentine?!
Liz
Now I find out that all this time he wanted to be my Boyfriend?! That wasn't part of the deal!
It's just a joke from Tyler.
Ha! He's so funny!
I wish.
Liz

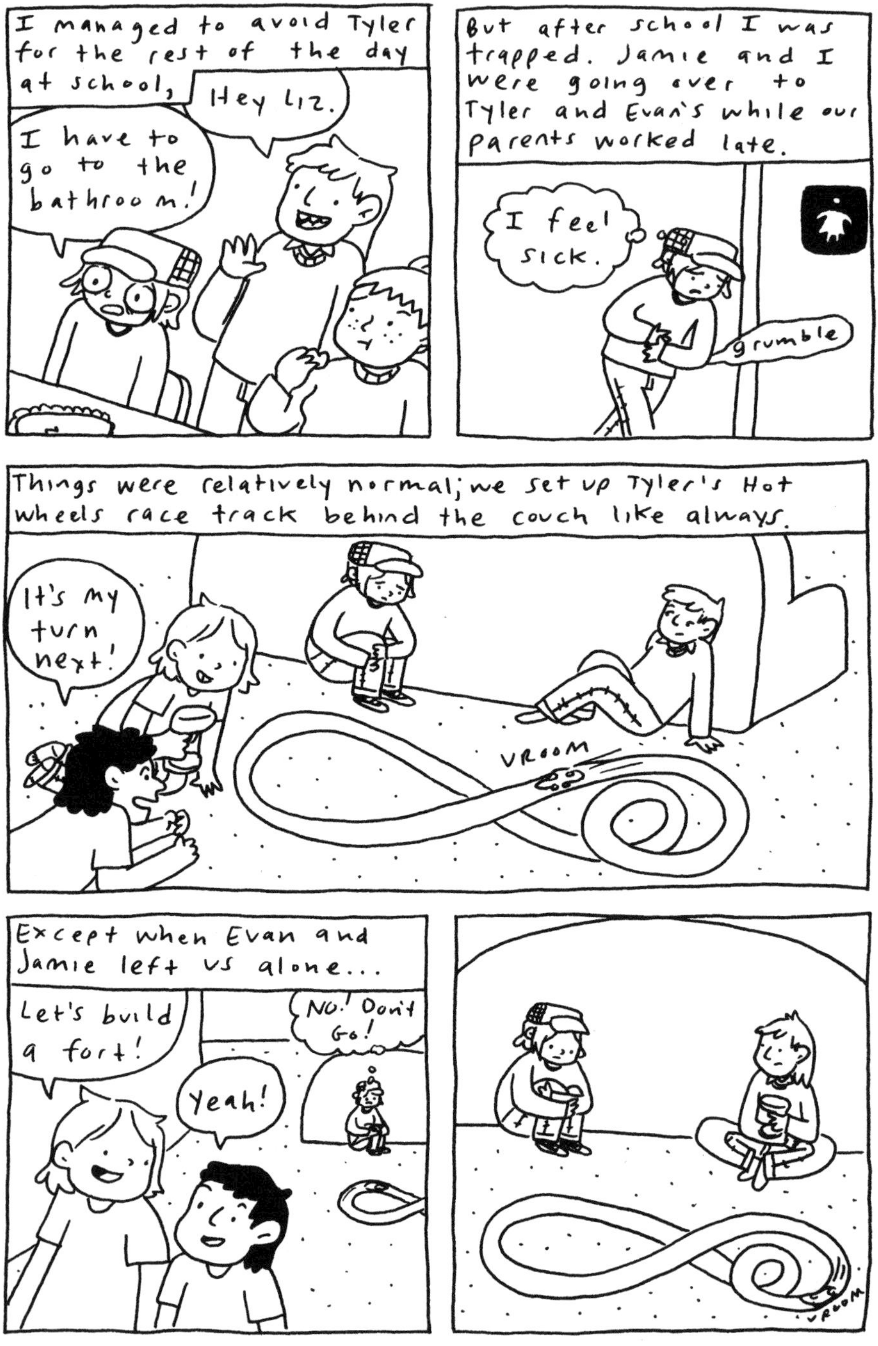
I managed to avoid Tyler for the rest of the day at school,
Hey Liz.
I have to go to the bathroom!
But after school I was trapped. Jamie and I were going over to Tyler and Evan's while our parents worked late.
I feel sick.
grumble
Things were relatively normal; we set up Tyler's Hot wheels race track behind the couch like always.
It's my turn next!
VROOM
Except when Evan and Jamie left us alone...
Let's build a fort!
NO! Don't Go!
Yeah!
VROOM

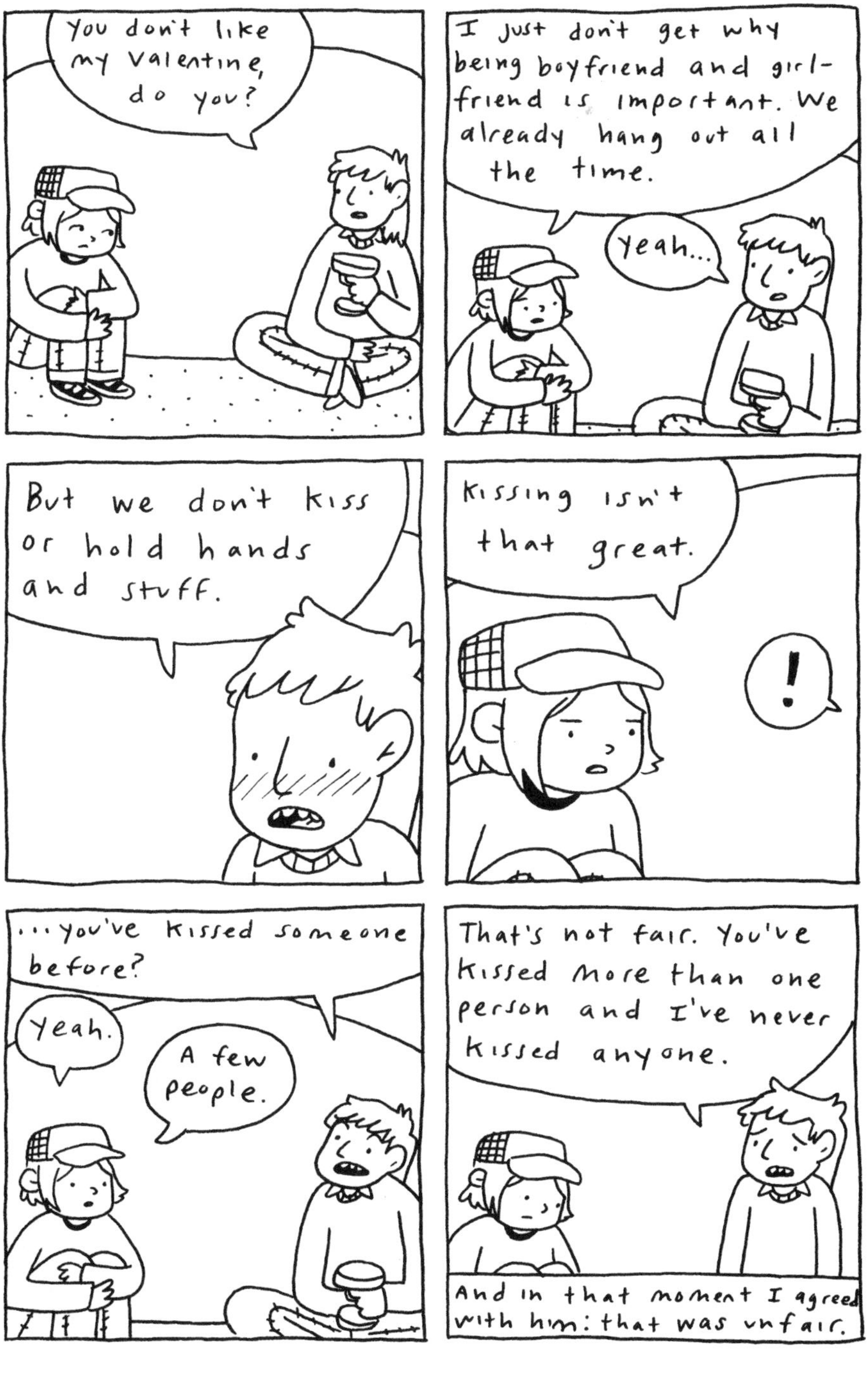
You don't like my valentine, do you?
I just don't get why being boyfriend and girlfriend is important. We already hang out all the time.
Yeah...
But we don't kiss or hold hands and stuff.
Kissing isn't that great.
!
...you've kissed someone before?
Yeah.
A few people.
That's not fair. You've kissed more than one person and I've never kissed anyone.
And in that moment I agreed with him: that was unfair.

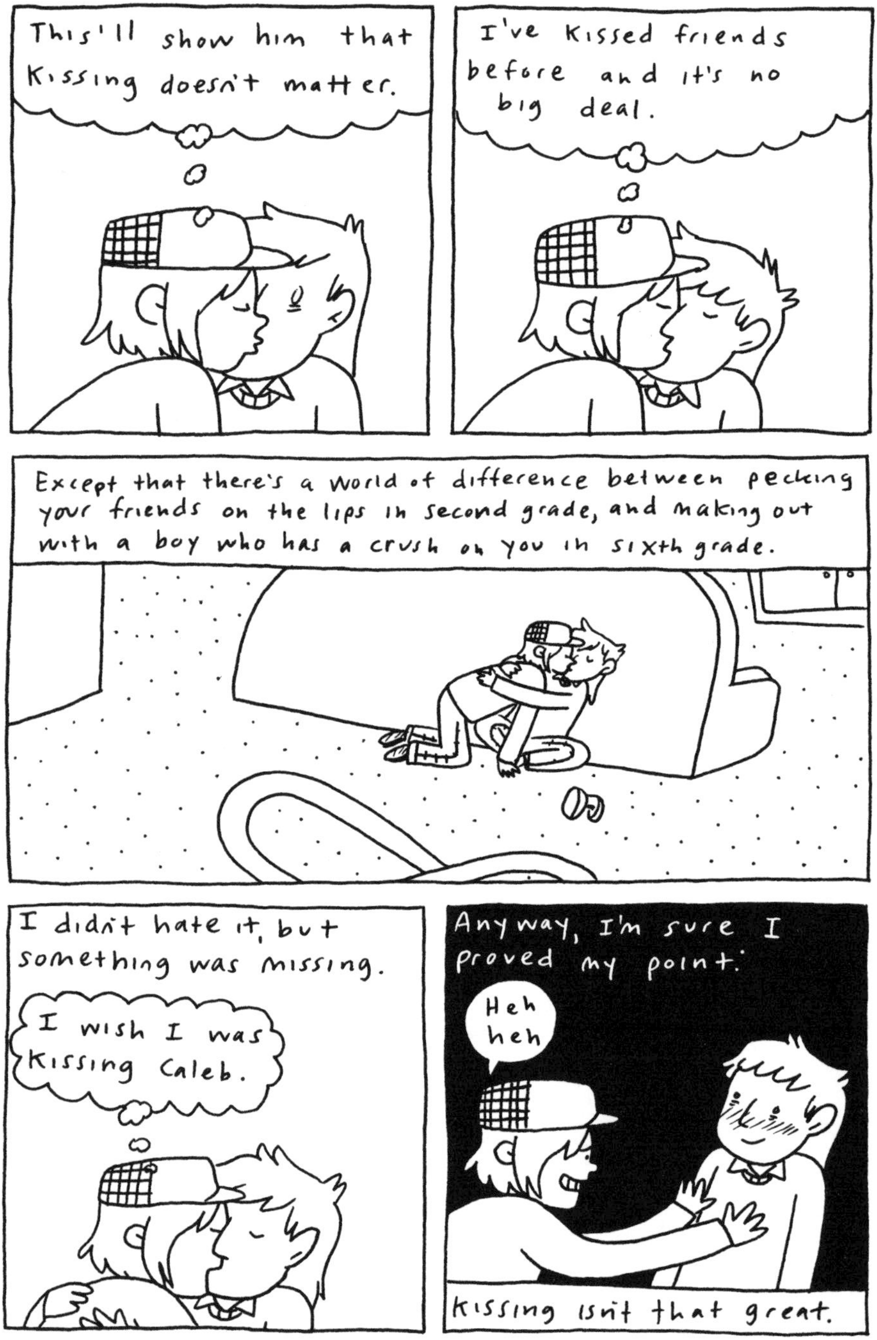
This'll show him that kissing doesn't matter.
I've kissed friends before and it's no big deal.
Except that there's a world of difference between pecking your friends on the lips in second grade, and making out with a boy who has a crush on you in sixth grade.
I didn't hate it, but something was missing.
I wish I was kissing Caleb.
Anyway, I'm sure I proved my point:
Heh heh
Kissing isn't that great.

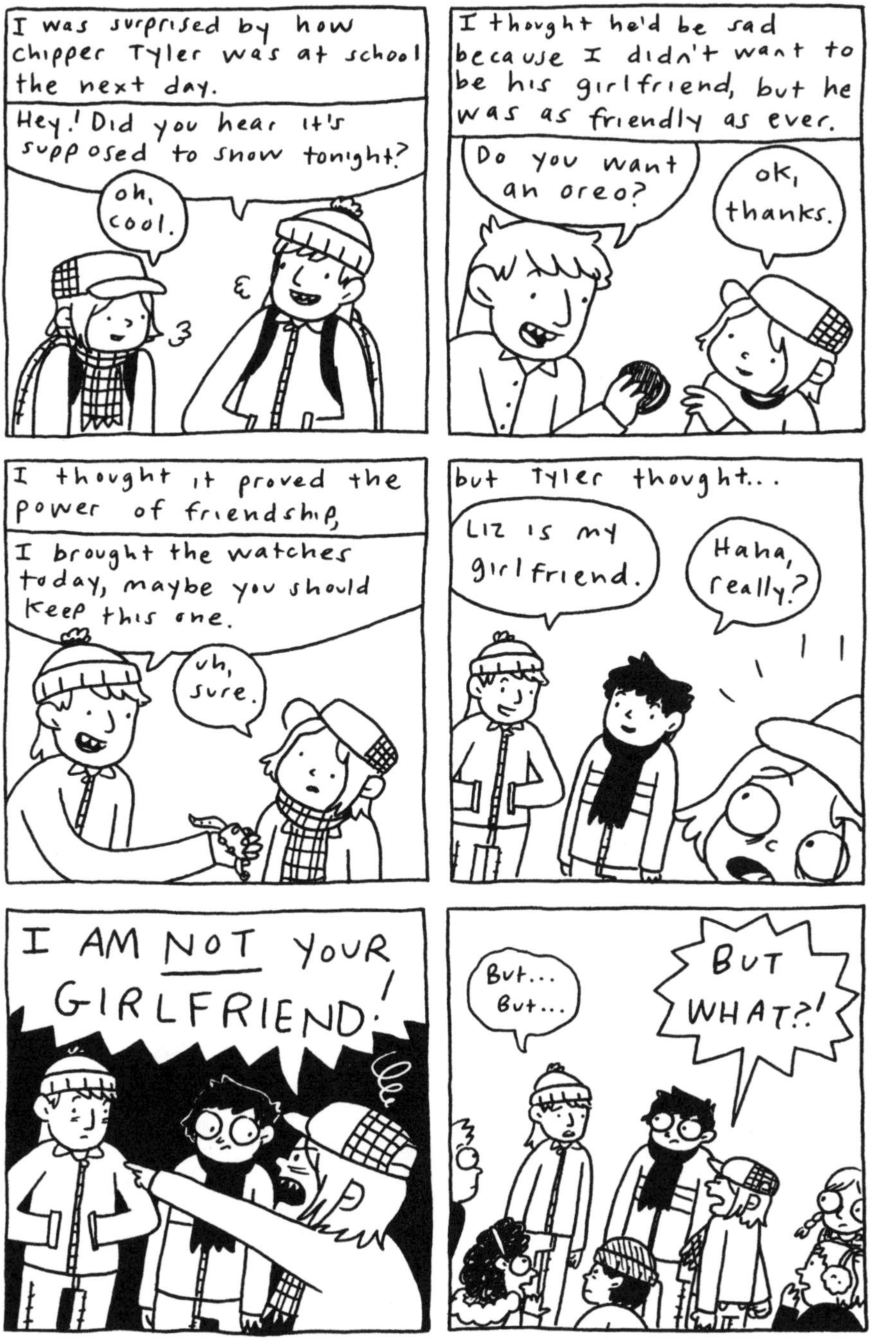
I was surprised by how chipper Tyler was at school the next day.
Hey! Did you hear it's supposed to snow tonight?
oh, cool.
I thought he'd be sad because I didn't want to be his girlfriend, but he was as friendly as ever.
Do you want an oreo?
ok, thanks.
I thought it proved the power of friendship,
I brought the watches today, maybe you should keep this one.
uh, sure.
but Tyler thought...
Liz is my girlfriend.
Haha, really?
I AM NOT YOUR GIRLFRIEND!
But... But...
BUT WHAT?!

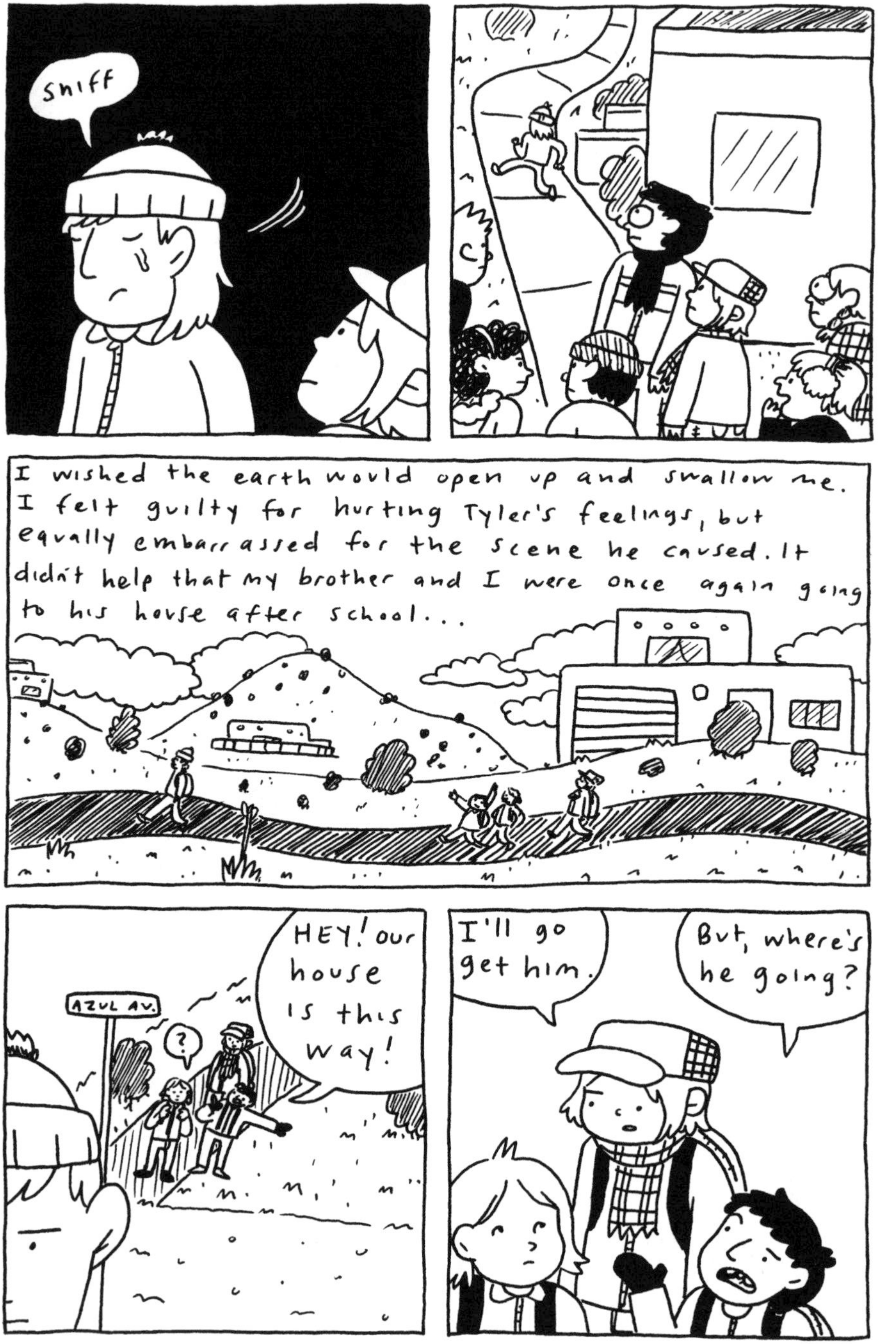
SNIFF
I wished the earth would open up and swallow me. I felt guilty for hurting Tyler's feelings, but equally embarrassed for the scene he caused. It didn't help that my brother and I were once again going to his house after school...
AZUL AV.
?
HEY! our house is this way!
I'll go get him.
But, where's he going?

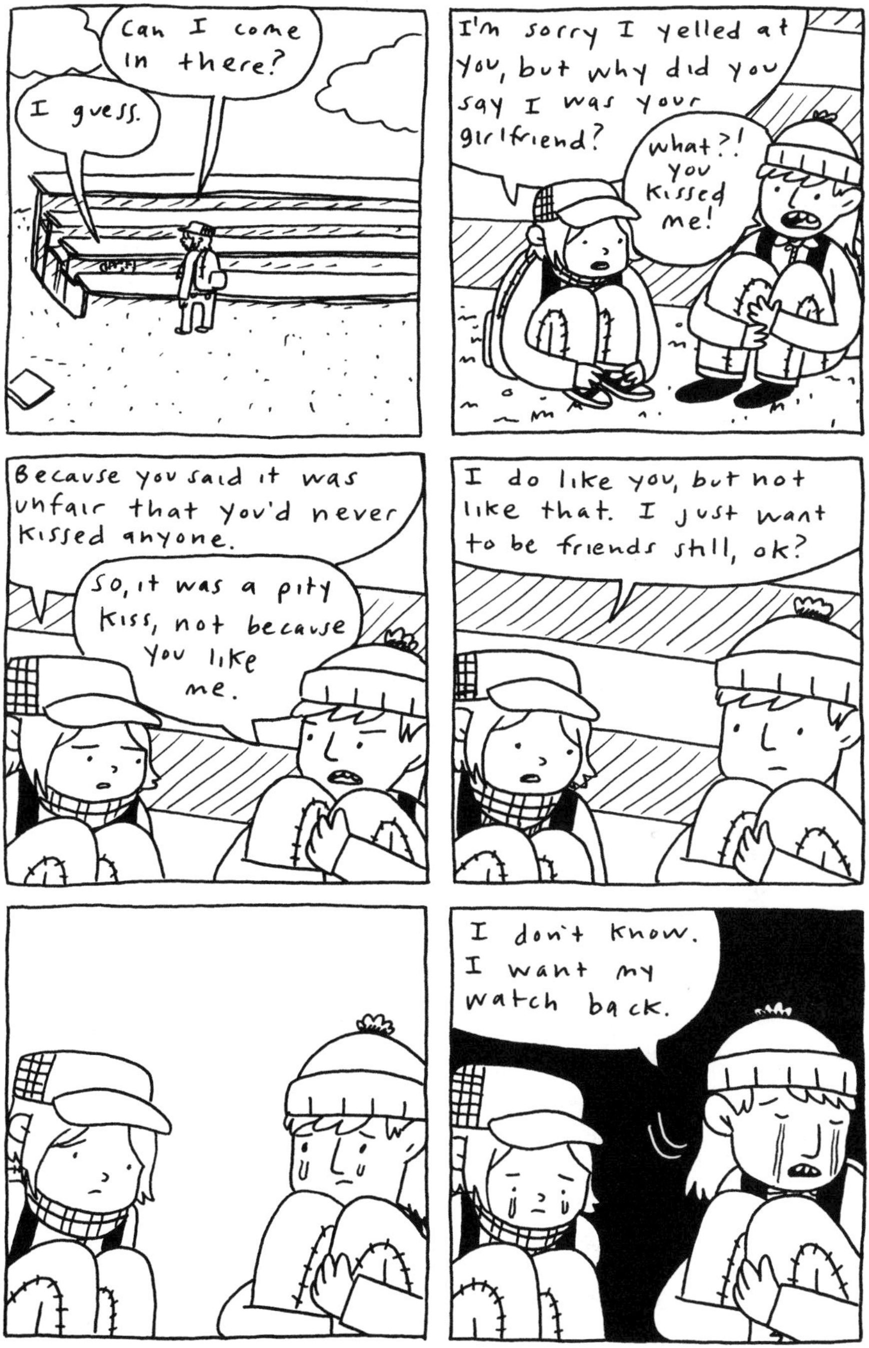
Can I come in there?
I guess.
I'm sorry I yelled at you, but why did you say I was your girlfriend?
what?! you kissed me!
Because you said it was unfair that you'd never kissed anyone.
So, it was a pity kiss, not because you like me.
I do like you, but not like that. I just want to be friends still, ok?
I don't know. I want my watch back.

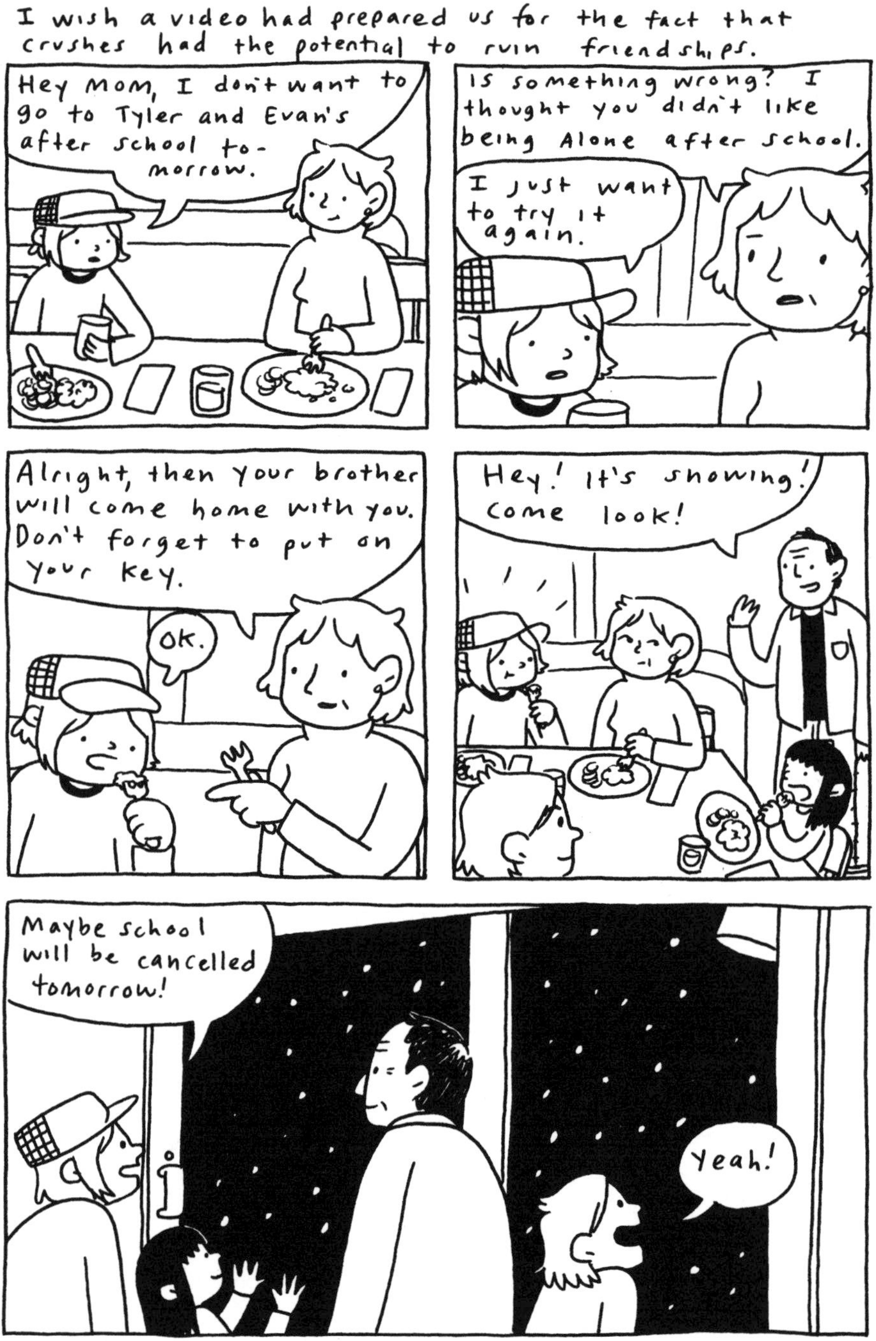
I wish a video had prepared us for the fact that crushes had the potential to ruin friendships.
Hey MOM, I don't want to go to Tyler and Evan's after school to-morrow.
Is something wrong? I thought you didn't like being Alone after school.
I just want to try it again.
Alright, then your brother will come home with you. Don't forget to put on your key.
OK.
Hey! It's snowing! Come look!
Maybe school will be cancelled tomorrow!
Yeah!

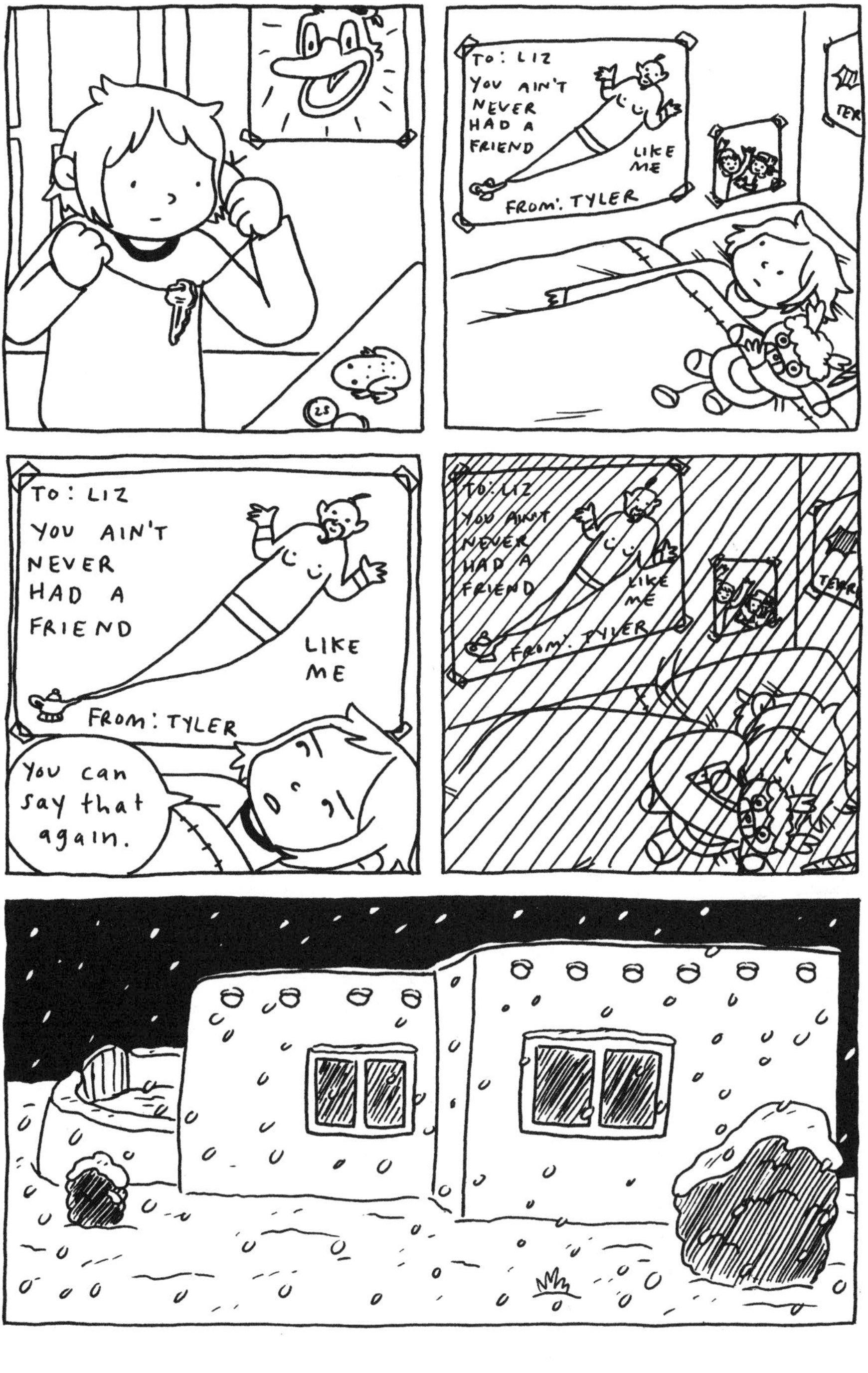
TO: LIZ
YOU AIN'T NEVER HAD A FRIEND LIKE ME
FROM: TYLER
TO: LIZ
YOU AIN'T NEVER HAD A FRIEND LIKE ME
FROM: TYLER
You can say that again.

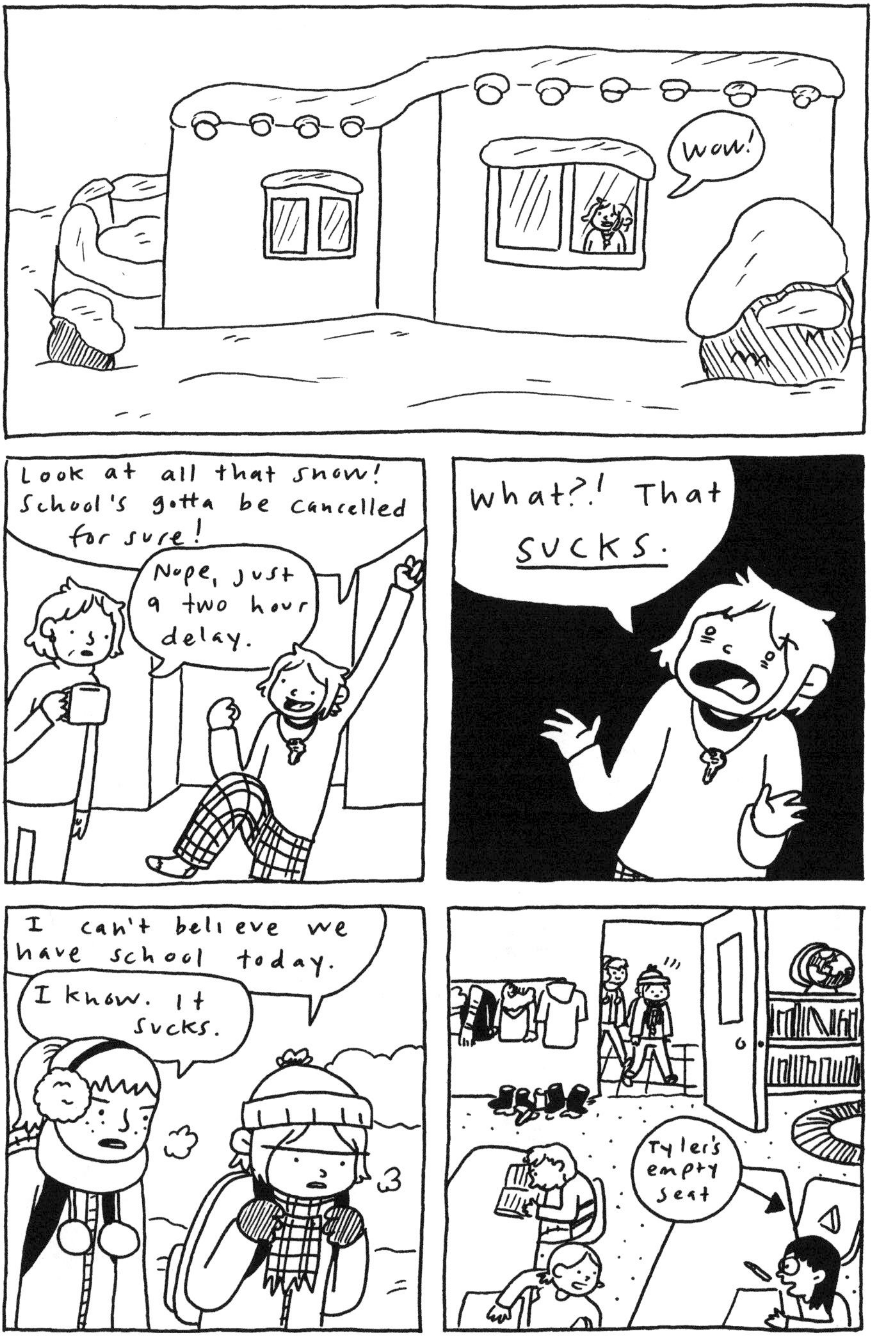
Wow!
Look at all that snow! School's gotta be cancelled for sure!
Nope, just a two hour delay.
What?! That SUCKS.
I can't believe we have school today.
I know. It sucks.
Tyler's empty seat

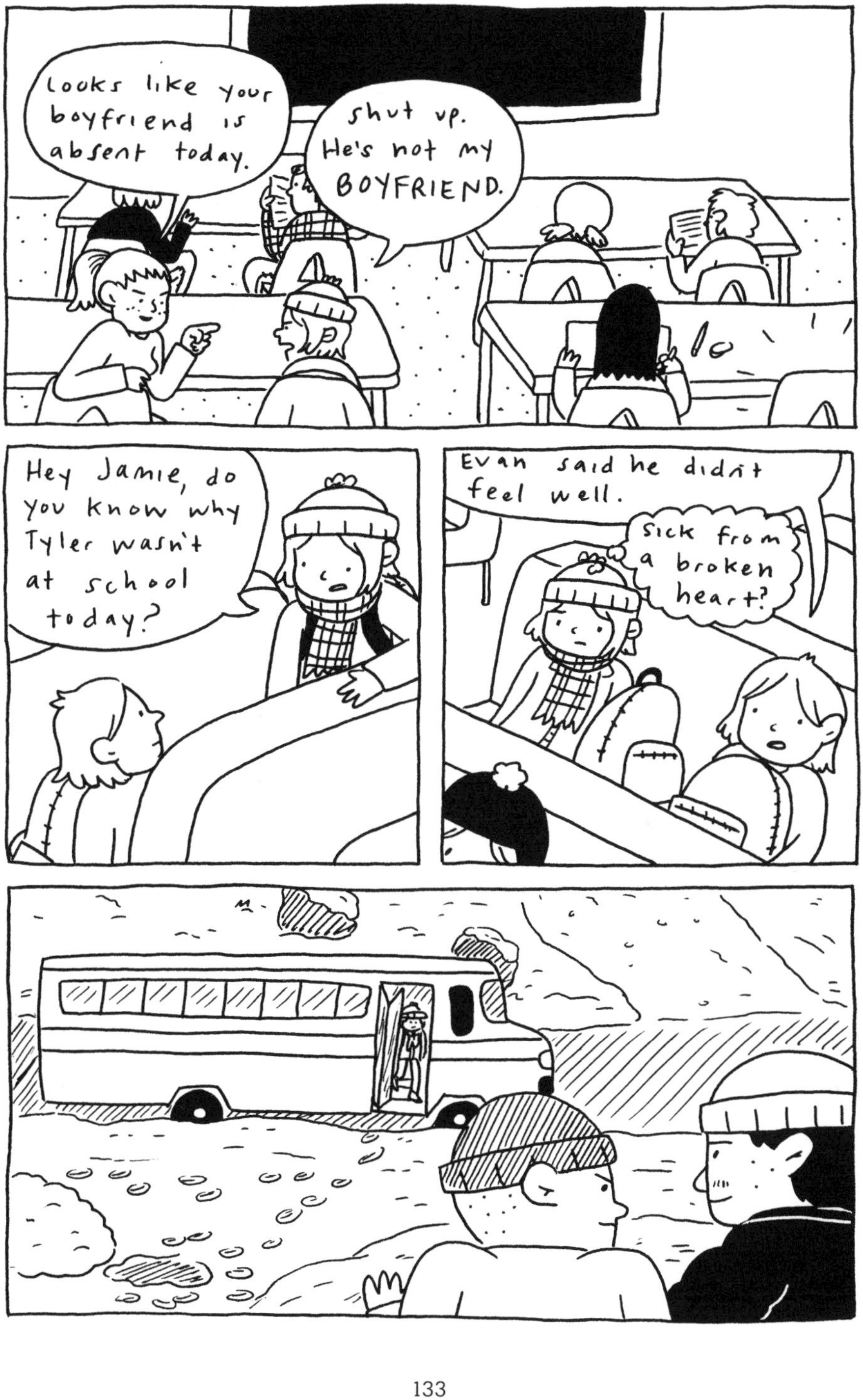
Looks like your boyfriend is absent today.
shut up. He's not my BOYFRIEND.
Hey Jamie, do you know why Tyler wasn't at school today?
Evan said he didn't feel well.
Sick from a broken heart?

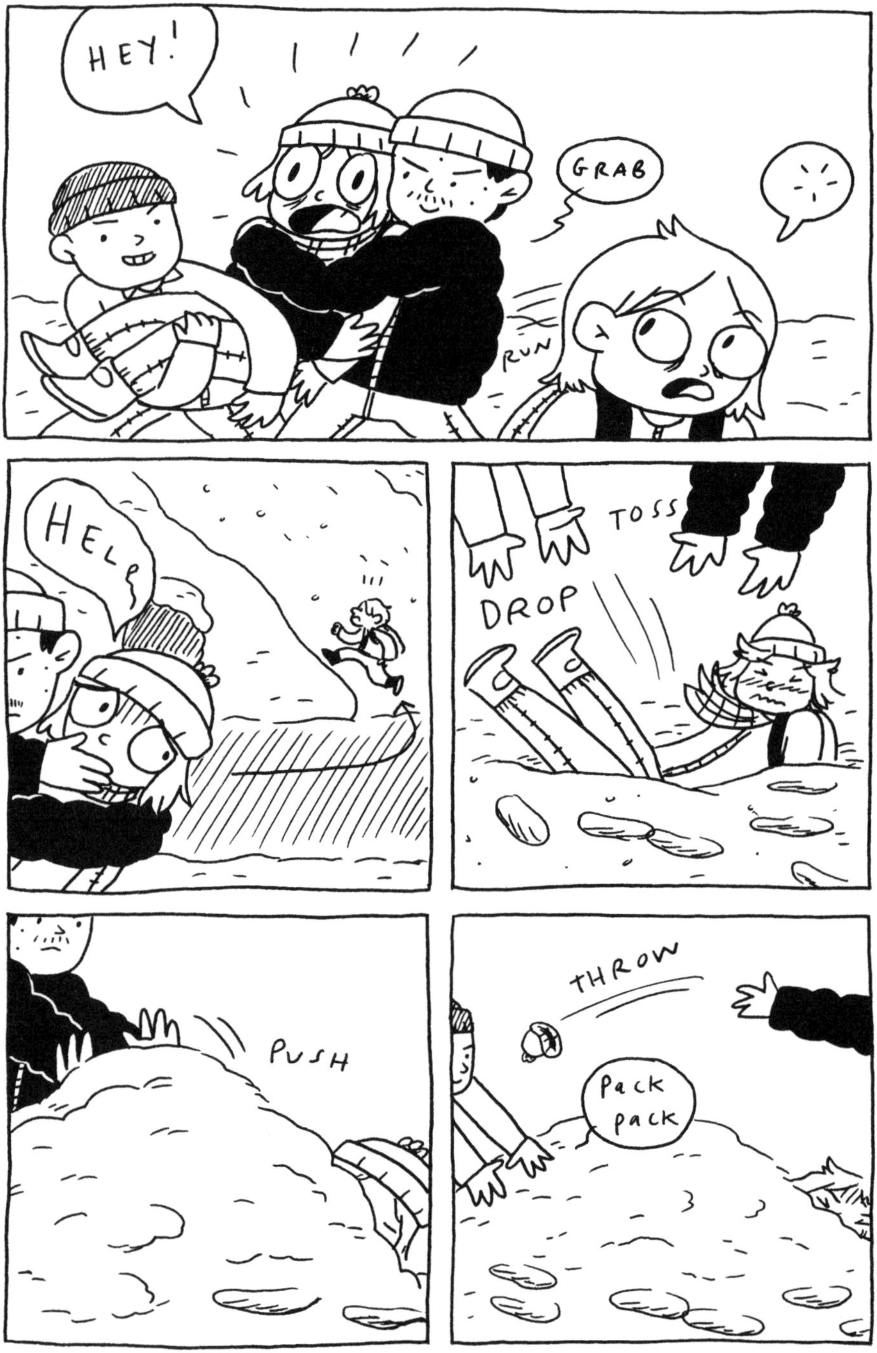
HEY!
GRAB
RUN
HELP
TOSS
DROP
PUSH
THROW
Pack pack

As my attackers fled, I could see that one of them was a highschool boy who lived on my street.

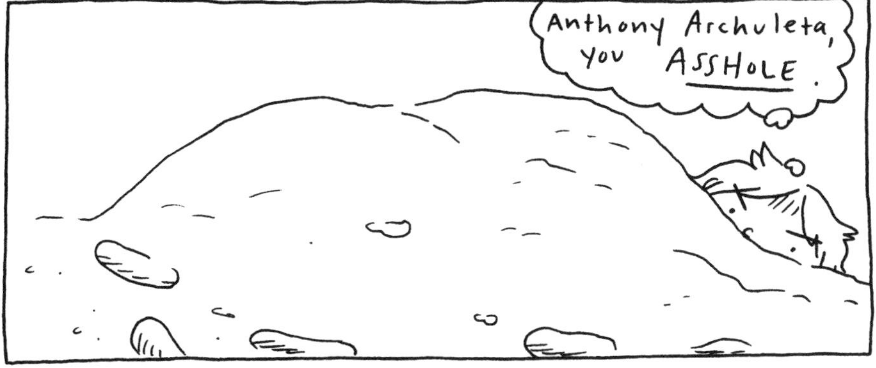
Anthony Archuleta, you ASSHOLE.

I was afraid to move: what if they were waiting for an excuse to bury me further?

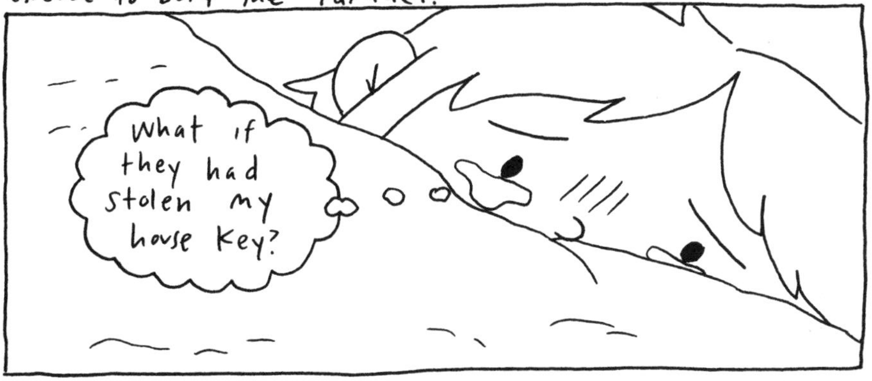
What if they had stolen my house key?

My left arm was twisted under me. It hurt so bad I thought it might be broken.

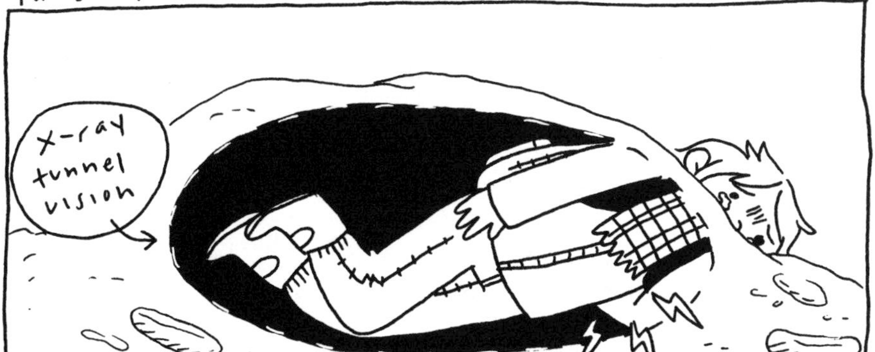
x-ray tunnel vision

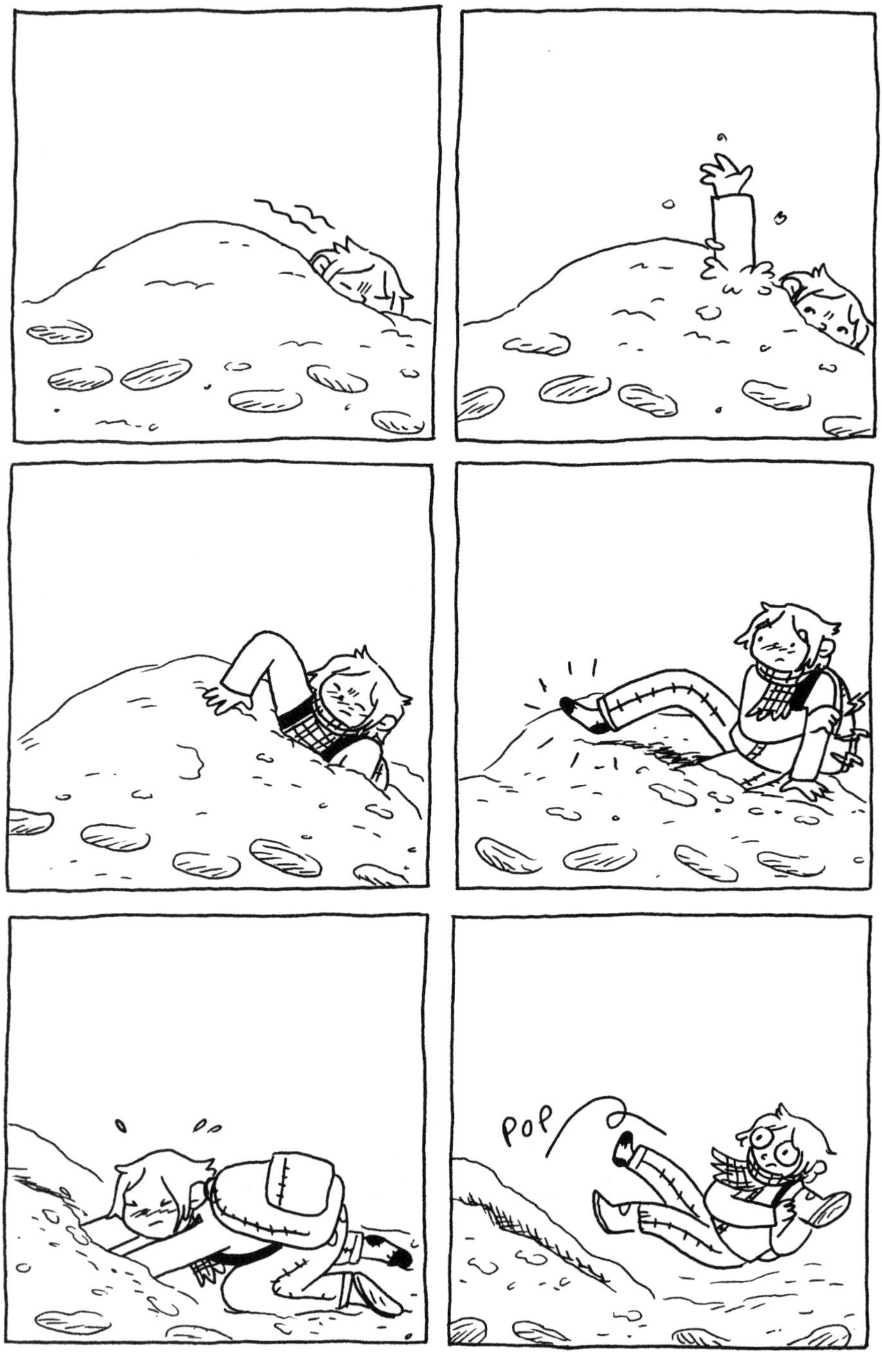
POP

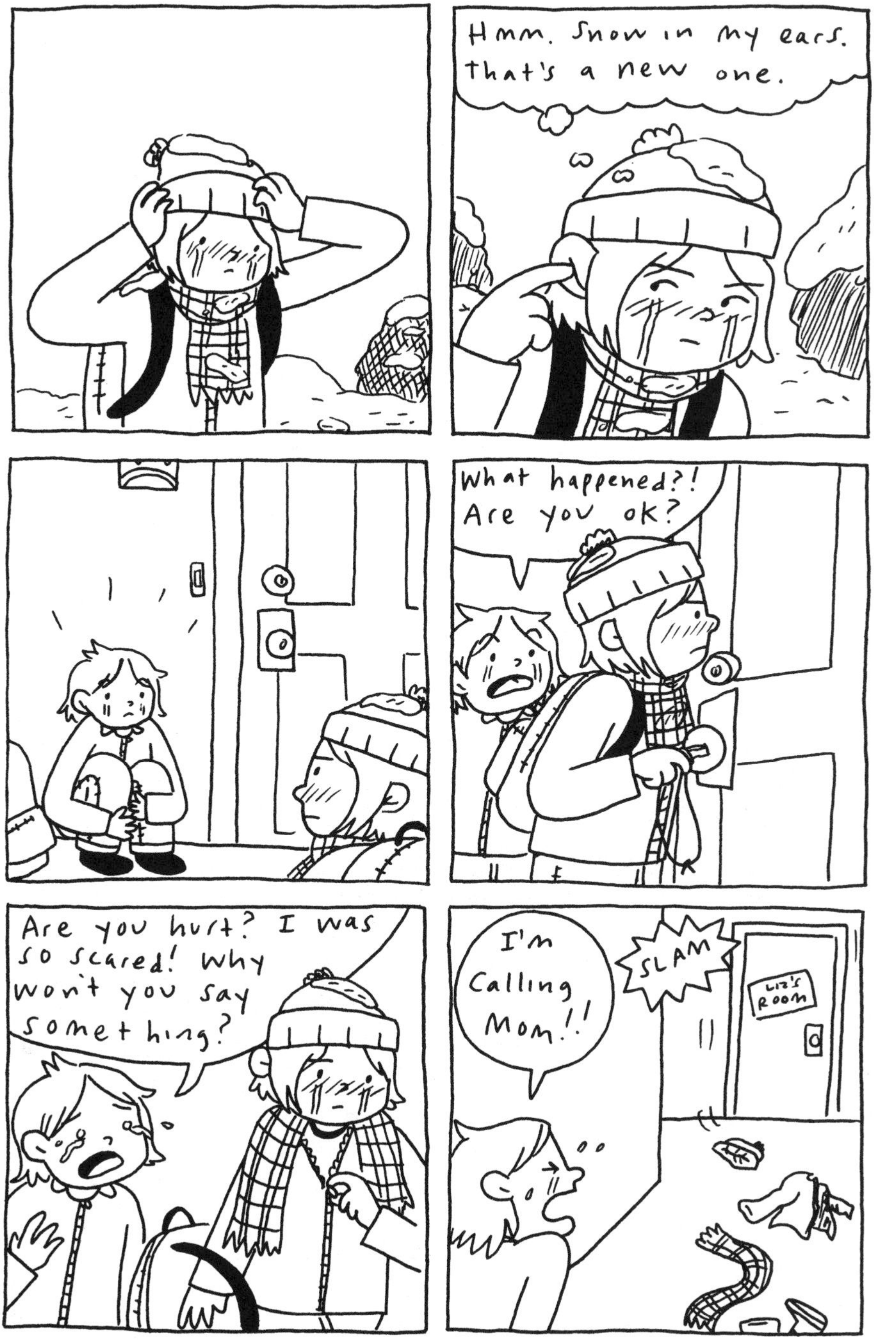
Hmm. Snow in my ears. That's a new one.
What happened?! Are you ok?
Are you hurt? I was so scared! Why won't you say something?
I'm Calling Mom!!
SLAM
LIZ'S ROOM

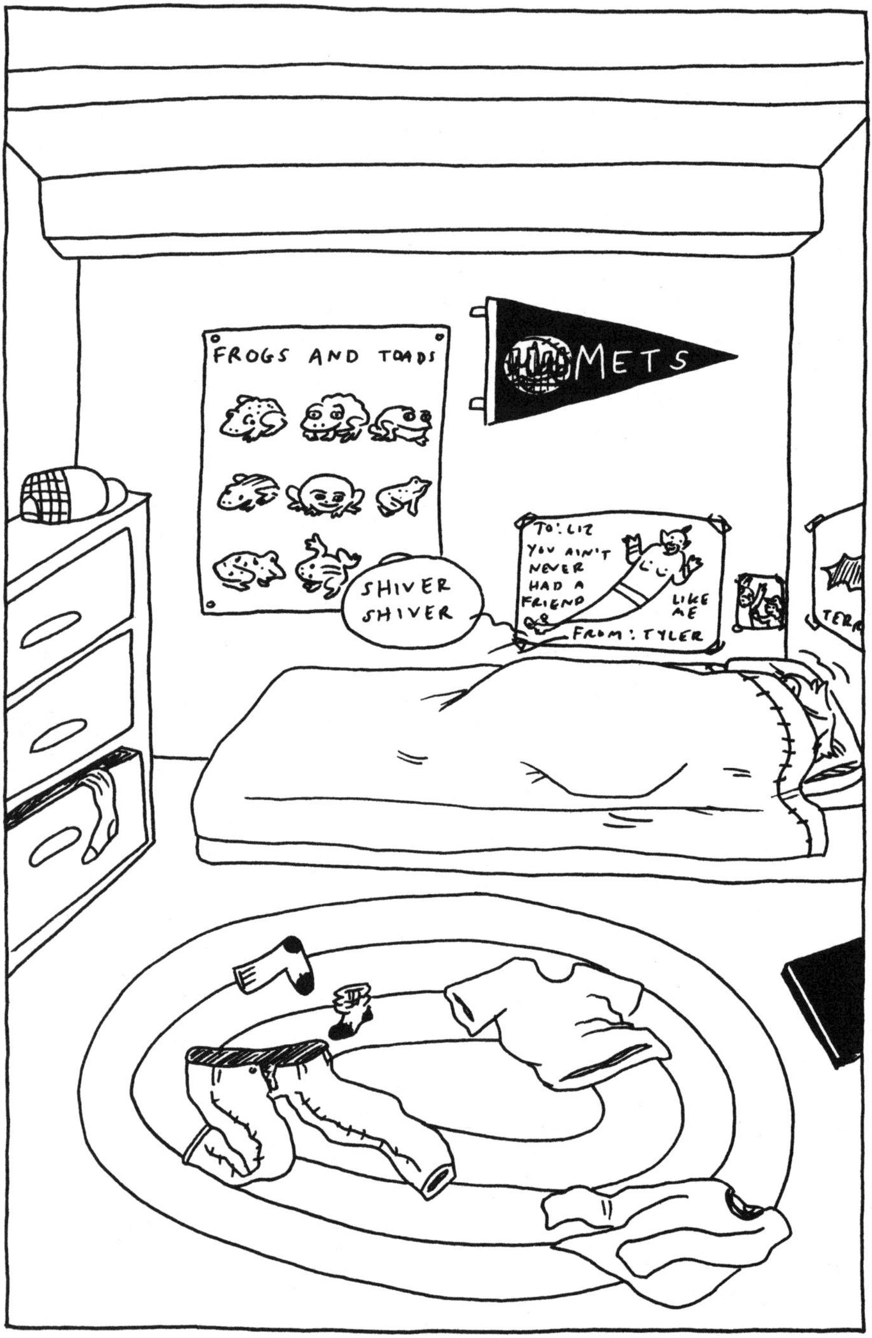
FROGS AND TOADS
METS
SHIVER SHIVER
TO: LIZ
YOU AIN'T NEVER HAD A FRIEND LIKE ME
FROM: TYLER

CHAPTER 7

Dear diary, Tyler isn't really my friend anymore. He spends all his time with this boy Billy.

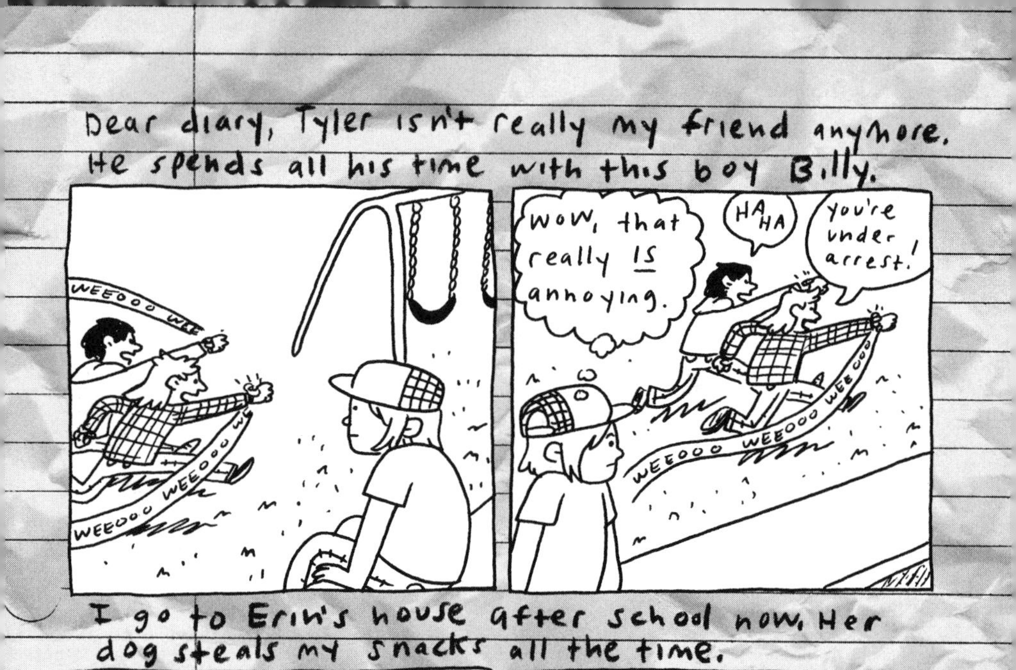
WEEOOO WEE
WEEOOO WEEOOO WEEOOO WE
Wow, that really IS annoying.
HA HA
You're under arrest!
WEEOOO WEEOOO WEEOOO

I go to Erin's house after school now. Her dog steals my snacks all the time.

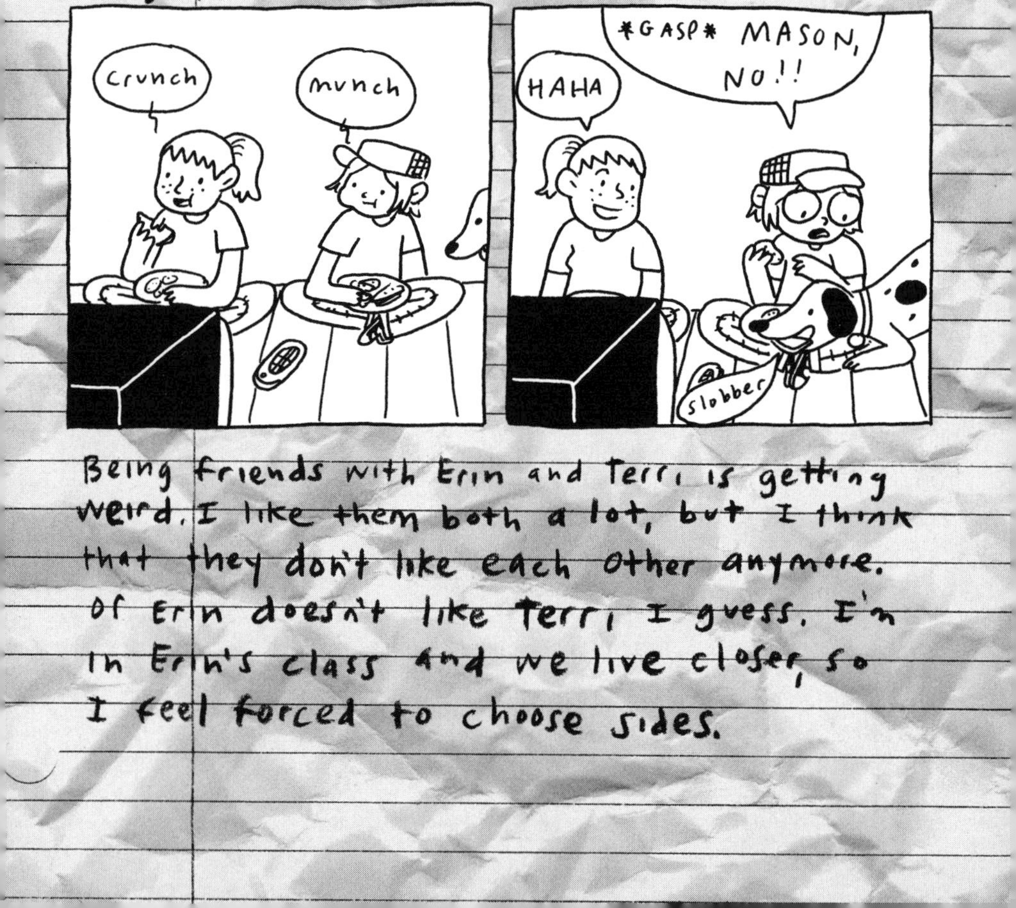
crunch
munch
HAHA
GASP MASON, NO!!
slobber

Being friends with Erin and Terri is getting weird. I like them both a lot, but I think that they don't like each other anymore. Or Erin doesn't like Terri, I guess. I'm in Erin's class and we live closer, so I feel forced to choose sides.

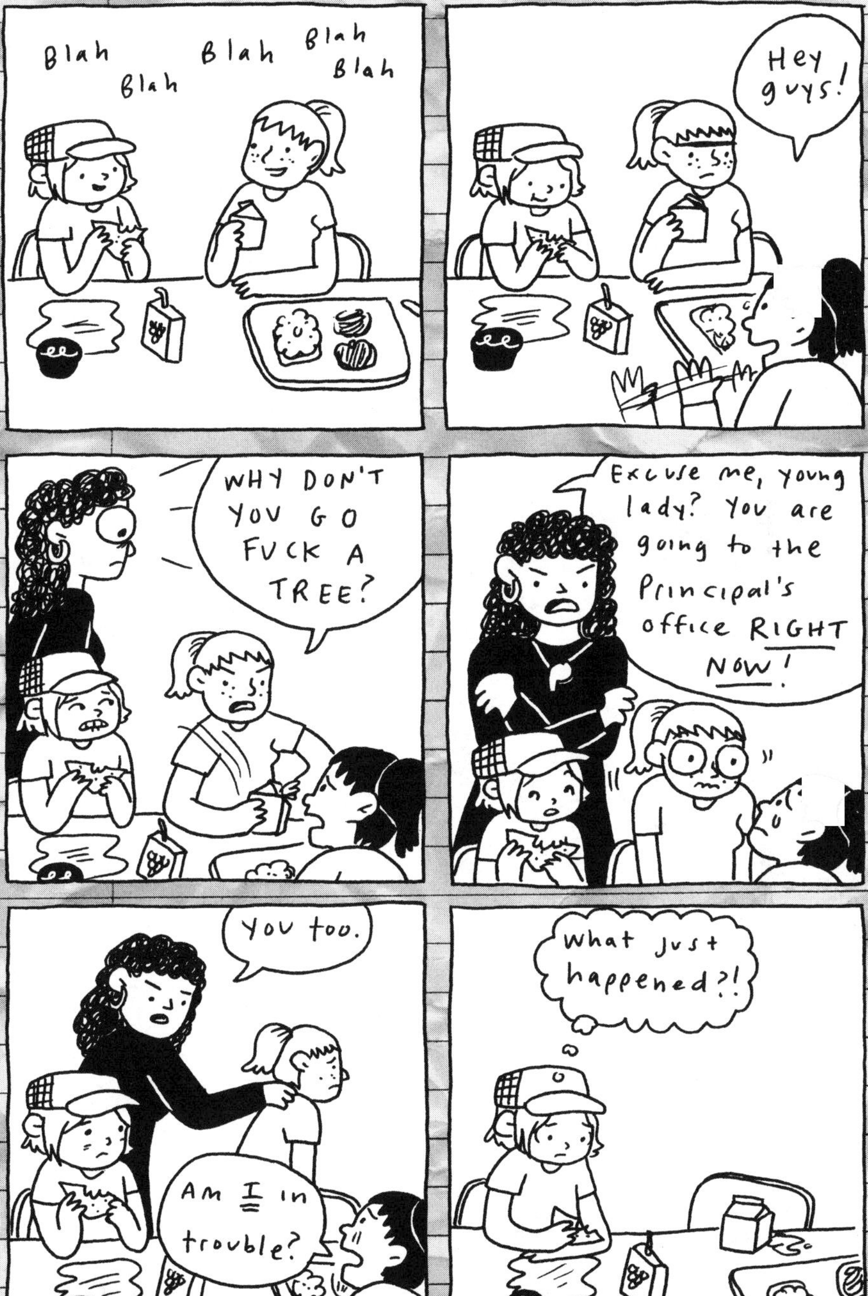
Blah Blah Blah Blah Blah
Hey guys!
WHY DON'T YOU GO FUCK A TREE?
Excuse me, young lady? You are going to the Principal's office RIGHT NOW!
You too.
Am I in trouble?
What just happened?!

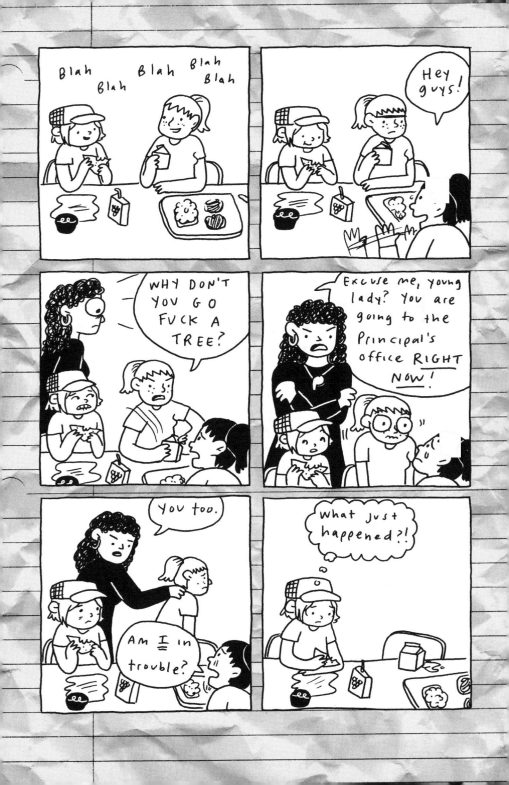

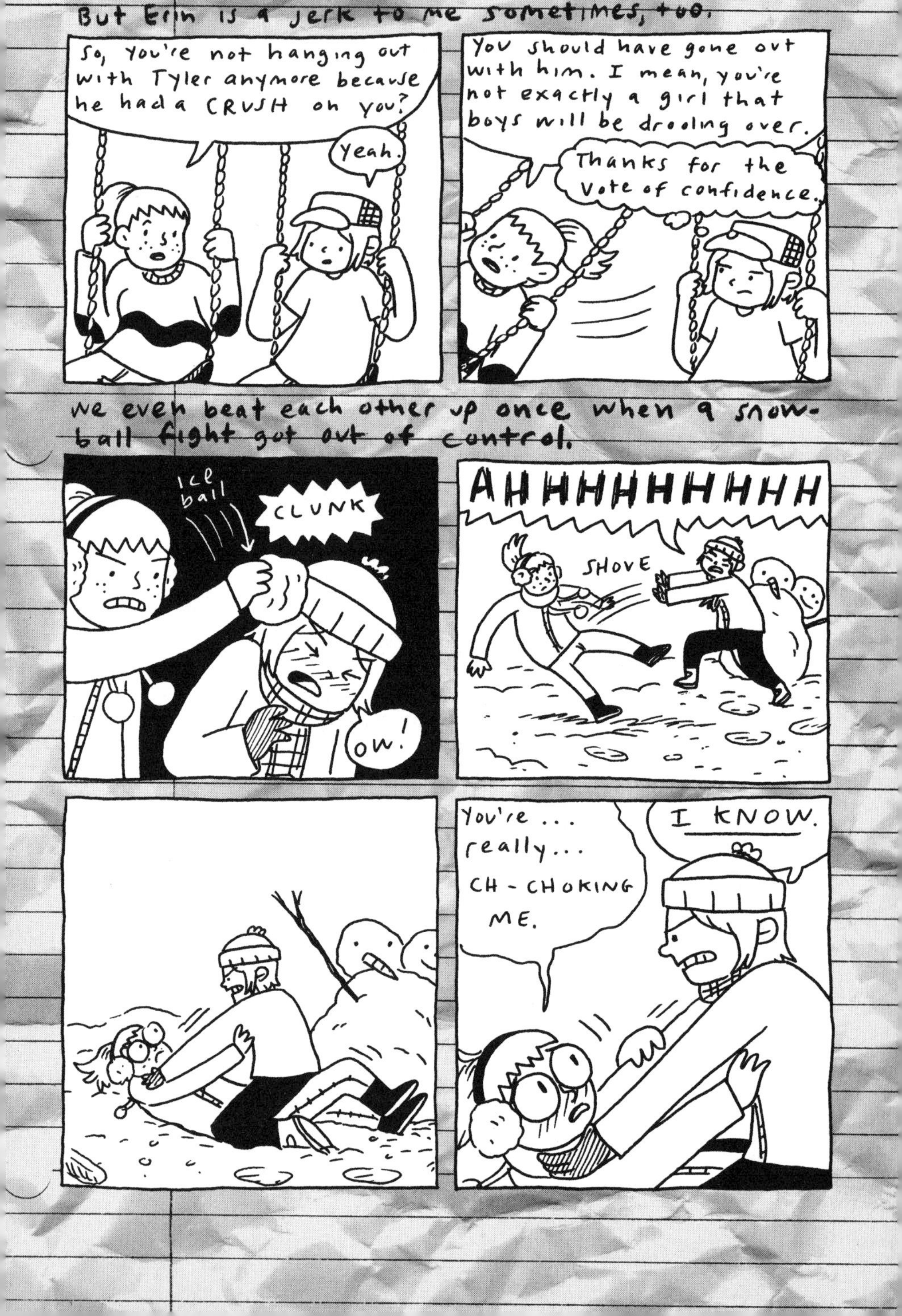
But Erin is a jerk to me sometimes, too.
So, you're not hanging out with Tyler anymore because he had a CRUSH on you?
Yeah.
You should have gone out with him. I mean, you're not exactly a girl that boys will be drooling over.
Thanks for the vote of confidence.
We even beat each other up once when a snow-ball fight got out of control.
Ice ball
CLUNK
OW!
AHHHHHHHHHH
SHOVE
You're ... really ... CH-CHOKING ME.
I KNOW.

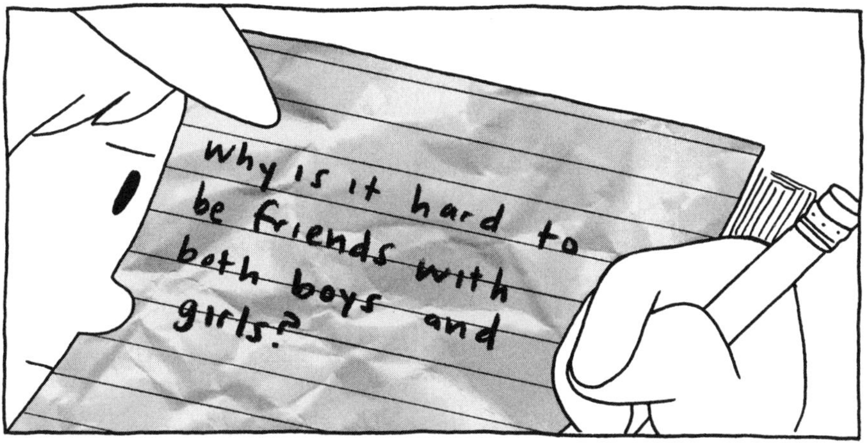
why is it hard to be friends with both boys and girls?

As the end of the school year approached, conversations about which middle school kids would be attending invaded the playground.

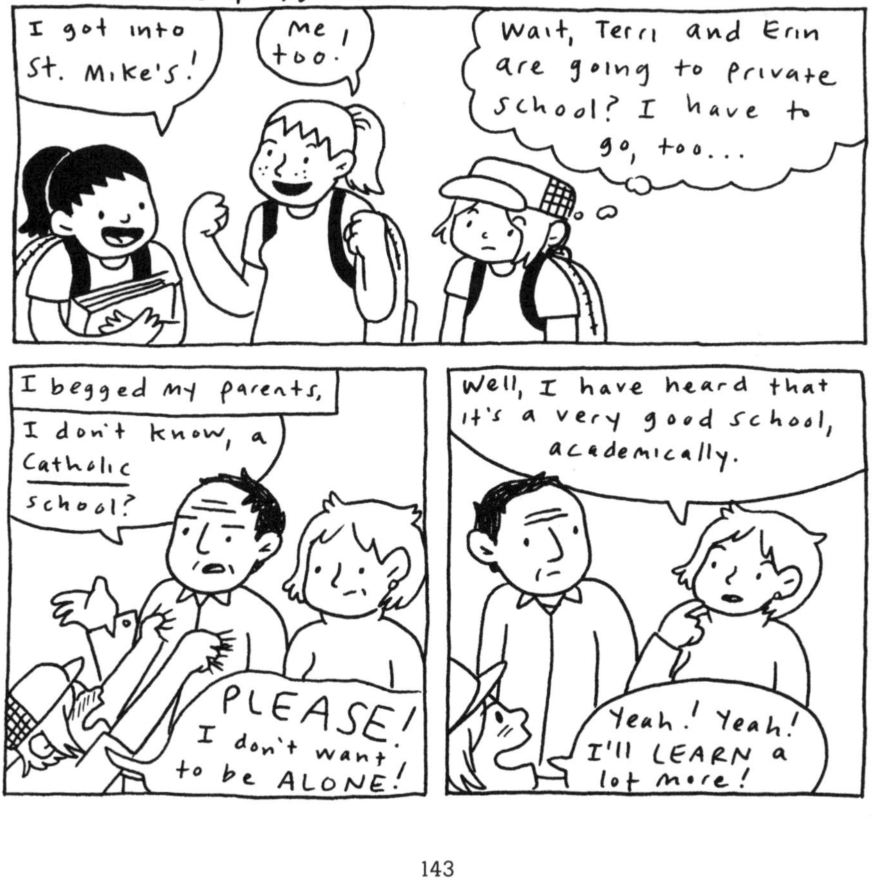
I got into St. Mike's!
Me, too!
Wait, Terri and Erin are going to private school? I have to go, too...
I begged my parents,
I don't know, a Catholic school?
PLEASE! I don't want to be ALONE!
Well, I have heard that it's a very good school, academically.
Yeah! Yeah! I'll LEARN a lot more!

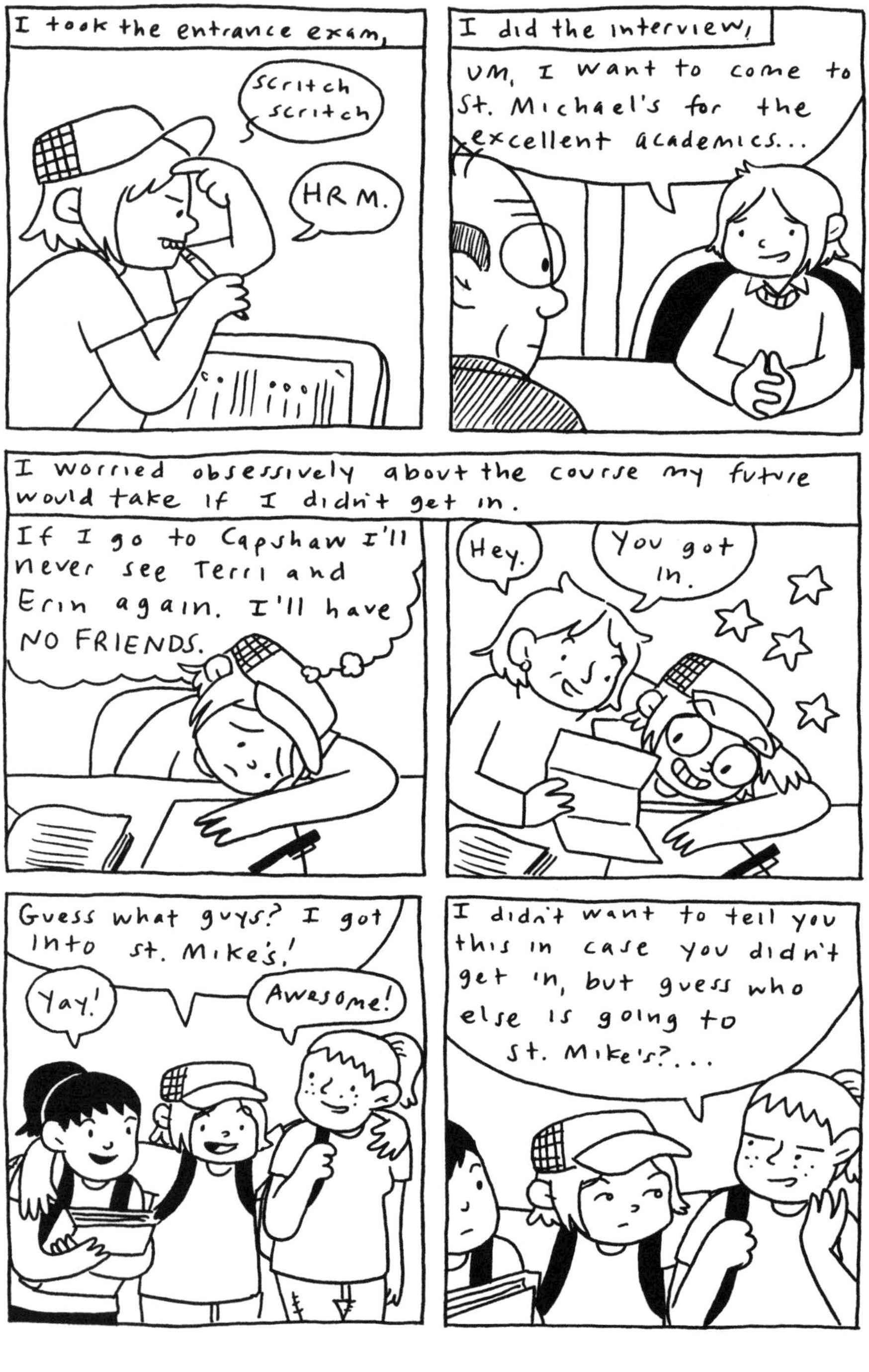
I took the entrance exam,
scritch scritch
HRM.
I did the interview,
UM, I want to come to St. Michael's for the excellent academics...
I worried obsessively about the course my future would take if I didn't get in.
If I go to Capshaw I'll never see Terri and Erin again. I'll have NO FRIENDS.
Hey.
You got in.
Guess what guys? I got into St. Mike's!
Yay!
Awesome!
I didn't want to tell you this in case you didn't get in, but guess who else is going to St. Mike's?...

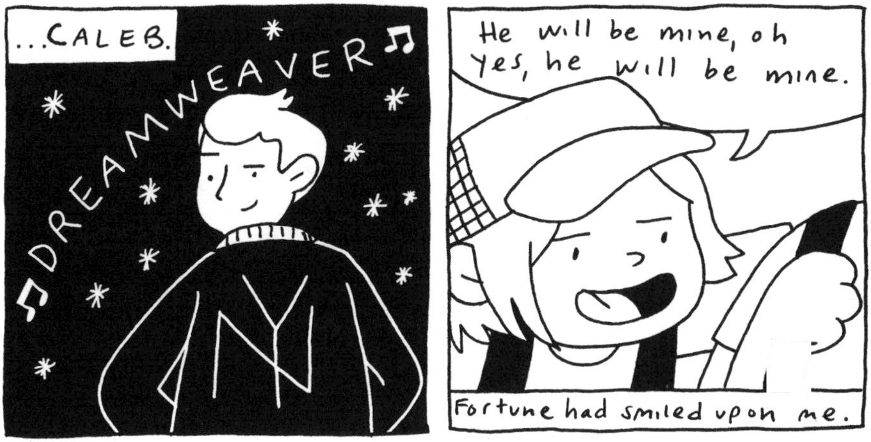
...CALEB.
♫DREAMWEAVER♫
He will be mine, oh yes, he will be mine.
Fortune had smiled upon me.

Through a game of pre-teen telephone, my crush on Caleb had been given a jolt of hope!

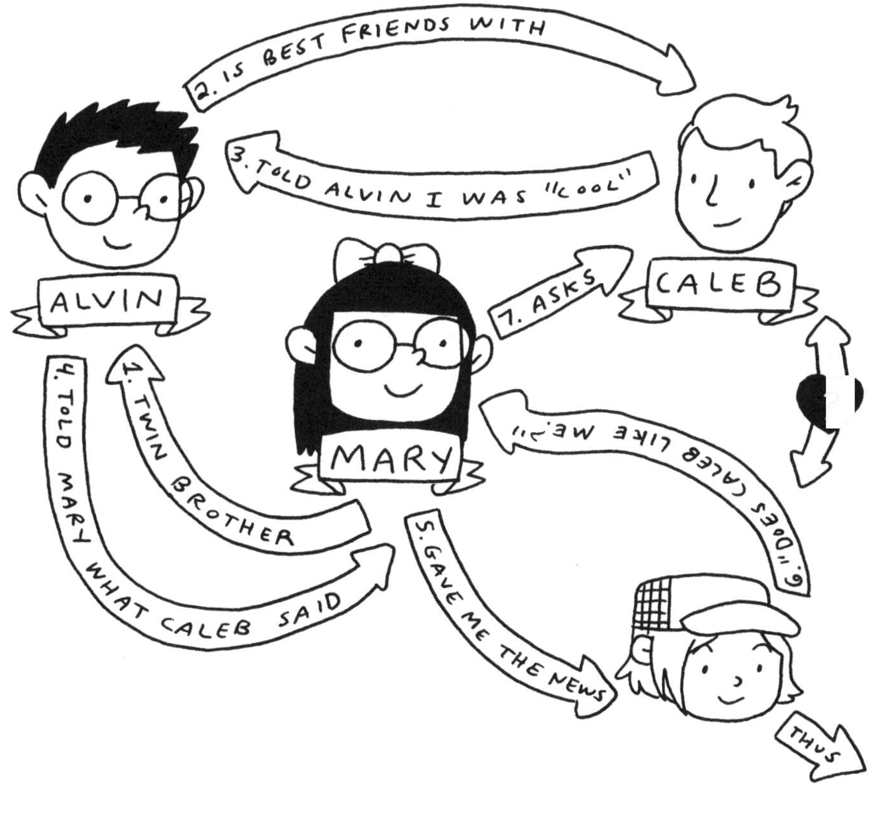
ALVIN
CALEB
MARY
1. TWIN BROTHER
2. IS BEST FRIENDS WITH
3. TOLD ALVIN I WAS "COOL"
4. TOLD MARY WHAT CALEB SAID
5. GAVE ME THE NEWS
6. "DOES CALEB LIKE ME?"
7. ASKS
THUS

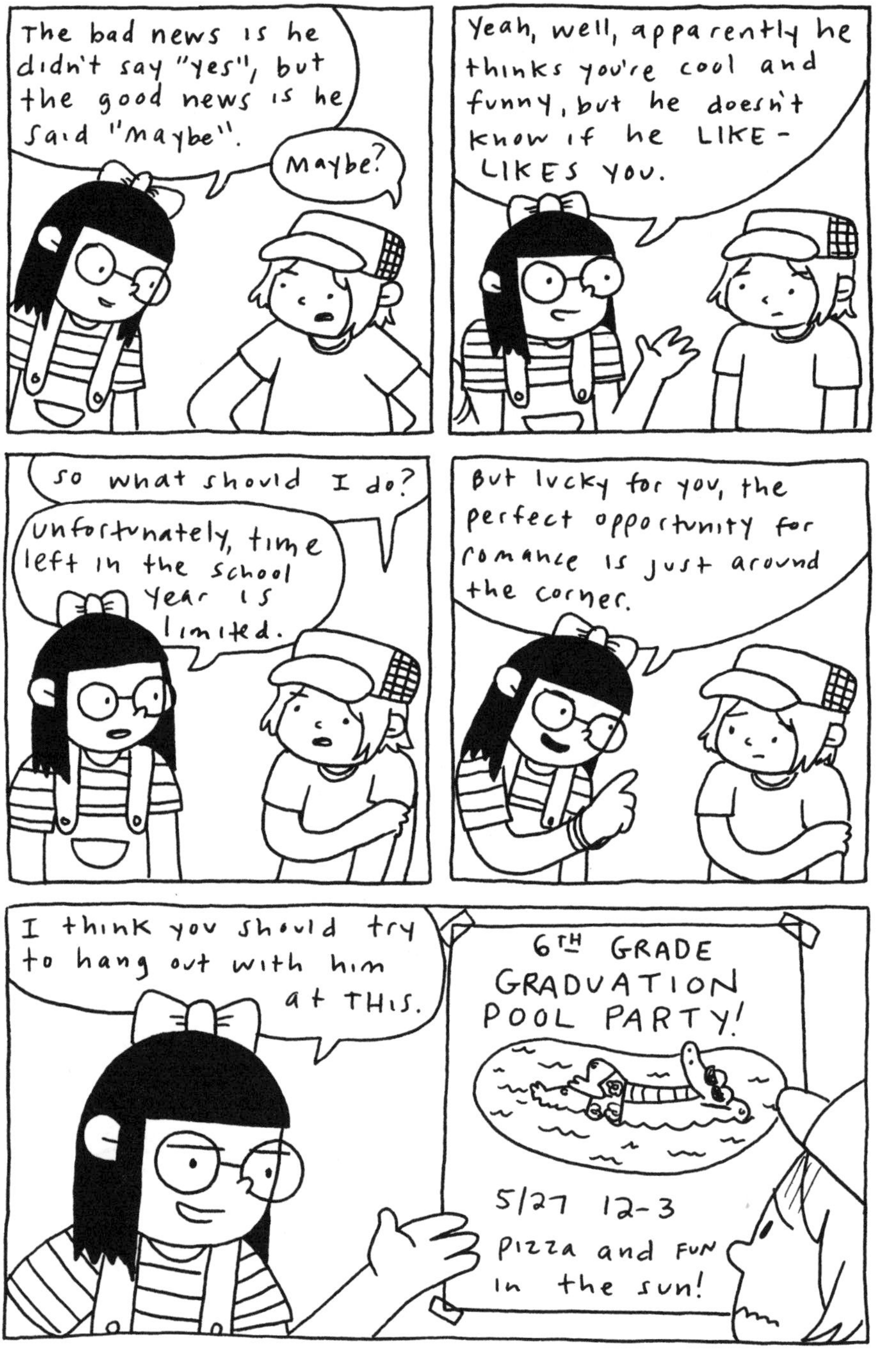
The bad news is he didn't say "yes", but the good news is he said "maybe".
Maybe?
Yeah, well, apparently he thinks you're cool and funny, but he doesn't know if he LIKE-LIKES you.
so what should I do?
unfortunately, time left in the school year is limited.
But lucky for you, the perfect opportunity for romance is just around the corner.
I think you should try to hang out with him at THIS.
6TH GRADE GRADUATION POOL PARTY!
5/27 12-3
pizza and FUN in the sun!

this was 1,000 times worse than Girl Scout Camp. At least there I didn't have to worry about what BOYS might think of my body. And I was supposed to try and flirt with someone, too? This was INSANITY.

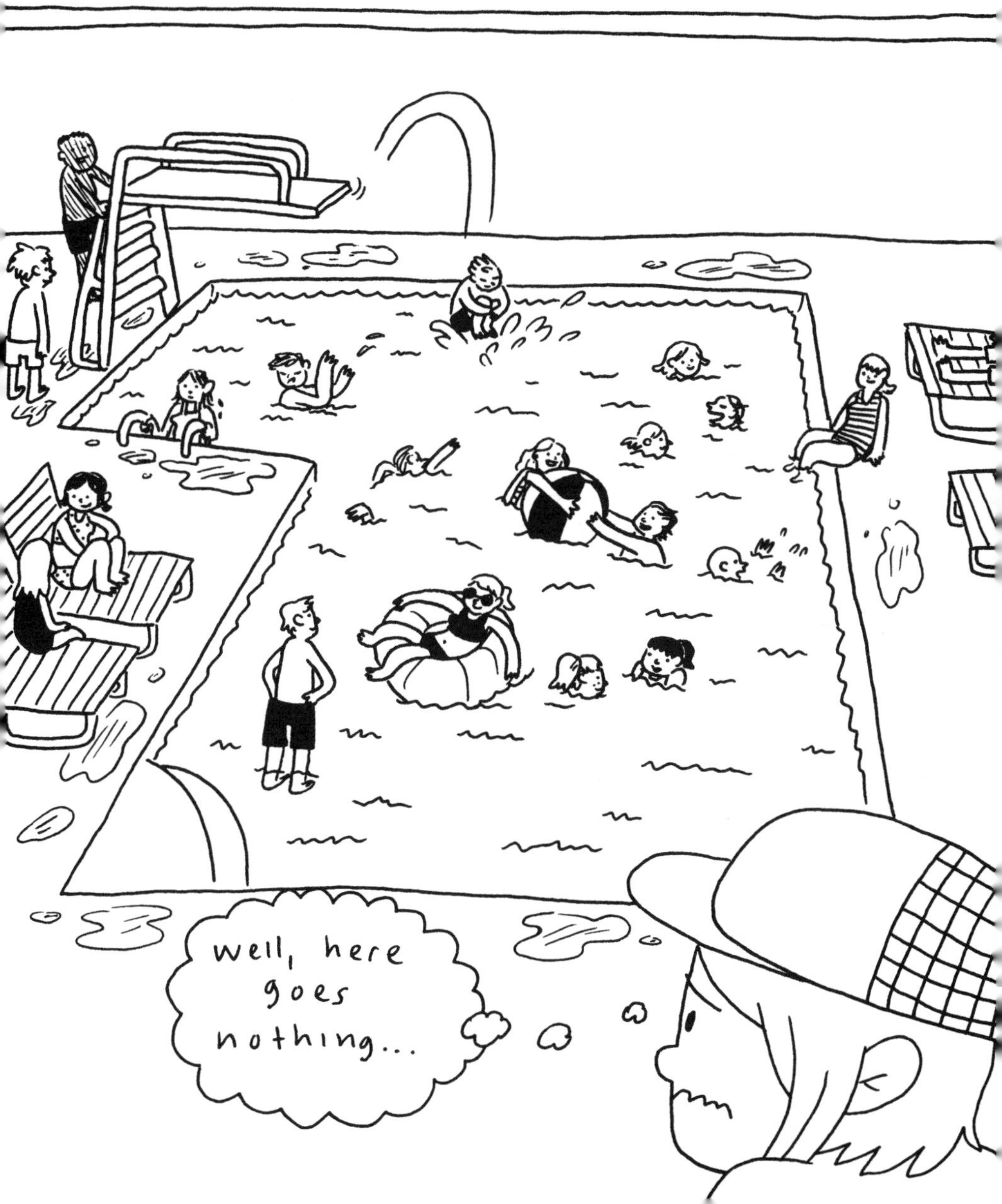
well, here goes nothing...

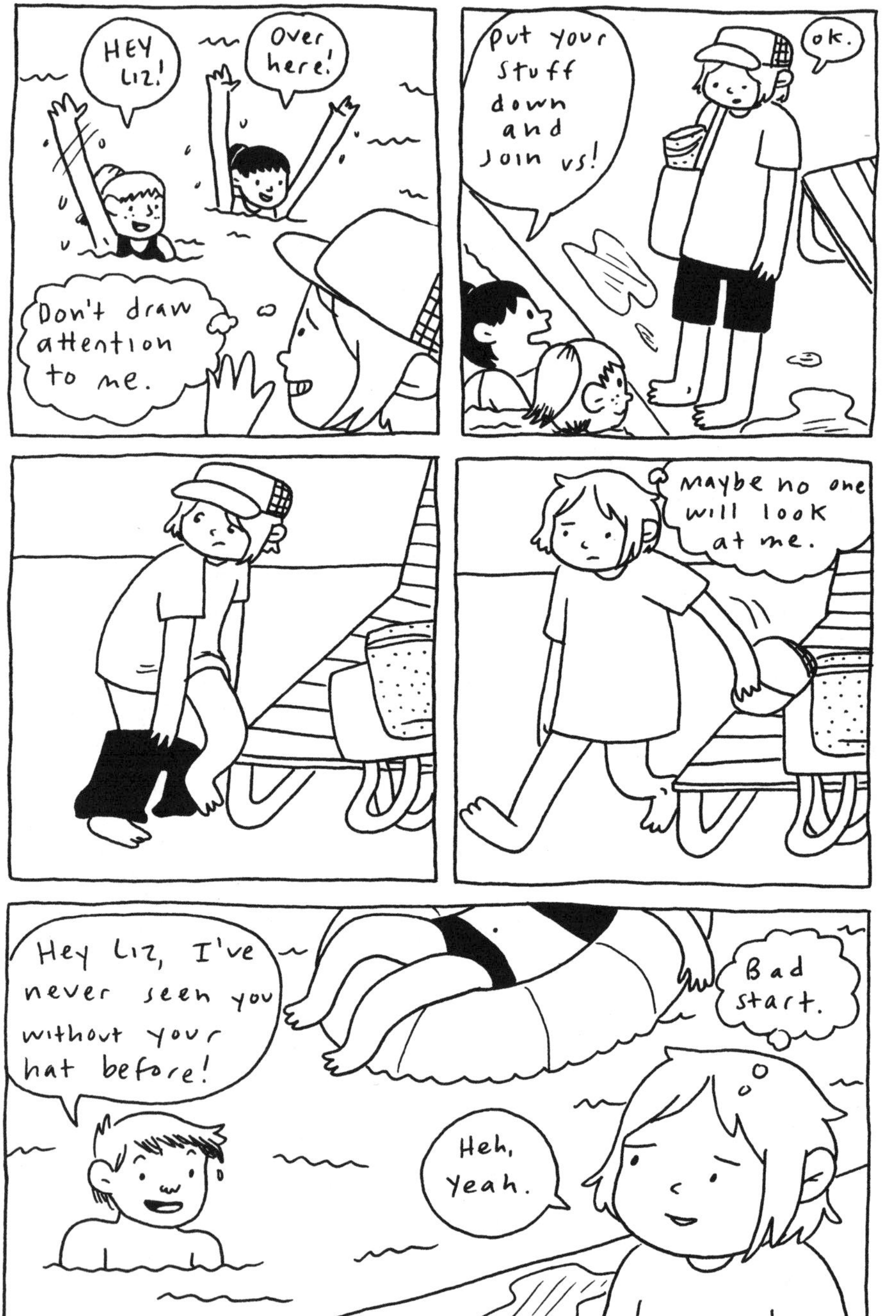
HEY LIZ!
Over here!
Don't draw attention to me.
Put your stuff down and join us!
ok.
Maybe no one will look at me.
Hey Liz, I've never seen you without your hat before!
Bad start.
Heh, yeah.

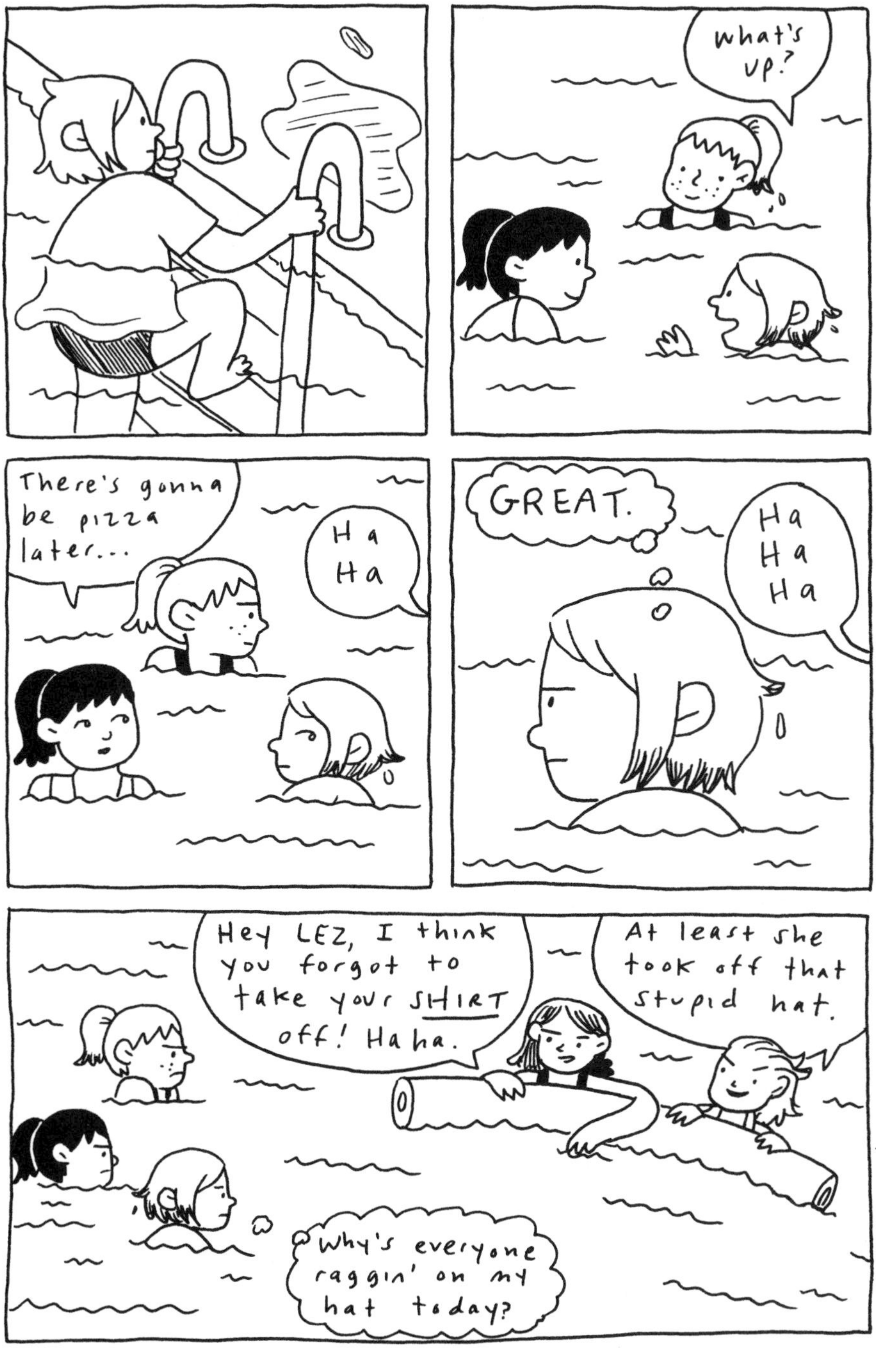
what's up?
There's gonna be pizza later...
Ha Ha
GREAT.
Ha Ha Ha
Hey LEZ, I think you forgot to take your SHIRT off! Haha.
At least she took off that stupid hat.
Why's everyone raggin' on my hat today?

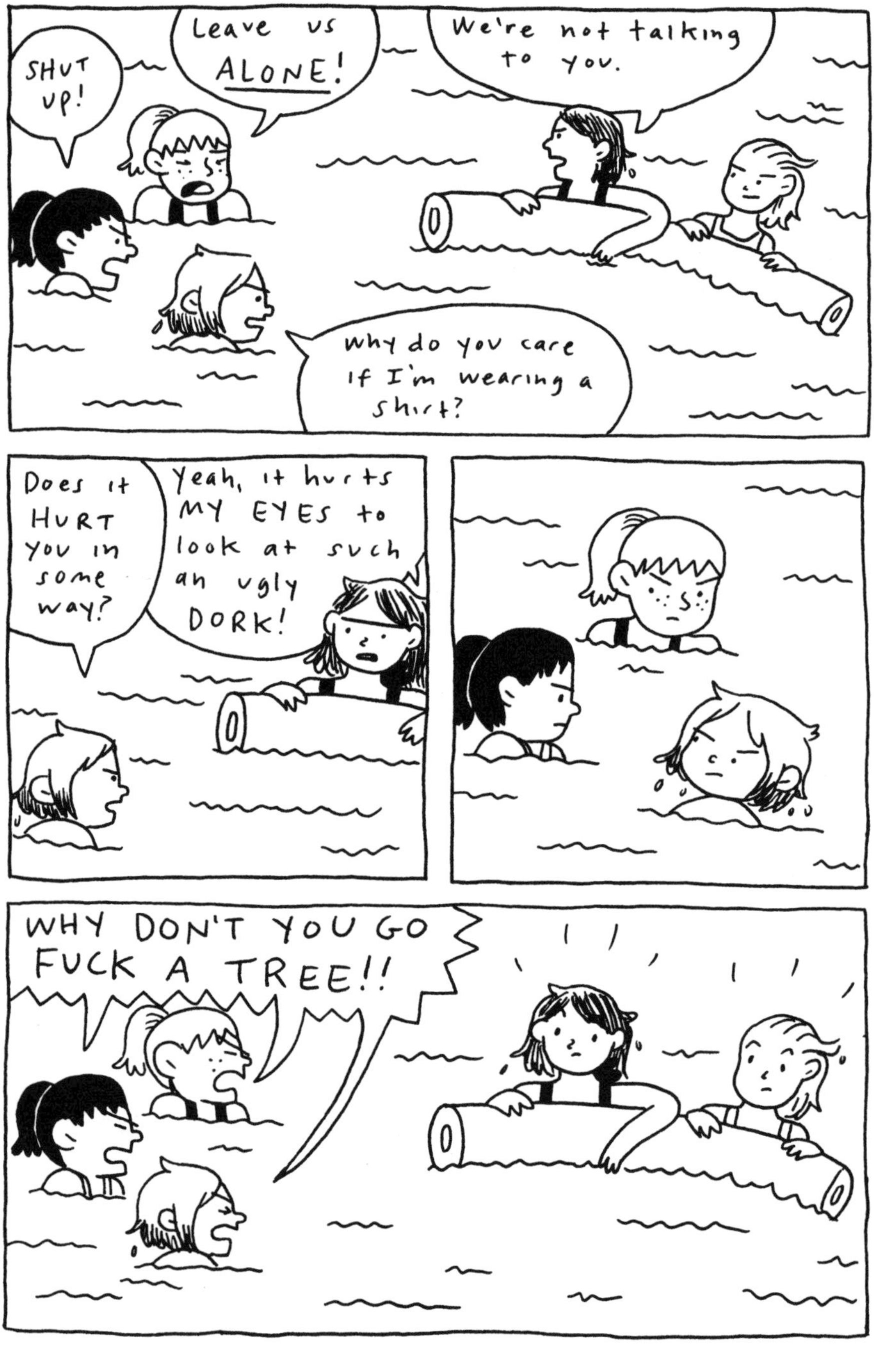
SHUT UP!
Leave us ALONE!
We're not talking to you.
Why do you care if I'm wearing a shirt?
Does it HURT you in some way?
Yeah, it hurts MY EYES to look at such an ugly DORK!
WHY DON'T YOU GO FUCK A TREE!!

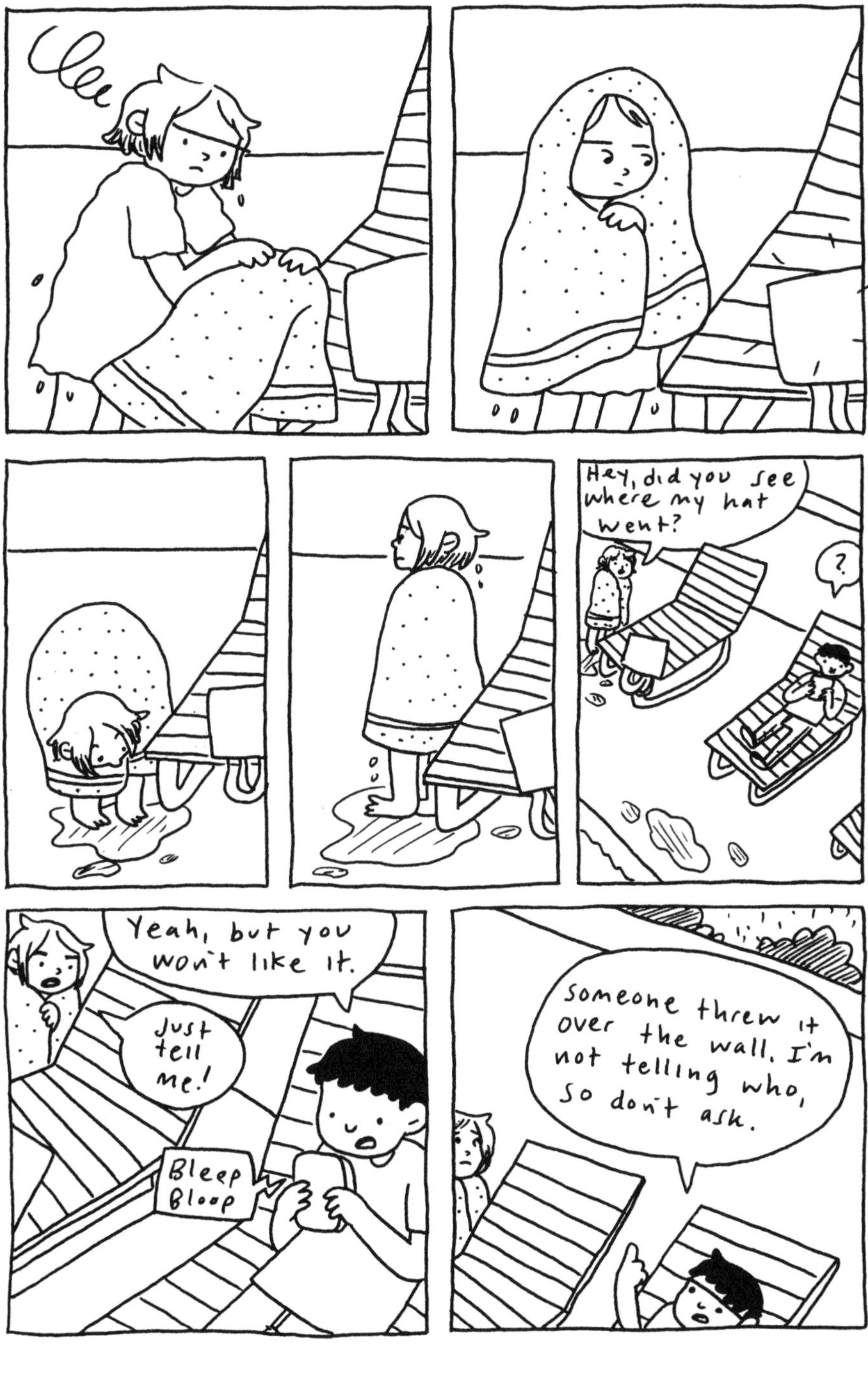
Hey, did you see where my hat went?
?
Yeah, but you won't like it.
Just tell me!
Bleep Bloop
Someone threw it over the wall. I'm not telling who, so don't ask.

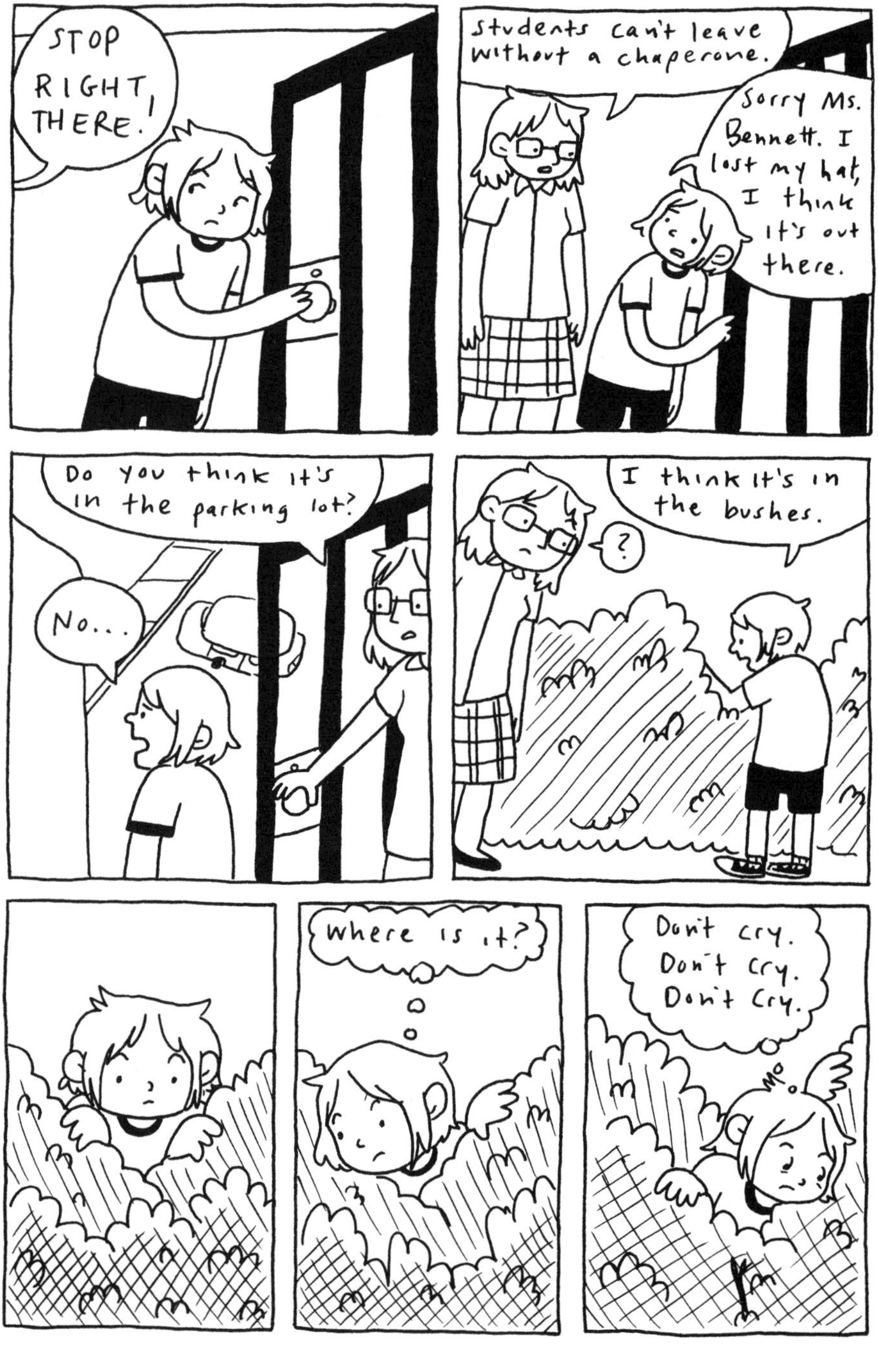

STOP RIGHT THERE.
Students can't leave without a chaperone.
Sorry Ms. Bennett. I lost my hat, I think it's out there.
Do you think it's in the parking lot?
No...
I think it's in the bushes.
?
Where is it?
Don't cry. Don't cry. Don't cry.

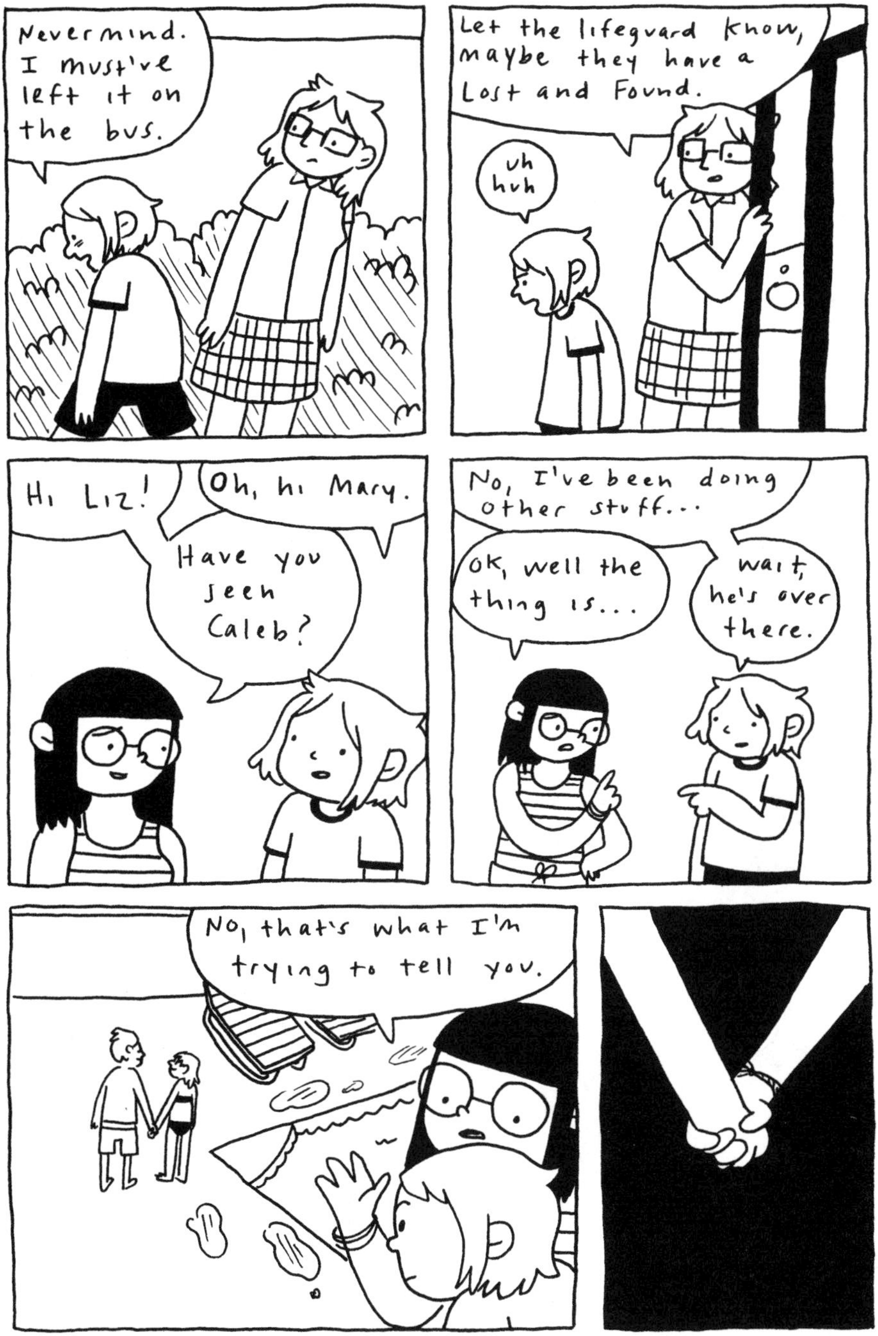
Nevermind. I must've left it on the bus.
Let the lifeguard know, maybe they have a Lost and Found.
uh huh
Hi Liz!
Oh, hi Mary.
Have you seen Caleb?
No, I've been doing other stuff...
ok, well the thing is...
wait, he's over there.
No, that's what I'm trying to tell you.

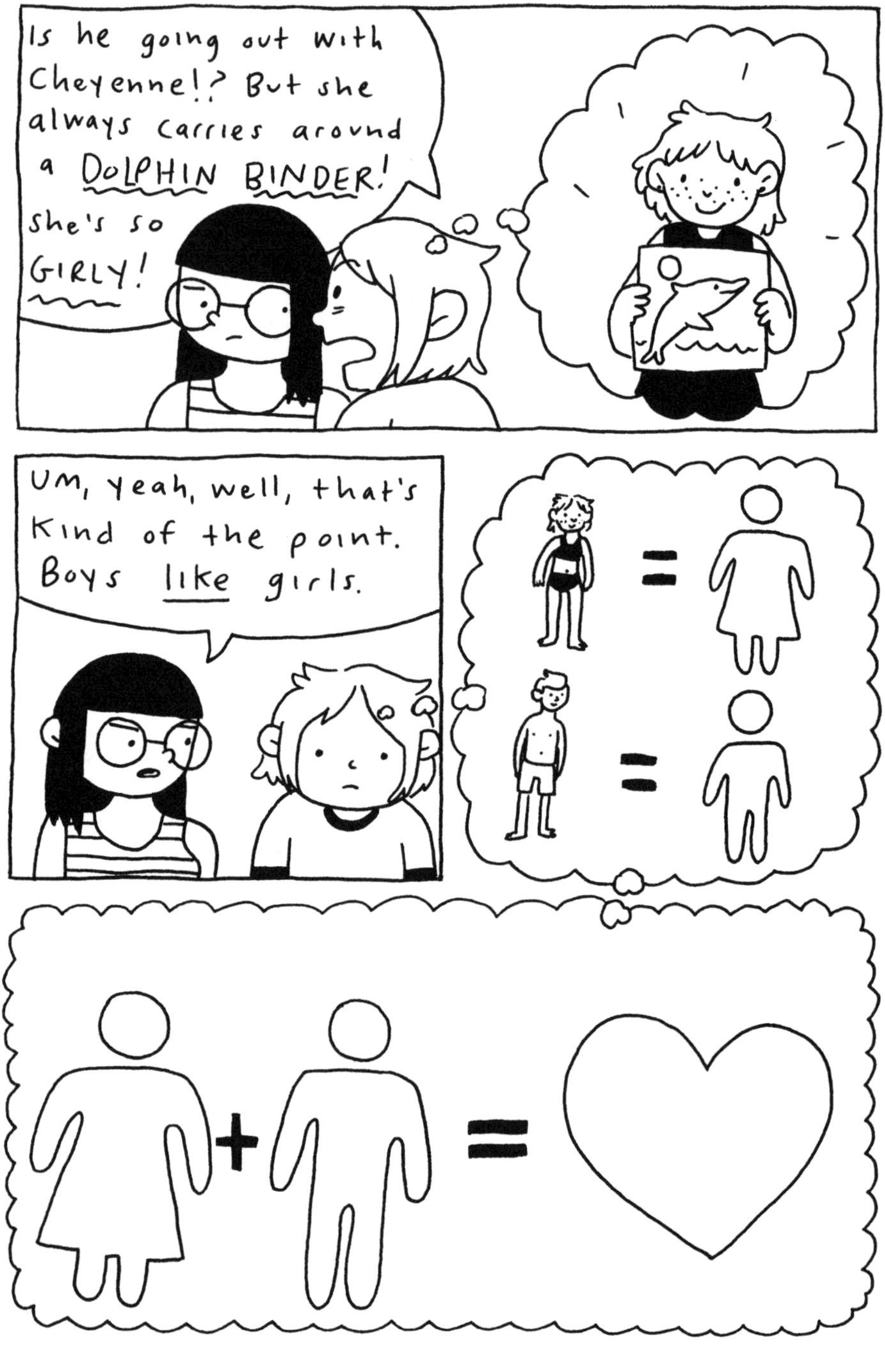

Is he going out with Cheyenne!? But she always carries around a DOLPHIN BINDER! She's so GIRLY!
Um, yeah, well, that's kind of the point. Boys like girls.

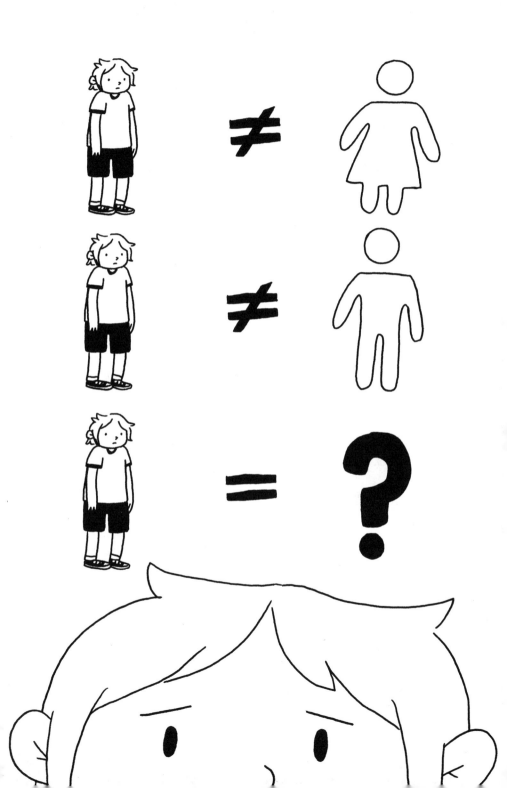

CHAPTER 8

It was surprisingly easy to make new friends in Middle School. I was still friends with Terri and Erin, but things were changing. We were eking out our own places in the social food chain.

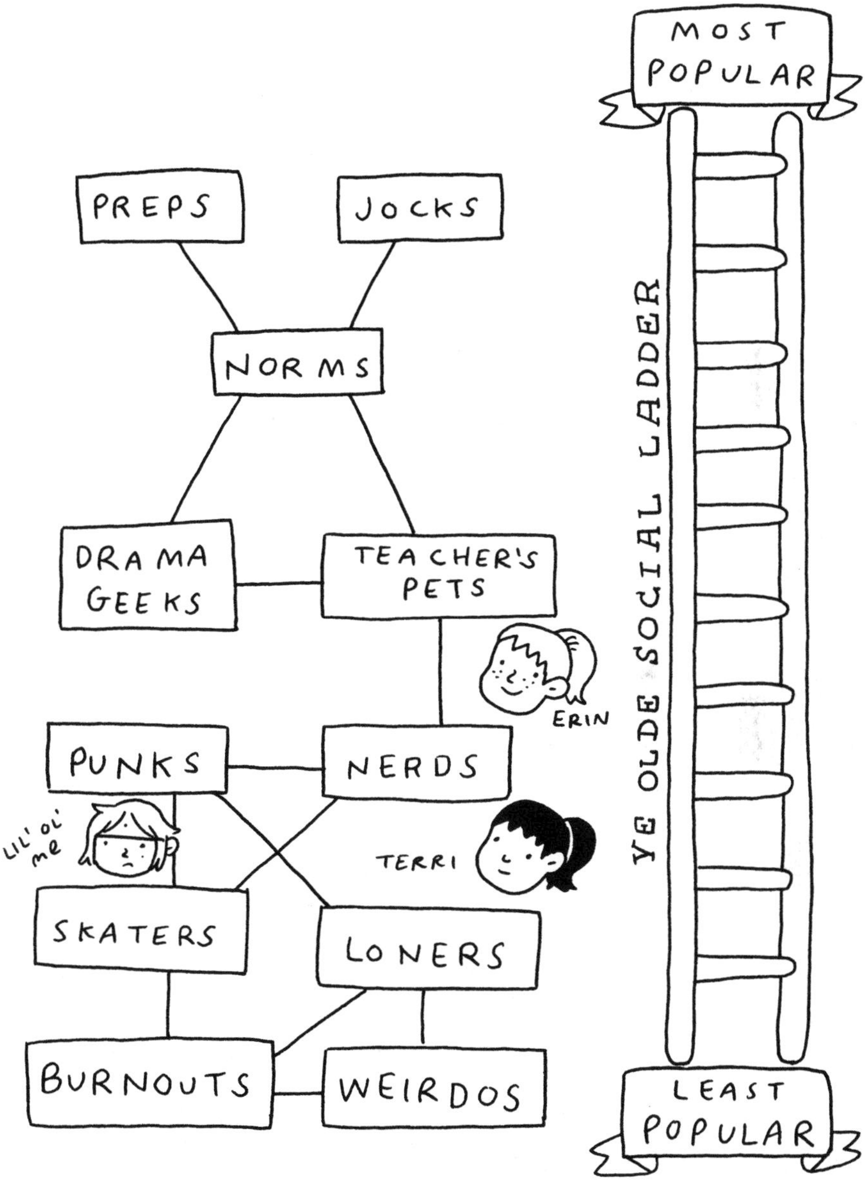

PREPS
JOCKS
NORMS
DRAMA GEEKS
TEACHER'S PETS
ERIN
PUNKS
NERDS
LIL' OL' ME
TERRI
SKATERS
LONERS
BURNOUTS
WEIRDOS
MOST POPULAR
YE OLDE SOCIAL LADDER
LEAST POPULAR

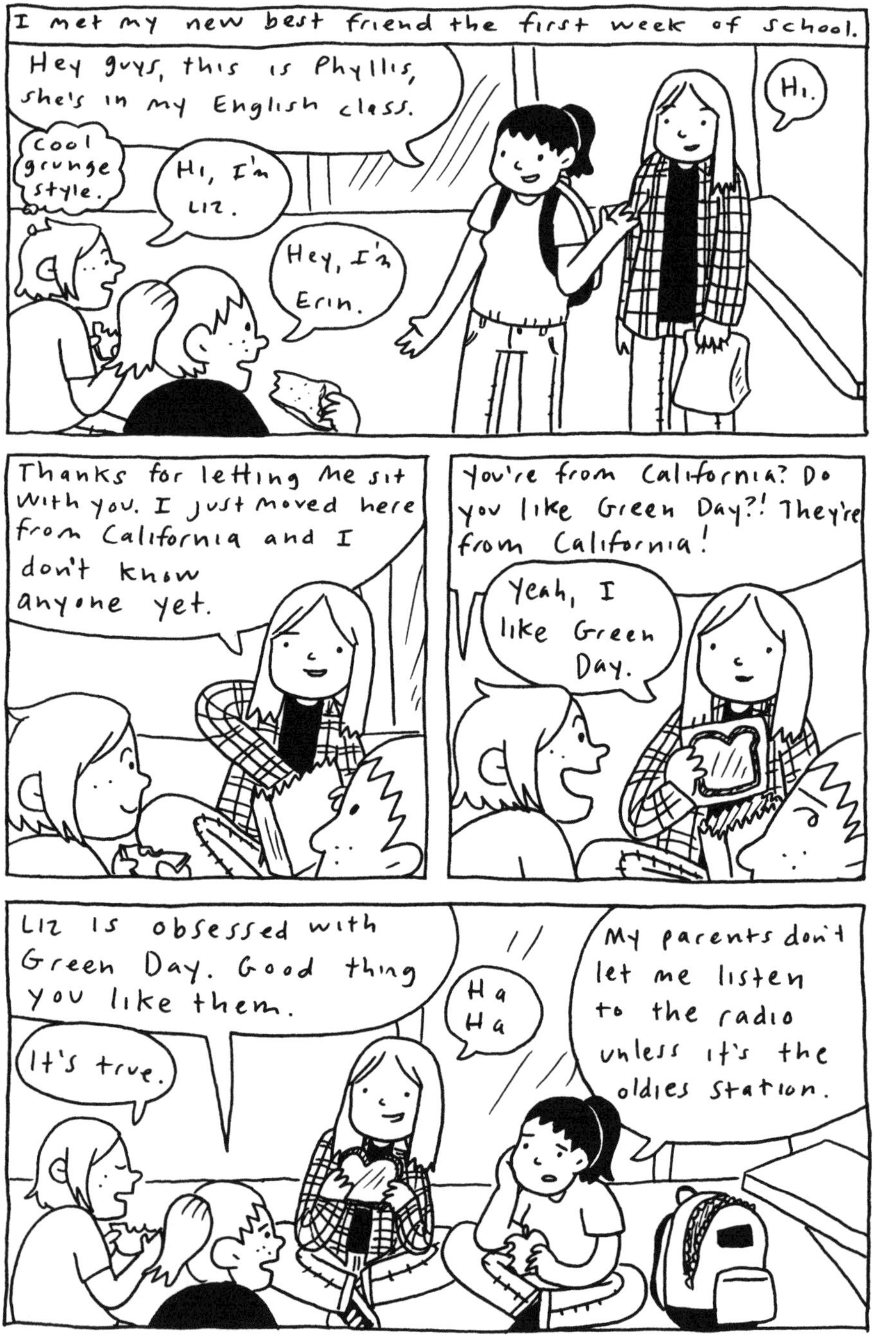
I met my new best friend the first week of school.
Hey guys, this is Phyllis, she's in my English class.
Hi.
Cool grunge style.
Hi, I'm Liz.
Hey, I'm Erin.
Thanks for letting me sit with you. I just moved here from California and I don't know anyone yet.
You're from California? Do you like Green Day?! They're from California!
Yeah, I like Green Day.
Liz is obsessed with Green Day. Good thing you like them.
It's true.
Ha Ha
My parents don't let me listen to the radio unless it's the oldies station.

Phyllis lived a block away from my Mom's toy store, so we rode the city bus across town together every day after school.

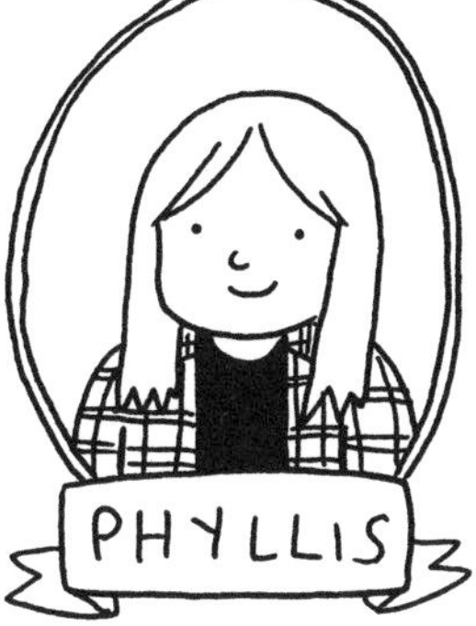
PHYLLIS

* Reads 1970s underground comics.
* Learned about graffiti art from her older brother.
* Is interested in skateboarding.
* Steals cigarettes from her mom.
* Is a lot less innocent than she looks.

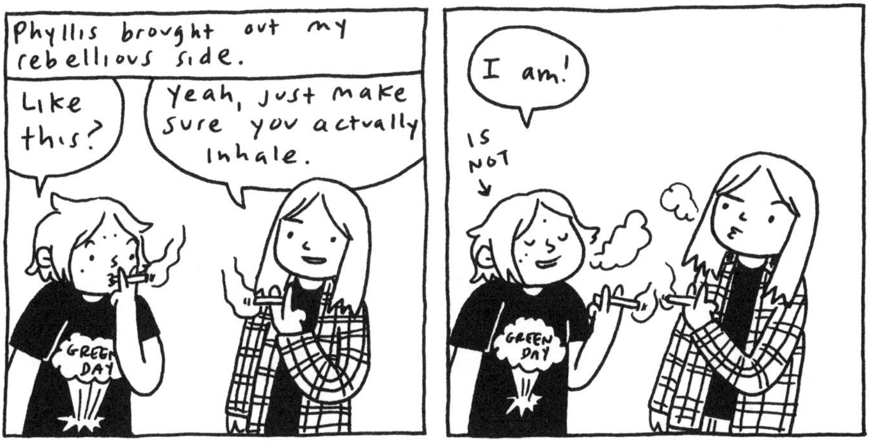
Phyllis brought out my rebellious side.
Like this?
Yeah, just make sure you actually inhale.
GREEN DAY
I am!
IS NOT
GREEN DAY

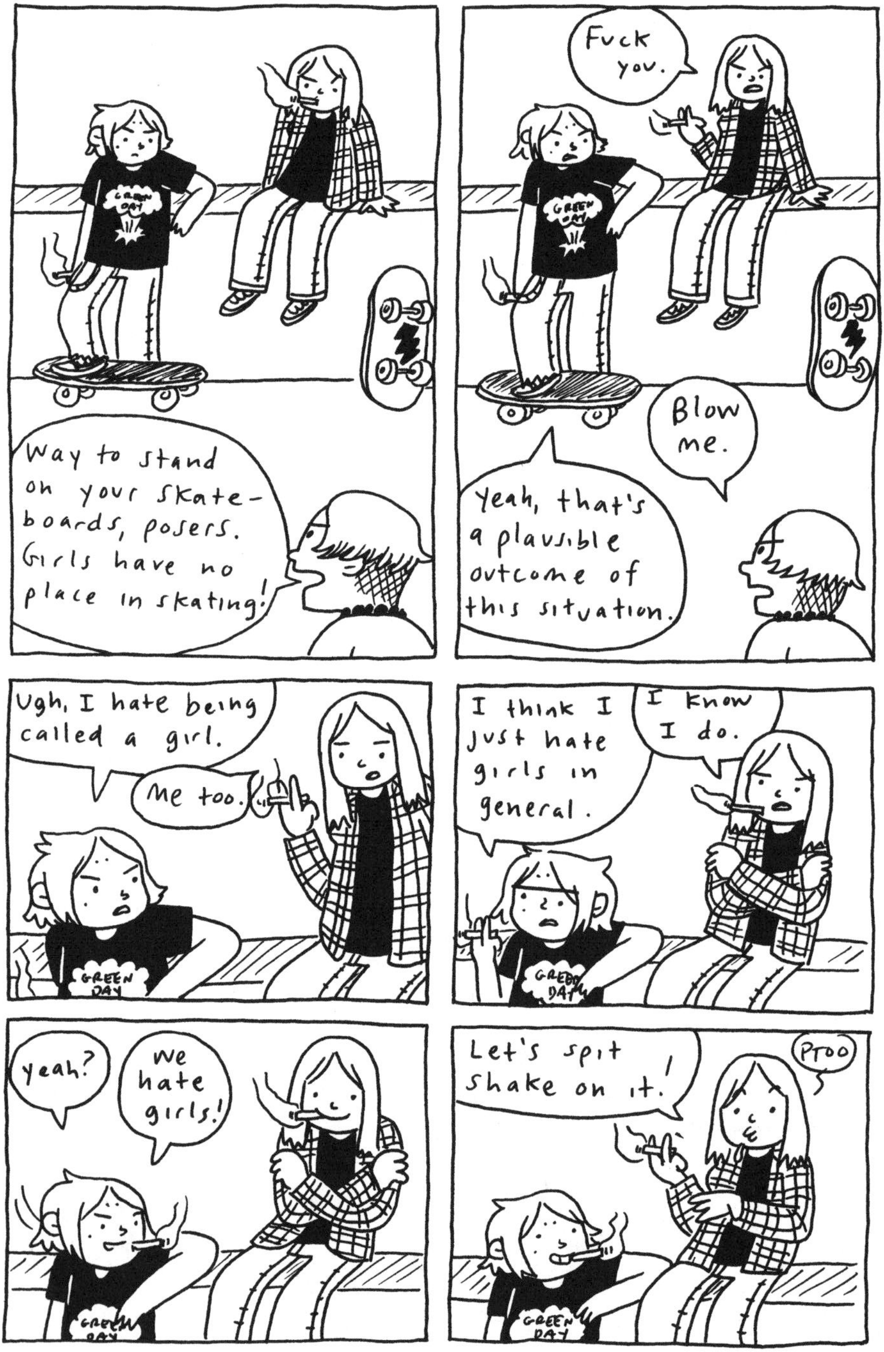
Way to stand on your skate-boards, posers. Girls have no place in skating!
Fuck you.
Blow me.
Yeah, that's a plausible outcome of this situation.
Ugh, I hate being called a girl.
Me too.
I think I just hate girls in general.
I know I do.
Yeah?
We hate girls!
Let's spit shake on it!
PTOO

It was true: I was starting to hate girls.

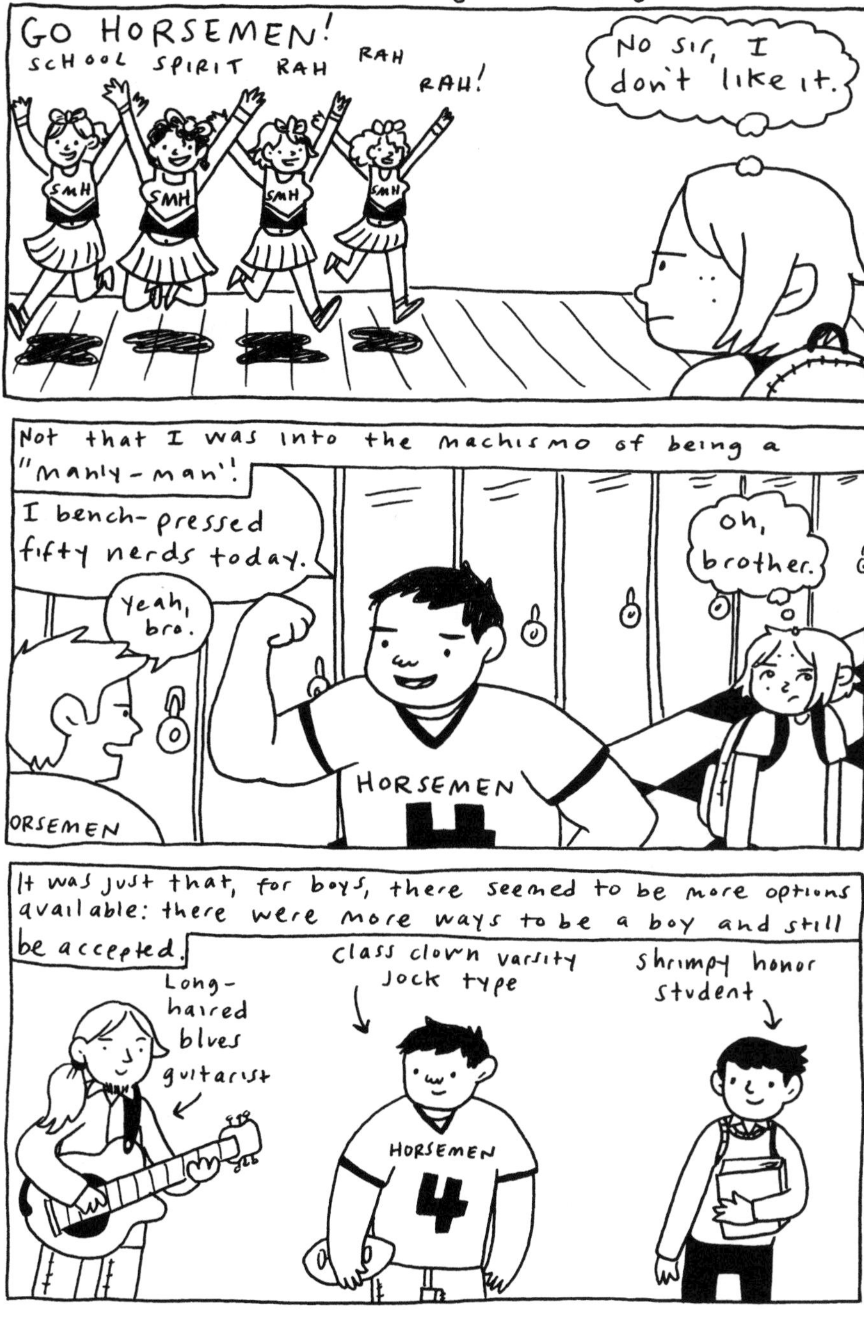
GO HORSEMEN!
SCHOOL SPIRIT RAH RAH RAH!
SMH
SMH
SMH
SMH
No sir, I don't like it.
Not that I was into the machismo of being a "manly-man"!
I bench-pressed fifty nerds today.
Yeah, bro.
Oh, brother.
ORSEMEN
HORSEMEN
It was just that, for boys, there seemed to be more options available: there were more ways to be a boy and still be accepted.
Long-haired blues guitarist
Class clown varsity jock type
Shrimpy honor student
HORSEMEN
4

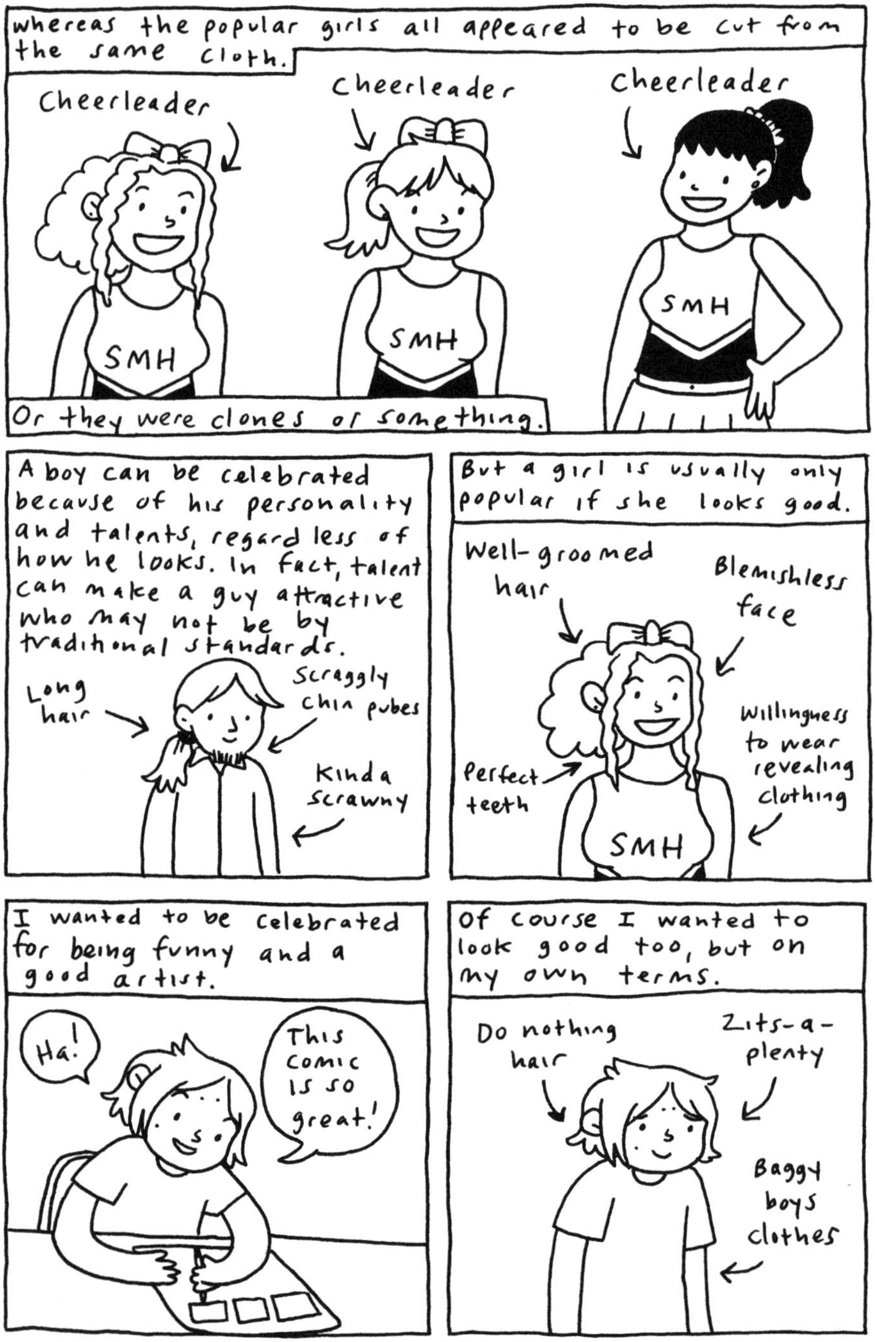
whereas the popular girls all appeared to be cut from the same cloth.
Cheerleader
Cheerleader
Cheerleader
SMH
SMH
SMH
Or they were clones or something.
A boy can be celebrated because of his personality and talents, regard less of how he looks. In fact, talent can make a guy attractive who may not be by traditional standards.
Long hair
Scraggly chin pubes
Kinda scrawny
But a girl is usually only popular if she looks good.
Well-groomed hair
Blemishless face
Willingness to wear revealing clothing
Perfect teeth
SMH
I wanted to be celebrated for being funny and a good artist.
Ha!
This comic is so great!
Of course I wanted to look good too, but on my own terms.
Do nothing hair
Zits-a-plenty
Baggy boys clothes

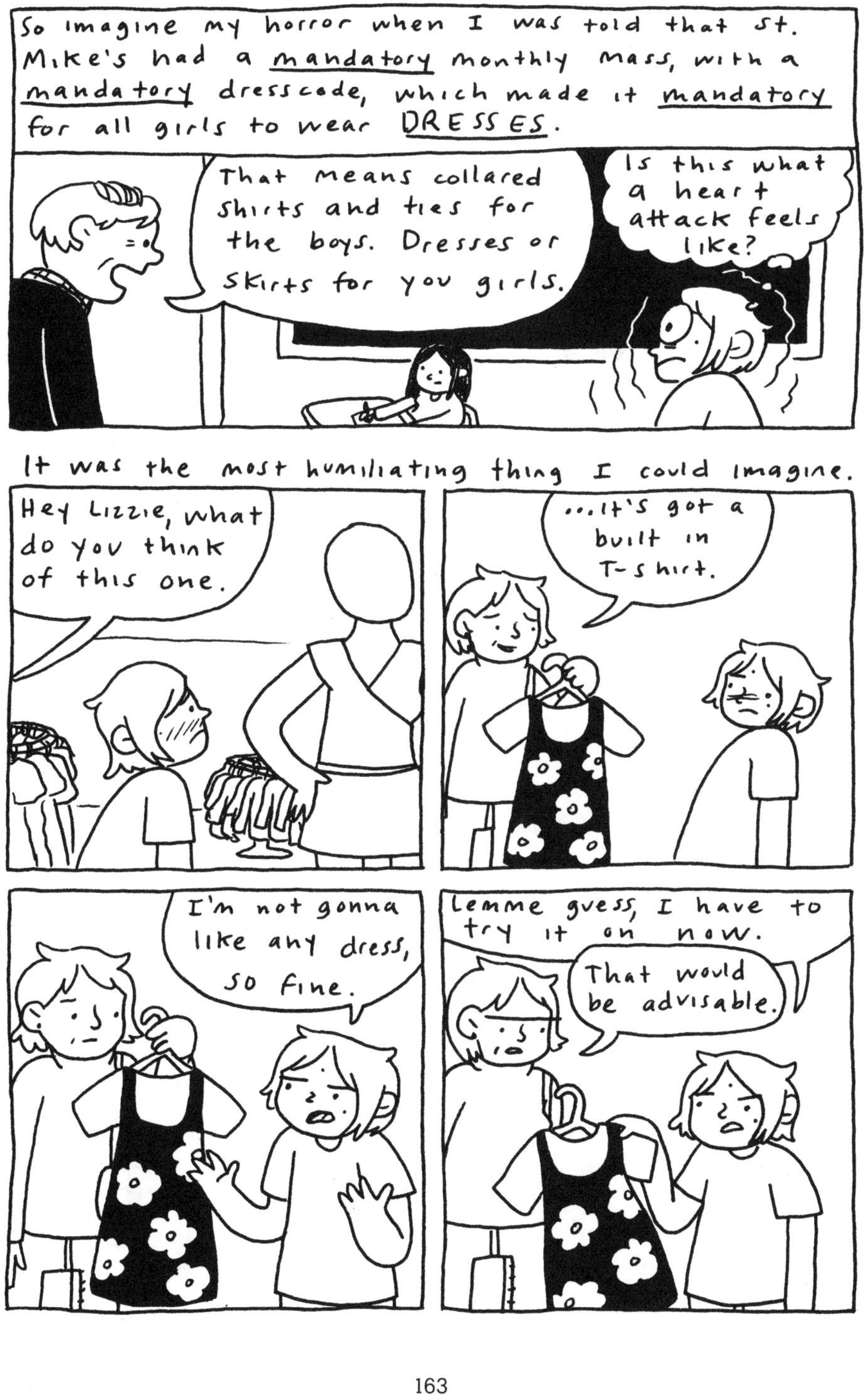
So imagine my horror when I was told that St. Mike's had a mandatory monthly mass, with a mandatory dresscode, which made it mandatory for all girls to wear DRESSES.
That means collared shirts and ties for the boys. Dresses or skirts for you girls.
Is this what a heart attack feels like?
It was the most humiliating thing I could imagine.
Hey Lizzie, what do you think of this one.
...It's got a built in T-shirt.
I'm not gonna like any dress, so fine.
Lemme guess, I have to try it on now.
That would be advisable.

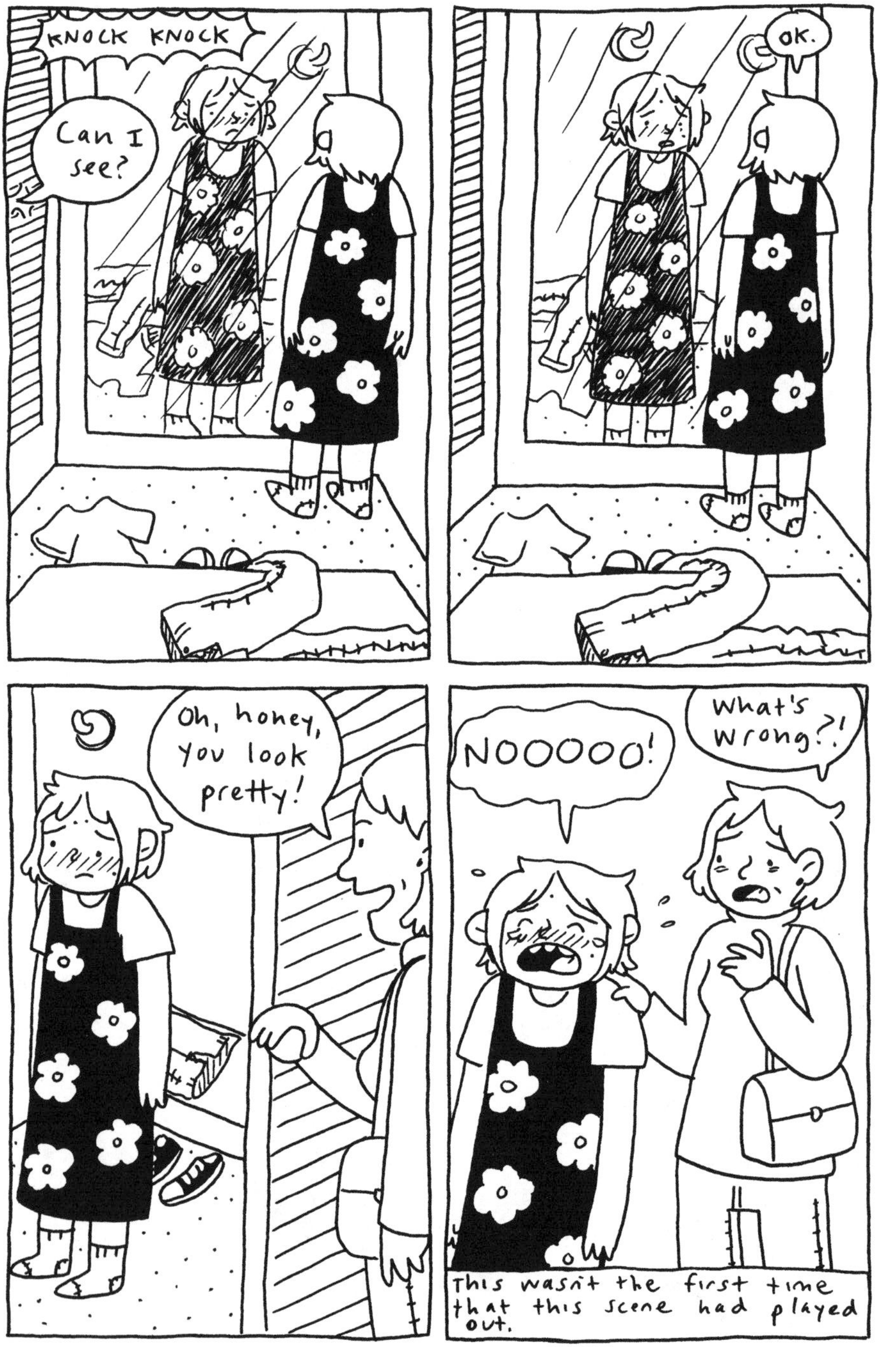
KNOCK KNOCK
Can I see?
OK.
Oh, honey, you look pretty!
NOOOOO!
What's wrong?!
This wasn't the first time that this scene had played out.

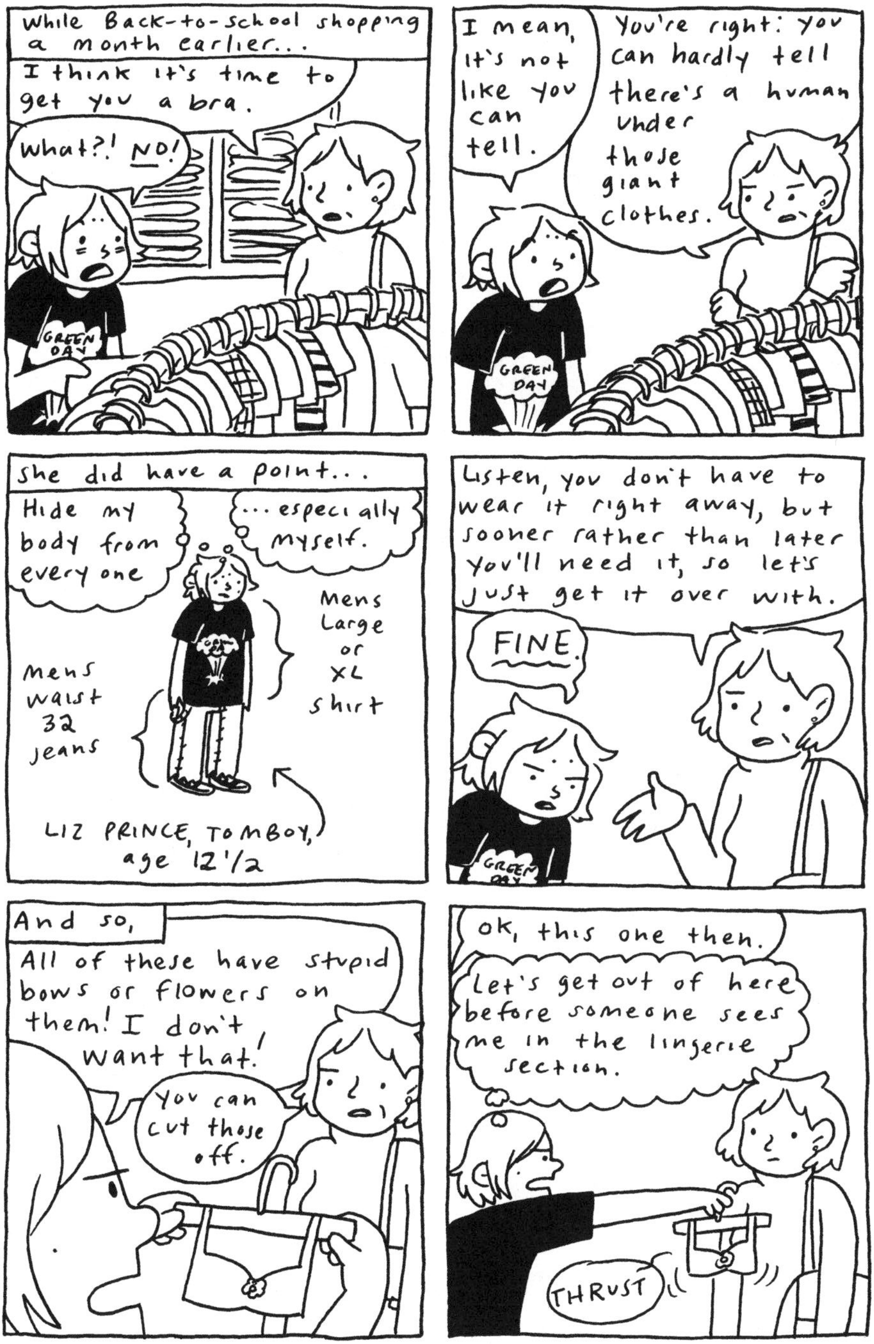
While Back-to-school shopping a month earlier...
I think it's time to get you a bra.
What?! NO!
GREEN DAY
I mean, it's not like you can tell.
You're right: you can hardly tell there's a human under those giant clothes.
GREEN DAY
She did have a point...
Hide my body from every one
...especially myself.
Mens Large or XL shirt
Mens waist 32 jeans
LIZ PRINCE, TOMBOY, age 12 1/2
Listen, you don't have to wear it right away, but sooner rather than later you'll need it, so let's just get it over with.
FINE.
And so,
All of these have stupid bows or flowers on them! I don't want that!
You can cut those off.
Ok, this one then.
Let's get out of here before someone sees me in the lingerie section.
THRUST

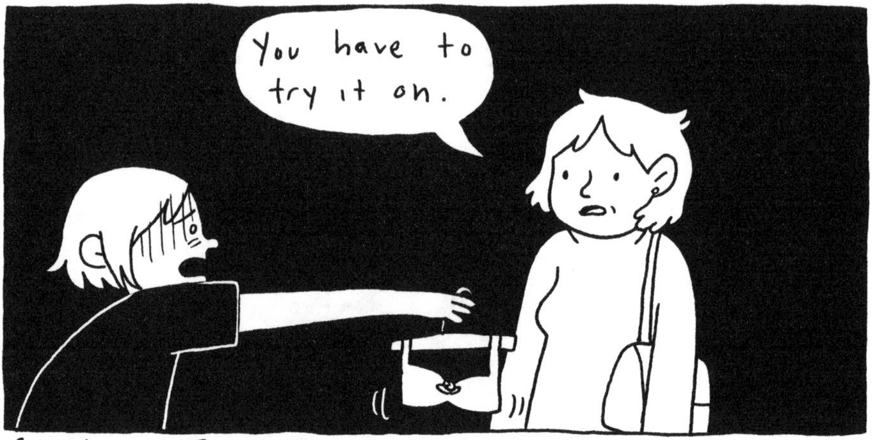
You have to try it on.

Sometimes I wondered if I was ruining this for my mom: Buying my first bra should've been a rite of passage.

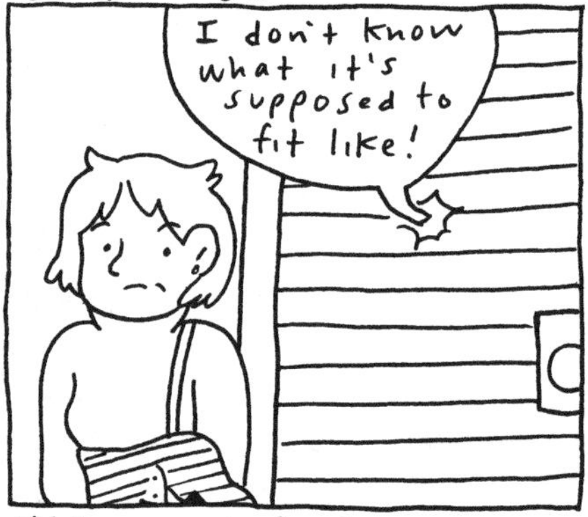
I don't know what it's supposed to fit like!

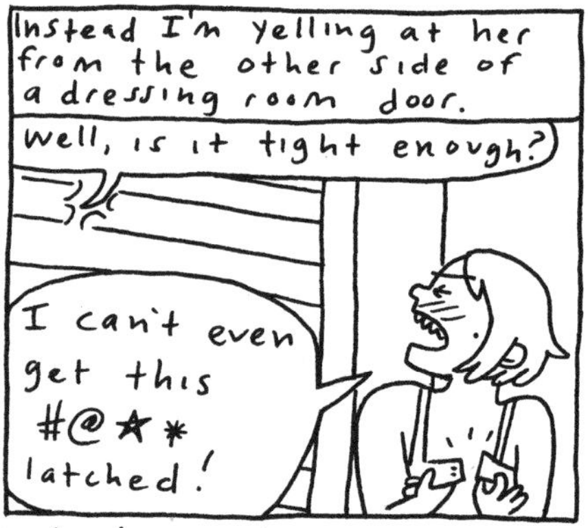
Instead I'm yelling at her from the other side of a dressing room door.
Well, is it tight enough?
I can't even get this #@★* latched!

It's a good thing my mom had my younger sister to properly fulfill the role of a daughter.

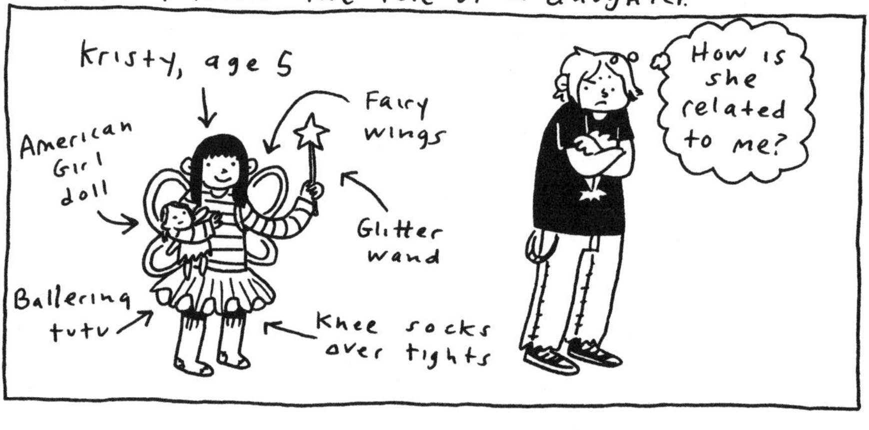
Kristy, age 5
Fairy wings
American Girl doll
Glitter wand
Ballerina tutu
Knee socks over tights
How is she related to me?

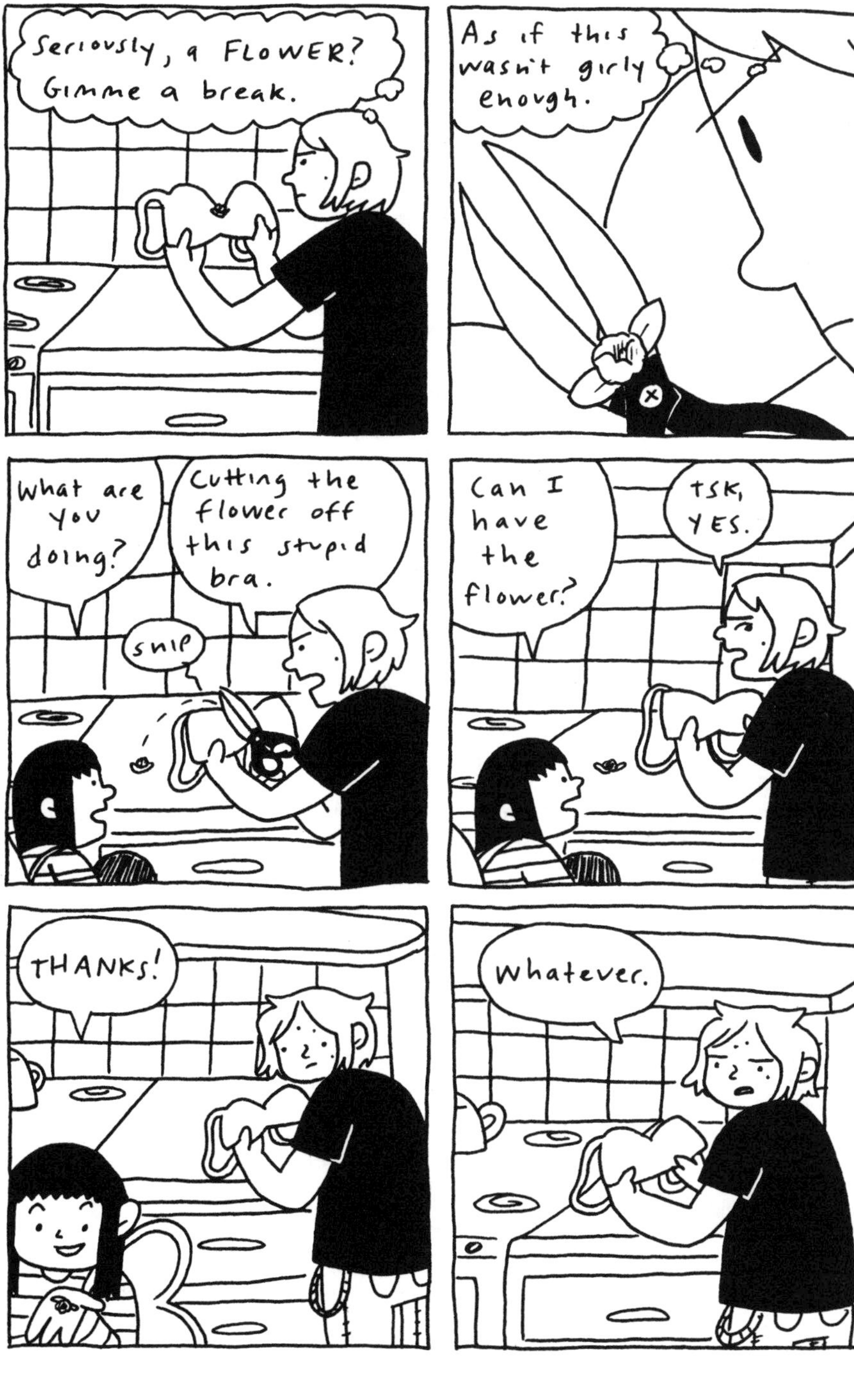
Seriously, a FLOWER? Gimme a break.
As if this wasn't girly enough.
What are you doing?
Cutting the flower off this stupid bra.
snip
Can I have the flower?
tsk, YES.
THANKS!
Whatever.

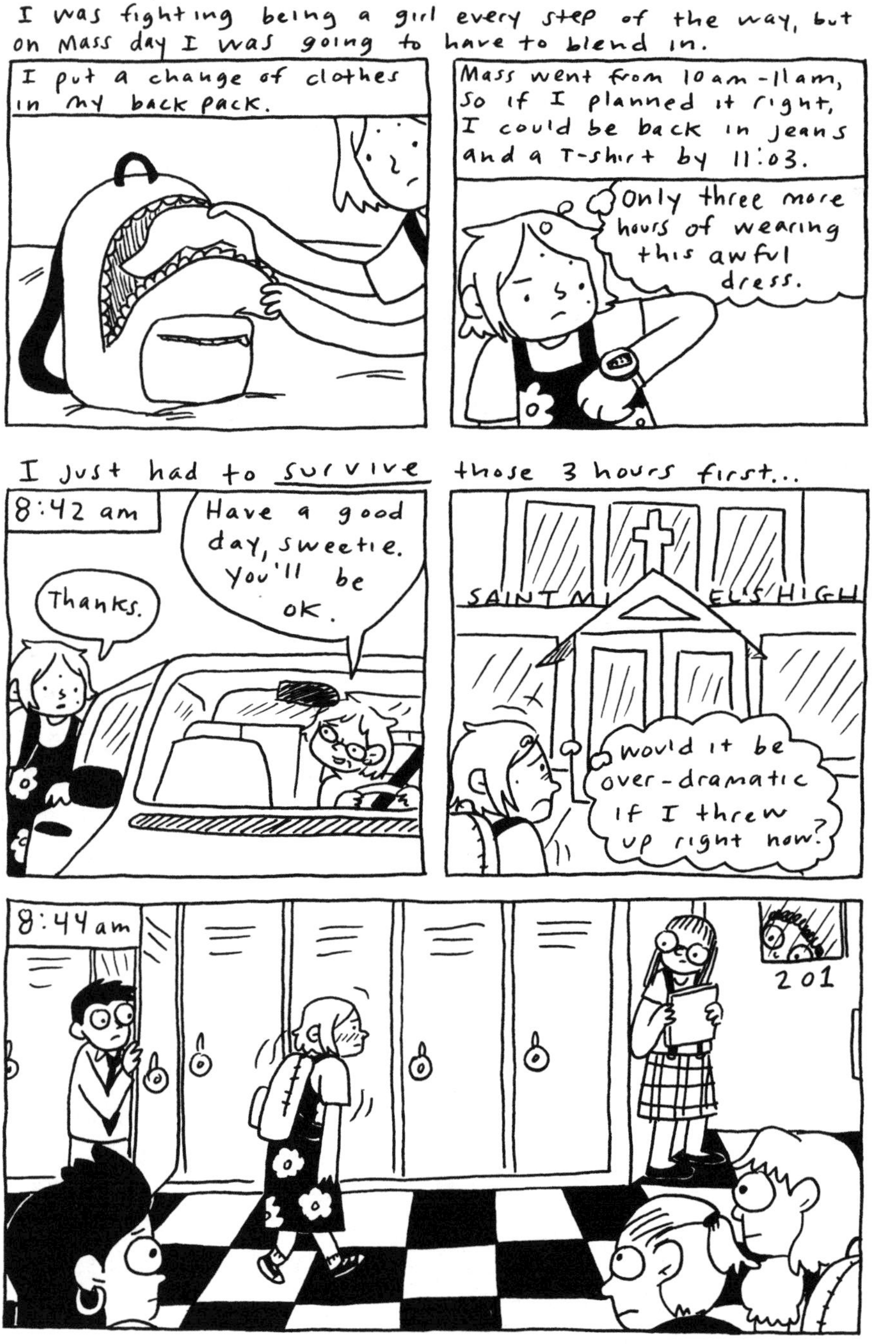
I was fighting being a girl every step of the way, but on Mass day I was going to have to blend in.
I put a change of clothes in my back pack.
Mass went from 10 am-11 am, So if I planned it right, I could be back in jeans and a T-shirt by 11:03.
Only three more hours of wearing this awful dress.
I just had to survive those 3 hours first...
8:42 am
Have a good day, sweetie. You'll be ok.
Thanks.
Would it be over-dramatic if I threw up right now?
8:44 am
201

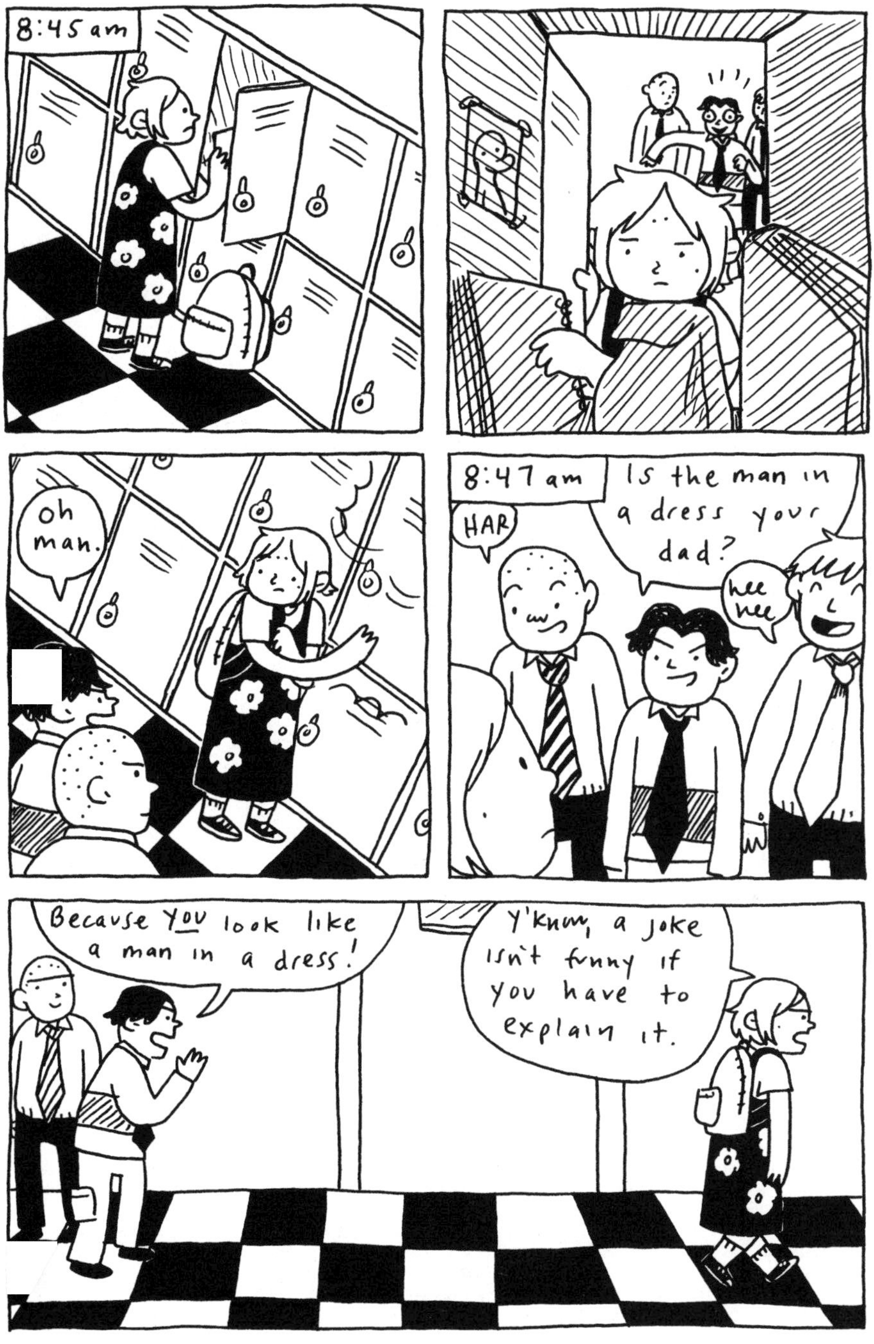
8:45 am
oh man.
8:47 am
HAR
Is the man in a dress your dad?
hee hee
Because YOU look like a man in a dress!
Y'know, a joke isn't funny if you have to explain it.

THE MAN IN THE DRESS IS SANTA FE'S URBAN LEGEND.

The story goes that his wife died suddenly, and that he wears her clothes as a tribute. He may have worked at Los Alamos Labs. I had been told that he wrote poetry on parchment scrolls, which he gives out to people who are willing to talk to him.

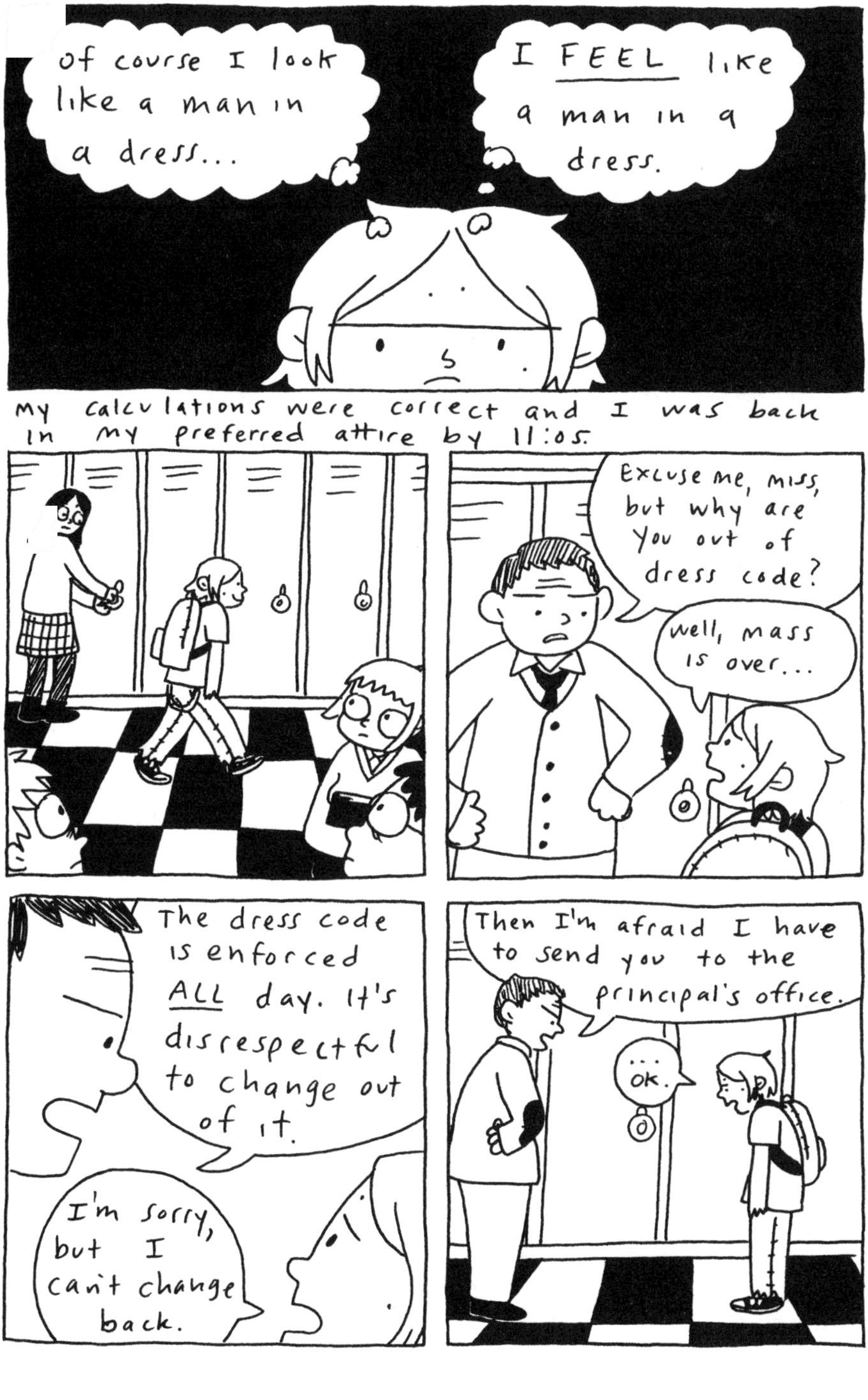
of course I look like a man in a dress...
I FEEL like a man in a dress.
My calculations were correct and I was back in my preferred attire by 11:05.
Excuse me, miss, but why are you out of dress code?
Well, mass is over...
The dress code is enforced ALL day. It's disrespectful to change out of it.
I'm sorry, but I can't change back.
Then I'm afraid I have to send you to the principal's office.
...OK.

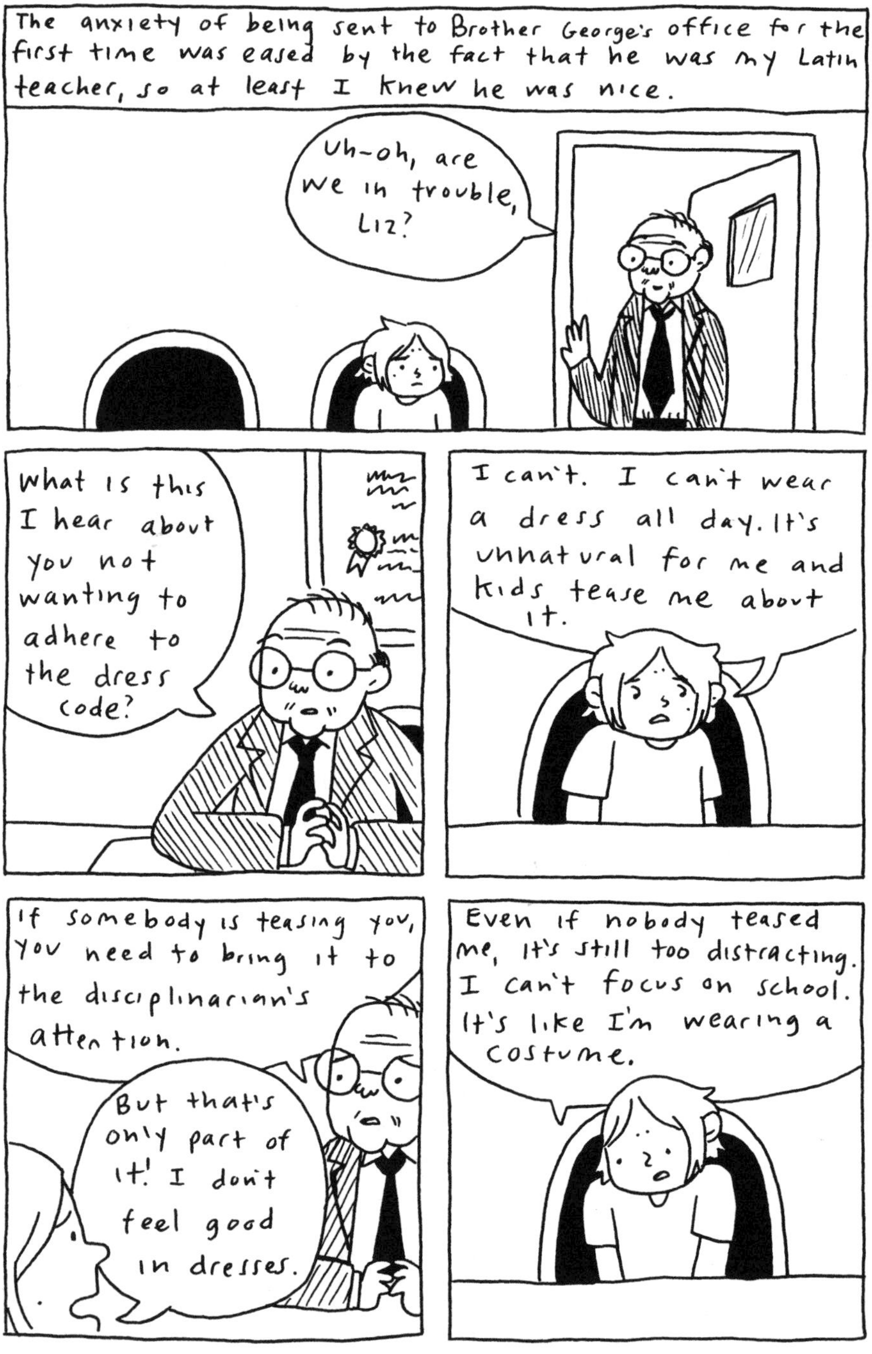
The anxiety of being sent to Brother George's office for the first time was eased by the fact that he was my Latin teacher, so at least I knew he was nice.
Uh-oh, are we in trouble, Liz?
What is this I hear about you not wanting to adhere to the dress code?
I can't. I can't wear a dress all day. It's unnatural for me and kids tease me about it.
If somebody is teasing you, you need to bring it to the disciplinarian's attention.
But that's only part of it! I don't feel good in dresses.
Even if nobody teased me, it's still too distracting. I can't focus on school. It's like I'm wearing a costume.

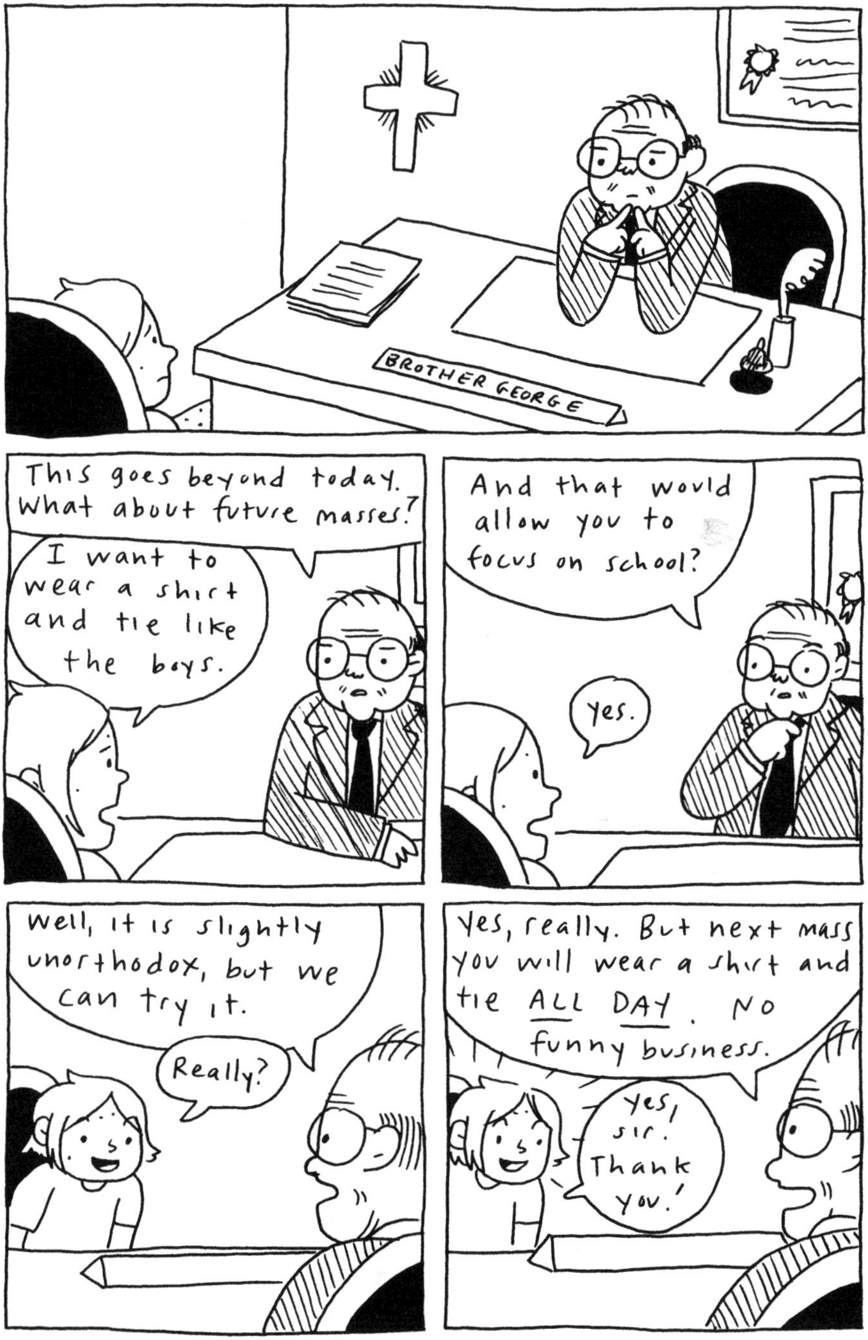
BROTHER GEORGE
This goes beyond today. What about future masses?
I want to wear a shirt and tie like the boys.
And that would allow you to focus on school?
Yes.
Well, it is slightly unorthodox, but we can try it.
Really?
Yes, really. But next mass you will wear a shirt and tie ALL DAY. No funny business.
Yes, sir. Thank you!

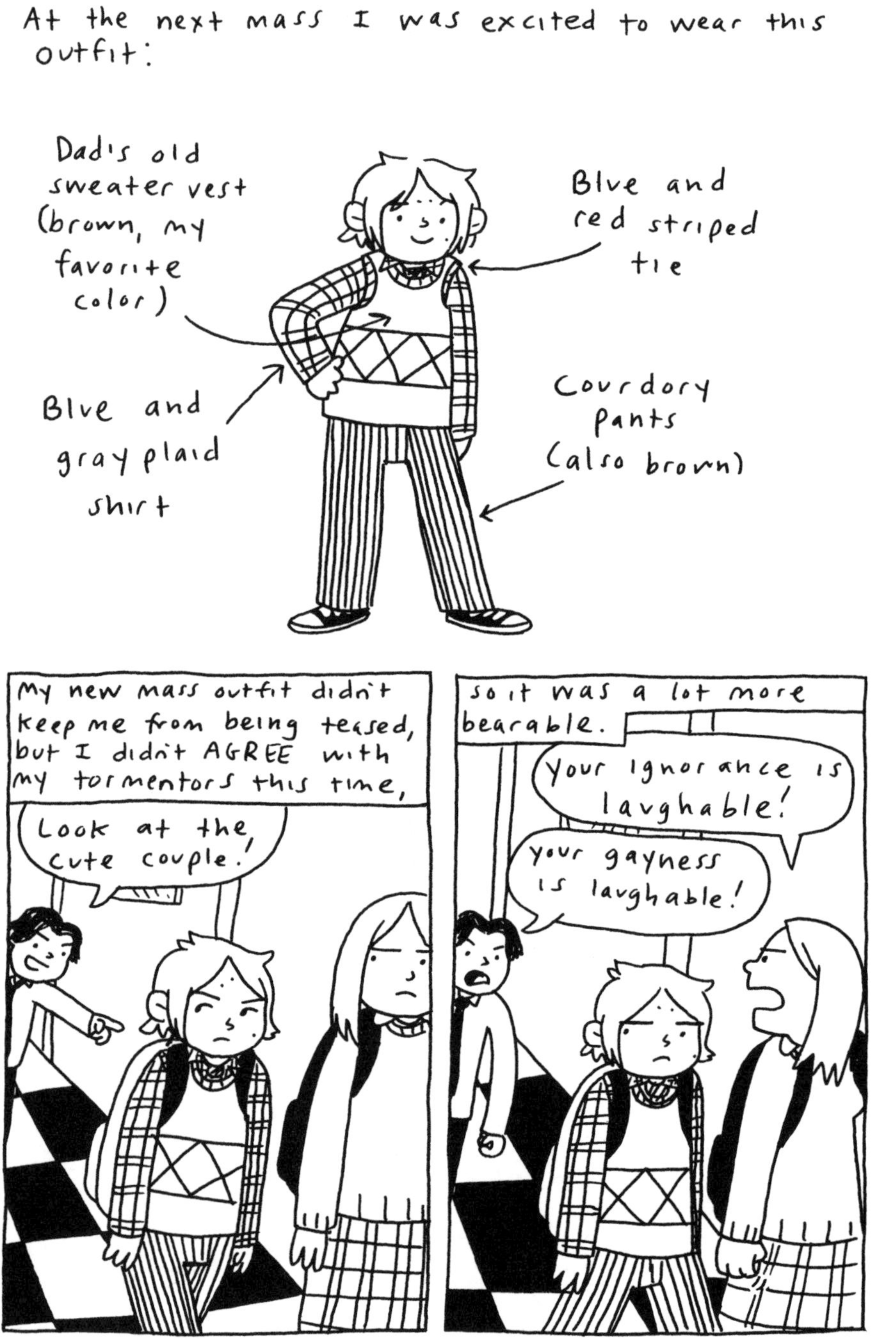
At the next mass I was excited to wear this outfit:
Dad's old sweater vest (brown, my favorite color)
Blue and red striped tie
Blue and gray plaid shirt
Courdory pants (also brown)
My new mass outfit didn't keep me from being teased, but I didn't AGREE with my tormentors this time,
Look at the cute couple!
so it was a lot more bearable.
Your ignorance is laughable!
Your gayness is laughable!

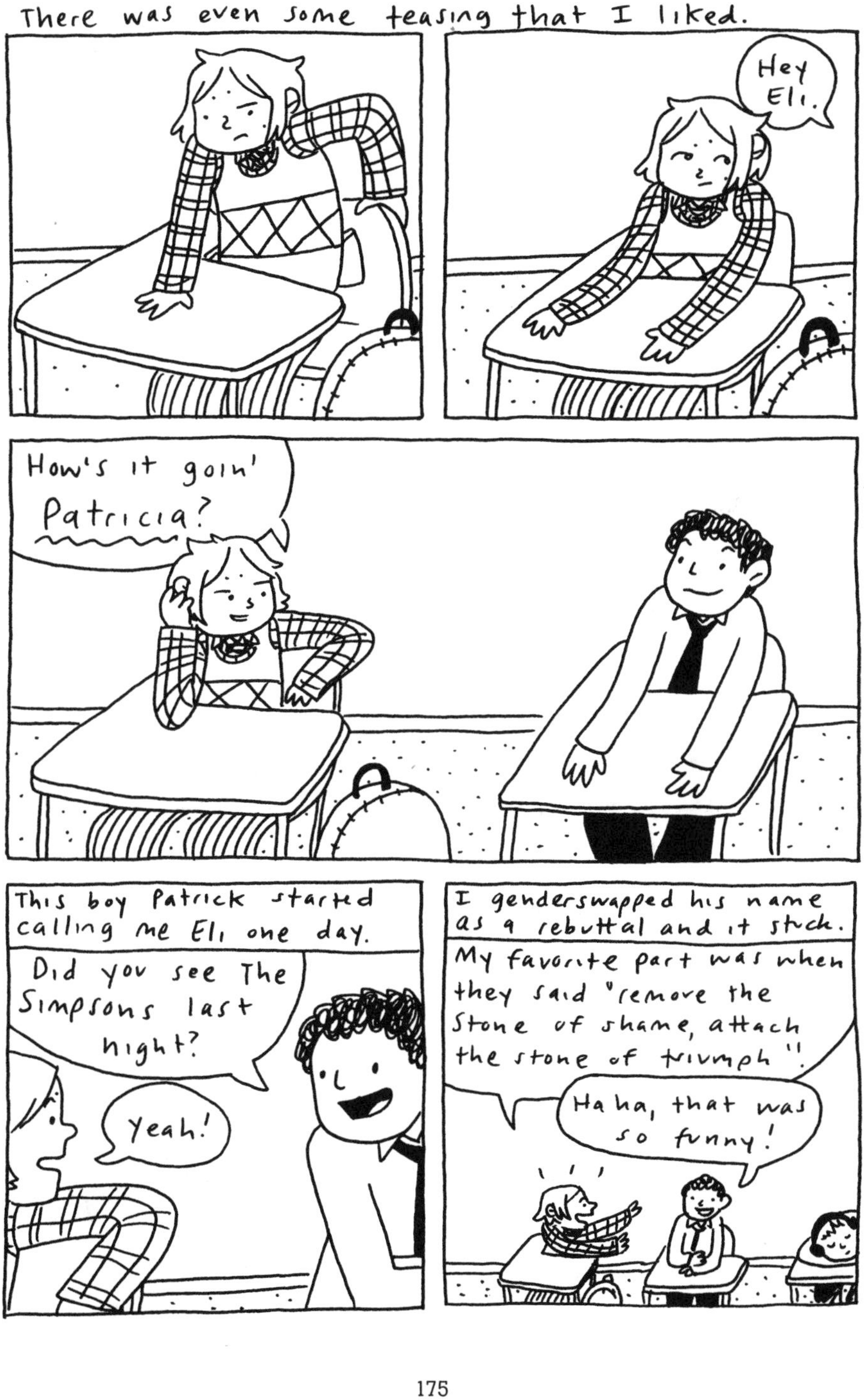
There was even some teasing that I liked.
Hey Eli.
How's it goin' Patricia?
This boy Patrick started calling me Eli one day.
Did you see The Simpsons last night?
Yeah!
I genderswapped his name as a rebuttal and it stuck.
My favorite part was when they said "remove the Stone of shame, attach the stone of triumph".
Haha, that was so funny!

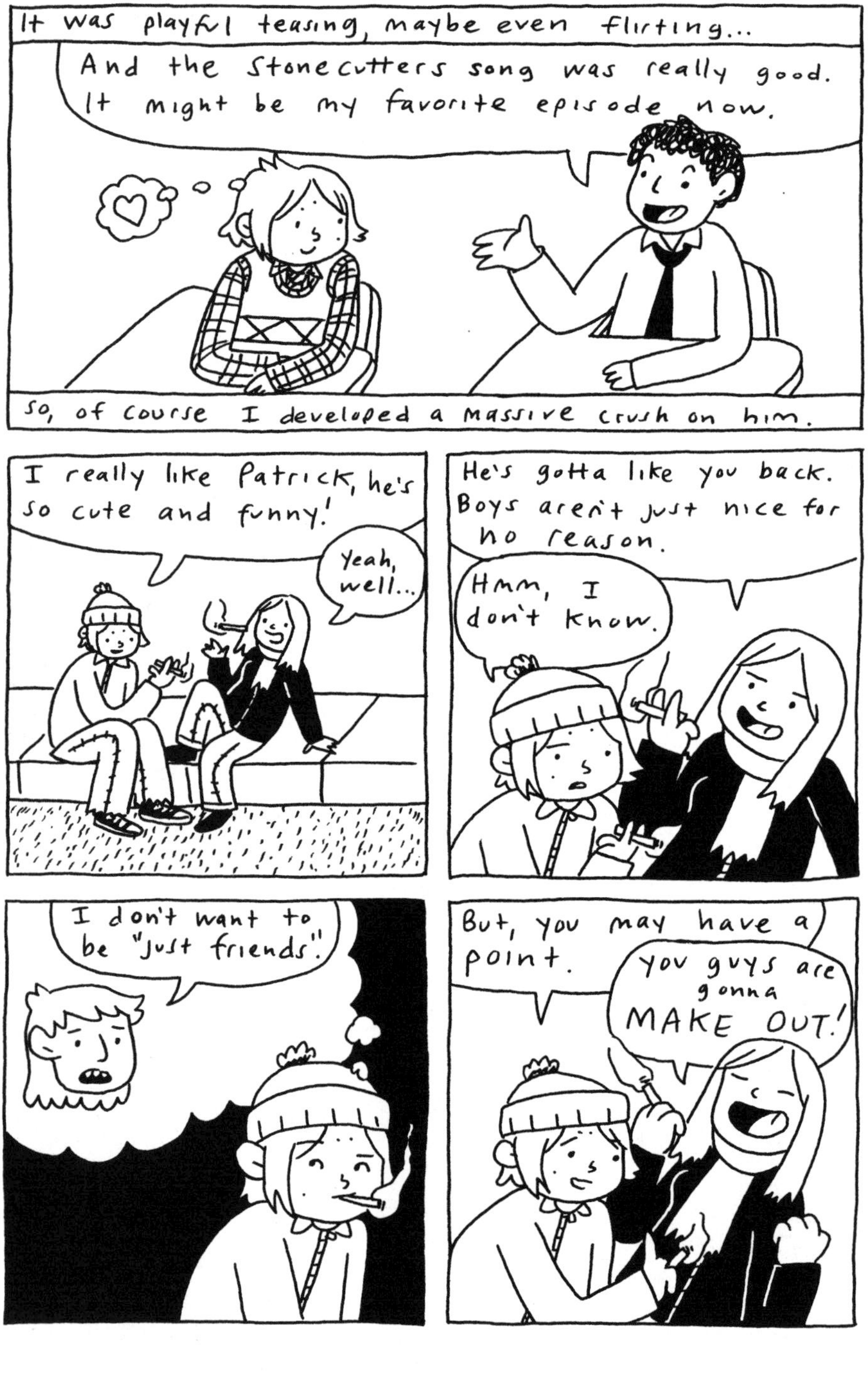
It was playful teasing, maybe even flirting...
And the Stonecutters song was really good. It might be my favorite episode now.
So, of course I developed a massive crush on him.
I really like Patrick, he's so cute and funny!
Yeah, well...
He's gotta like you back. Boys aren't just nice for no reason.
Hmm, I don't know.
I don't want to be "just friends".
But, you may have a point.
You guys are gonna MAKE OUT!

CHAPTER 9

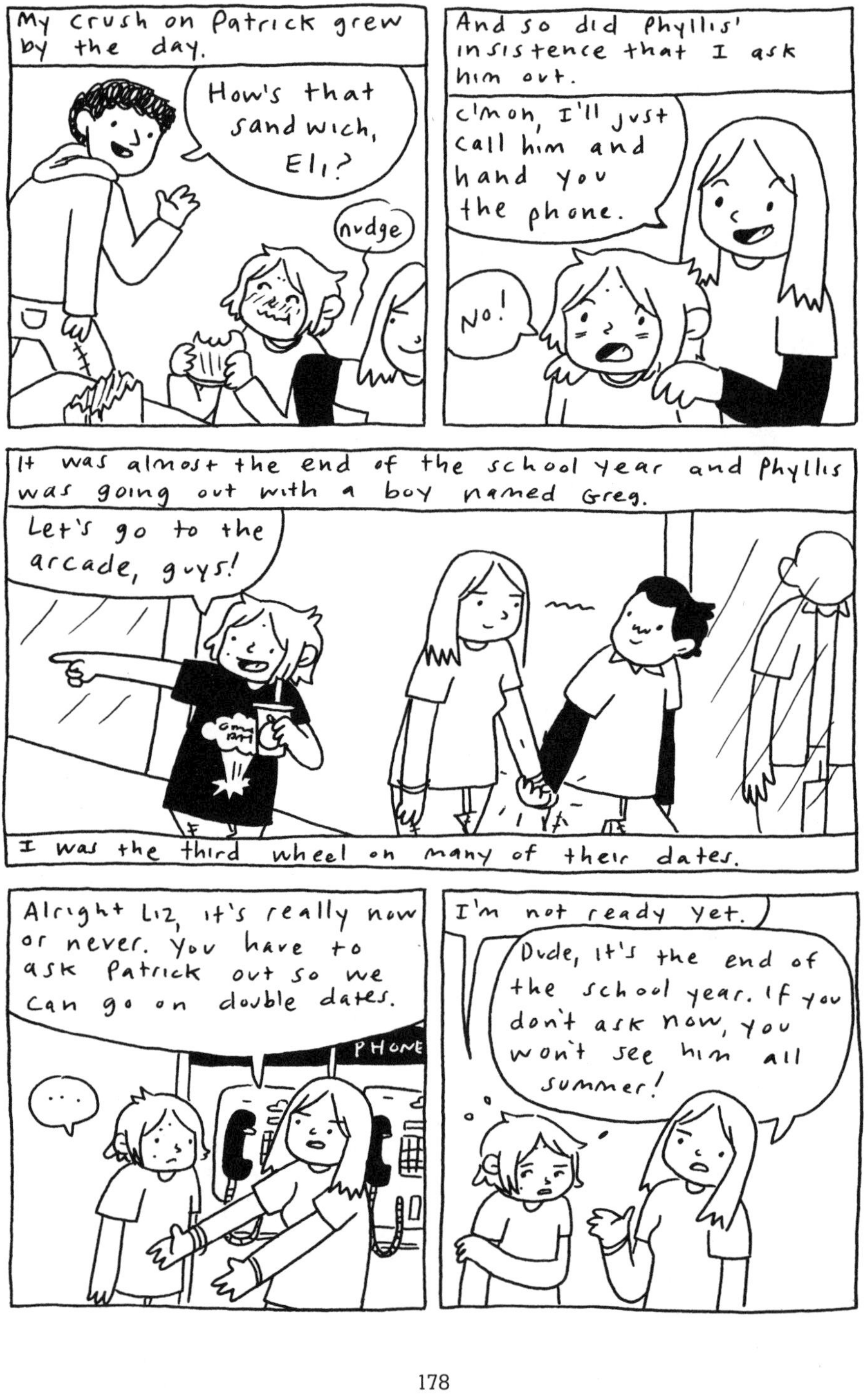
My crush on Patrick grew by the day.
How's that sandwich, Eli?
nudge
And so did Phyllis' insistence that I ask him out.
c'mon, I'll just call him and hand you the phone.
No!
It was almost the end of the school year and Phyllis was going out with a boy named Greg.
Let's go to the arcade, guys!
I was the third wheel on many of their dates.
Alright Liz, it's really now or never. You have to ask Patrick out so we can go on double dates.
...
PHONE
I'm not ready yet.
Dude, it's the end of the school year. If you don't ask now, you won't see him all summer!

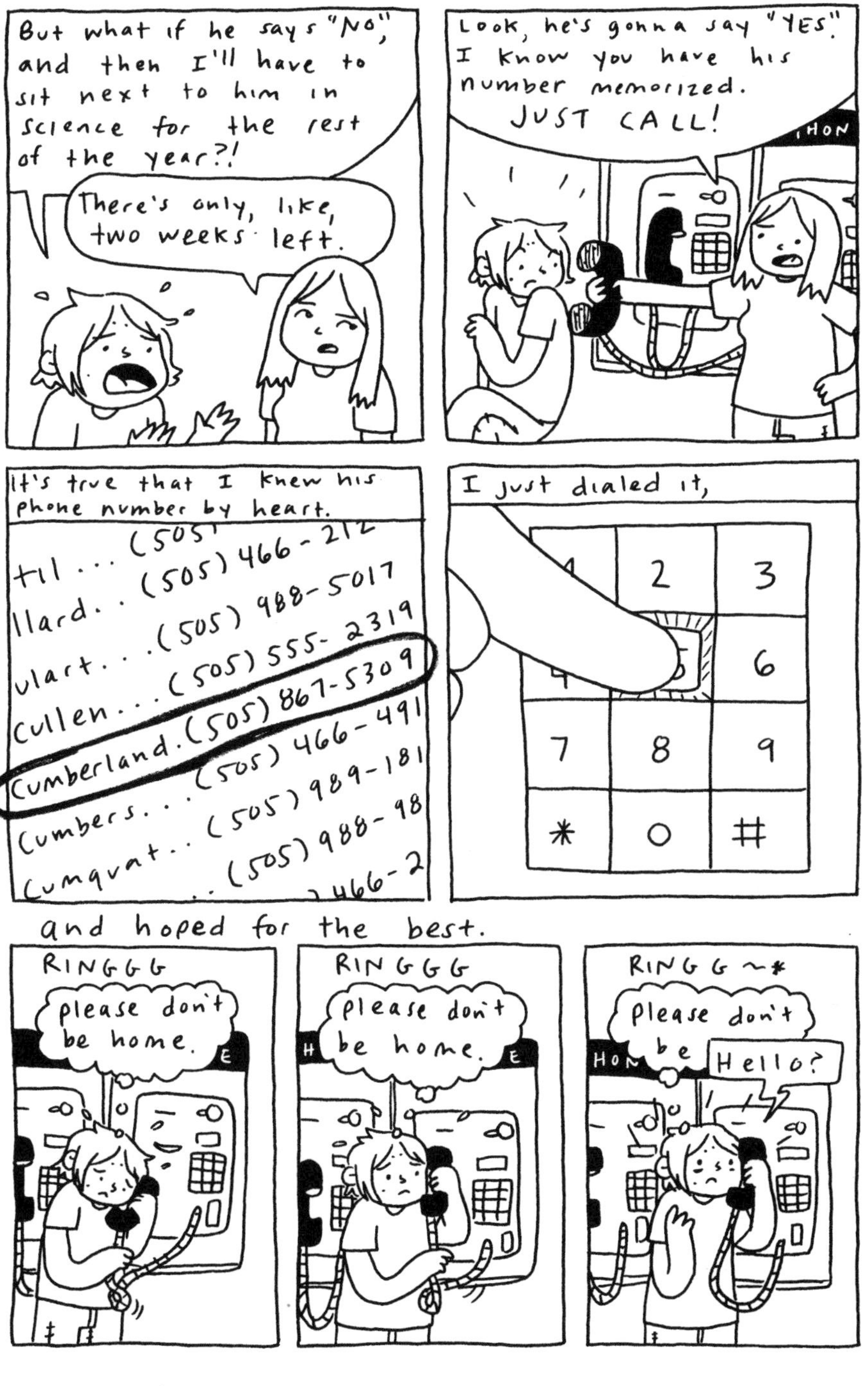
But what if he says "NO", and then I'll have to sit next to him in science for the rest of the year?!
There's only, like, two weeks left.
Look, he's gonna say "YES". I know you have his number memorized.
JUST CALL!
It's true that I knew his phone number by heart.
(505) 466-212
llard.. (505) 988-5017
ulart... (505) 555-2319
Cullen... (505) 867-5309
Cumberland. (505) 466-491
Cumbers... (505) 989-181
Cumquat.. (505) 988-98
I just dialed it,
1 2 3
6
7 8 9
* 0 #
and hoped for the best.
RINGGG
please don't be home.
RINGGG
please don't be home.
RINGG~*
please don't be
Hello?

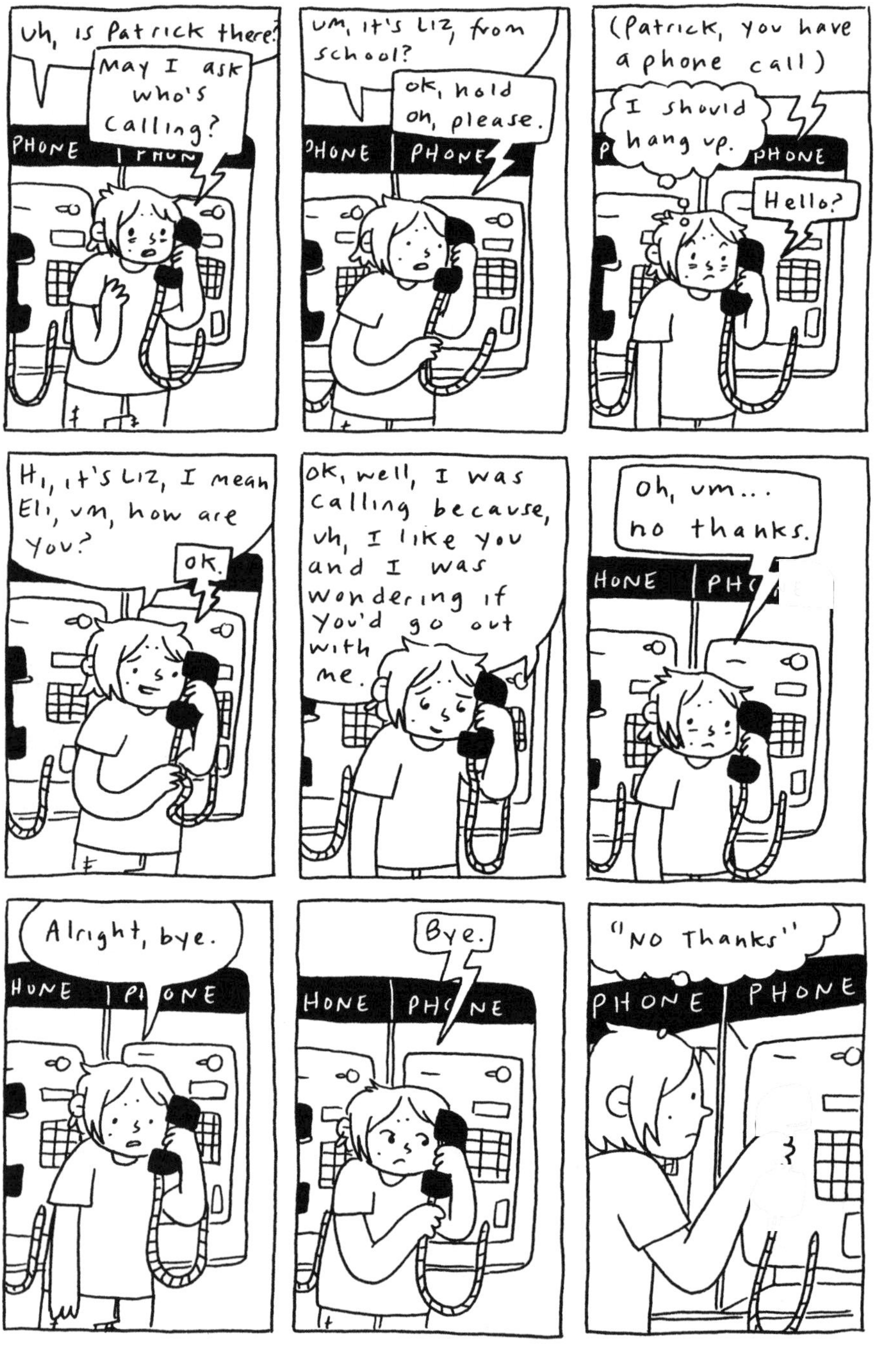
uh, is Patrick there?
May I ask who's calling?
um, it's Liz, from school?
ok, hold on, please.
(Patrick, you have a phone call)
I should hang up.
Hello?
Hi, it's Liz, I mean Eli, um, how are you?
ok.
ok, well, I was calling because, uh, I like you and I was wondering if you'd go out with me.
Oh, um... no thanks.
Alright, bye.
Bye.
"No Thanks"

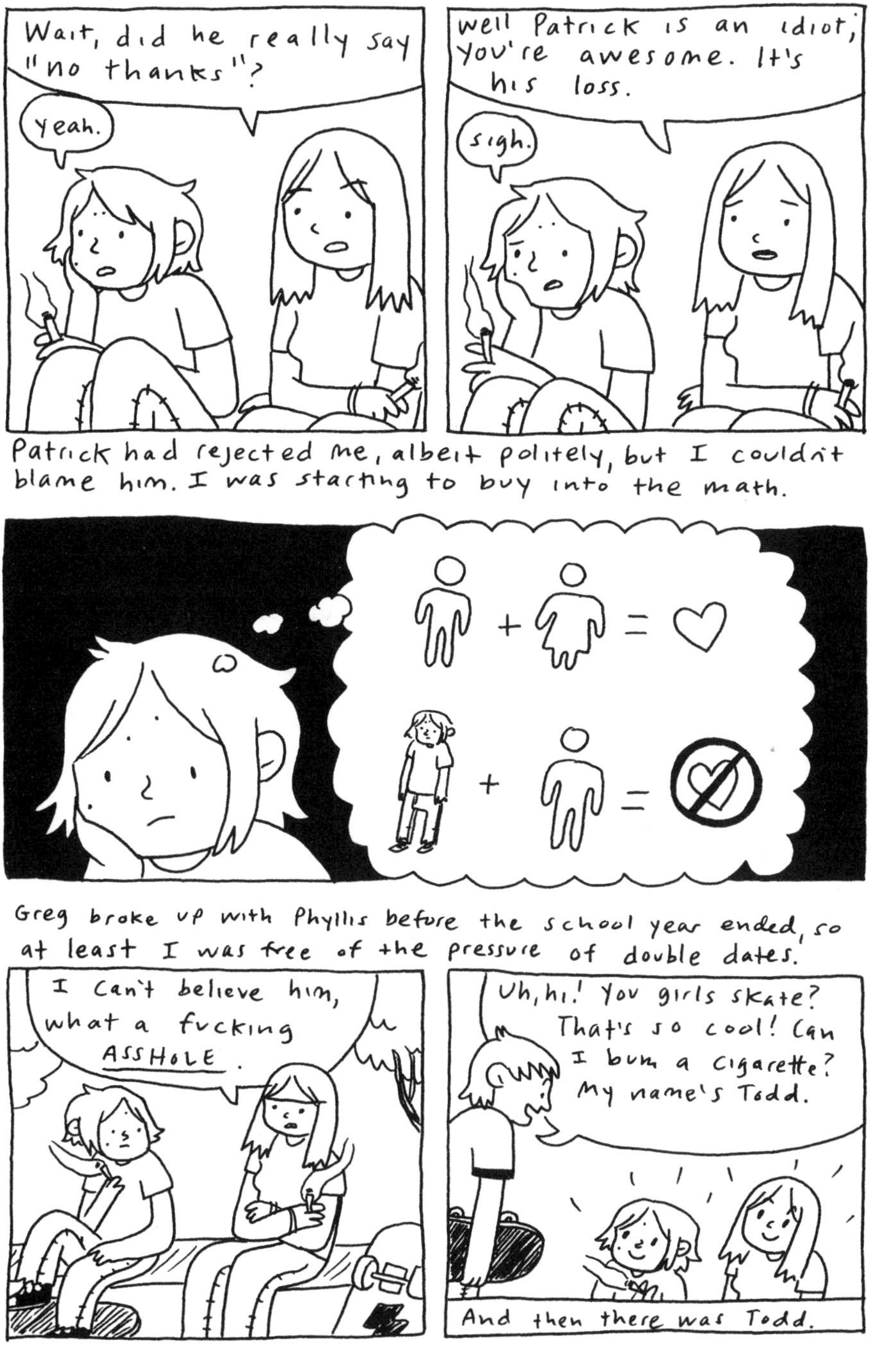
Wait, did he really say "no thanks"?
yeah.
well Patrick is an idiot; you're awesome. It's his loss.
sigh.
Patrick had rejected me, albeit politely, but I couldn't blame him. I was starting to buy into the math.
+
=
+
=
Greg broke up with Phyllis before the school year ended, so at least I was free of the pressure of double dates.
I can't believe him, what a fucking ASSHOLE.
Uh, hi! You girls skate? That's so cool! Can I bum a cigarette? My name's Todd.
And then there was Todd.

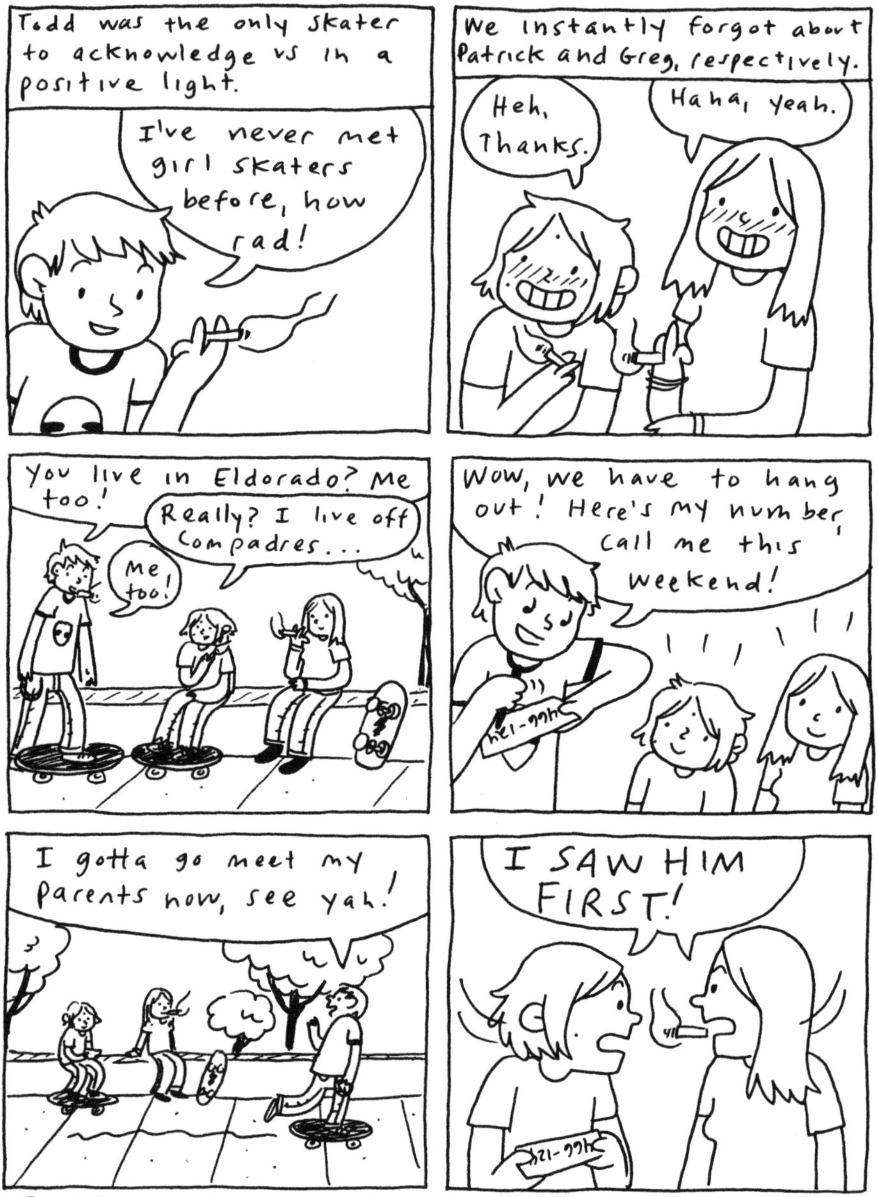
Todd was the only skater to acknowledge us in a positive light.
I've never met girl skaters before, how rad!
We instantly forgot about Patrick and Greg, respectively.
Heh, Thanks.
Haha, yeah.
You live in Eldorado? Me too!
Really? I live off Compadres...
Me too!
Wow, we have to hang out! Here's my number, call me this weekend!
I gotta go meet my parents now, see yah!
I SAW HIM FIRST!

I didn't really consider myself in competition with Phyllis, I knew given a choice between the two of us, I'd likely lose. Instead I hoped that Todd wouldn't like either of us and we'd all just be friends.

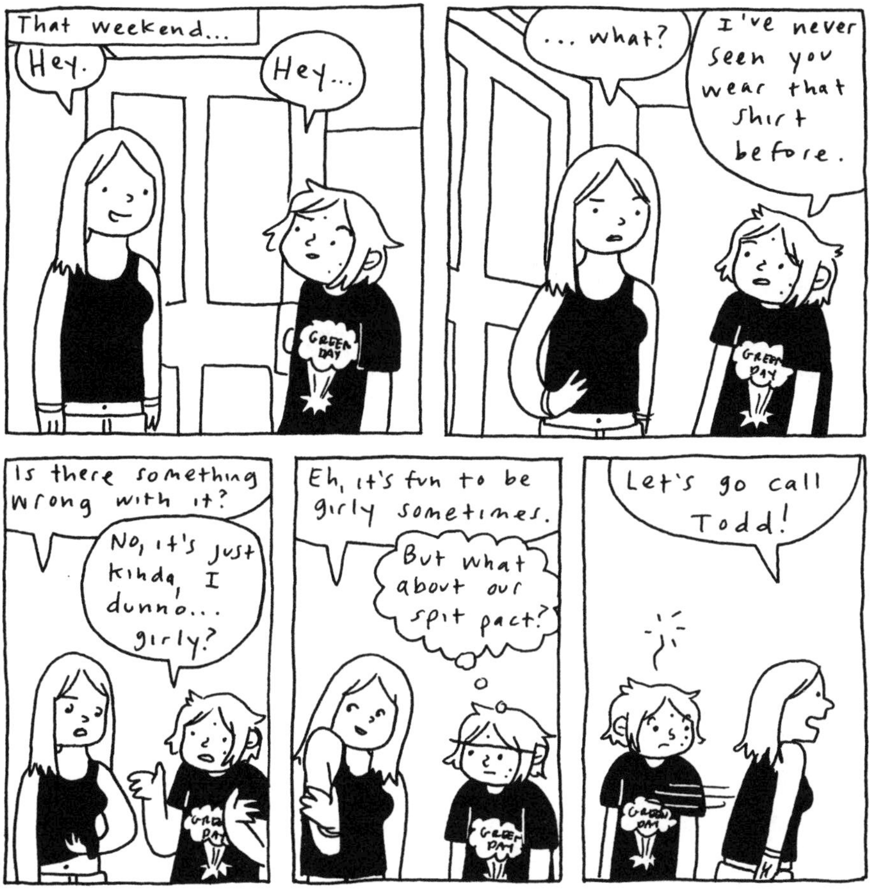
That weekend...
Hey.
Hey...
GREEN DAY
... what?
I've never seen you wear that shirt before.
Is there something wrong with it?
No, it's just kinda, I dunno... girly?
Eh, it's fun to be girly sometimes.
But what about our spit pact?
Let's go call Todd!

we met Todd in a field between his house and mine: being neighbors in Eldorado was relative. He lived a twenty-minute walk from me.

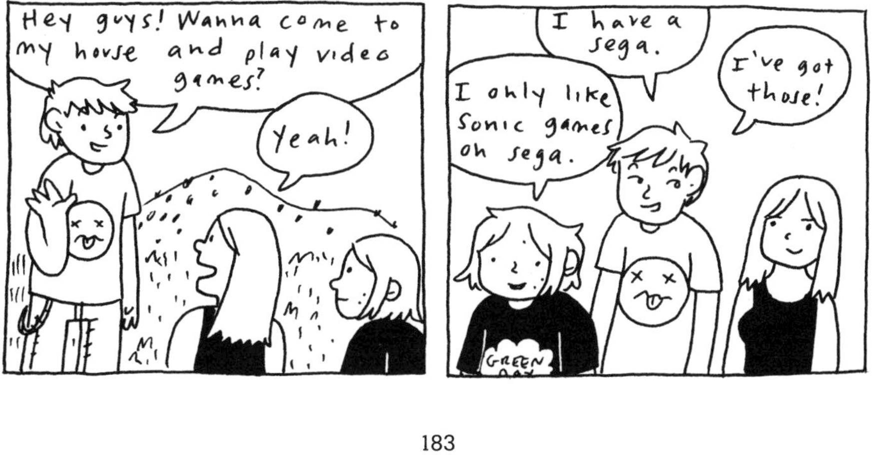
Hey guys! Wanna come to my house and play video games?
Yeah!
I have a sega.
I only like Sonic games on sega.
I've got those!
GREEN DAY

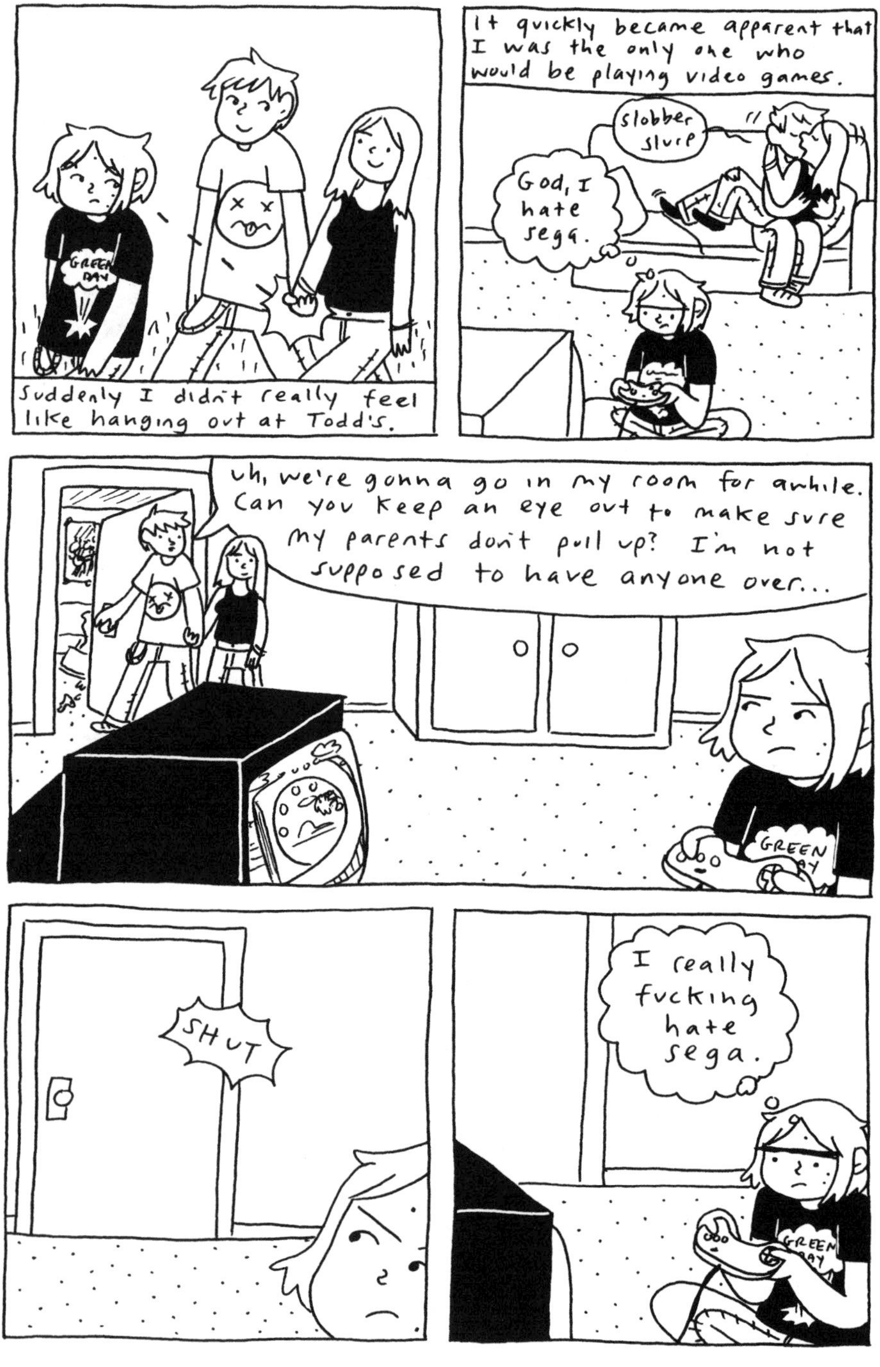
Suddenly I didn't really feel like hanging out at Todd's.
GREEN DAY
It quickly became apparent that I was the only one who would be playing video games.
slobber slurp
God, I hate sega.
Uh, we're gonna go in my room for awhile. Can you keep an eye out to make sure my parents don't pull up? I'm not supposed to have anyone over...
GREEN DAY
SHUT
I really fucking hate sega.
GREEN DAY

dear diary, Yesterday Phyllis slept over at my house and it was awful. we went to hang out at Todd's and they instantly ditched me to make out in his bedroom.

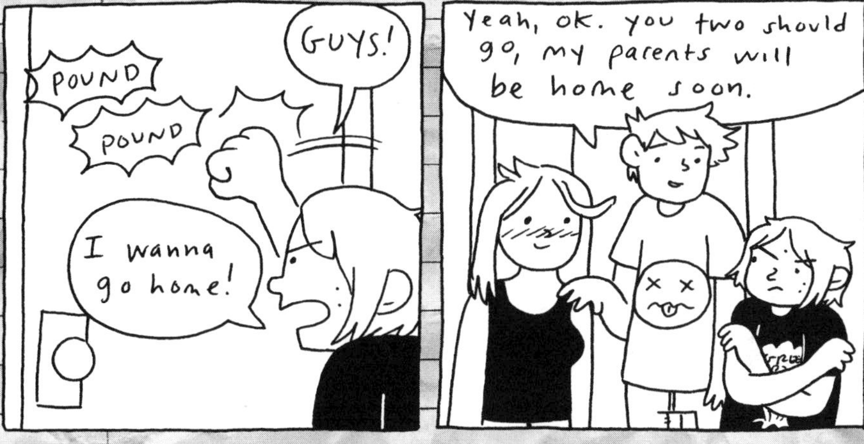
POUND
POUND
GUYS!
I wanna go home!
Yeah, OK. you two should go, my parents will be home soon.
EW, you have a HICKEY.
OH NO! I'm so gonna have to hide that from my mom.
GREEN
I'm surprised there's not more, he put his hand up my shirt and...
Please kill me.

It's really lame that she would suck his face off in front of me. But the worst part is that she was dressed up like a girl for his benefit. Yuck. Am I the last tomboy on earth?

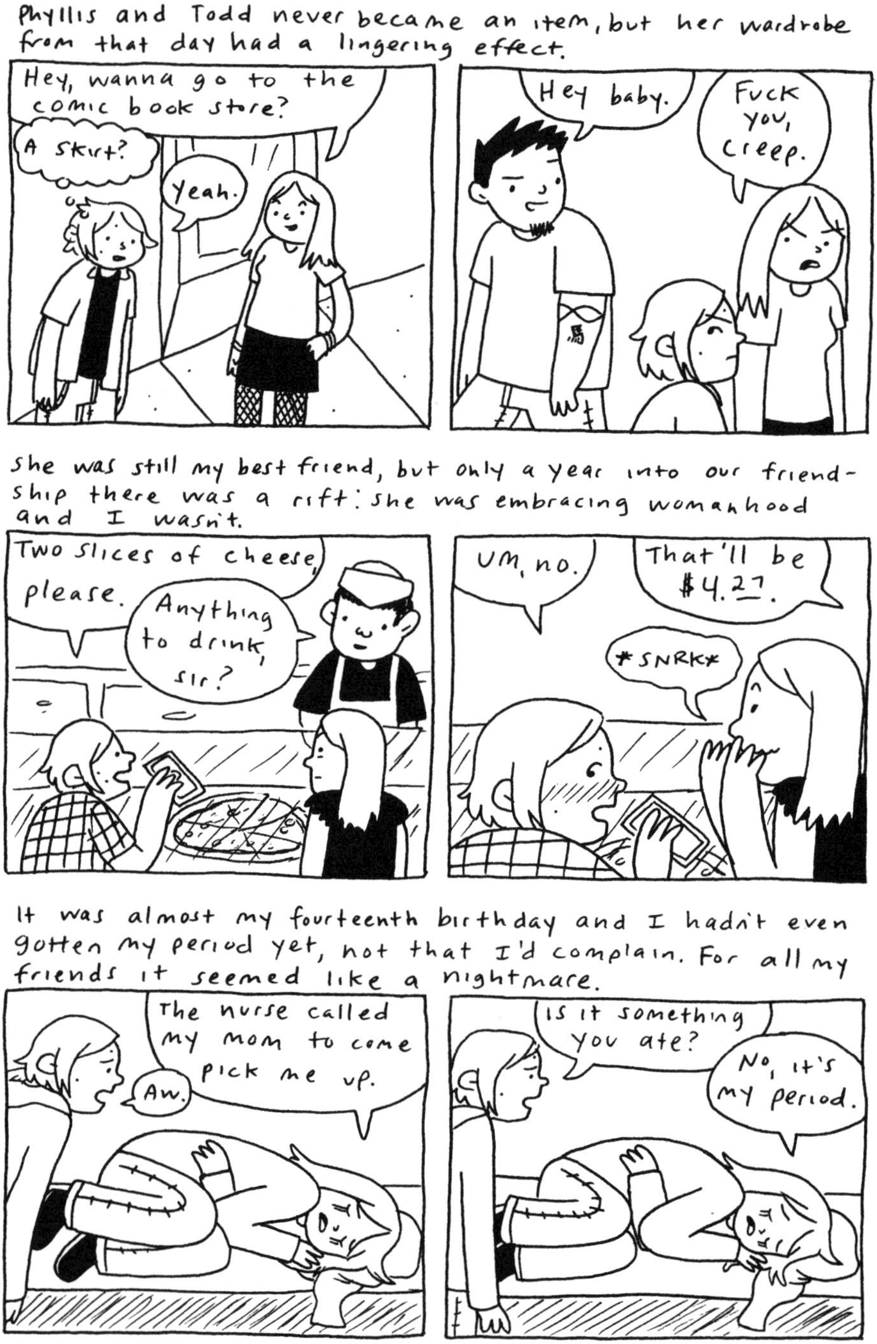
Phyllis and Todd never became an item, but her wardrobe from that day had a lingering effect.
Hey, wanna go to the comic book store?
A skirt?
Yeah.
Hey baby.
Fuck you, creep.
She was still my best friend, but only a year into our friendship there was a rift: she was embracing womanhood and I wasn't.
Two slices of cheese, please.
Anything to drink, sir?
Um, no.
That'll be $4.27.
SNRK
It was almost my fourteenth birthday and I hadn't even gotten my period yet, not that I'd complain. For all my friends it seemed like a nightmare.
The nurse called my mom to come pick me up.
Aw.
Is it something you ate?
No, it's my period.

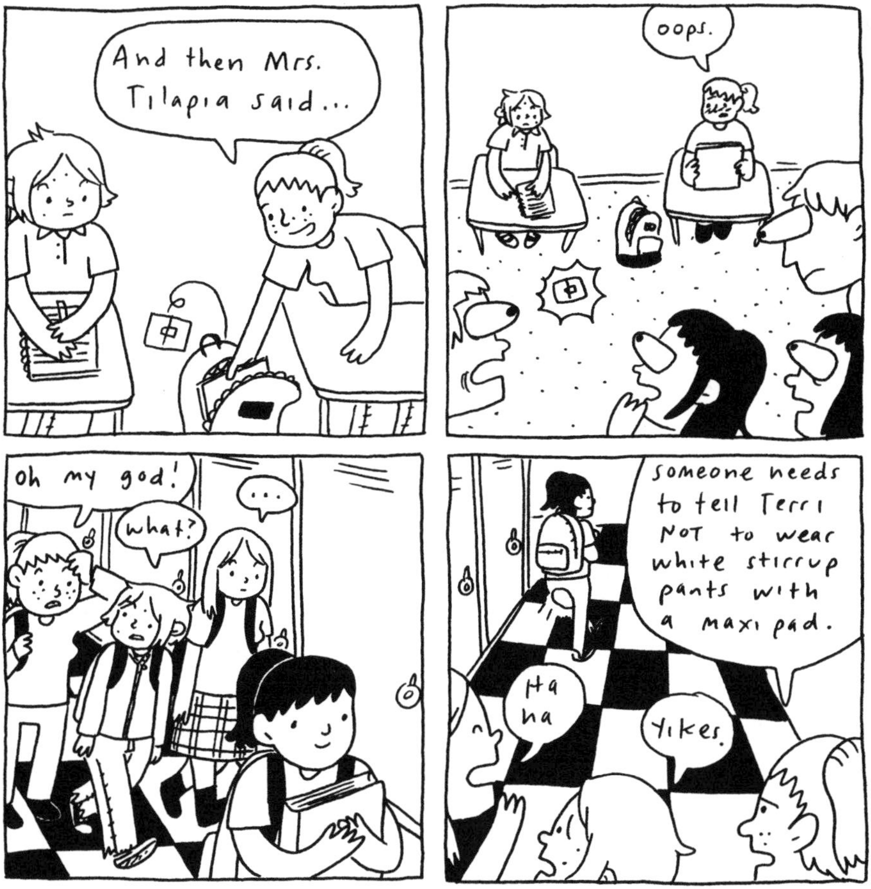
And then Mrs. Tilapia said...
oops.
oh my god!
what?
...
Someone needs to tell Terri NOT to wear white stirrup pants with a maxi pad.
Ha ha
Yikes.

I was afraid that getting my period would change me. All my friends certainly seemed more feminine afterward.

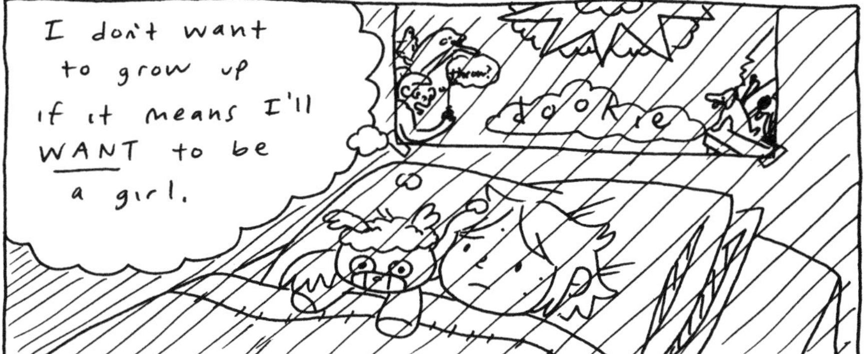
I don't want to grow up if it means I'll WANT to be a girl.

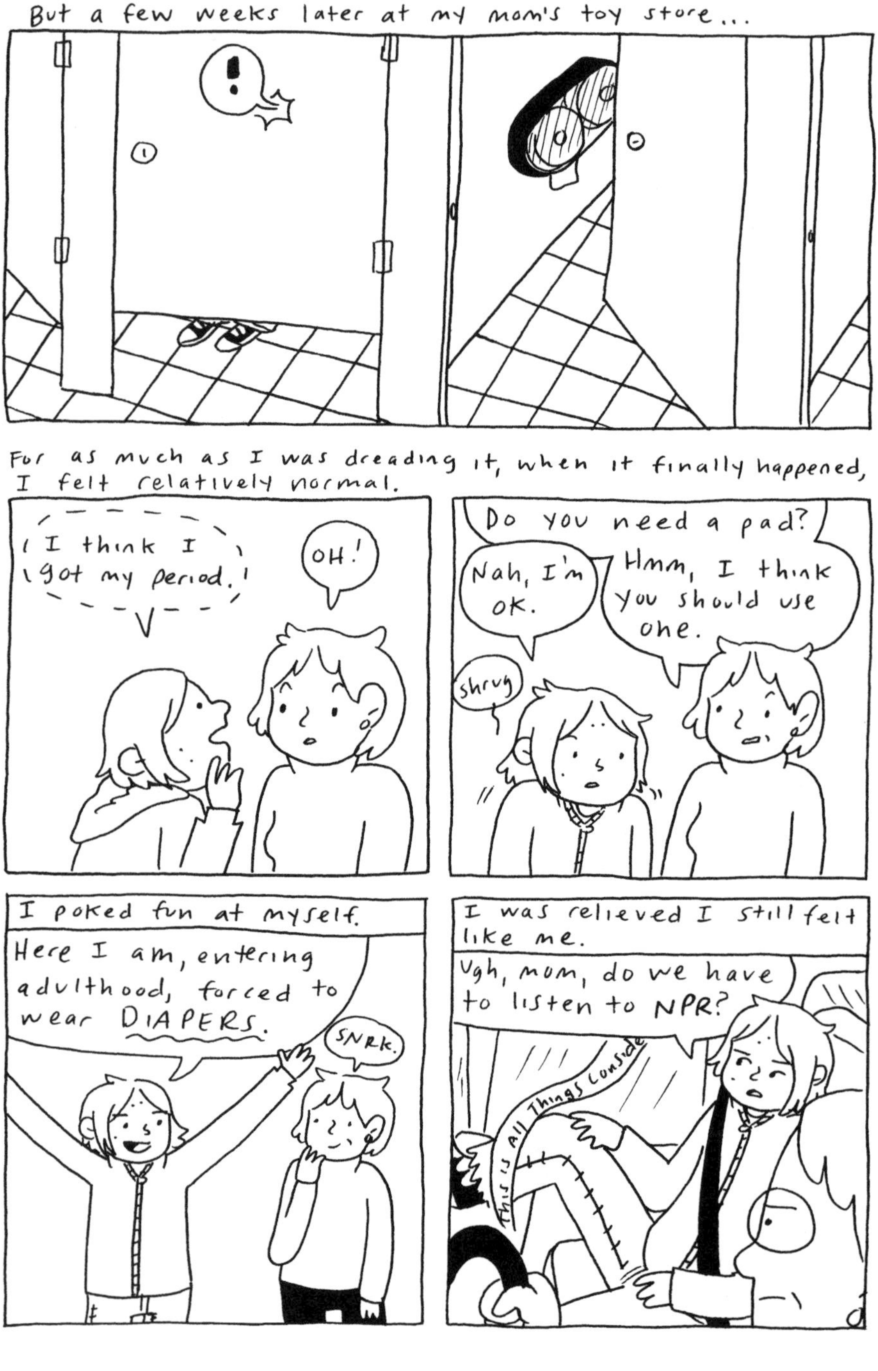
But a few weeks later at my mom's toy store...
!
For as much as I was dreading it, when it finally happened, I felt relatively normal.
I think I got my period.
OH!
Do you need a pad?
Nah, I'm OK.
Hmm, I think you should use one.
shrug
I poked fun at myself.
Here I am, entering adulthood, forced to wear DIAPERS.
SNRK.
I was relieved I still felt like me.
Ugh, mom, do we have to listen to NPR?
This is All Things Conside

Unfortunately, a big part of being me meant that I was mortified by how this new burden of womanhood further set me back from my goal of being "one of the boys"!

1. Boys don't have to carry around embarrassing feminine hygiene products.

Could these be any more pink?

2. Boys don't have to buy embarrassing feminine hygiene products.

Far worse than bra and dress shopping combined.

TO THE MAX
Banana Boats
FRESH ONES
SUPER LONGS
heavy flow
Summ 2 Eve
emega embarrassing
PLUG IT! WITH TAMPONS!
Regular
O.d.b. procomfy

3. Boys don't have to worry about changing embarrassing feminine hygiene products in public restrooms.

must open as quietly as possible.

RIP

4. Boys don't have to worry about bleeding through their pants.

Would anyone tell me, or would I just know from the laughing and pointing?

5. Boys don't get horrible, debilitating menstrual cramps.

dookie

To top it off, I was experiencing my own particular brand of body issues.

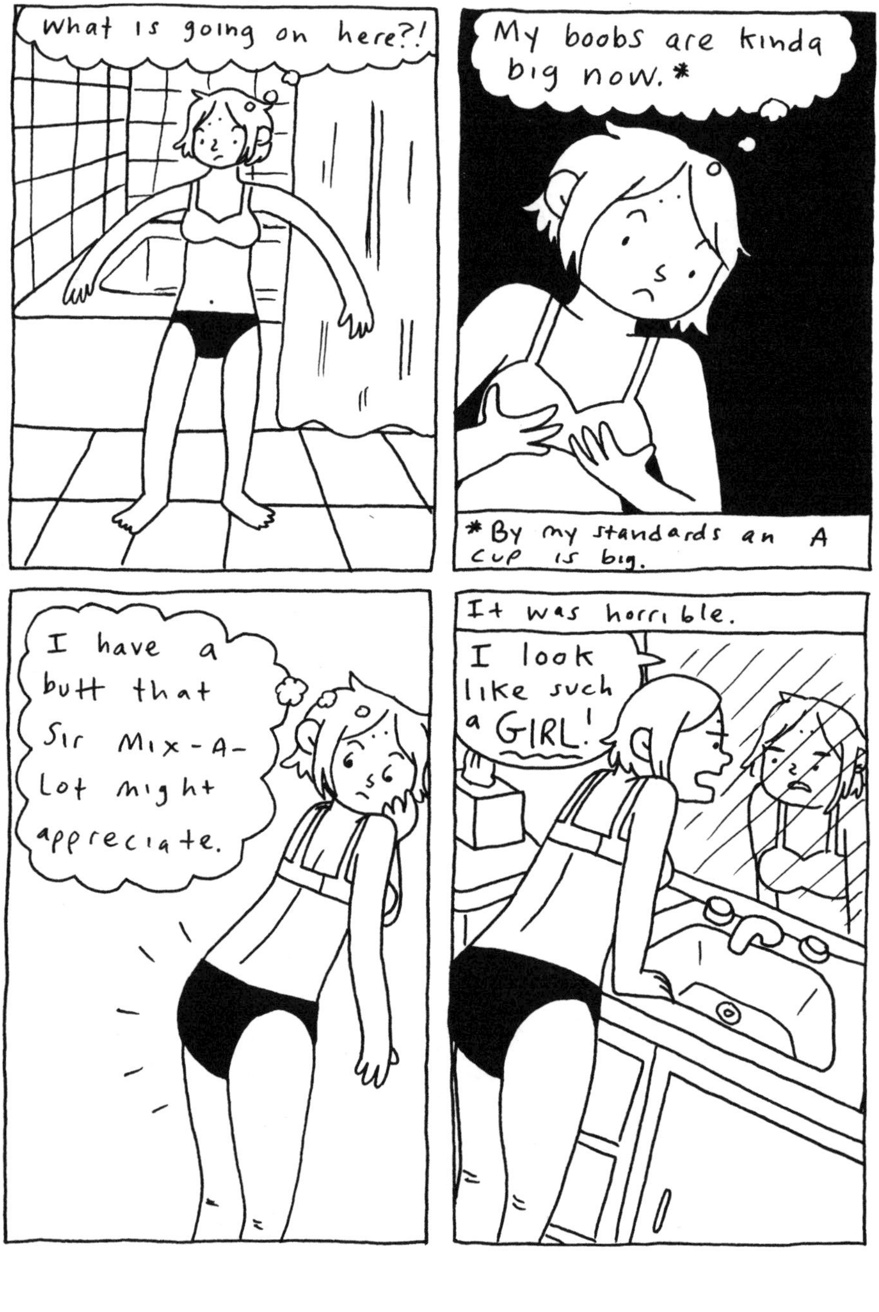

What is going on here?!
My boobs are kinda big now.*
* By my standards an A cup is big.
I have a butt that Sir Mix-A-Lot might appreciate.
It was horrible.
I look like such a GIRL!

CHAPTER 10

I was spending a lot of afternoons at my mom's store without Phyllis (because her family had moved to a different neighborhood). Around that same time a woman named Harley started working for my Mom.

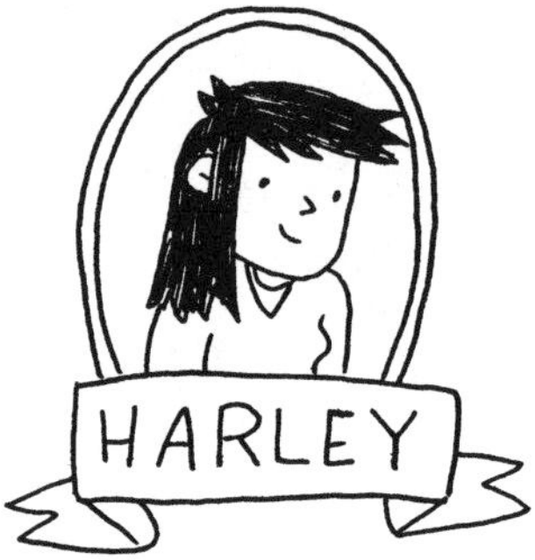
HARLEY

* Is my parents' age, but never had kids of her own.
* Self-publishes an anthology zine.
* Is the first person who wasn't a family member or a friend to take an interest in my comics.
* Is the coolest adult.

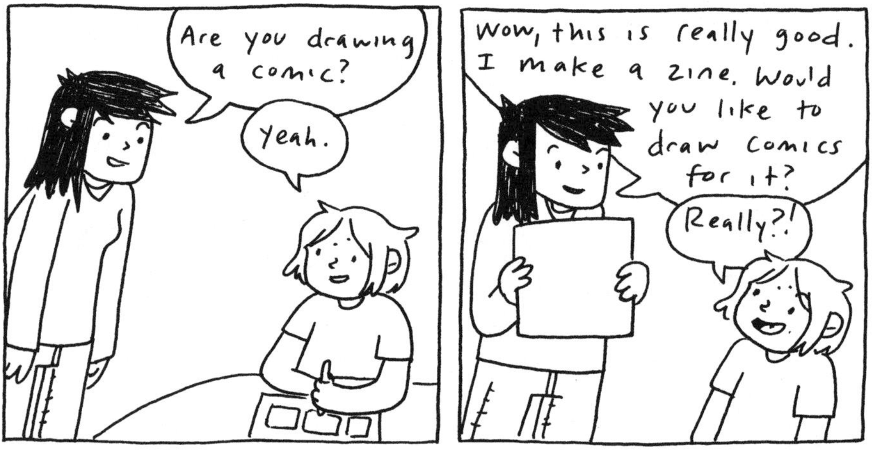
Are you drawing a comic?
Yeah.
Wow, this is really good. I make a zine. Would you like to draw comics for it?
Really?!

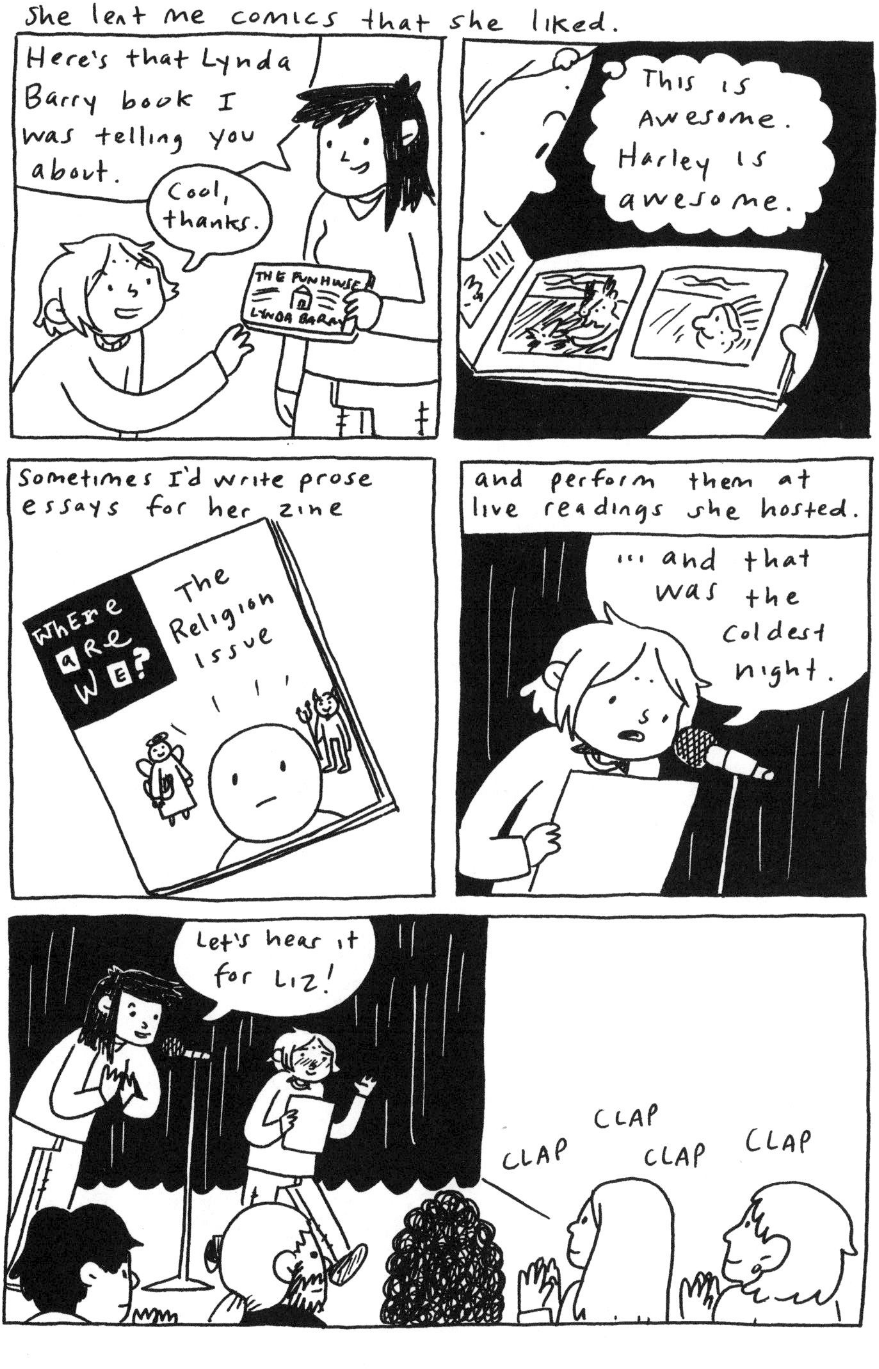
She lent me comics that she liked.
Here's that Lynda Barry book I was telling you about.
Cool, thanks.
THE FUNHOUSE
LYNDA BARRY
This is awesome. Harley is awesome.
Sometimes I'd write prose essays for her zine
Where are we?
The Religion Issue
and perform them at live readings she hosted.
... and that was the coldest night.
Let's hear it for Liz!
CLAP
CLAP
CLAP
CLAP

I felt genuinely celebrated for being an individual,

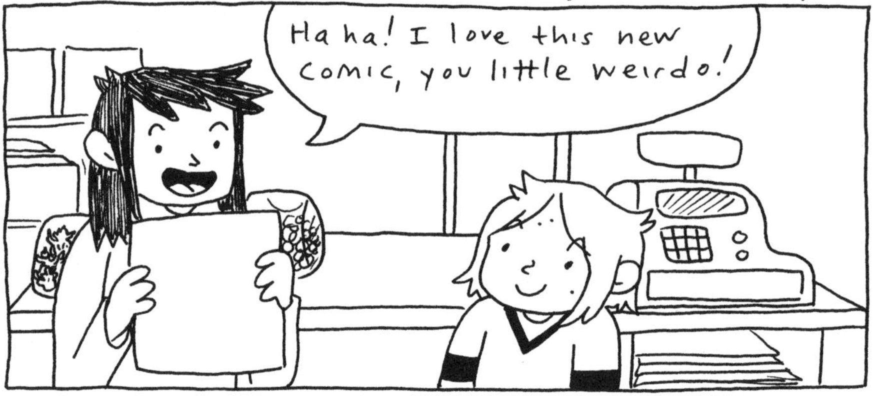
Ha ha! I love this new comic, you little weirdo!

which was a nice change of pace.

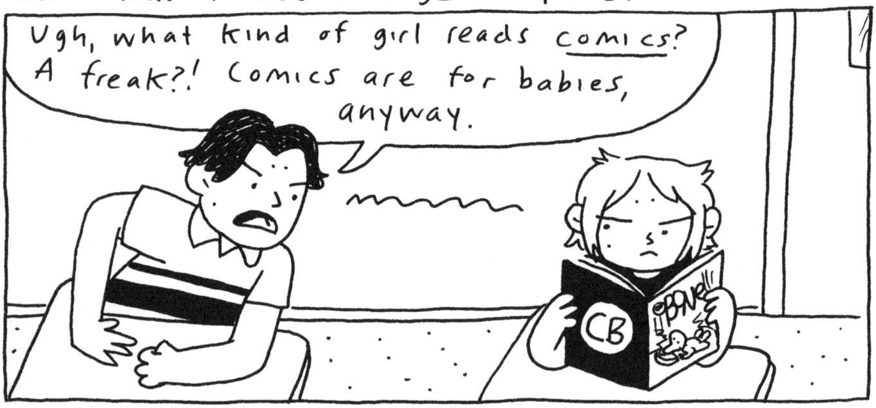
Ugh, what kind of girl reads comics? A freak?! Comics are for babies, anyway.
CB

By the time 9th grade started, Terri and Erin had both moved away, making Phyllis the only real friend I had left at school.

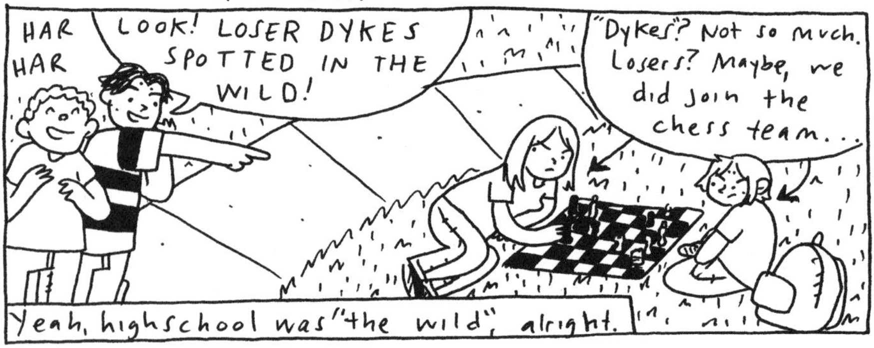
HAR HAR
LOOK! LOSER DYKES SPOTTED IN THE WILD!
"Dykes"? Not so much. Losers? Maybe, we did join the chess team...
Yeah, highschool was "the wild", alright.

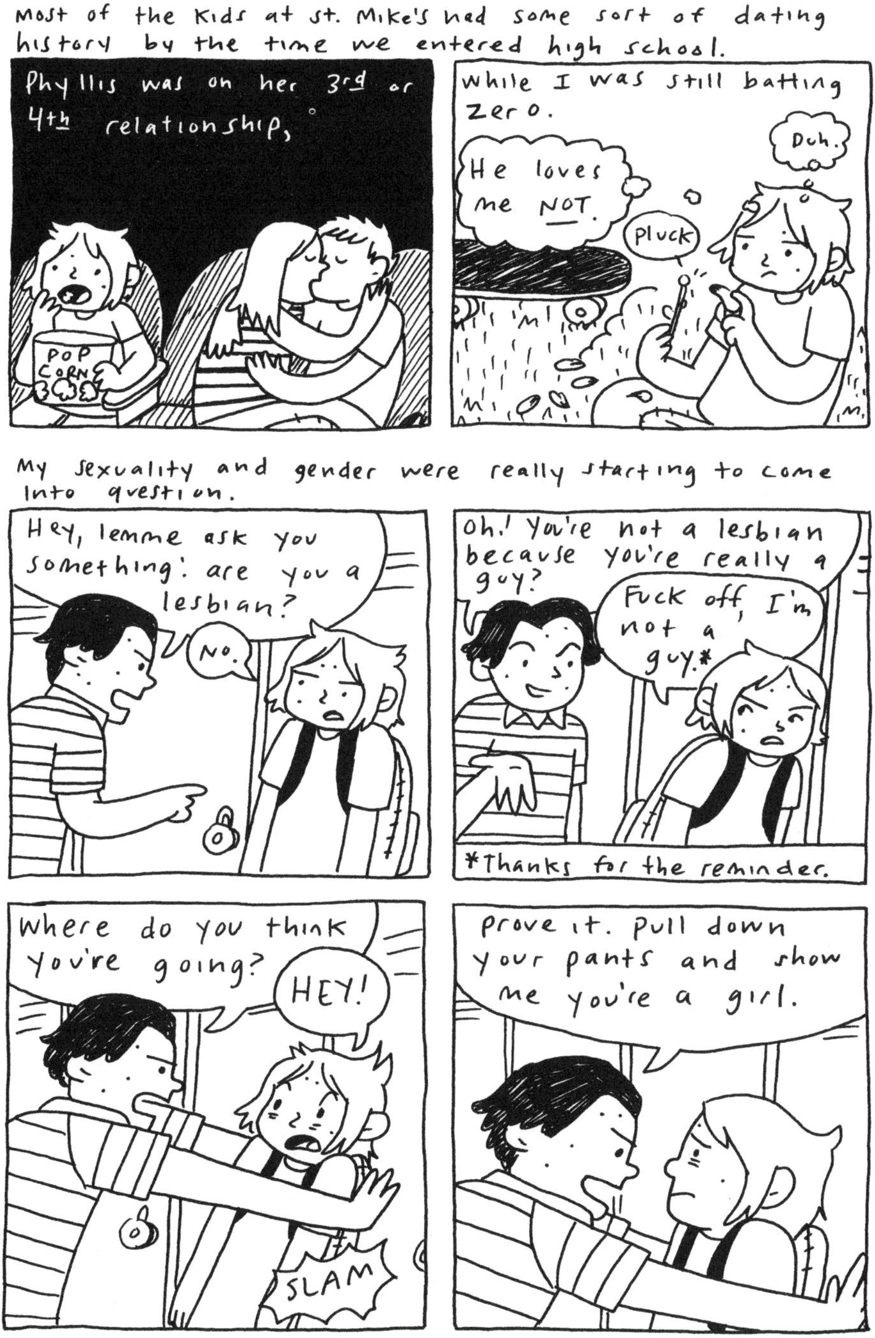
Most of the kids at St. Mike's had some sort of dating history by the time we entered high school.
Phyllis was on her 3rd or 4th relationship,
while I was still batting zero.
He loves me NOT.
PLUCK
Duh.
POP CORN
My sexuality and gender were really starting to come into question.
Hey, lemme ask you something: are you a lesbian?
No.
Oh! You're not a lesbian because you're really a guy?
Fuck off, I'm not a guy.*
*Thanks for the reminder.
Where do you think you're going?
HEY!
SLAM
Prove it. Pull down your pants and show me you're a girl.

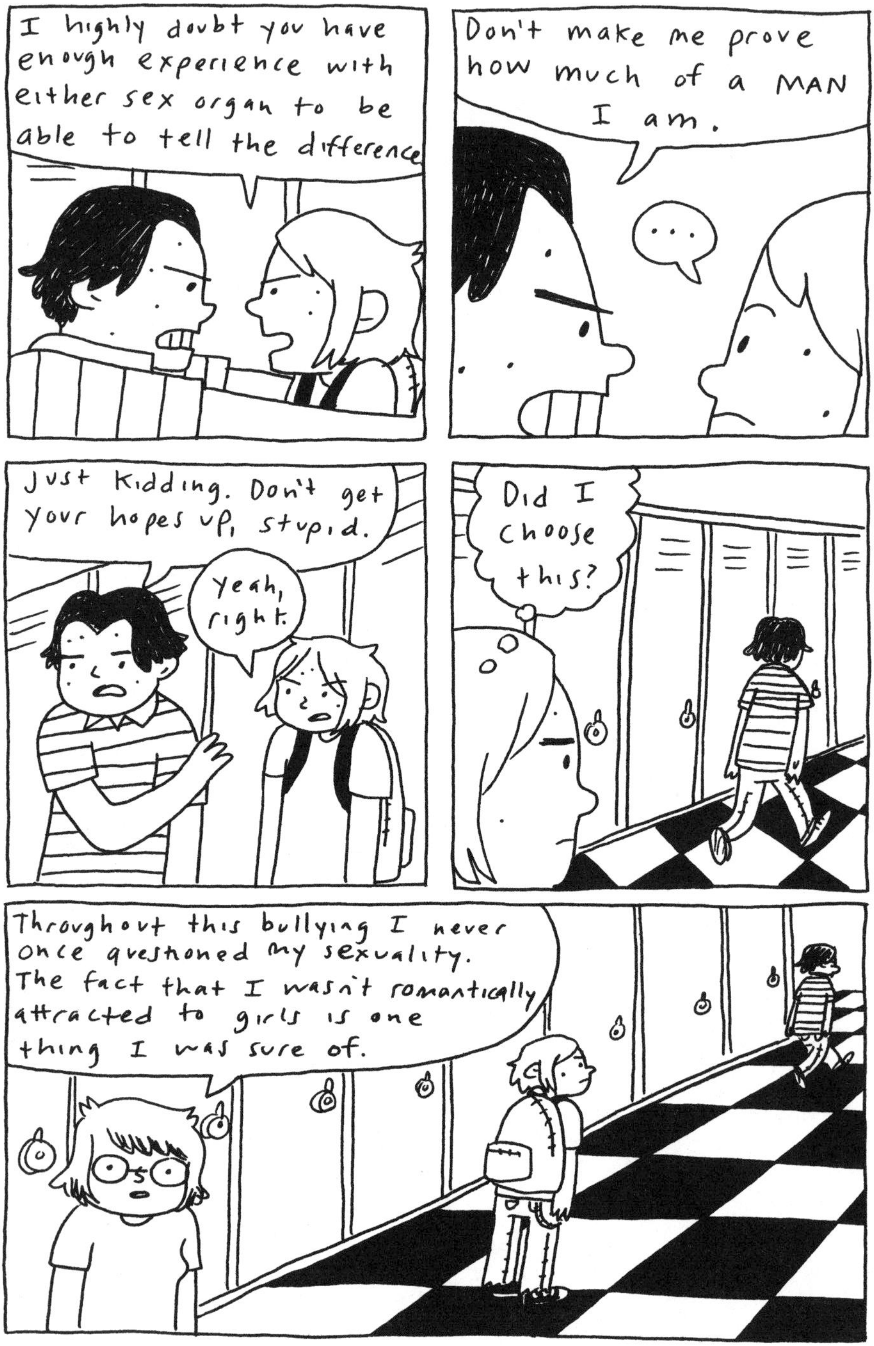
I highly doubt you have enough experience with either sex organ to be able to tell the difference
Don't make me prove how much of a MAN I am.
...
Just kidding. Don't get your hopes up, stupid.
Yeah, right.
Did I choose this?
Throughout this bullying I never once questioned my sexuality. The fact that I wasn't romantically attracted to girls is one thing I was sure of.

The stereotype of the butch lesbian has plagued me my whole life, but I don't dress like a boy to attract girls: I dress like a boy because it feels natural to me.

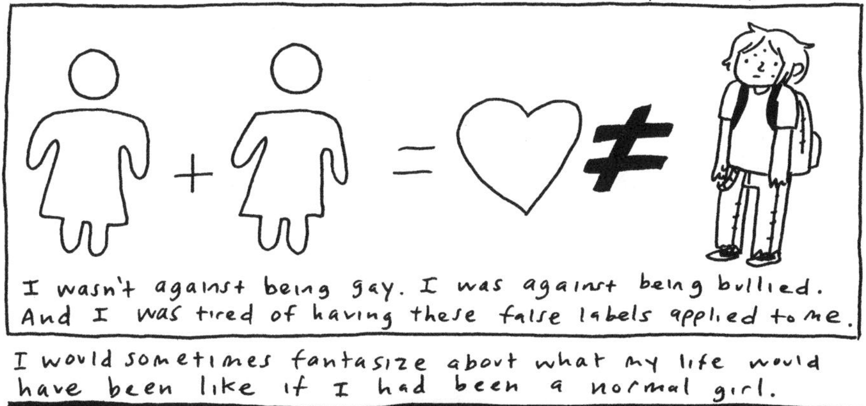
I wasn't against being gay. I was against being bullied.
And I was tired of having these false labels applied to me.

I would sometimes fantasize about what my life would have been like if I had been a normal girl.

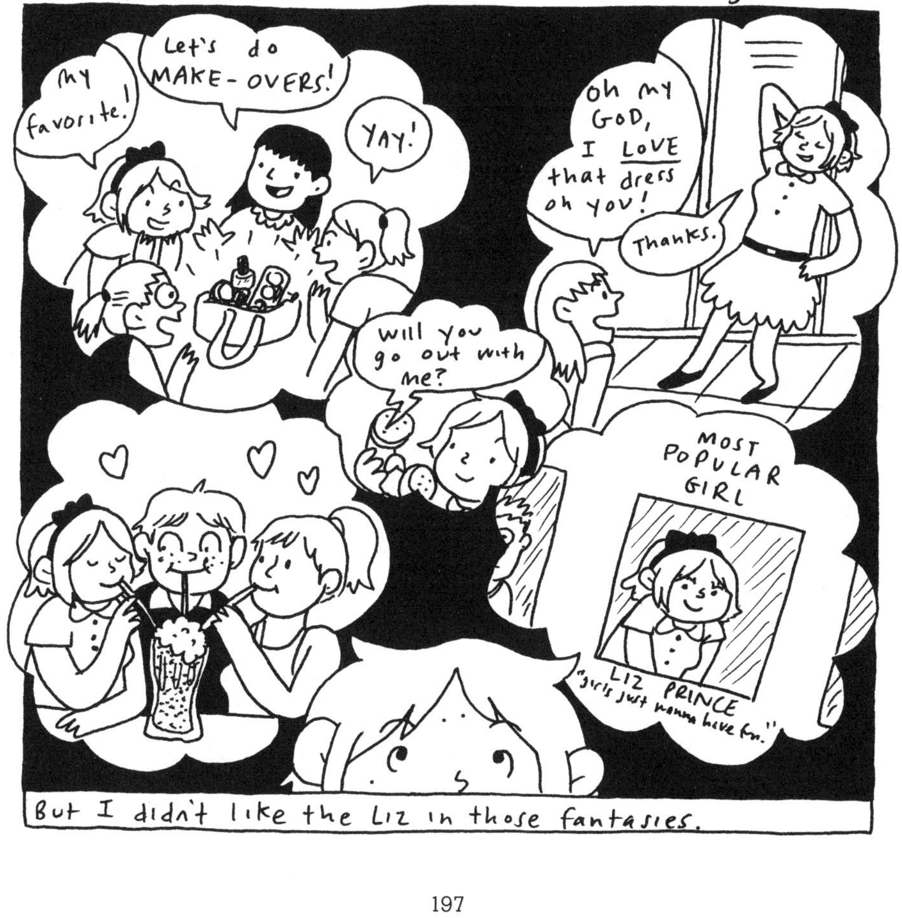
Let's do MAKE-OVERS!
My favorite!
YAY!
Oh my GOD, I LOVE that dress on you!
Thanks.
Will you go out with me?
MOST POPULAR GIRL
LIZ PRINCE
"girls just wanna have fun."
But I didn't like the Liz in those fantasies.

I liked the Liz that I was. Being a normal girl was just never an option for me.

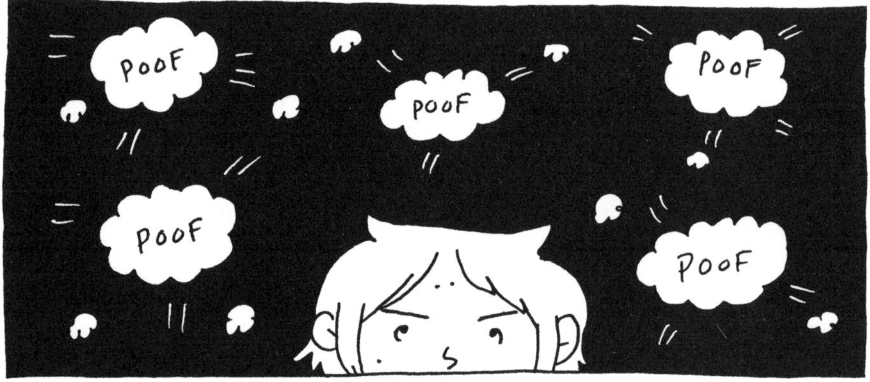
POOF
POOF
POOF
POOF
POOF

Instead of wearing me down, the teasing made me all the more desperate to avoid feminine things.

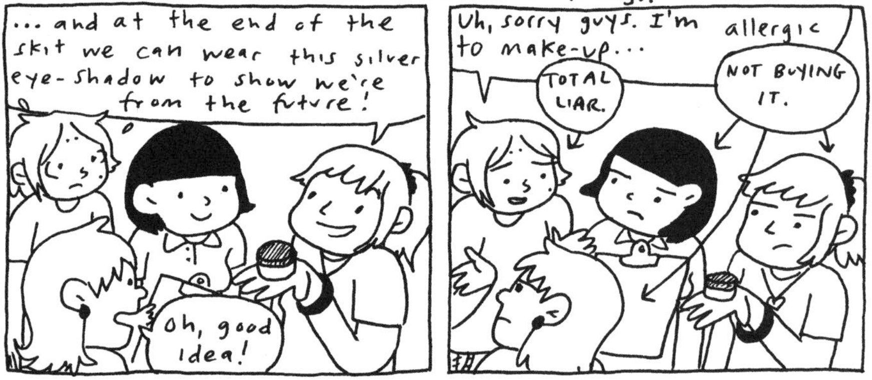
... and at the end of the skit we can wear this silver eye-shadow to show we're from the future!
Oh, good idea!
Uh, sorry guys. I'm allergic to make-up...
TOTAL LIAR.
NOT BUYING IT.

Even a new teacher mistook me for a boy.

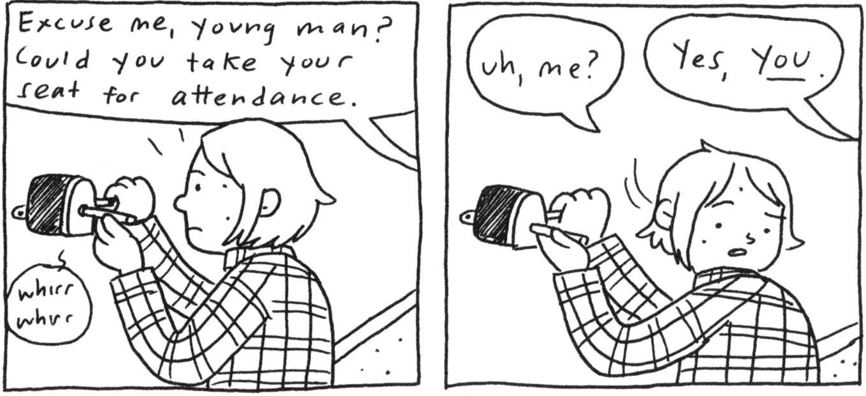
Excuse me, young man? Could you take your seat for attendance.
whirr whirr
uh, me?
Yes, YOU.

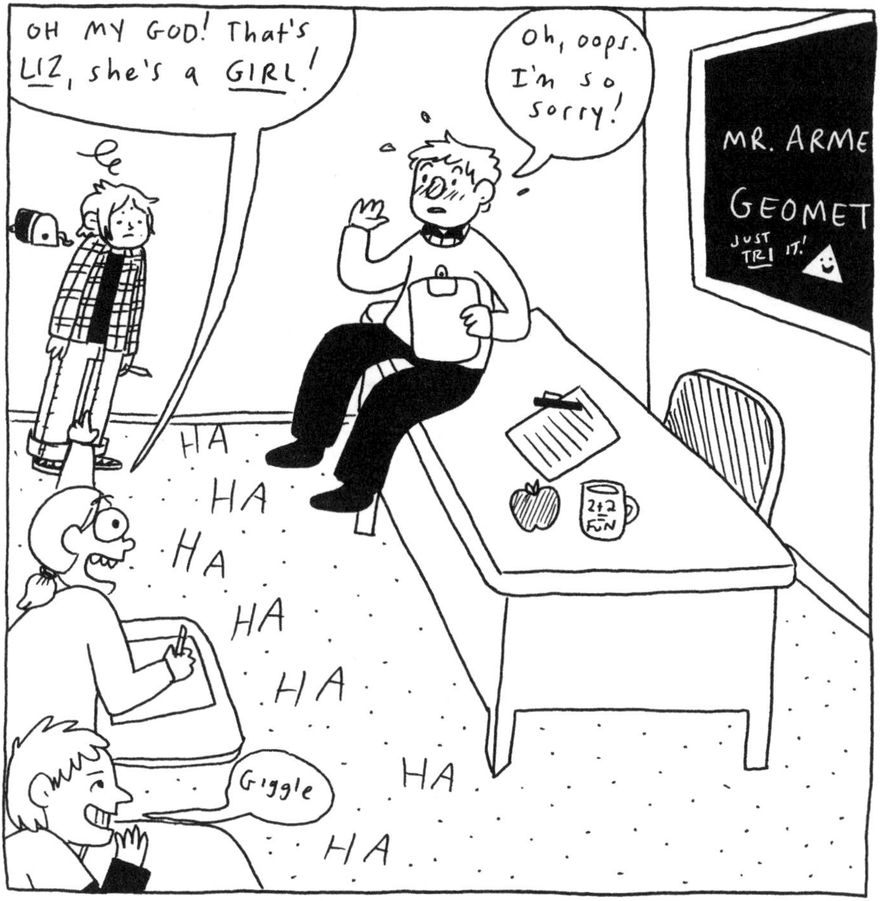
OH MY GOD! That's LIZ, she's a GIRL!
Oh, oops. I'm so sorry!
MR. ARME
GEOMET
JUST TRI IT!
2+2 = FUN
HA HA HA HA HA HA HA
Giggle

It seemed unlikely that I'd find a boy at St. Mike's oblivious enough of my reputation to date me.

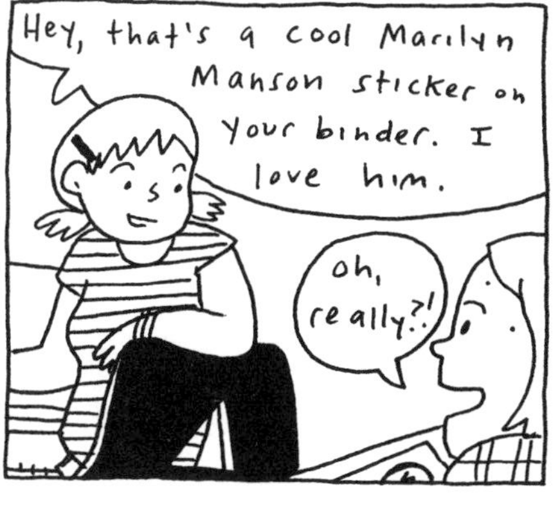
Hey, that's a cool Marilyn Manson sticker on your binder. I love him.
Oh, really?!

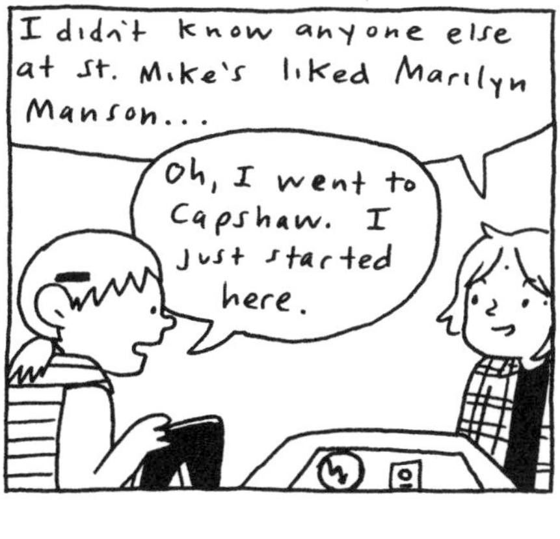
I didn't know anyone else at St. Mike's liked Marilyn Manson...
Oh, I went to Capshaw. I just started here.

Bree began hanging out with Phyllis and me. She had a mysterious past that intrigued us.

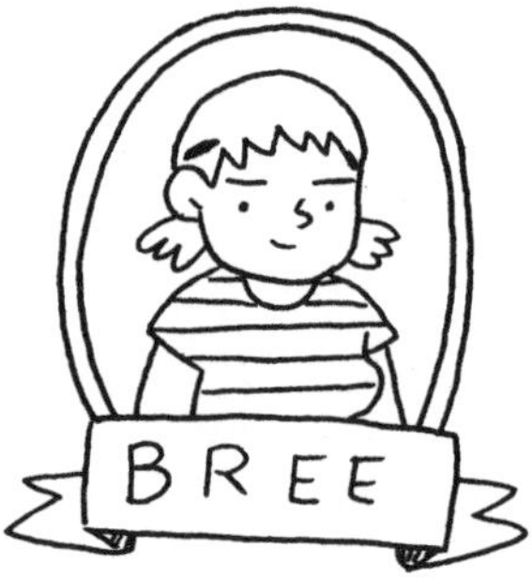
BREE

Stories she told us included:

* She's a recovering meth addict (ten years before Breaking Bad).
* She's in an on-again, off-again relationship with a 20-year-old.
* She was the most popular girl at Capshaw, and her best friend is Ian, the most popular boy at Santa Fe High.

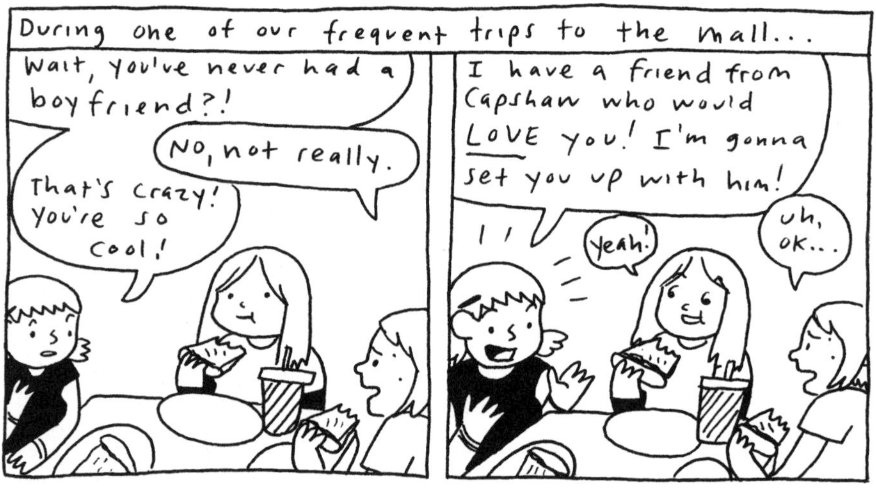
During one of our frequent trips to the mall...
Wait, you've never had a boyfriend?!
No, not really.
That's crazy! You're so cool!
I have a friend from Capshaw who would LOVE you! I'm gonna set you up with him!
Yeah!
Uh, ok...

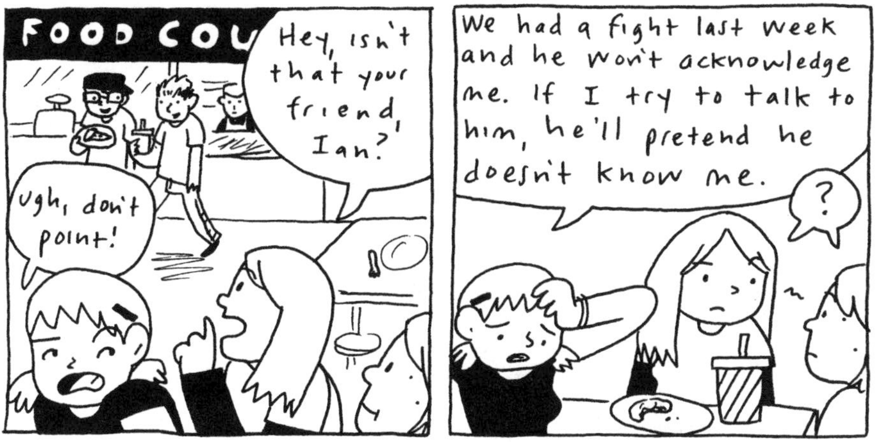
FOOD COU
Hey, isn't that your friend, Ian?
Ugh, don't point!
We had a fight last week and he won't acknowledge me. If I try to talk to him, he'll pretend he doesn't know me.
?

A few days later Bree's friend, Will, called me.

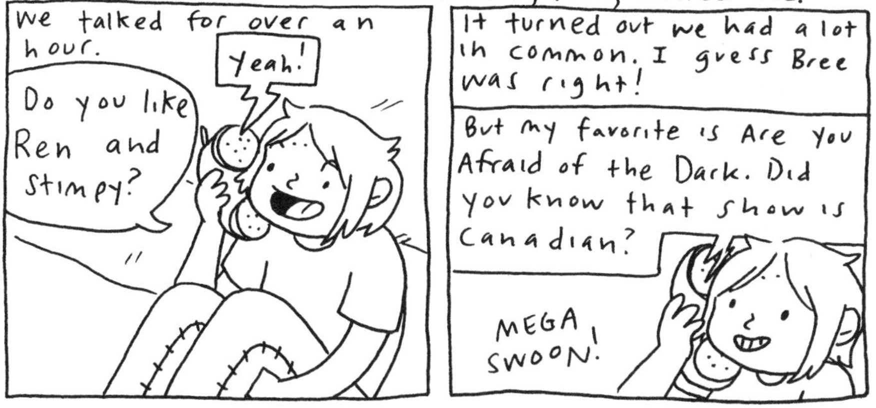
We talked for over an hour.
Do you like Ren and Stimpy?
Yeah!
It turned out we had a lot in common. I guess Bree was right!
But my favorite is Are you Afraid of the Dark. Did you know that show is Canadian?
MEGA SWOON!

Will suggested we meet at the mall that weekend: Phyllis would come as a date for Will's brother, and Bree would come because she was the facilitator.

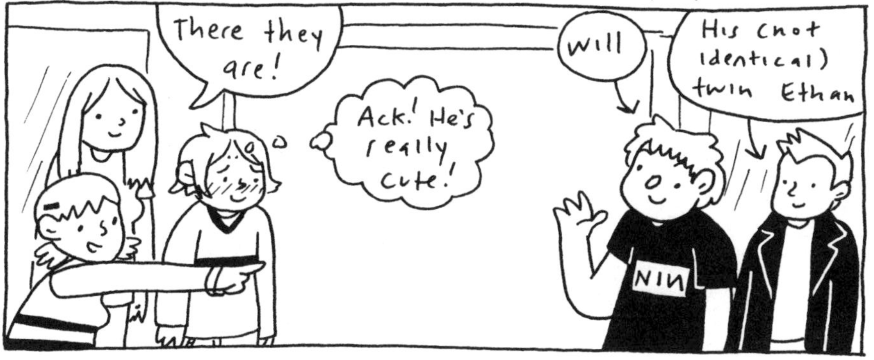
There they are!
Ack! He's really cute!
Will
His (not identical) twin Ethan
NIN

dear diary, For the first time in my life a boy I like likes me back! Will is my boyfriend! He's really cute and funny.

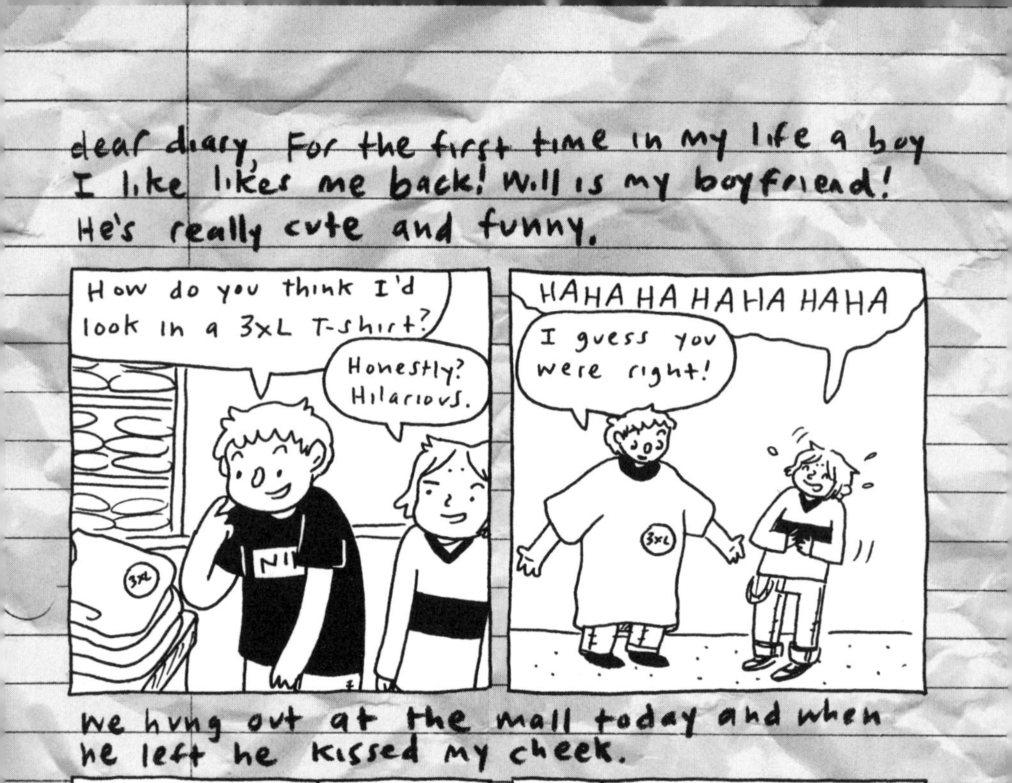
How do you think I'd look in a 3XL T-shirt?
Honestly? Hilarious.
3XL
HAHA HA HAHA HAHA
I guess you were right!
3XL

we hung out at the mall today and when he left he kissed my cheek.

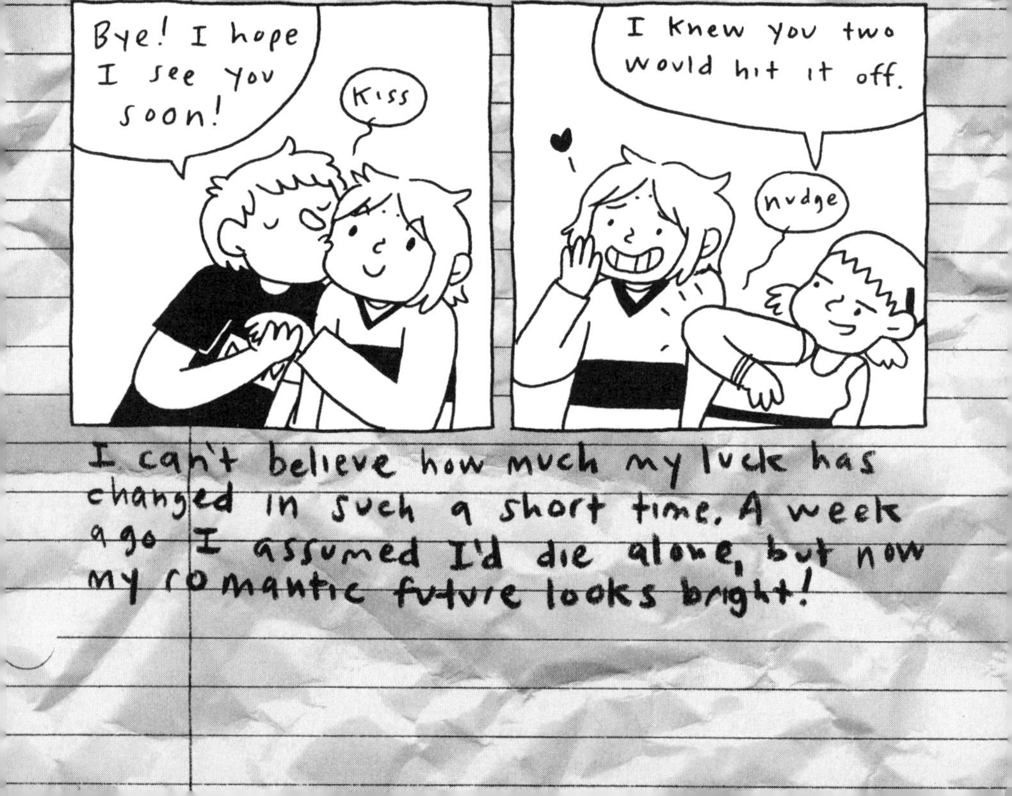
Bye! I hope I see you soon!
Kiss
I knew you two would hit it off.
nudge

I can't believe how much my luck has changed in such a short time. A week ago I assumed I'd die alone, but now my romantic future looks bright!

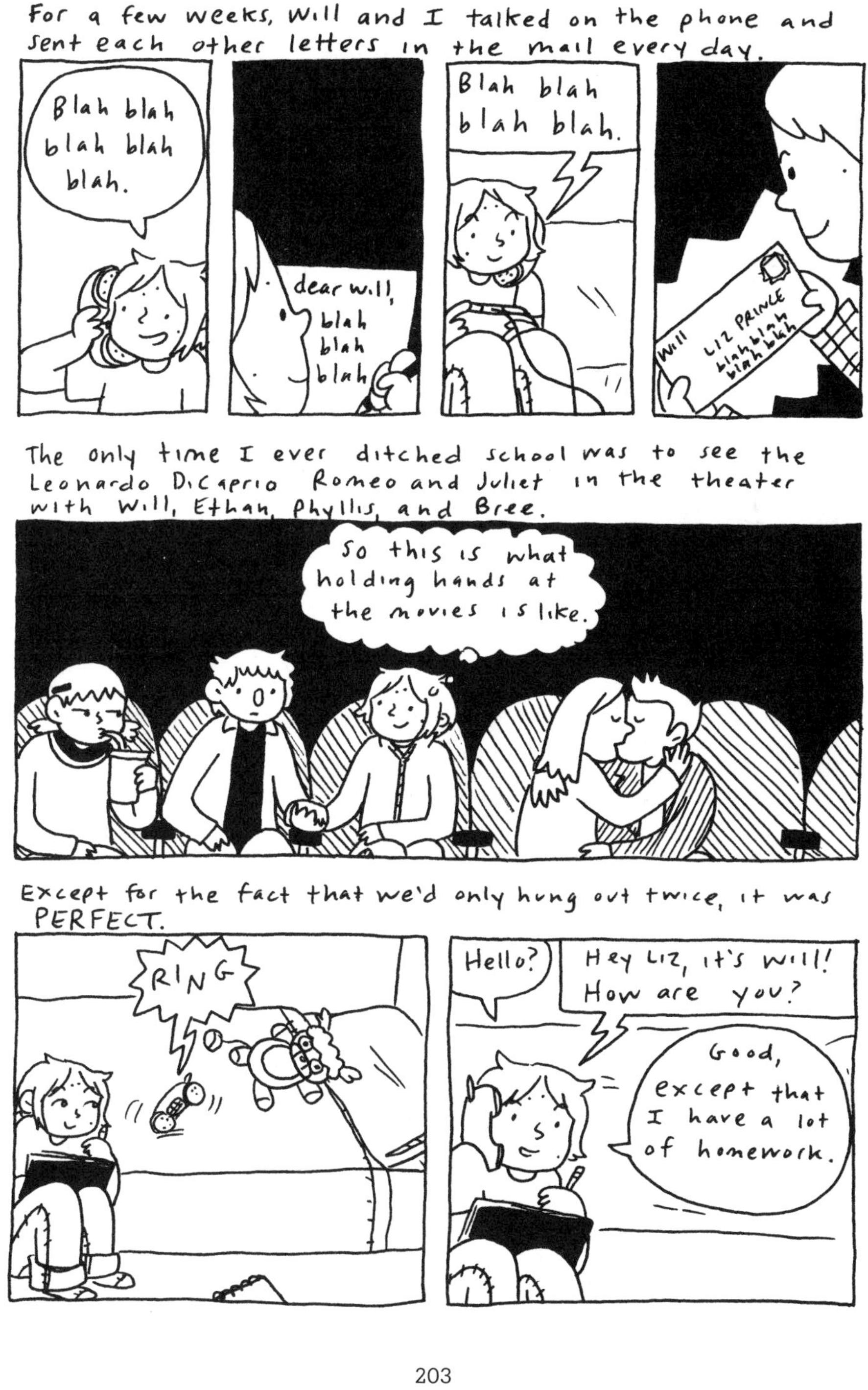
For a few weeks, Will and I talked on the phone and sent each other letters in the mail every day.
Blah blah blah blah blah.
dear will, blah blah blah
Blah blah blah blah.
LIZ PRINCE blah blah blah blah
Will
The only time I ever ditched school was to see the Leonardo DiCaprio Romeo and Juliet in the theater with Will, Ethan, Phyllis, and Bree.
So this is what holding hands at the movies is like.
Except for the fact that we'd only hung out twice, it was PERFECT.
RING
Hello?
Hey Liz, it's Will! How are you?
Good, except that I have a lot of homework.

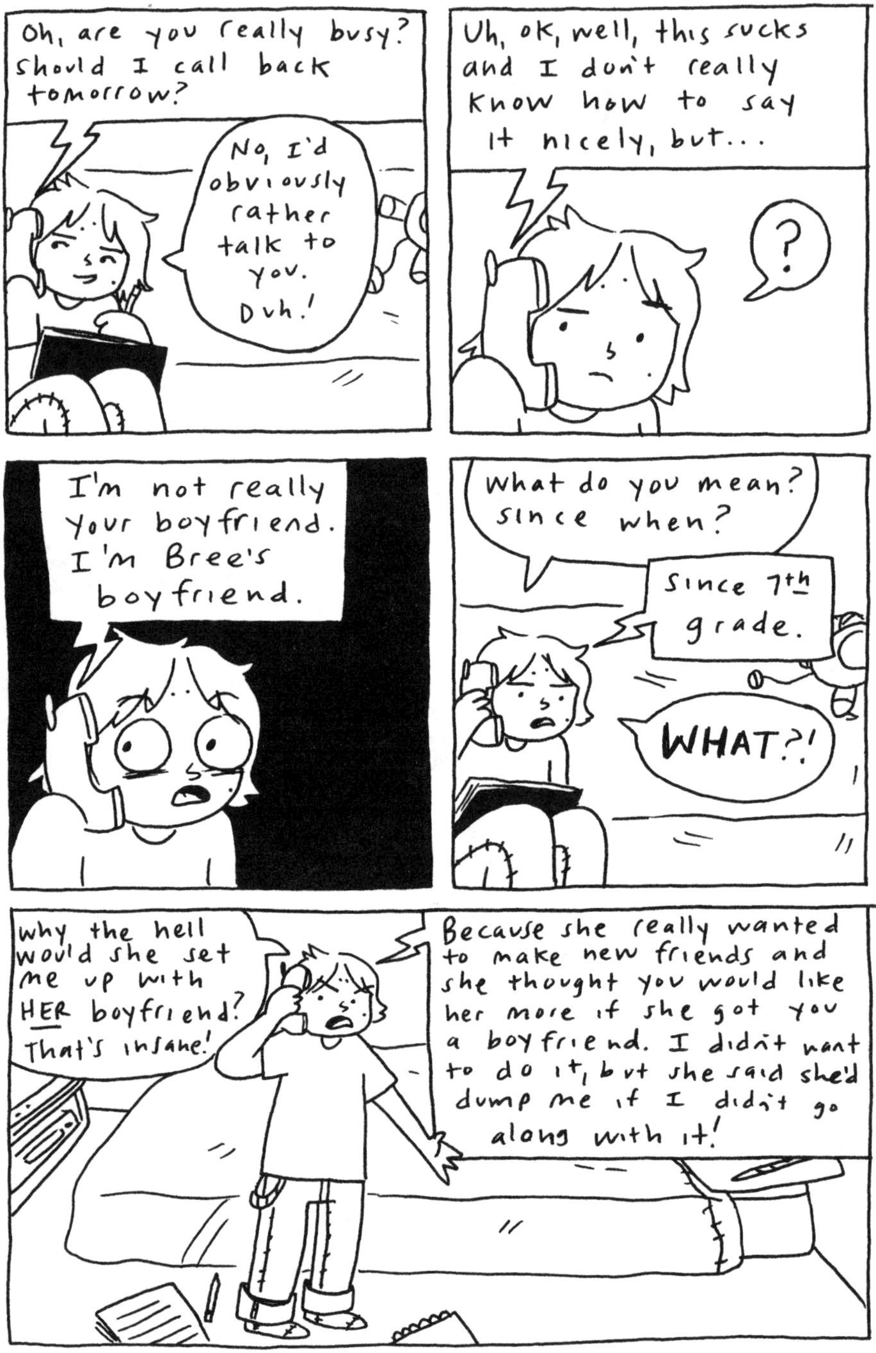

Oh, are you really busy? Should I call back tomorrow?
No, I'd obviously rather talk to you. Duh!
Uh, ok, well, this sucks and I don't really know how to say it nicely, but...
?
I'm not really your boyfriend. I'm Bree's boyfriend.
What do you mean? Since when?
Since 7th grade.
WHAT?!
Why the hell would she set me up with HER boyfriend? That's insane!
Because she really wanted to make new friends and she thought you would like her more if she got you a boyfriend. I didn't want to do it, but she said she'd dump me if I didn't go along with it!

I'm so humiliated, of course the only boyfriend I could get would be fake.

I feel really bad, I mean, she used BOTH of us, and she thought you wouldn't like me, but then you did and she got jealous and I tried to tell...

DIE!

The stupid thing is that I wouldn't even know Will if Bree hadn't introduced us. It's like she forced me to have a crush on him just so she could take it away. I guess what I thought all along is true: NO BOY WILL EVER LIKE ME.

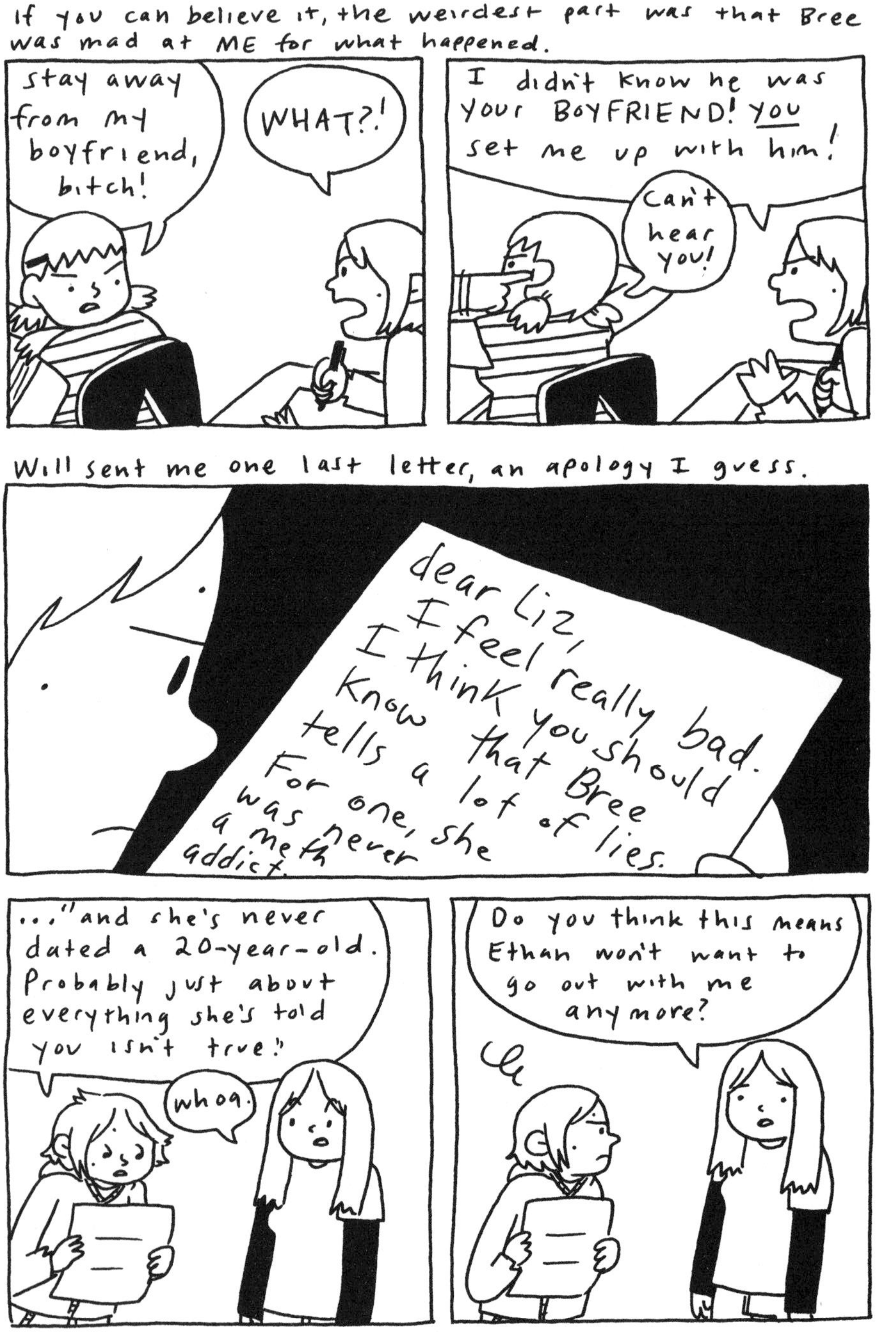

If you can believe it, the weirdest part was that Bree was mad at ME for what happened.
Stay away from my boyfriend, bitch!
WHAT?!
I didn't know he was your BOYFRIEND! YOU set me up with him!
Can't hear you!
Will sent me one last letter, an apology I guess.
dear Liz,
I feel really bad.
I think you should know that Bree tells a lot of lies.
For one, she was never a meth addict.
..."and she's never dated a 20-year-old. Probably just about everything she's told you isn't true."
whoa.
Do you think this means Ethan won't want to go out with me anymore?

CHAPTER 11

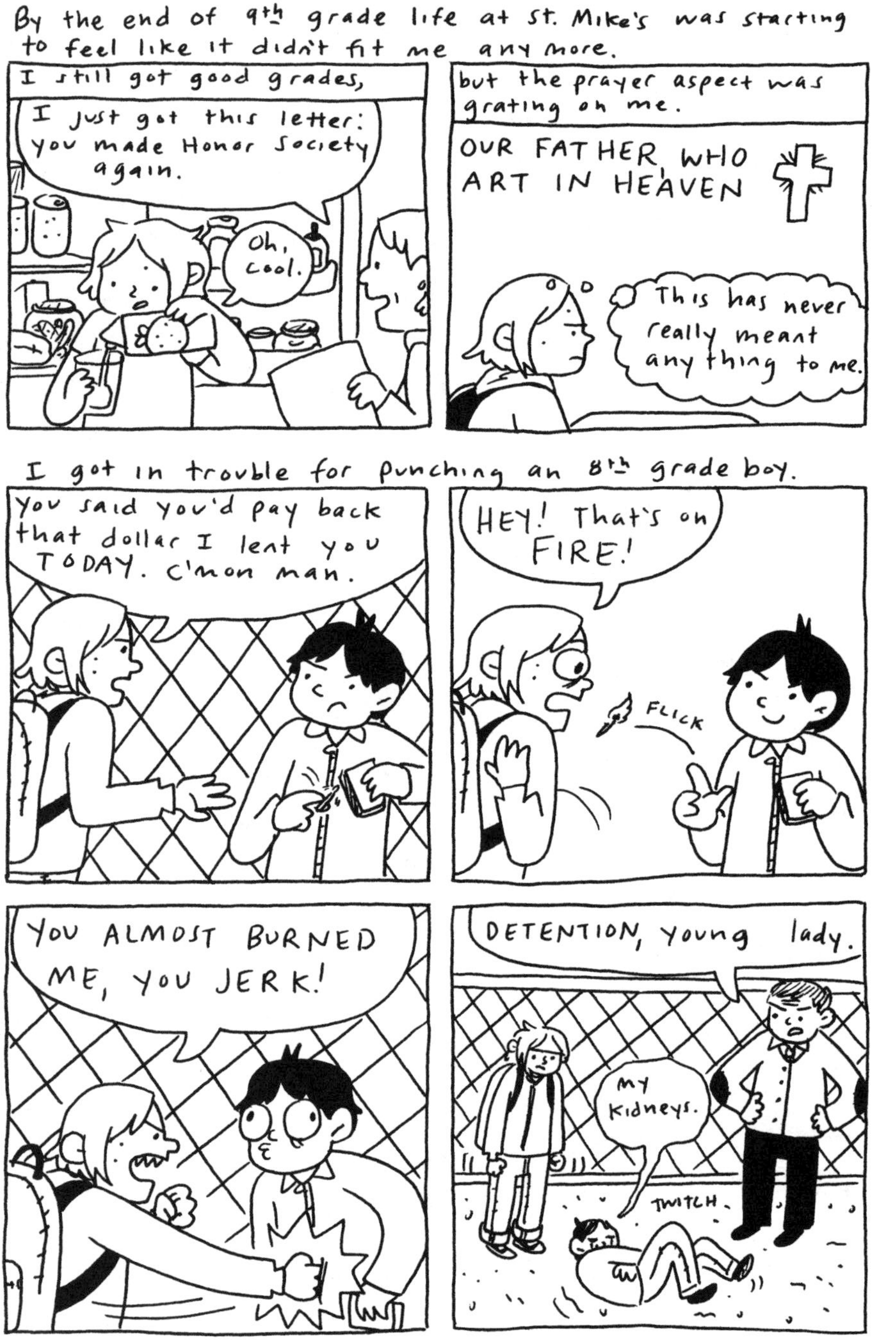
By the end of 9th grade life at St. Mike's was starting to feel like it didn't fit me any more.
I still got good grades,
I just got this letter: you made Honor Society again.
Oh, cool.
but the prayer aspect was grating on me.
OUR FATHER WHO ART IN HEAVEN
This has never really meant anything to me.
I got in trouble for punching an 8th grade boy.
You said you'd pay back that dollar I lent you TODAY. C'mon man.
HEY! That's on FIRE!
FLICK
YOU ALMOST BURNED ME, YOU JERK!
DETENTION, young lady.
My kidneys.
TWITCH

then drug dogs found pot in Phyllis' locker.

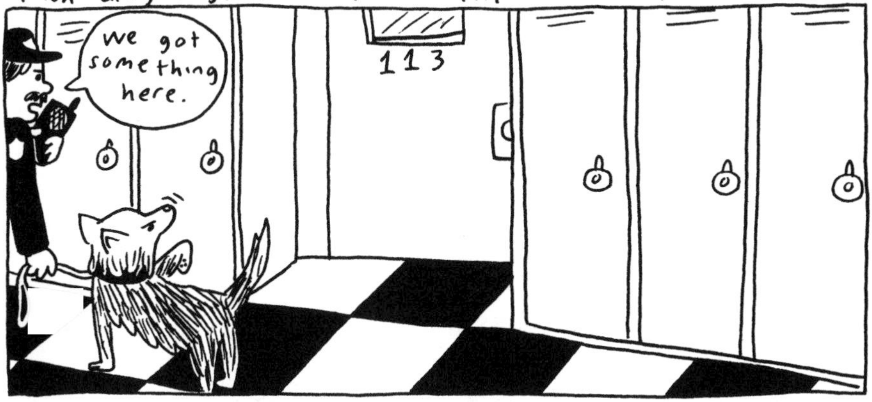
113
we got something here.

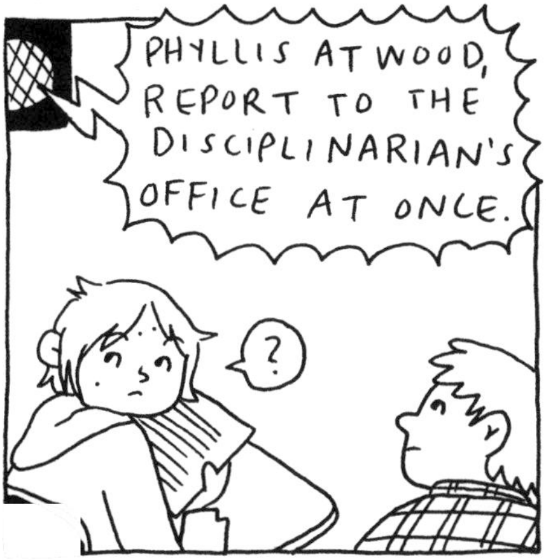
PHYLLIS ATWOOD, REPORT TO THE DISCIPLINARIAN'S OFFICE AT ONCE.
?

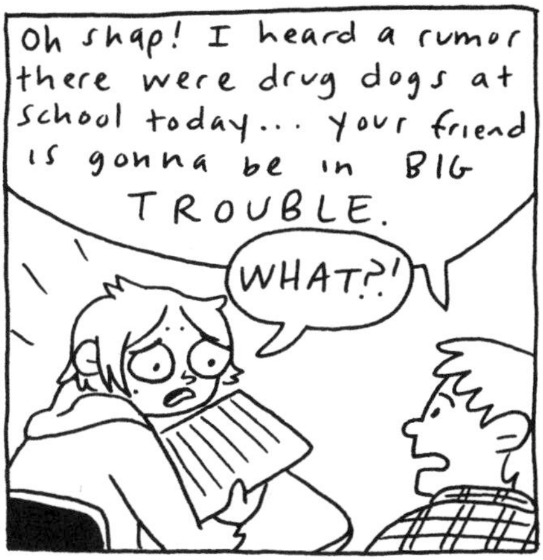
Oh snap! I heard a rumor there were drug dogs at school today... your friend is gonna be in BIG TROUBLE.
WHAT?!

she was in BIG TROUBLE, but somehow she didn't get expelled. Instead she was suspended for two weeks and grounded for much longer.

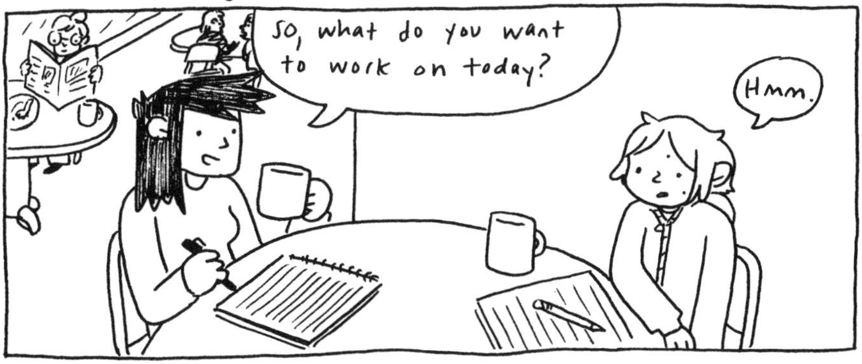
So, what do you want to work on today?
Hmm.

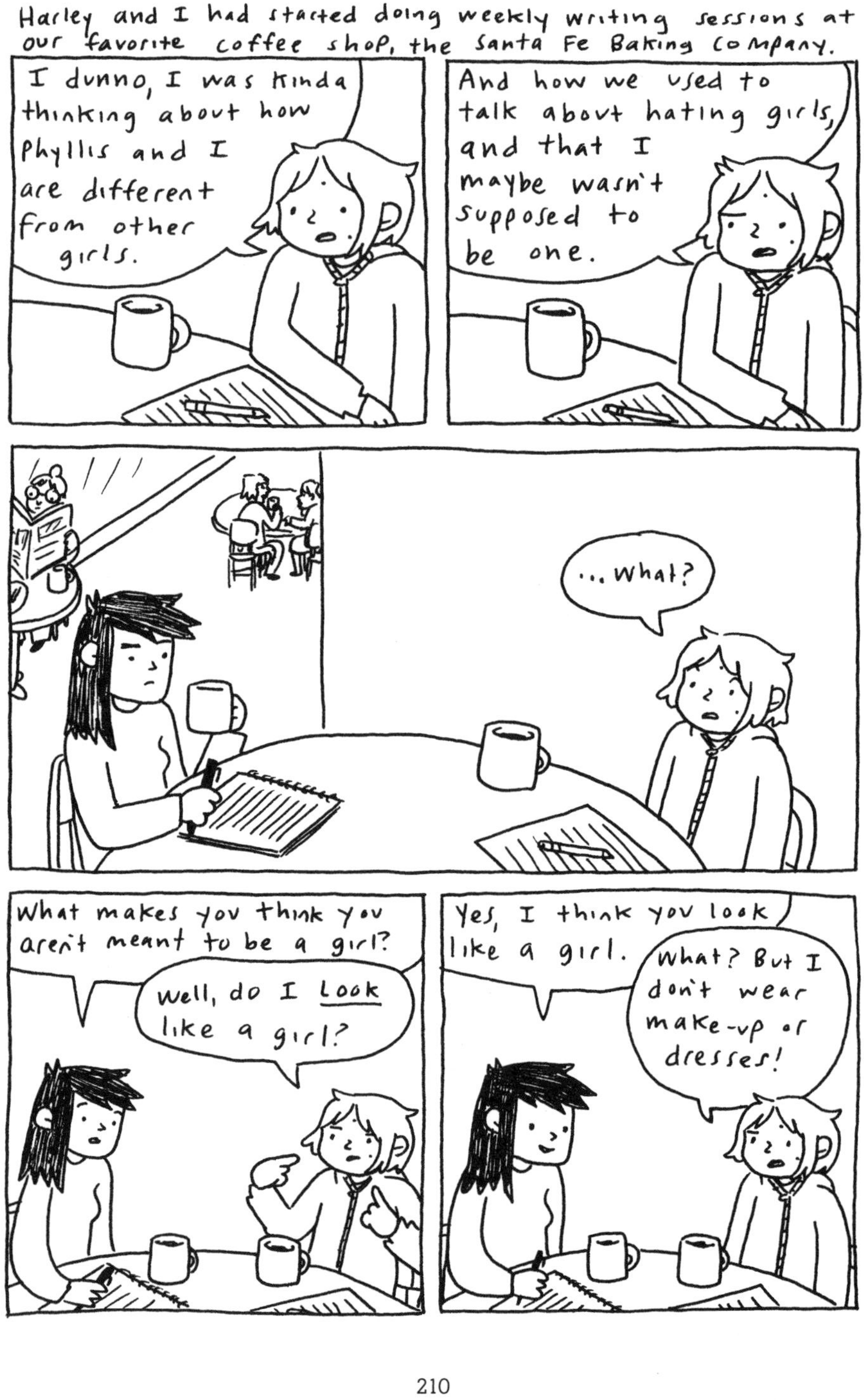
Harley and I had started doing weekly writing sessions at our favorite coffee shop, the Santa Fe Baking Company.
I dunno, I was kinda thinking about how Phyllis and I are different from other girls.
And how we used to talk about hating girls, and that I maybe wasn't supposed to be one.
...What?
What makes you think you aren't meant to be a girl?
Well, do I LOOK like a girl?
Yes, I think you look like a girl.
What? But I don't wear make-up or dresses!

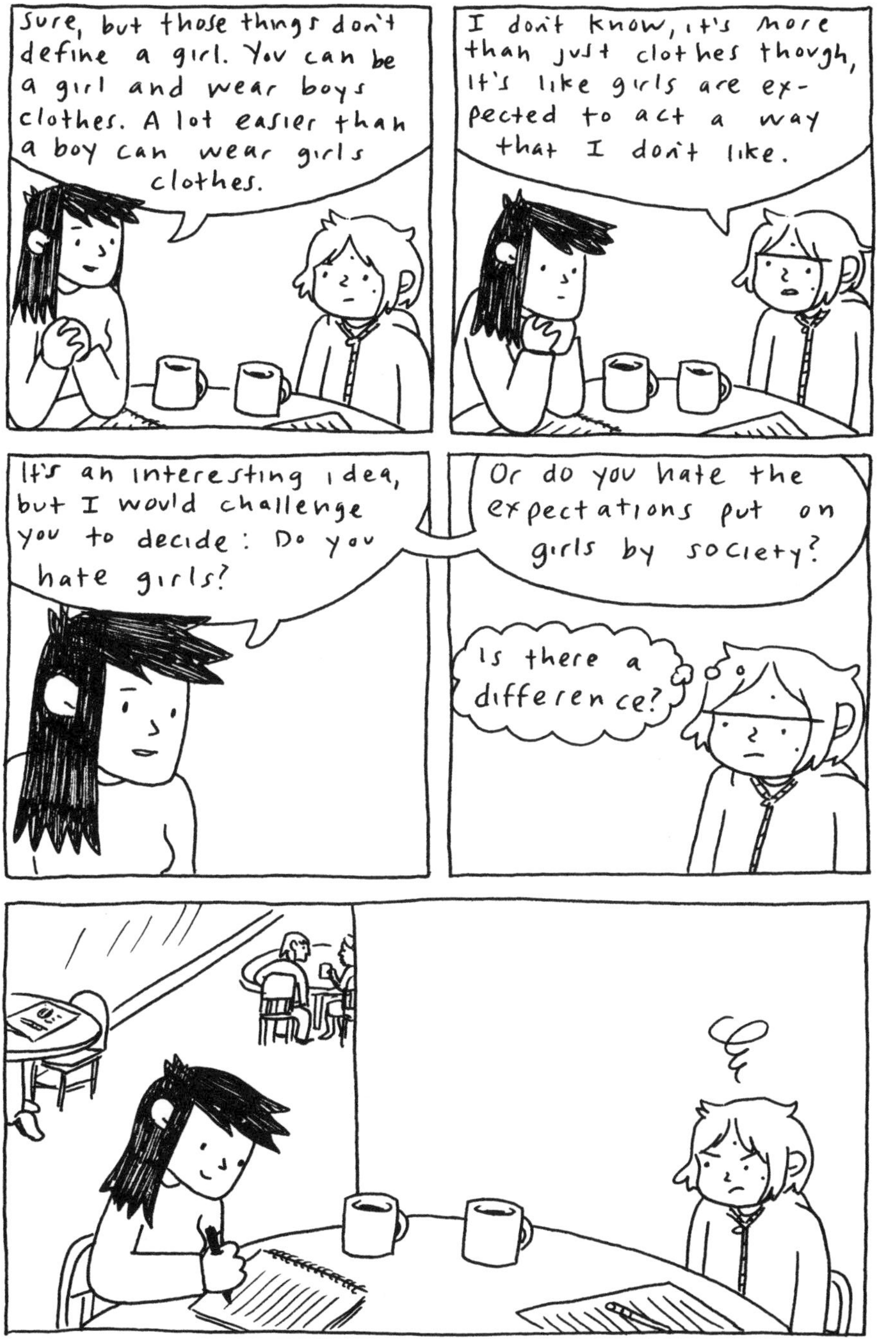
Sure, but those things don't define a girl. You can be a girl and wear boys clothes. A lot easier than a boy can wear girls clothes.
I don't know, it's more than just clothes though, It's like girls are expected to act a way that I don't like.
It's an interesting idea, but I would challenge you to decide: Do you hate girls?
Or do you hate the expectations put on girls by society?
Is there a difference?

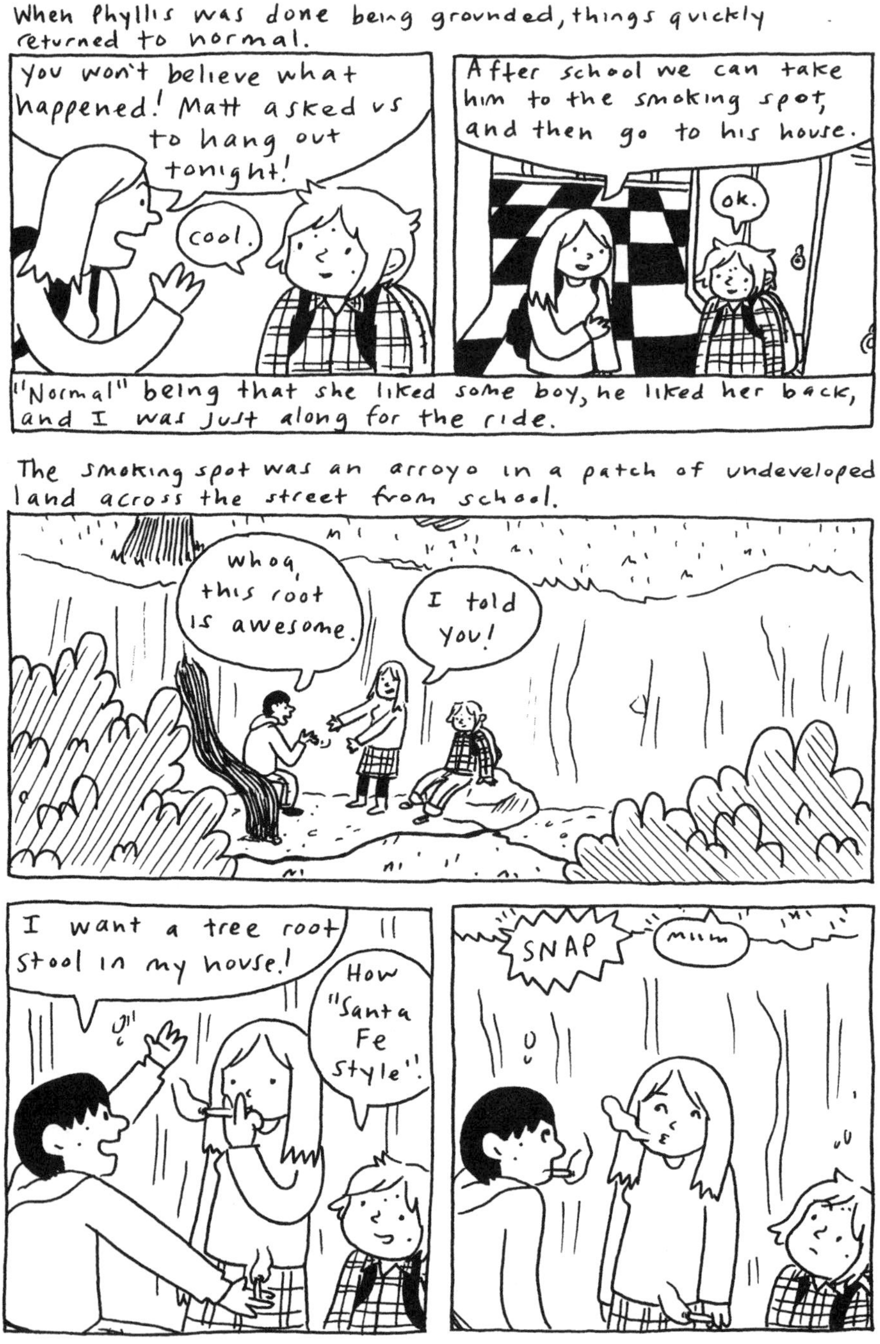

When Phyllis was done being grounded, things quickly returned to normal.
You won't believe what happened! Matt asked us to hang out tonight!
cool.
After school we can take him to the smoking spot, and then go to his house.
ok.
"Normal" being that she liked some boy, he liked her back, and I was just along for the ride.
The smoking spot was an arroyo in a patch of undeveloped land across the street from school.
Whoa, this root is awesome.
I told you!
I want a tree root stool in my house!
How "Santa Fe Style"!
SNAP

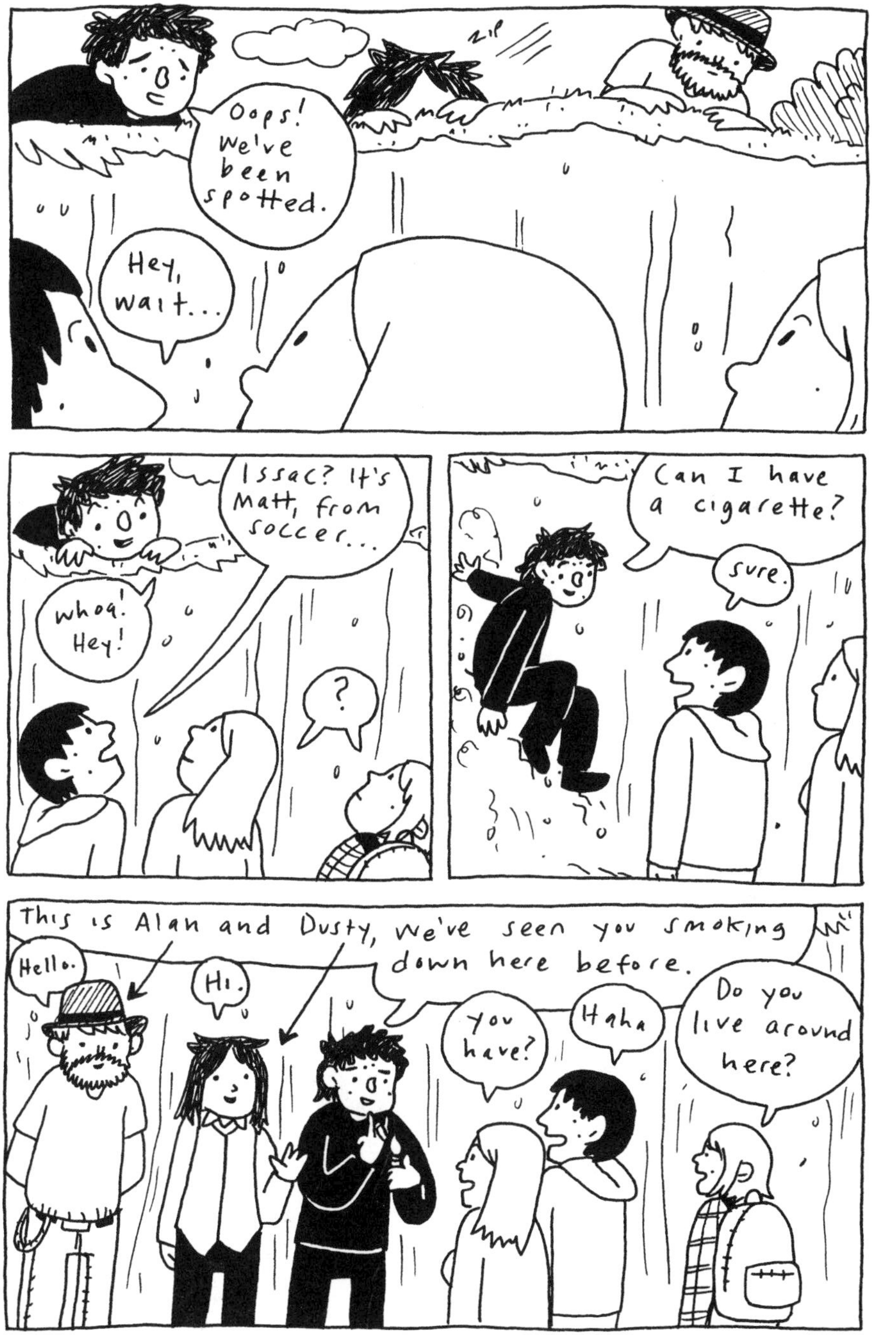
zip
Oops! We've been spotted.
Hey, wait...
Issac? It's Matt, from soccer...
whoa! Hey!
?
Can I have a cigarette?
sure.
This is Alan and Dusty, we've seen you smoking down here before.
Hello.
Hi.
you have?
Haha
Do you live around here?

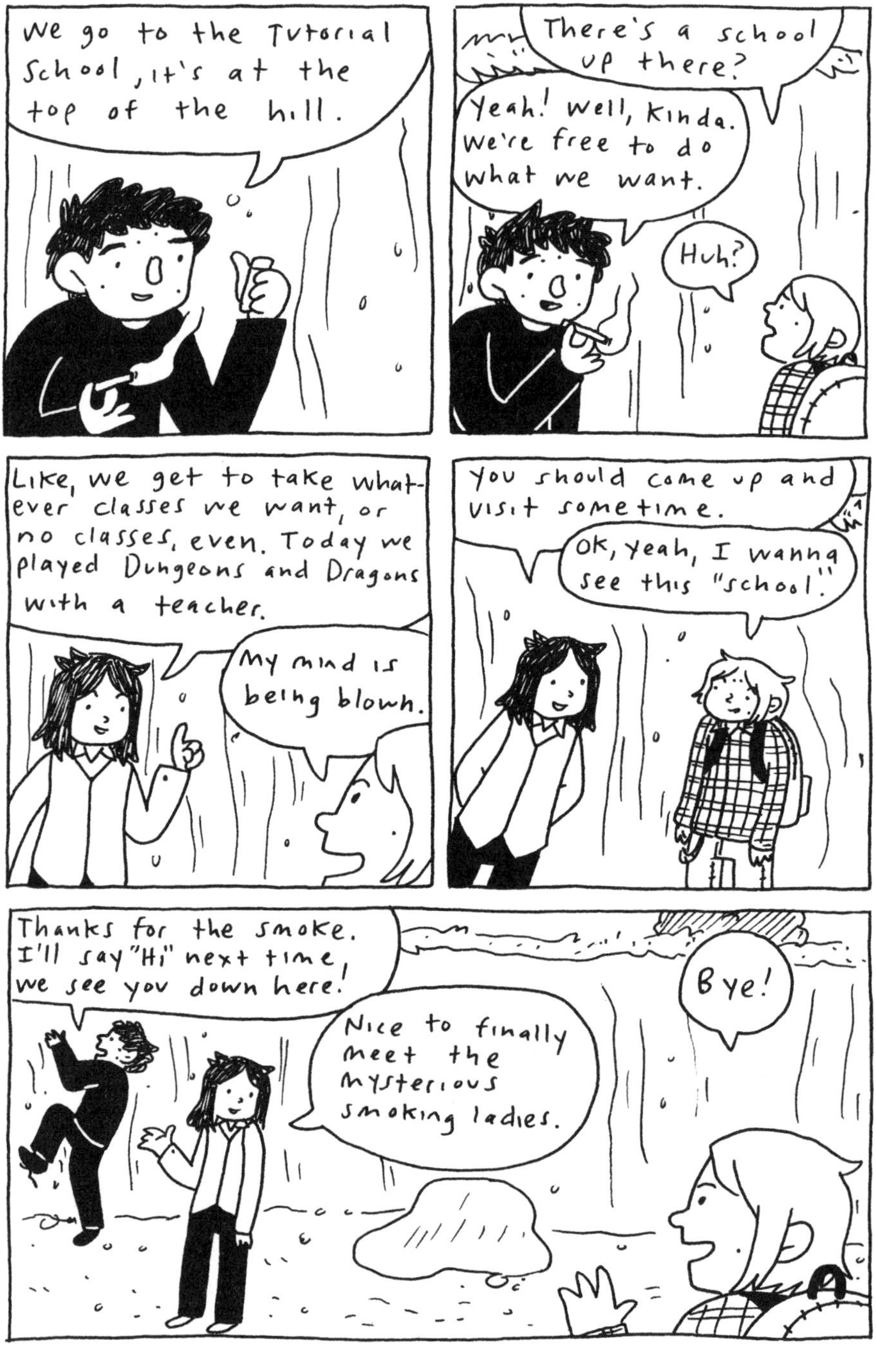
We go to the Tutorial School, it's at the top of the hill.
There's a school up there?
Yeah! Well, kinda. We're free to do what we want.
Huh?
Like, we get to take whatever classes we want, or no classes, even. Today we played Dungeons and Dragons with a teacher.
My mind is being blown.
You should come up and visit sometime.
Ok, yeah, I wanna see this "school".
Thanks for the smoke. I'll say "Hi" next time we see you down here!
Nice to finally meet the mysterious smoking ladies.
Bye!

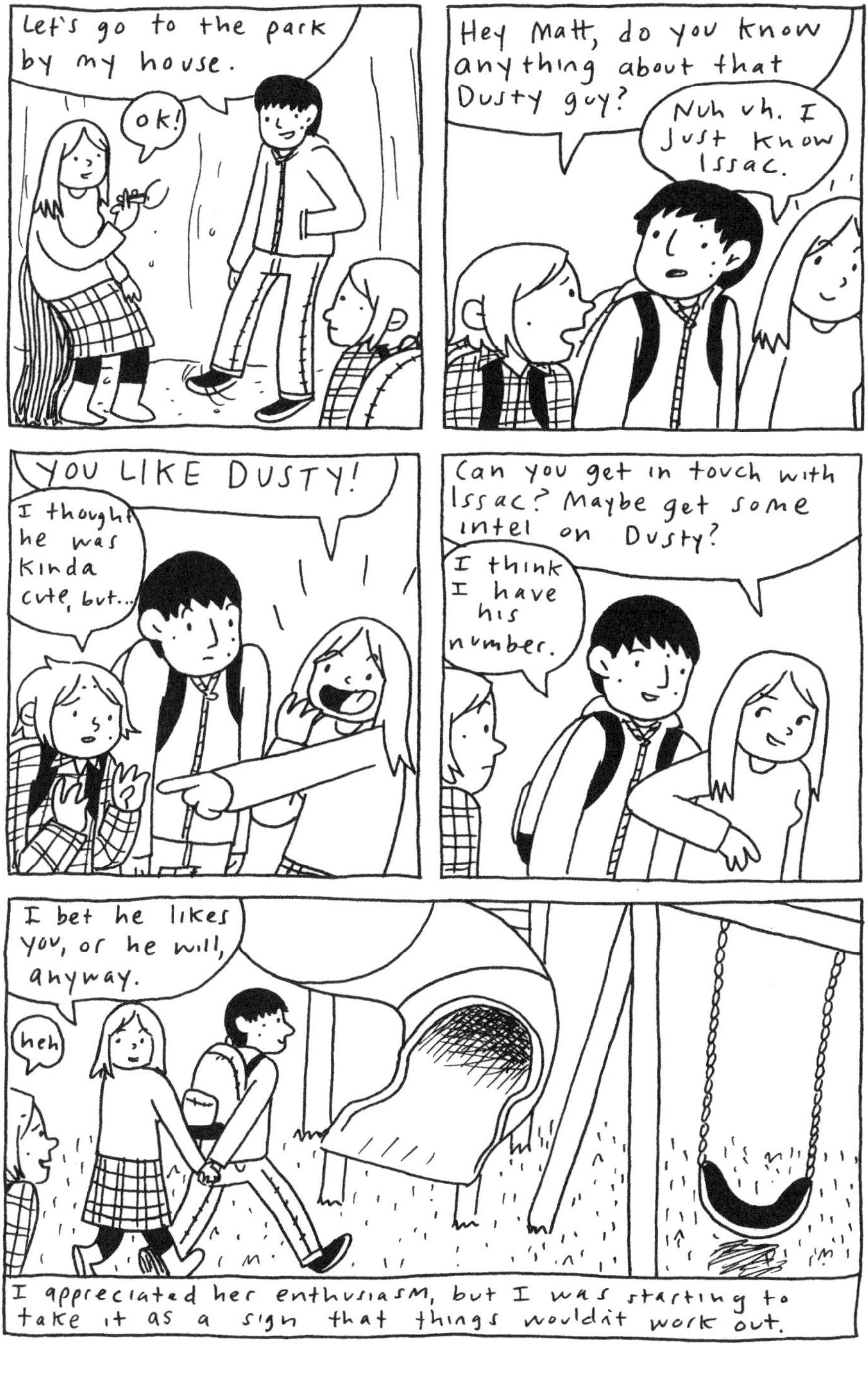

Let's go to the park by my house.
ok!
Hey Matt, do you know anything about that Dusty guy?
Nuh uh. I just know Issac.
YOU LIKE DUSTY!
I thought he was kinda cute, but...
Can you get in touch with Issac? Maybe get some intel on Dusty?
I think I have his number.
I bet he likes you, or he will, anyway.
heh
I appreciated her enthusiasm, but I was starting to take it as a sign that things wouldn't work out.

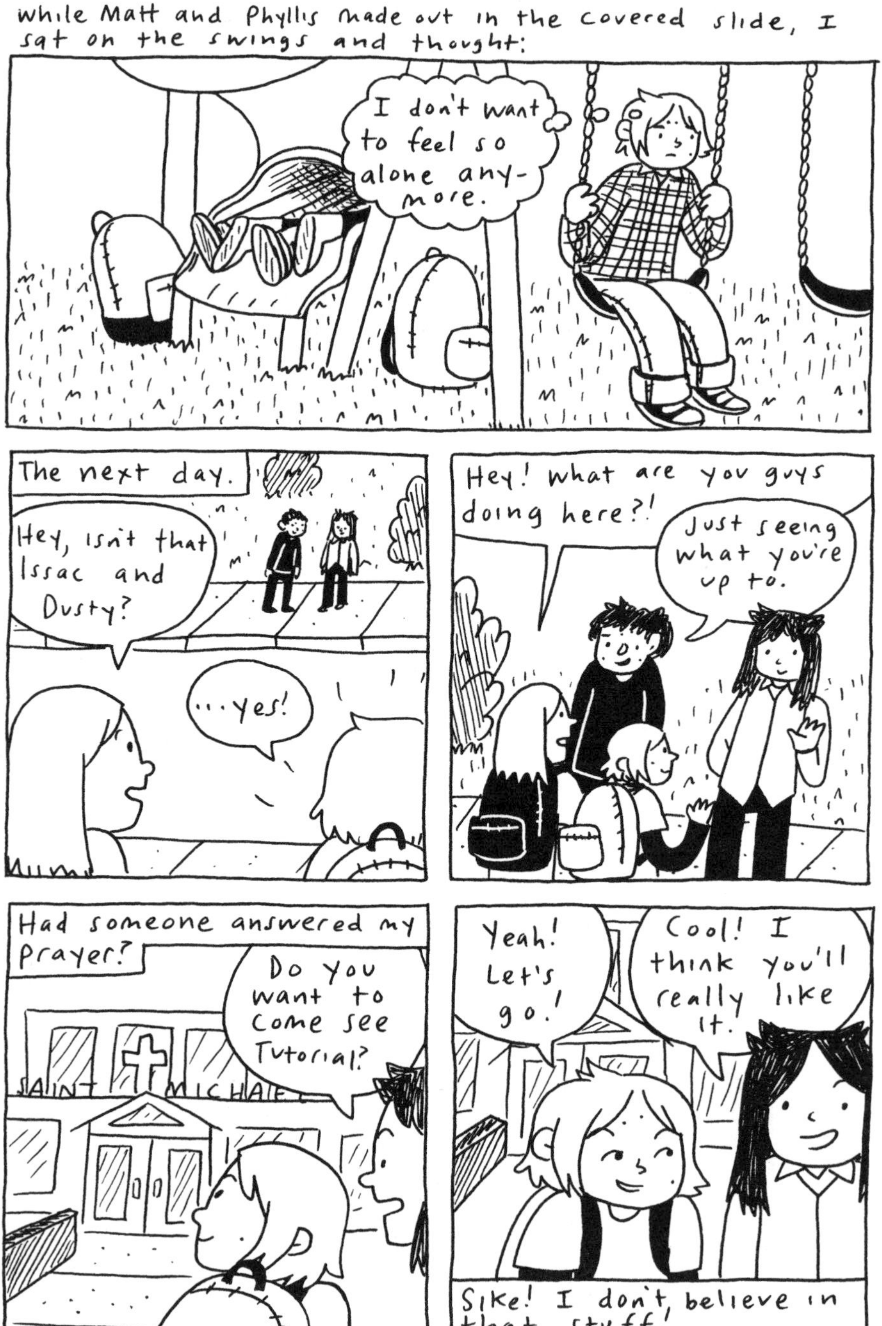
While Matt and Phyllis made out in the covered slide, I sat on the swings and thought:
I don't want to feel so alone any-more.
The next day.
Hey, isn't that Issac and Dusty?
...yes!
Hey! What are you guys doing here?!
Just seeing what you're up to.
Had someone answered my prayer?
Do you want to come see Tutorial?
SAINT MICHAEL
Yeah! Let's go!
Cool! I think you'll really like it.
Sike! I don't believe in that stuff!

CHAPTER 12

dear diary, I am beyond excited that school is over! my last year at St. Mike's! I can't believe my parents are letting me go to Tutorial next year. I'm going to a new school with a new boyfriend!

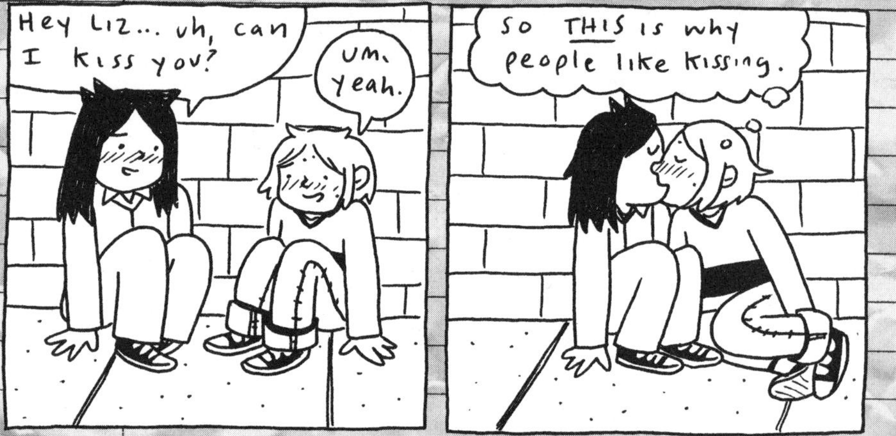
Hey Liz... uh, can I kiss you?
Um, yeah.
So THIS is why people like kissing.

So far we've been dating for a month and it hasn't turned out to be a hoax. It's been great! The only annoying thing is that I'm already feeling pressured into sex stuff, but not by Dusty.

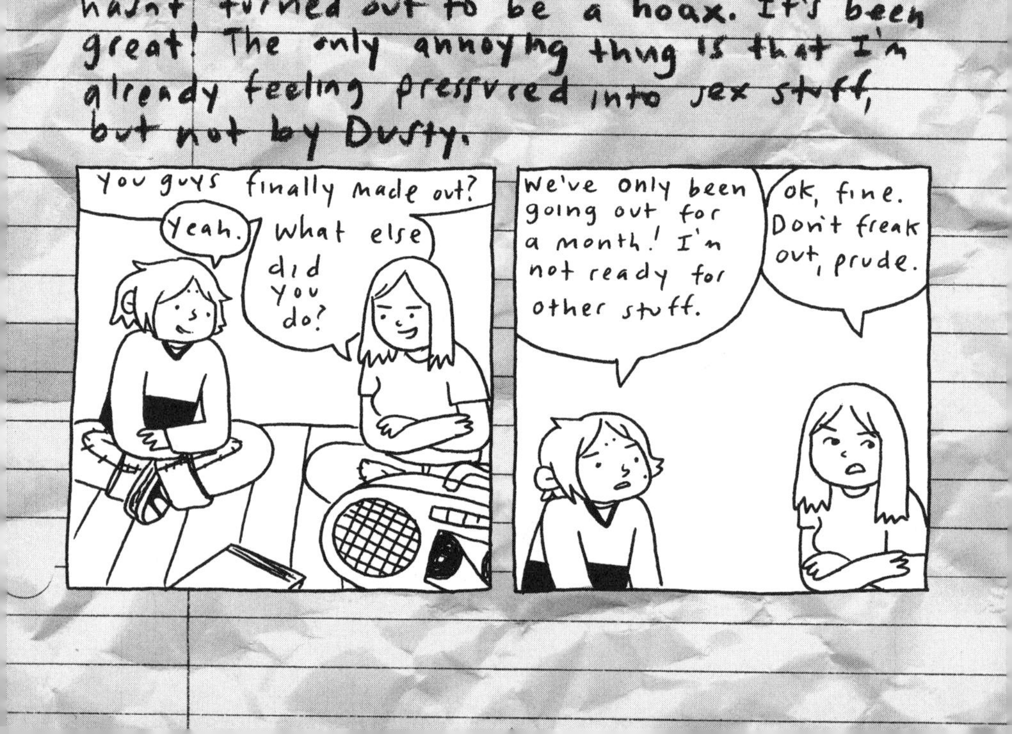
You guys finally made out?
Yeah.
What else did you do?
We've only been going out for a month! I'm not ready for other stuff.
Ok, fine. Don't freak out, prude.

Phyllis and I have been sneaking out a lot when I sleep over. It was really scary the first few times.

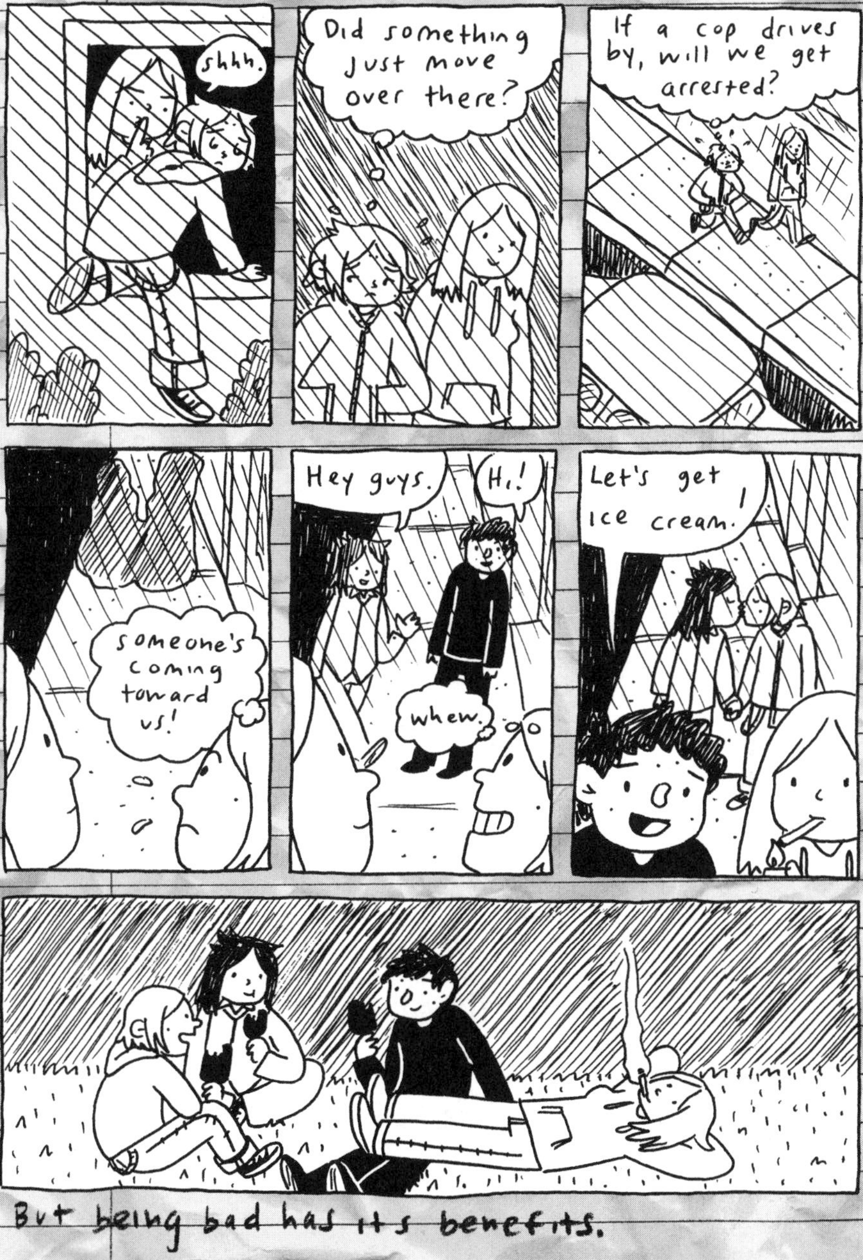
shhh.
Did something just move over there?
If a cop drives by, will we get arrested?
someone's coming toward us!
Hey guys.
Hi!
whew.
Let's get ice cream!

But being bad has its benefits.

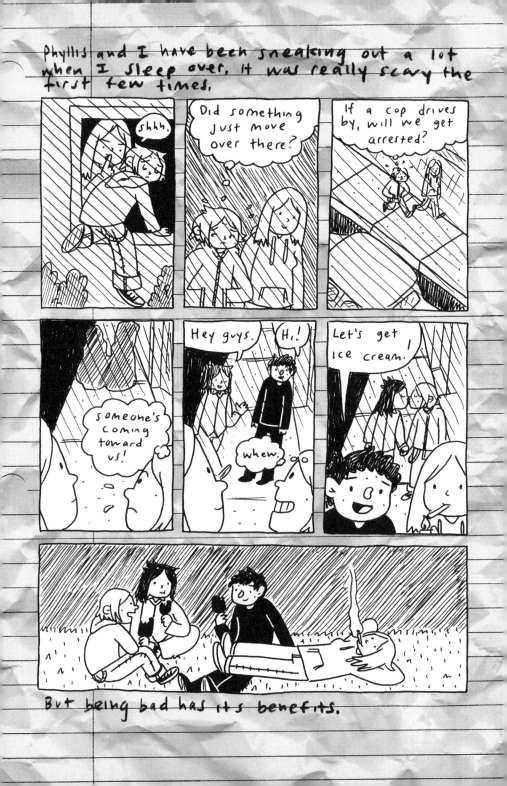

I was on a roll, everything was coming up Liz, and right before my 16th birthday another of my lifelong dreams came true.

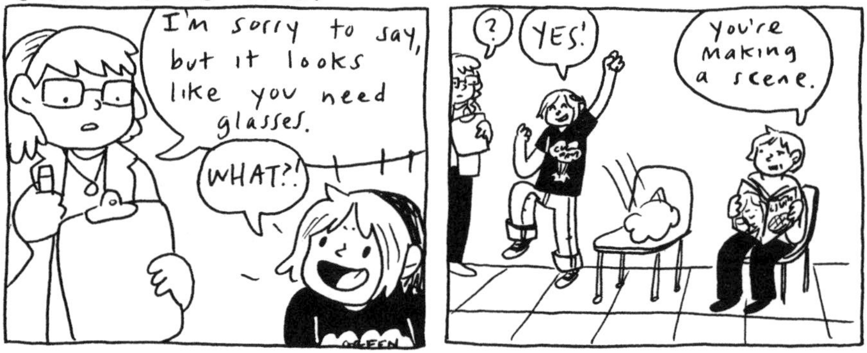
I'm sorry to say, but it looks like you need glasses.
WHAT?!
?
YES!
You're making a scene.

Ever since my childhood infatuation with Egon Spengler, glasses had been a sign of sophistication that I longed to acquire and now they were MINE. All those years of sitting too close to the TV paid off.

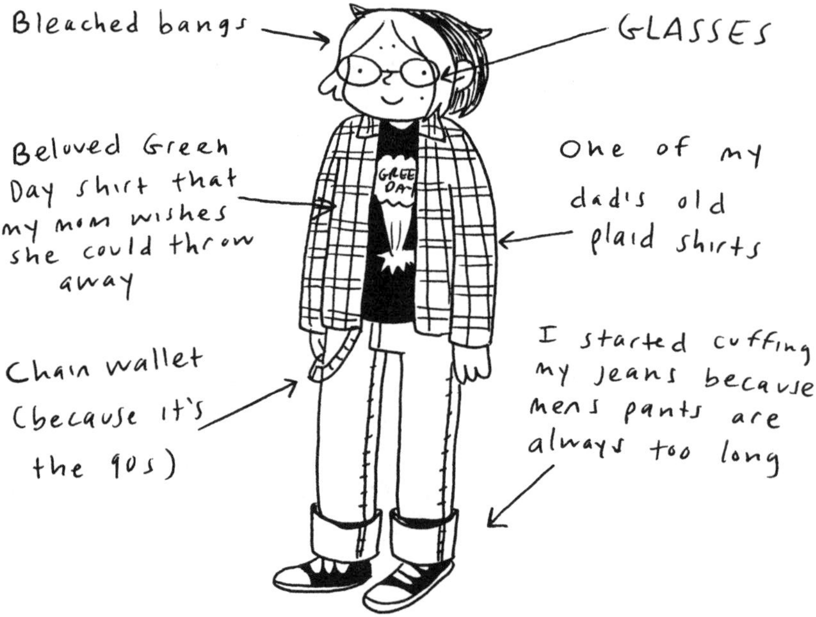
Bleached bangs
GLASSES
Beloved Green Day shirt that my mom wishes she could throw away
One of my dad's old plaid shirts
Chain wallet (because it's the 90s)
I started cuffing my jeans because mens pants are always too long

LIZ PRINCE, Tomboy, age 16

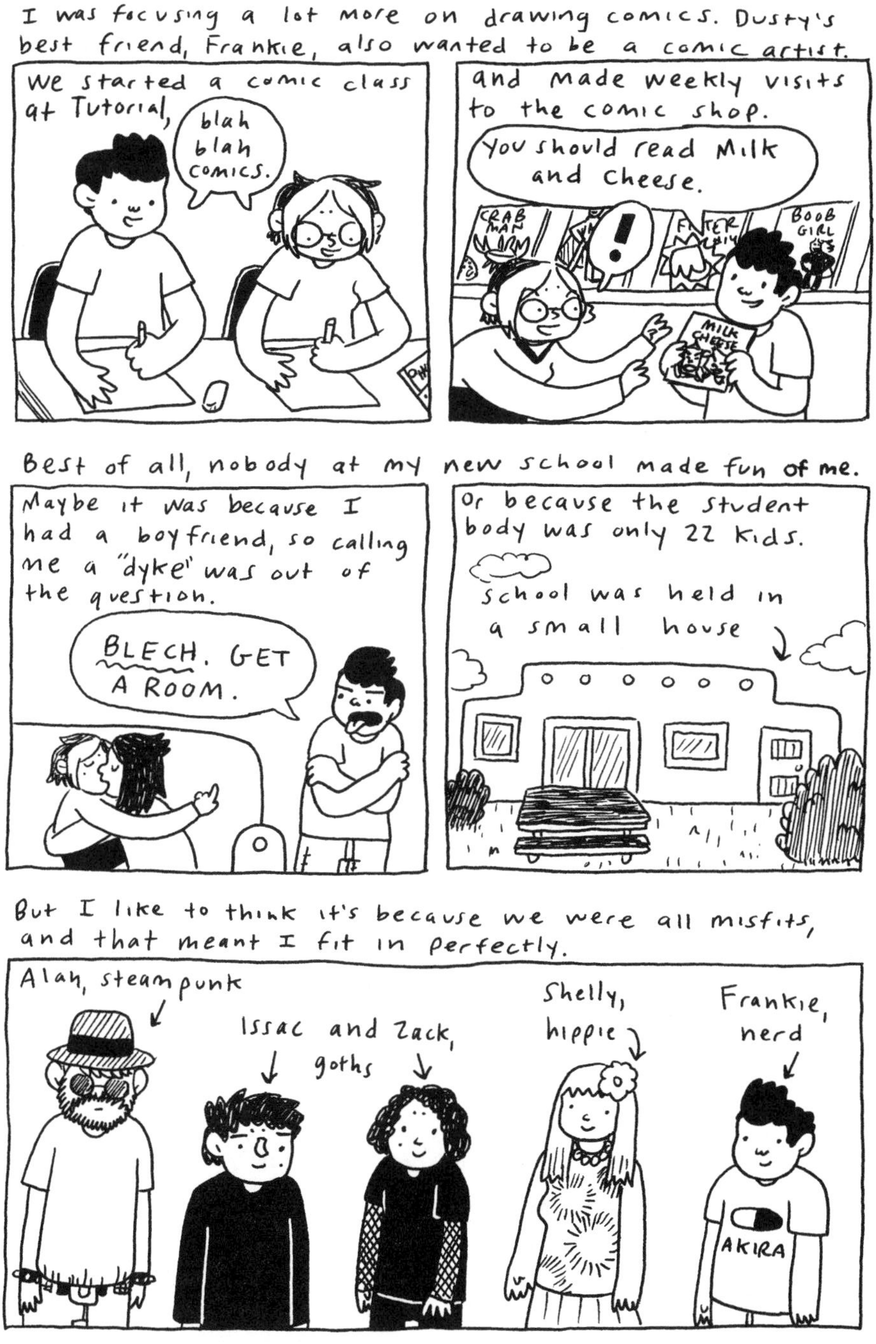
I was focusing a lot more on drawing comics. Dusty's best friend, Frankie, also wanted to be a comic artist.
We started a comic class at Tutorial,
blah blah comics.
and made weekly visits to the comic shop.
You should read Milk and Cheese.
CRAB MAN
BOOB GIRL
!
MILK CHEESE
Best of all, nobody at my new school made fun of me.
Maybe it was because I had a boyfriend, so calling me a "dyke" was out of the question.
BLECH. GET A ROOM.
Or because the student body was only 22 kids.
School was held in a small house
But I like to think it's because we were all misfits, and that meant I fit in perfectly.
Alan, steampunk
Issac and Zack, goths
Shelly, hippie
Frankie, nerd
AKIRA

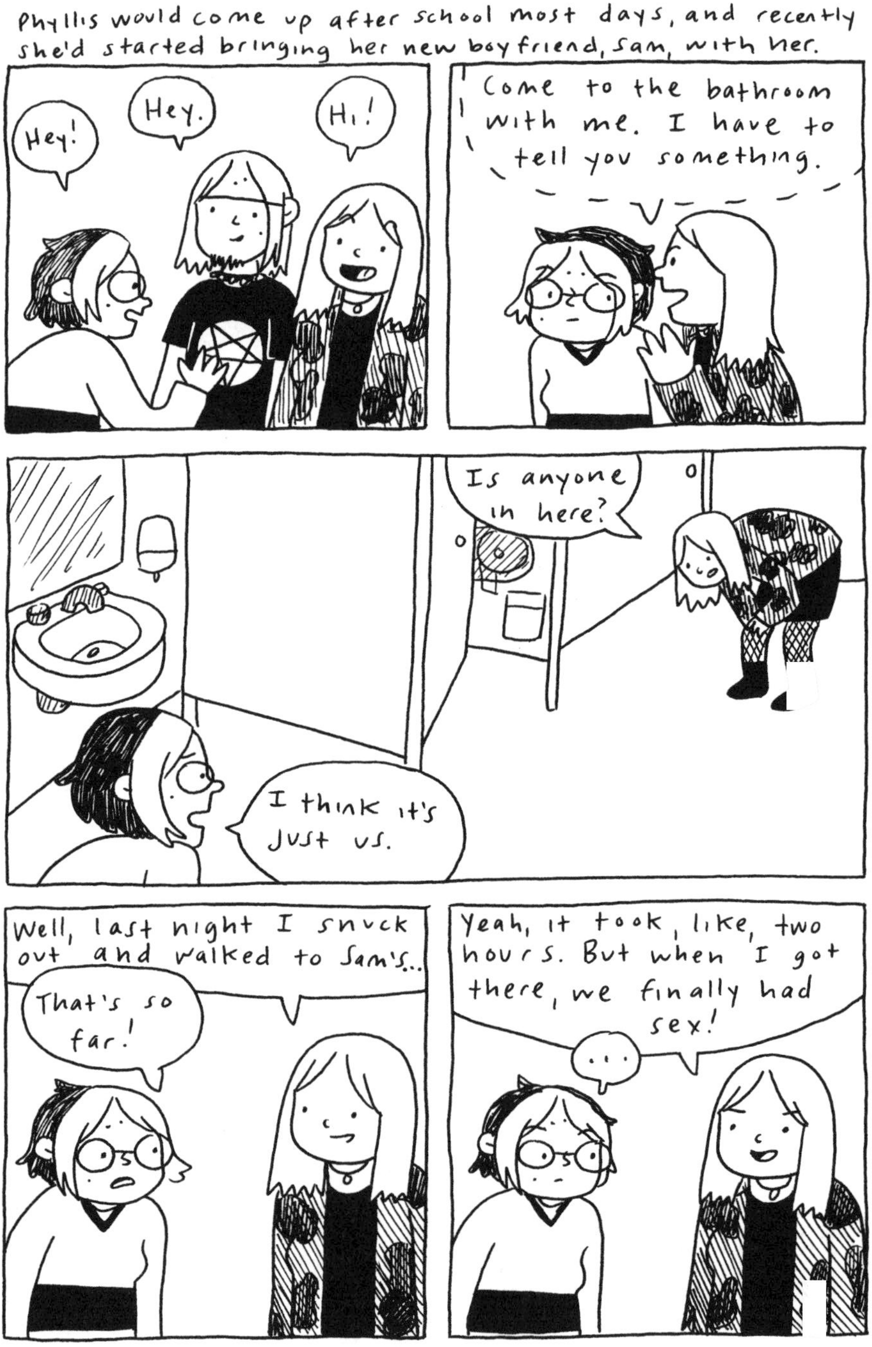
Phyllis would come up after school most days, and recently she'd started bringing her new boyfriend, Sam, with her.
Hey!
Hey.
Hi!
Come to the bathroom with me. I have to tell you something.
Is anyone in here?
I think it's just us.
Well, last night I snuck out and walked to Sam's...
That's so far!
Yeah, it took, like, two hours. But when I got there, we finally had sex!
...

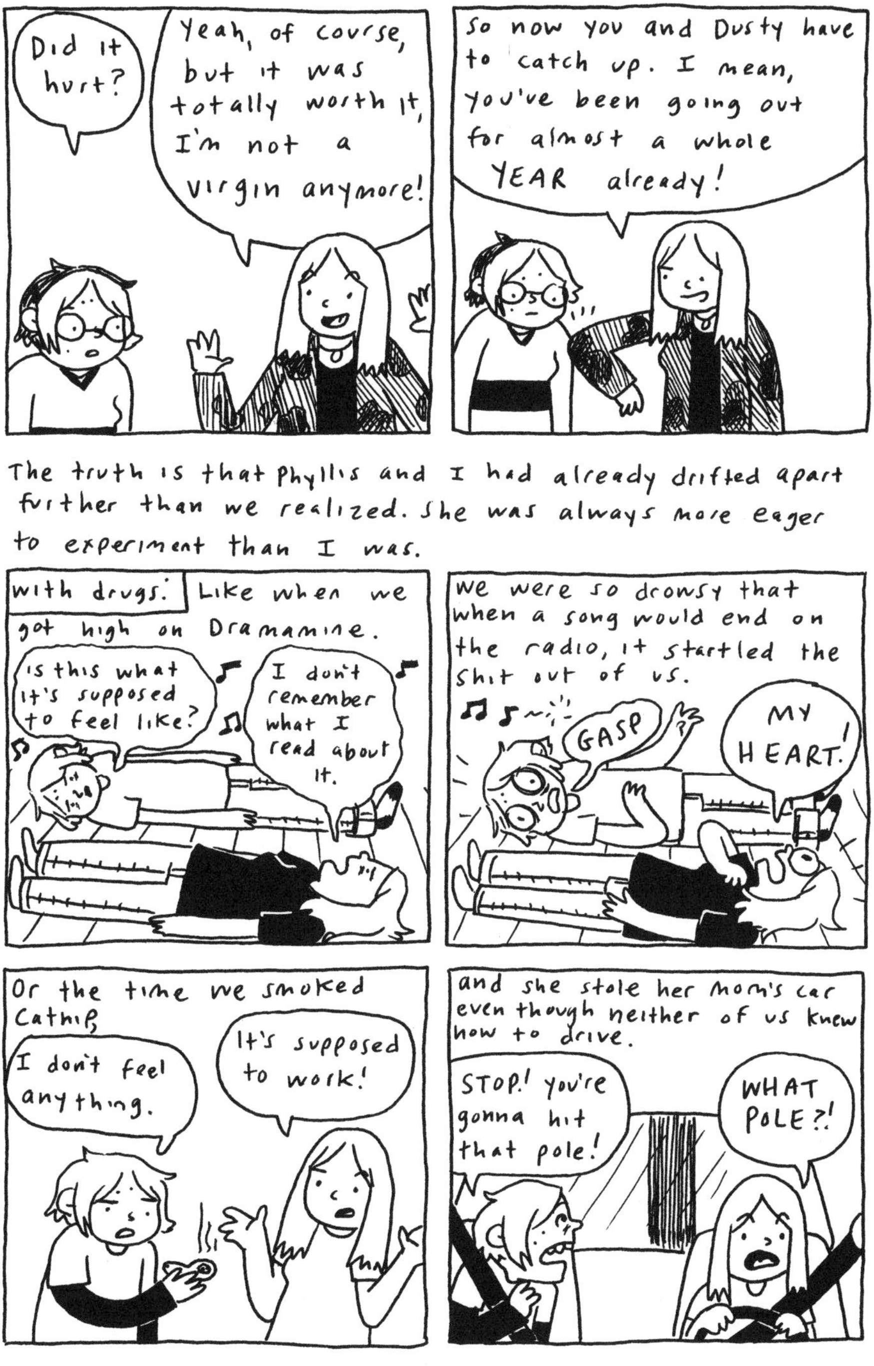
Did it hurt?
Yeah, of course, but it was totally worth it, I'm not a virgin anymore!
So now you and Dusty have to catch up. I mean, you've been going out for almost a whole YEAR already!
The truth is that Phyllis and I had already drifted apart further than we realized. She was always more eager to experiment than I was.
with drugs. Like when we got high on Dramamine.
is this what it's supposed to feel like?
I don't remember what I read about it.
we were so drowsy that when a song would end on the radio, it startled the shit out of us.
GASP
MY HEART!
Or the time we smoked Catnip,
I don't feel anything.
It's supposed to work!
and she stole her mom's car even though neither of us knew how to drive.
STOP! you're gonna hit that pole!
WHAT POLE?!

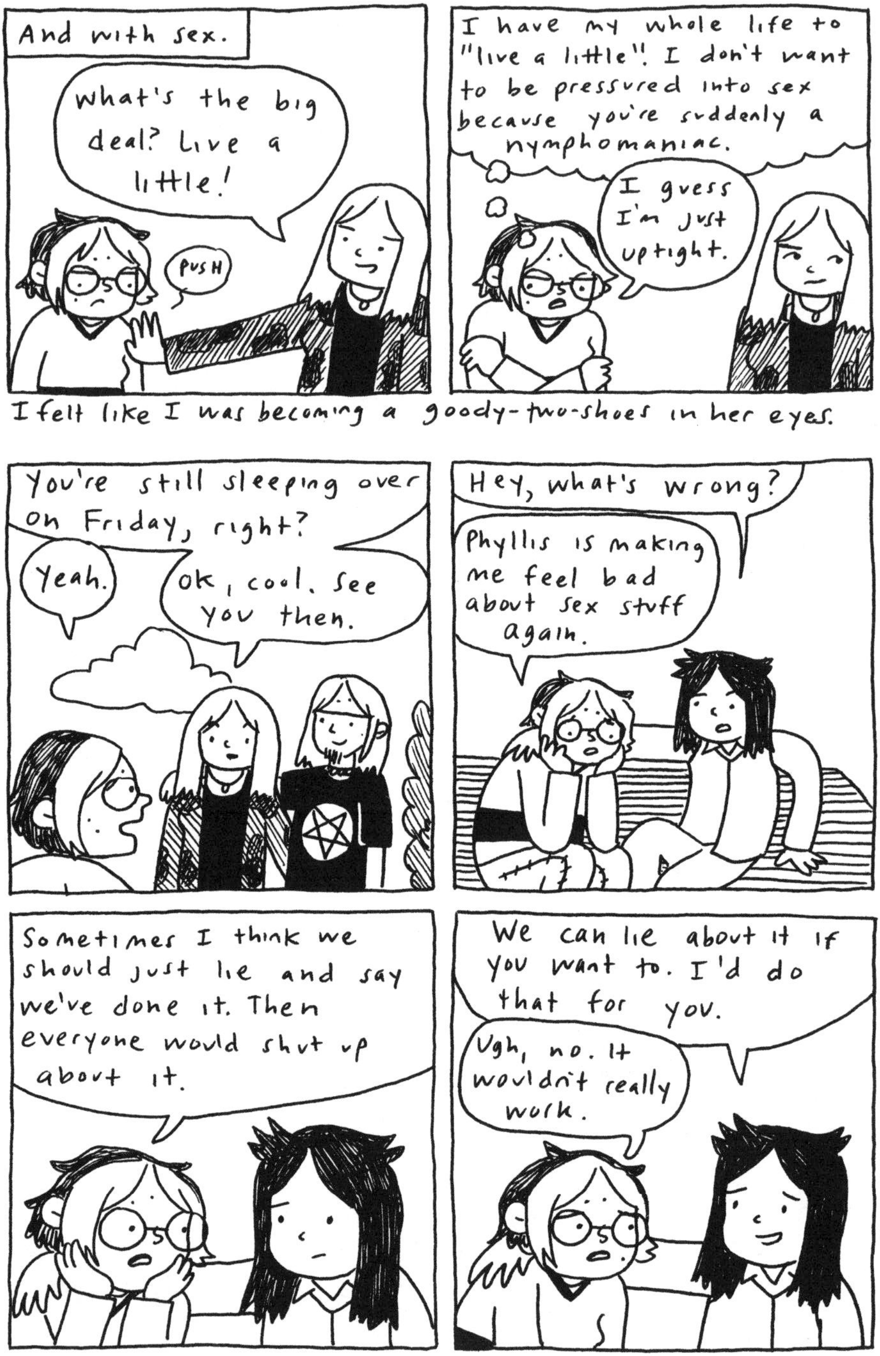
And with sex.
What's the big deal? Live a little!
PUSH
I have my whole life to "live a little"! I don't want to be pressured into sex because you're suddenly a nymphomaniac.
I guess I'm just uptight.
I felt like I was becoming a goody-two-shoes in her eyes.
You're still sleeping over on Friday, right?
Yeah.
Ok, cool. See you then.
Hey, what's wrong?
Phyllis is making me feel bad about sex stuff again.
Sometimes I think we should just lie and say we've done it. Then everyone would shut up about it.
We can lie about it if you want to. I'd do that for you.
Ugh, no. It wouldn't really work.

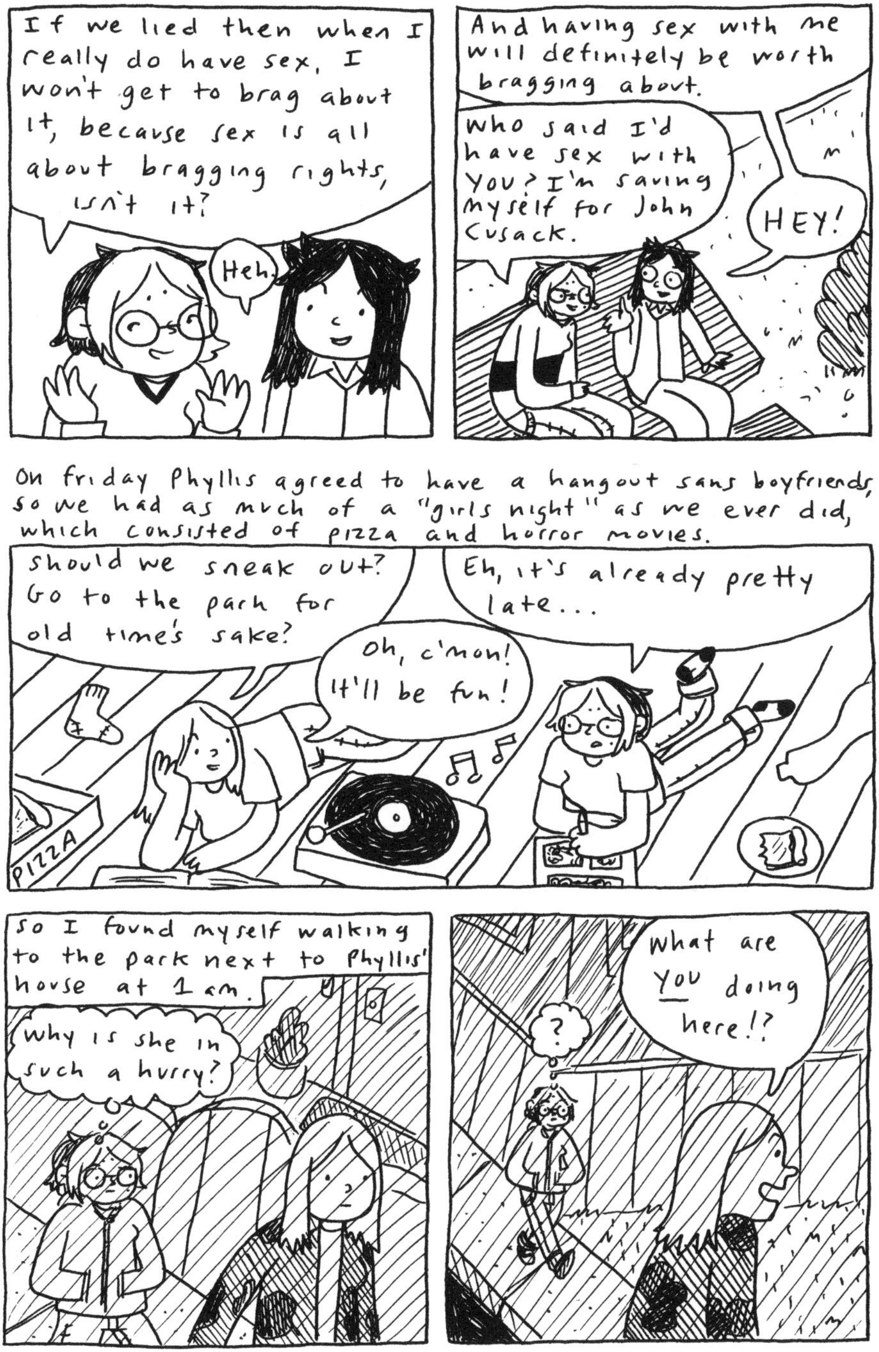
If we lied then when I really do have sex, I won't get to brag about it, because sex is all about bragging rights, isn't it?
Heh.
And having sex with me will definitely be worth bragging about.
Who said I'd have sex with you? I'm saving myself for John Cusack.
HEY!
On friday Phyllis agreed to have a hangout sans boyfriends, so we had as much of a "girls night" as we ever did, which consisted of pizza and horror movies.
Should we sneak out? Go to the park for old time's sake?
Eh, it's already pretty late...
Oh, c'mon! It'll be fun!
PIZZA
So I found myself walking to the park next to Phyllis' house at 1 am.
Why is she in such a hurry?
?
What are YOU doing here!?

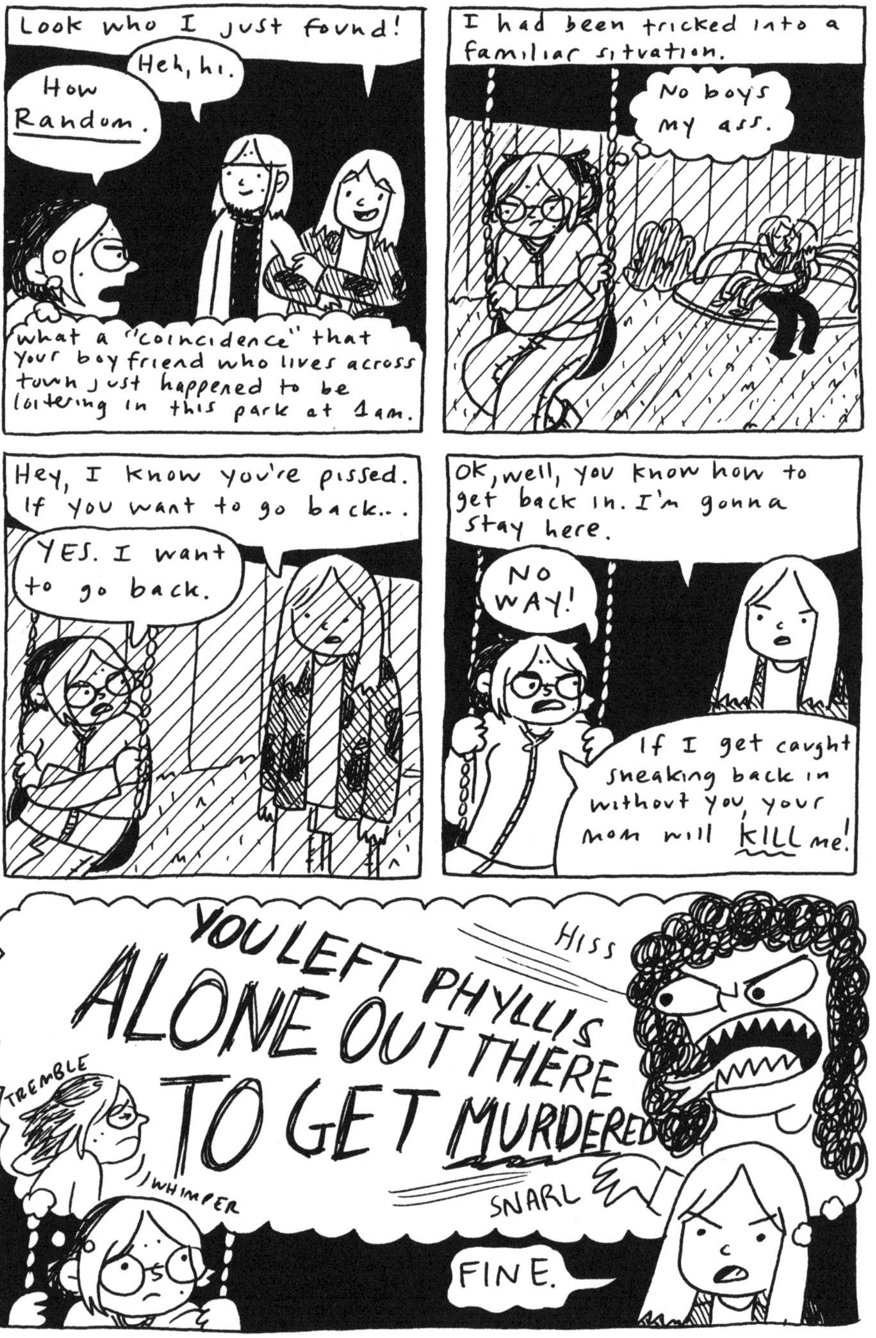
Look who I just found!
Heh, hi.
How Random.
what a "coincidence" that your boyfriend who lives across town just happened to be loitering in this park at 1am.
I had been tricked into a familiar situation.
No boys my ass.
Hey, I know you're pissed. If you want to go back...
YES. I want to go back.
Ok, well, you know how to get back in. I'm gonna stay here.
NO WAY!
If I get caught sneaking back in without you, your mom will KILL me!
YOU LEFT PHYLLIS ALONE OUT THERE TO GET MURDERED
HISS
TREMBLE
WHIMPER
SNARL
FINE.

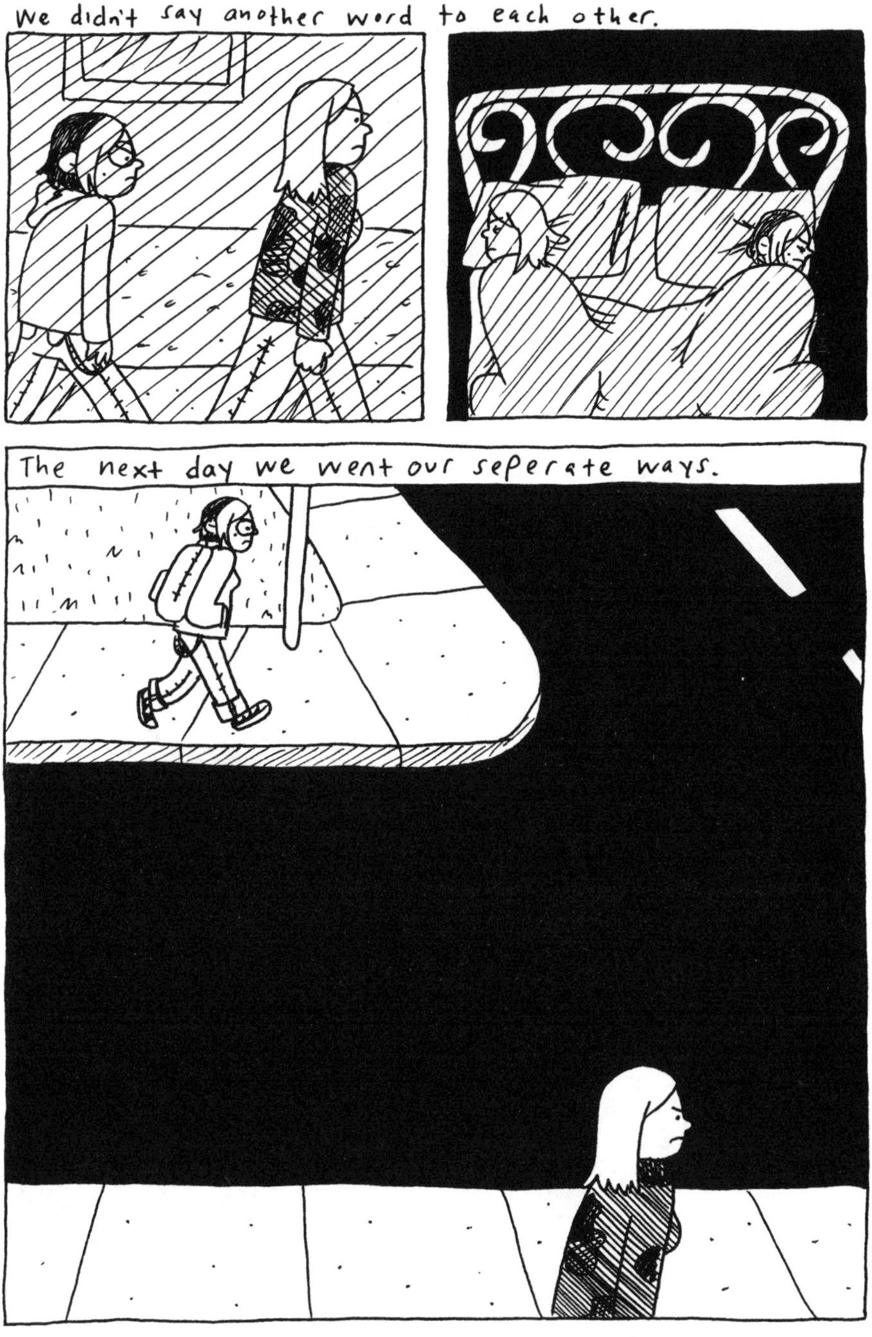
We didn't say another word to each other.
The next day we went our seperate ways.

CHAPTER 13

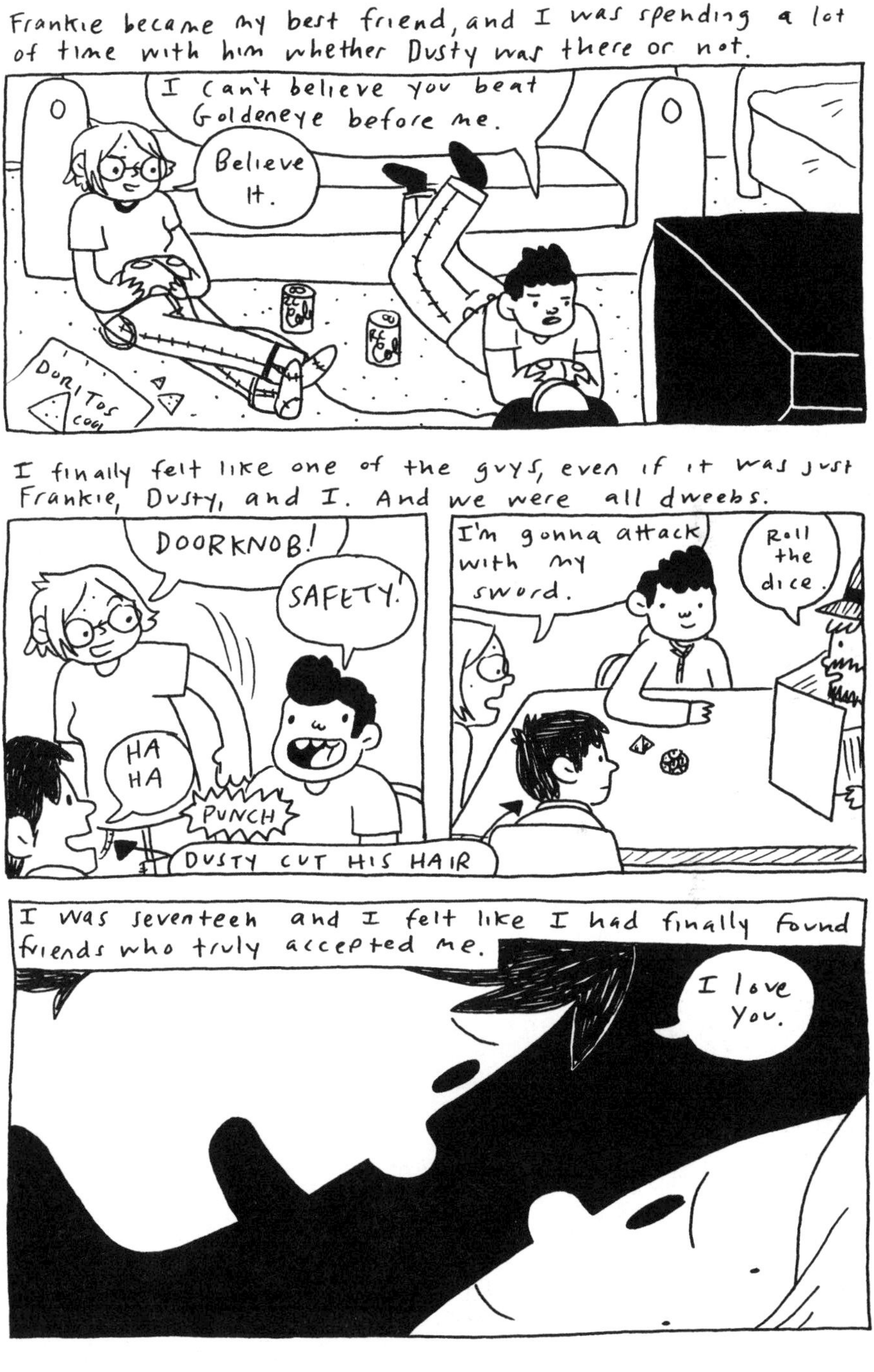
Frankie became my best friend, and I was spending a lot of time with him whether Dusty was there or not.
I can't believe you beat Goldeneye before me.
Believe it.
DORITOS
I finally felt like one of the guys, even if it was just Frankie, Dusty, and I. And we were all dweebs.
DOORKNOB!
SAFETY!
HA HA
PUNCH
DUSTY CUT HIS HAIR
I'm gonna attack with my sword.
Roll the dice.
I was seventeen and I felt like I had finally found friends who truly accepted me.
I love you.

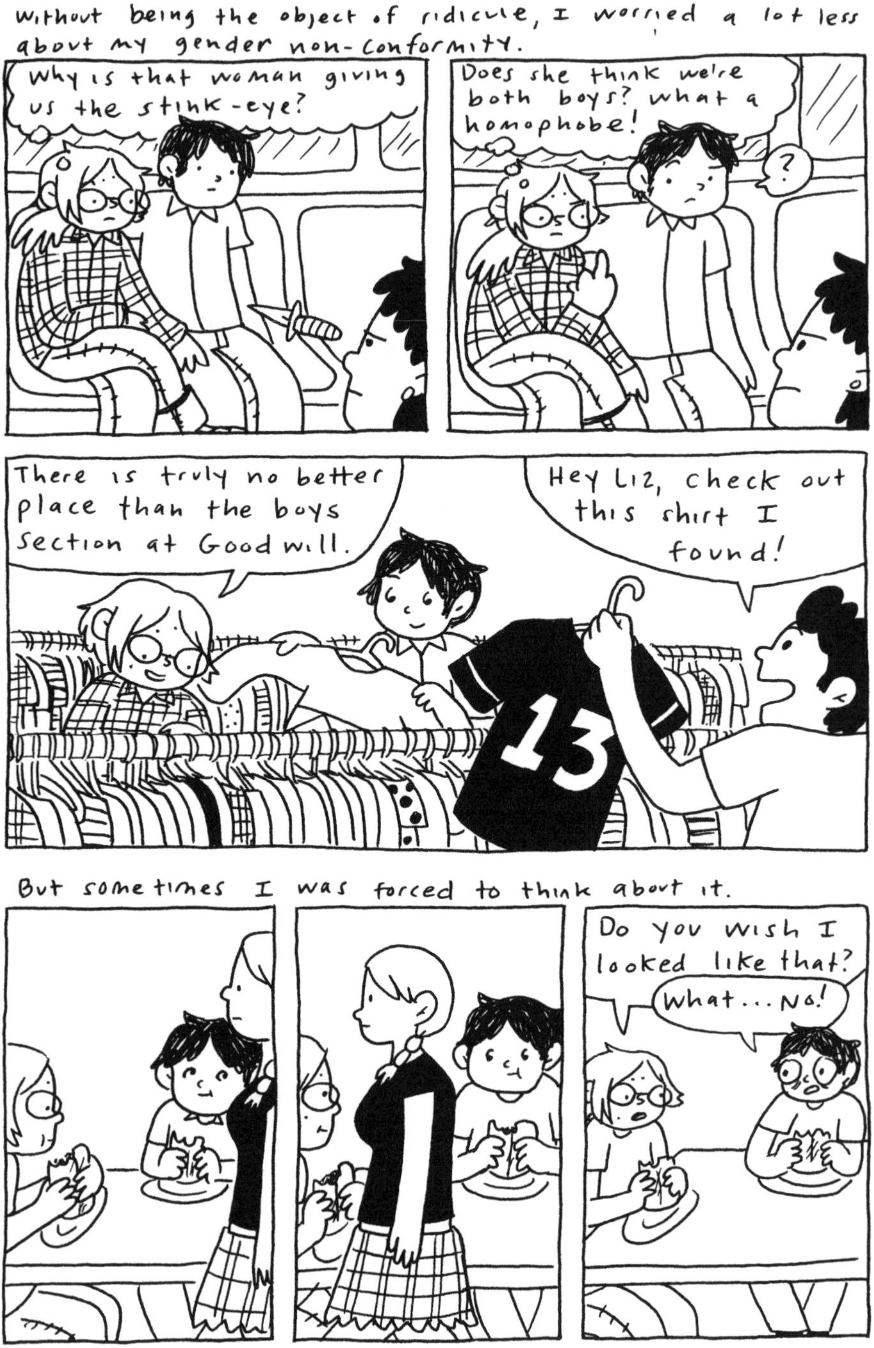
without being the object of ridicule, I worried a lot less about my gender non-conformity.
Why is that woman giving us the stink-eye?
Does she think we're both boys? what a homophobe!
?
There is truly no better place than the boys section at Goodwill.
Hey Liz, check out this shirt I found!
13
But sometimes I was forced to think about it.
Do you wish I looked like that?
What... No!

I rarely met other girls who looked like me, and it was doubly rare to see girls who looked like me in movies, on TV, or in advertisements.

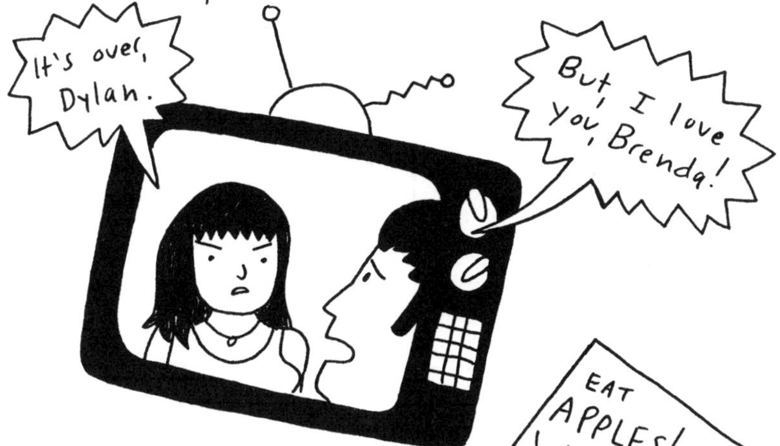
It's over, Dylan.
But, I love you, Brenda!

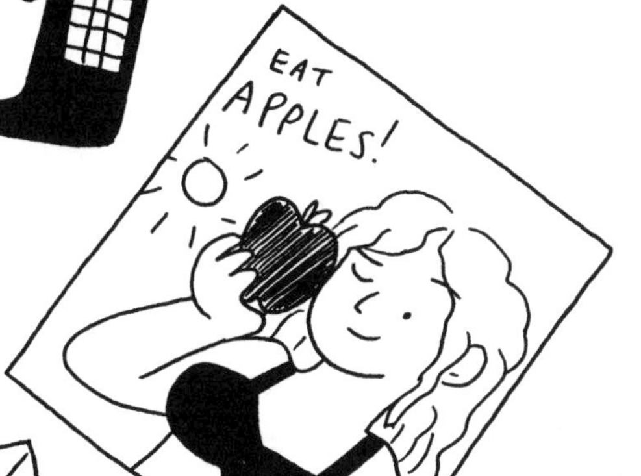
EAT APPLES!

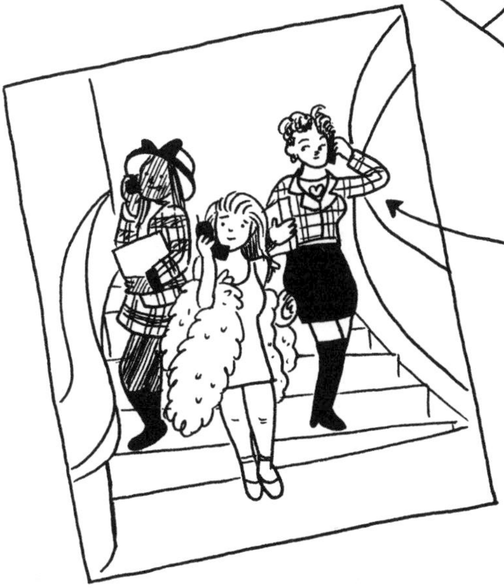

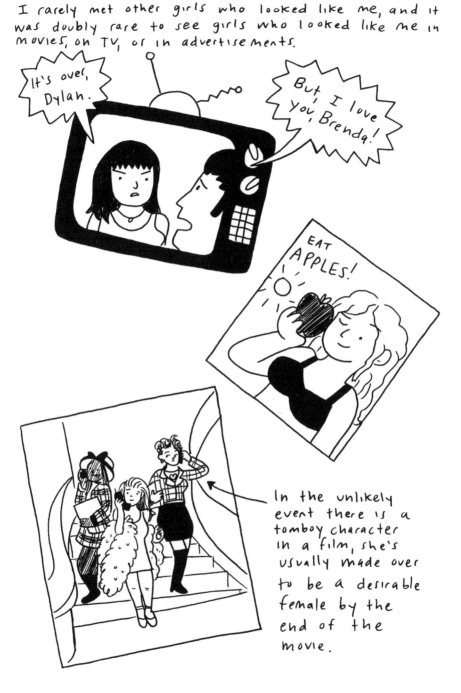

In the unlikely event there is a tomboy character in a film, she's usually made over to be a desirable female by the end of the movie.

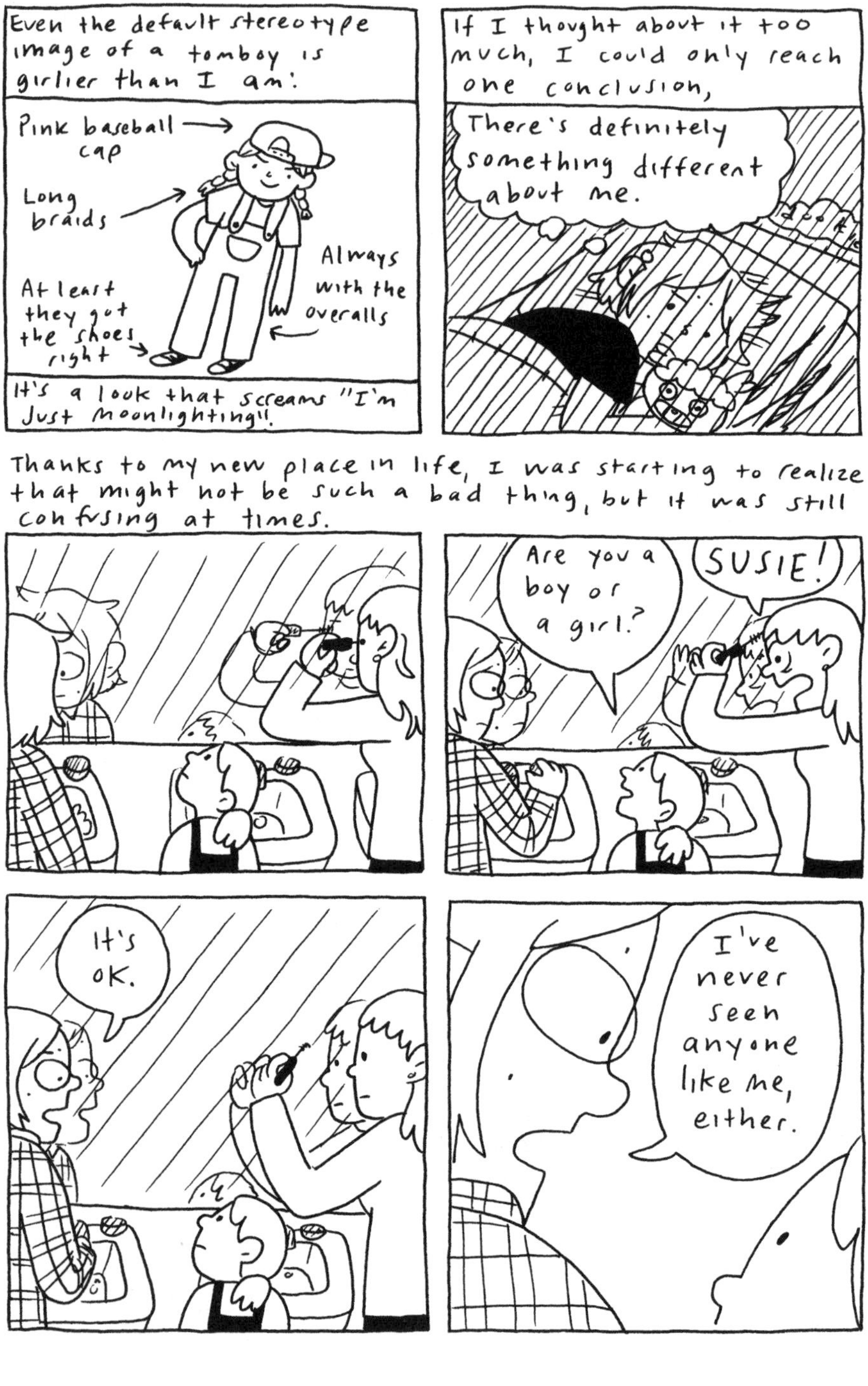
Even the default stereotype image of a tomboy is girlier than I am:
Pink baseball cap
Long braids
Always with the overalls
At least they got the shoes right
It's a look that screams "I'm just moonlighting".
If I thought about it too much, I could only reach one conclusion,
There's definitely something different about me.
Thanks to my new place in life, I was starting to realize that might not be such a bad thing, but it was still confusing at times.
Are you a boy or a girl?
SUSIE!
It's ok.
I've never seen anyone like me, either.

We were encouraged to do community service or volunteer work through school, so I chose to help out at a teen art center called Warehouse 21. My contact was a girl my age:

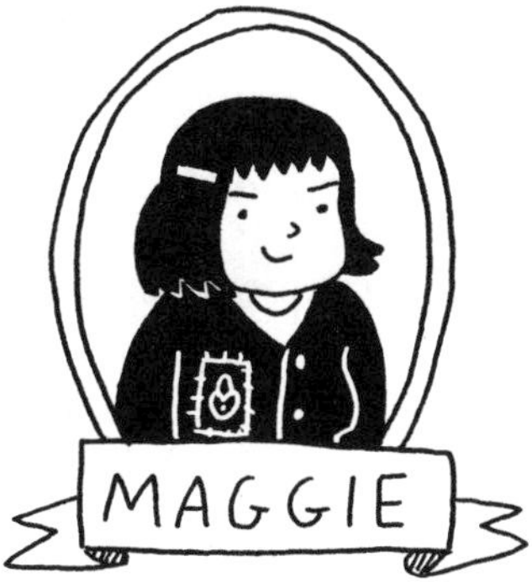
MAGGIE

* Is a punk.
* Plays piano and bass and probably any other instrument you put in front of her.
* Drives a big, wood-paneled truck.
* Doesn't take shit from anyone.

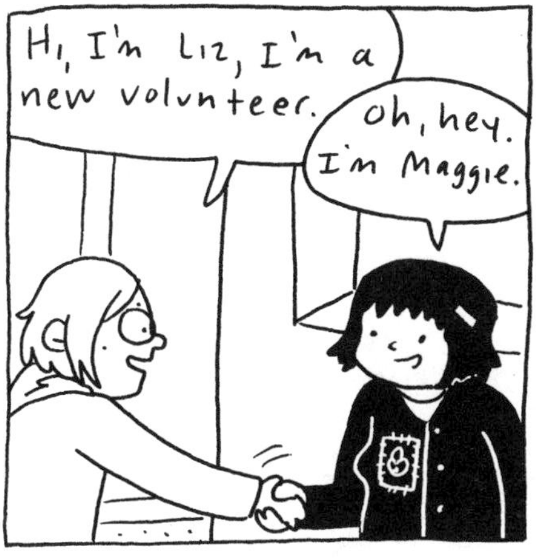
Hi, I'm Liz, I'm a new volunteer.
Oh, hey. I'm Maggie.

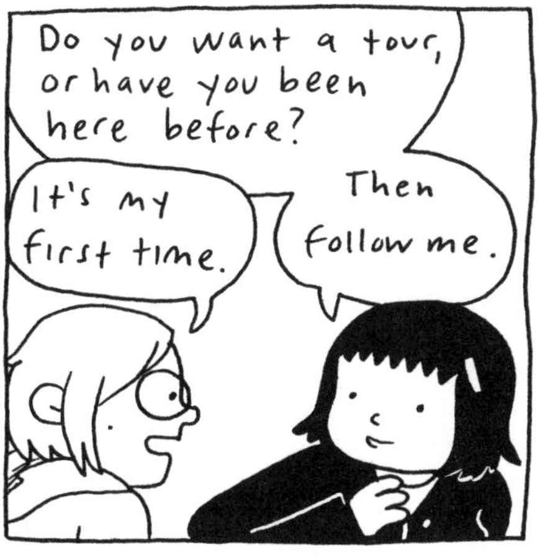
Do you want a tour, or have you been here before?
It's my first time.
Then follow me.

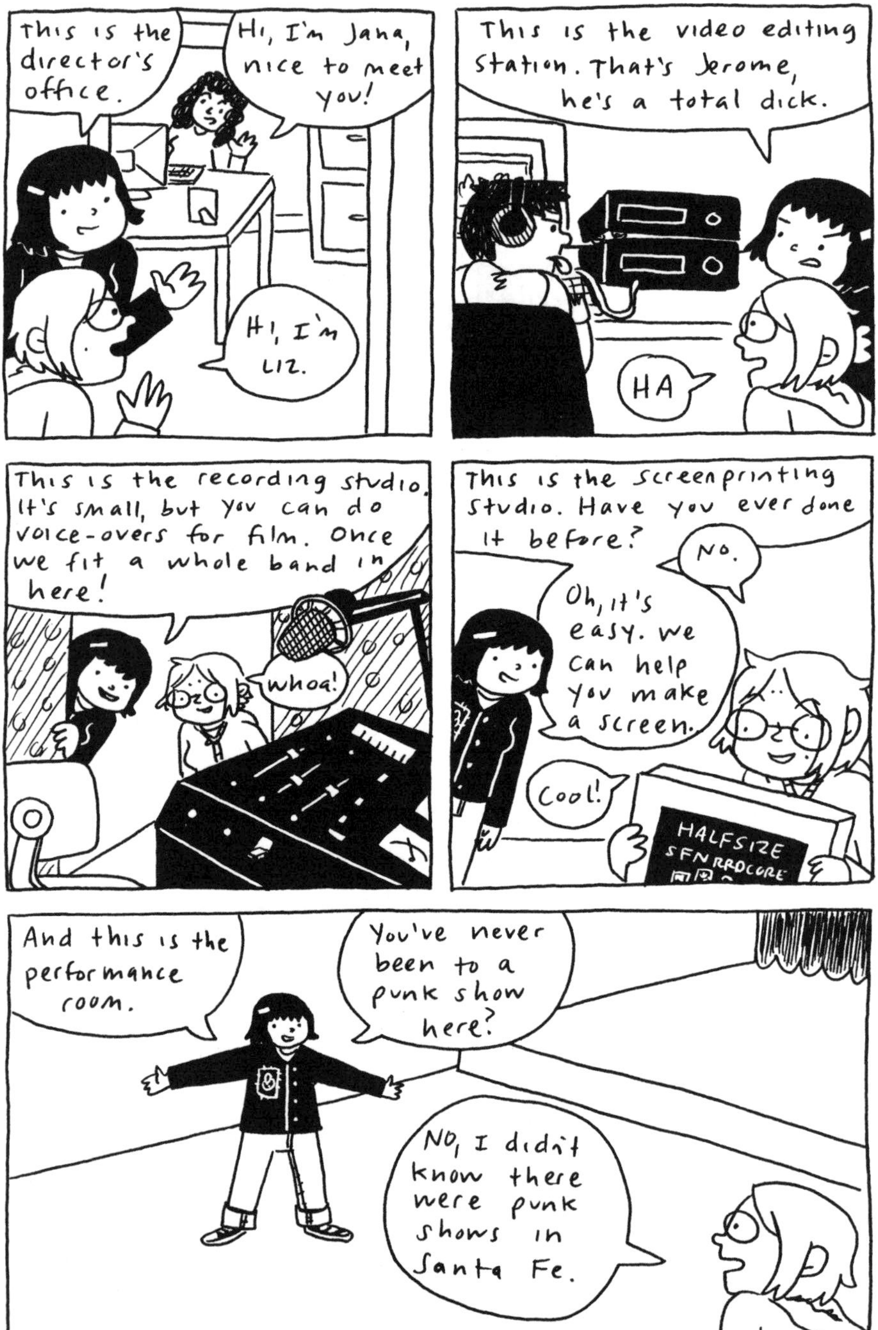
This is the director's office.
Hi, I'm Jana, nice to meet you!
Hi, I'm Liz.
This is the video editing station. That's Jerome, he's a total dick.
HA
This is the recording studio. It's small, but you can do voice-overs for film. Once we fit a whole band in here!
whoa!
This is the screenprinting studio. Have you ever done it before?
No.
Oh, it's easy. we can help you make a screen.
Cool!
HALFSIZE
And this is the performance room.
You've never been to a punk show here?
No, I didn't know there were punk shows in Santa Fe.

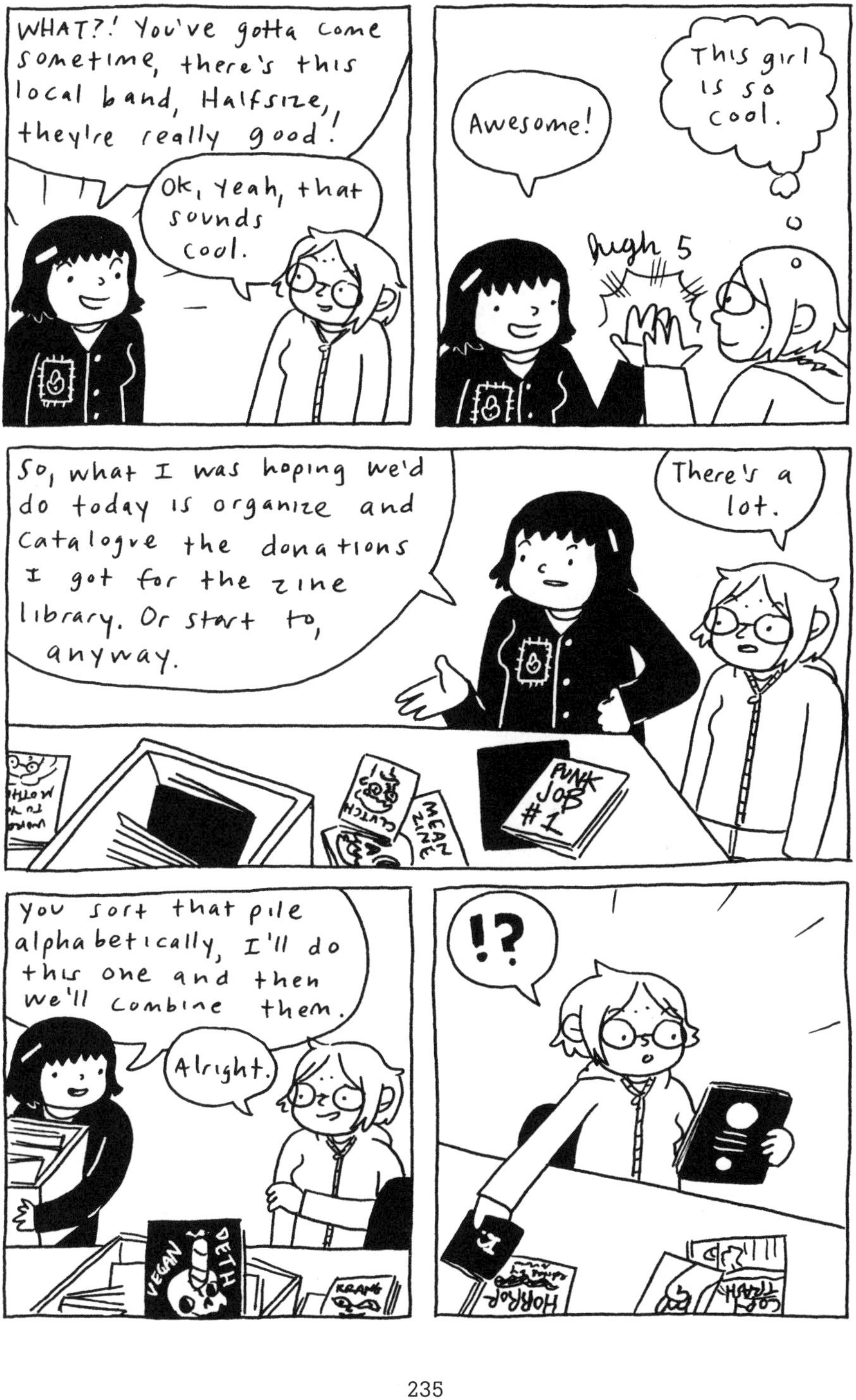
WHAT?! You've gotta come sometime, there's this local band, Halfsize, they're really good!
Ok, yeah, that sounds cool.
Awesome!
This girl is so cool.
high 5
So, what I was hoping we'd do today is organize and catalogue the donations I got for the zine library. Or start to, anyway.
There's a lot.
PUNK JOB #1
MEAN ZINE
You sort that pile alphabetically, I'll do this one and then we'll combine them.
Alright.
VEGAN DETH
KRANG
!?

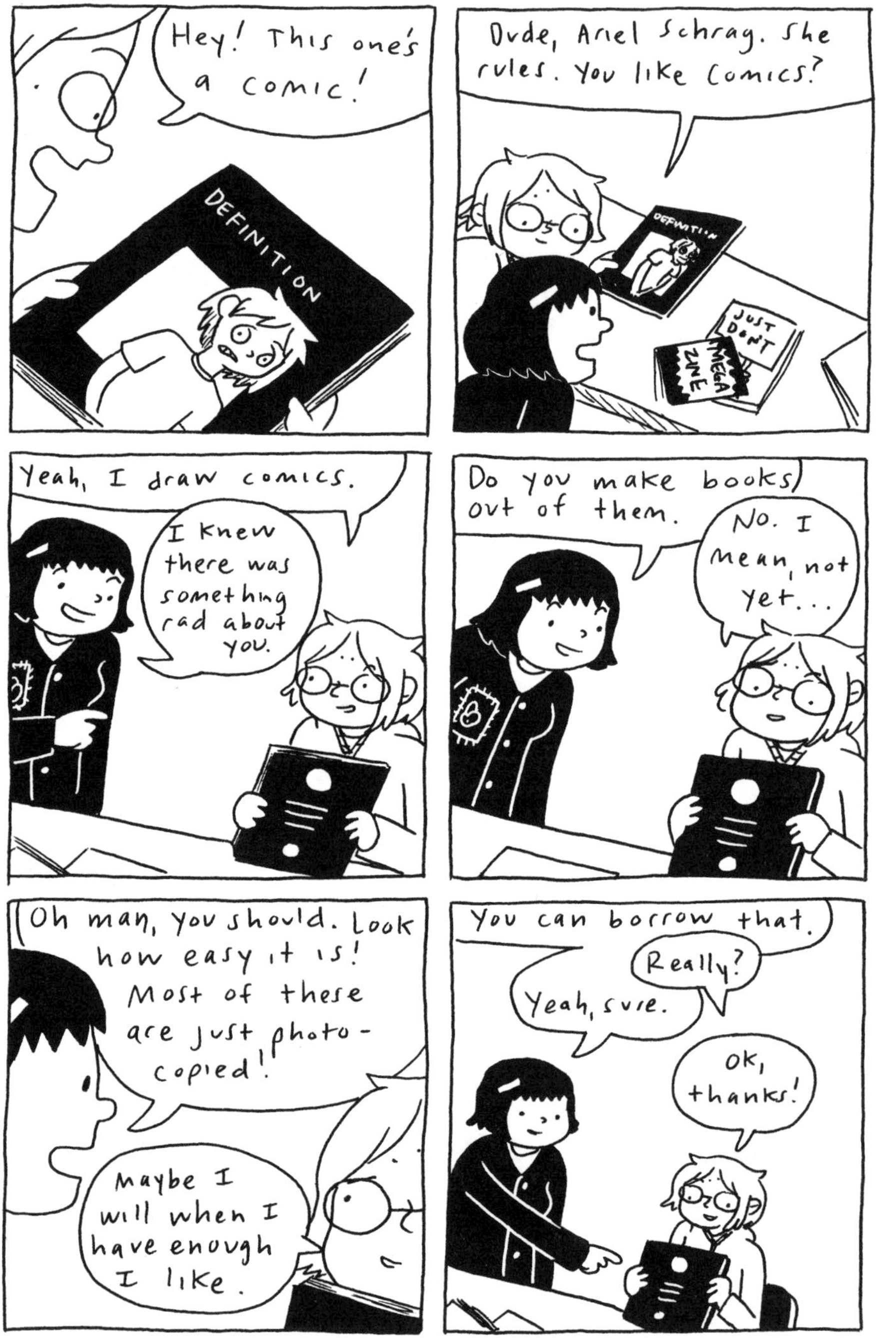
Hey! This one's a comic!
DEFINITION
Dude, Ariel Schrag. She rules. You like comics?
DEFINITION
JUST DON'T
MEGA ZINE
Yeah, I draw comics.
I knew there was something rad about you.
Do you make books out of them.
No. I mean, not yet...
Oh man, you should. Look how easy it is! Most of these are just photo-copied!
Maybe I will when I have enough I like.
You can borrow that.
Really?
Yeah, sure.
Ok, thanks!

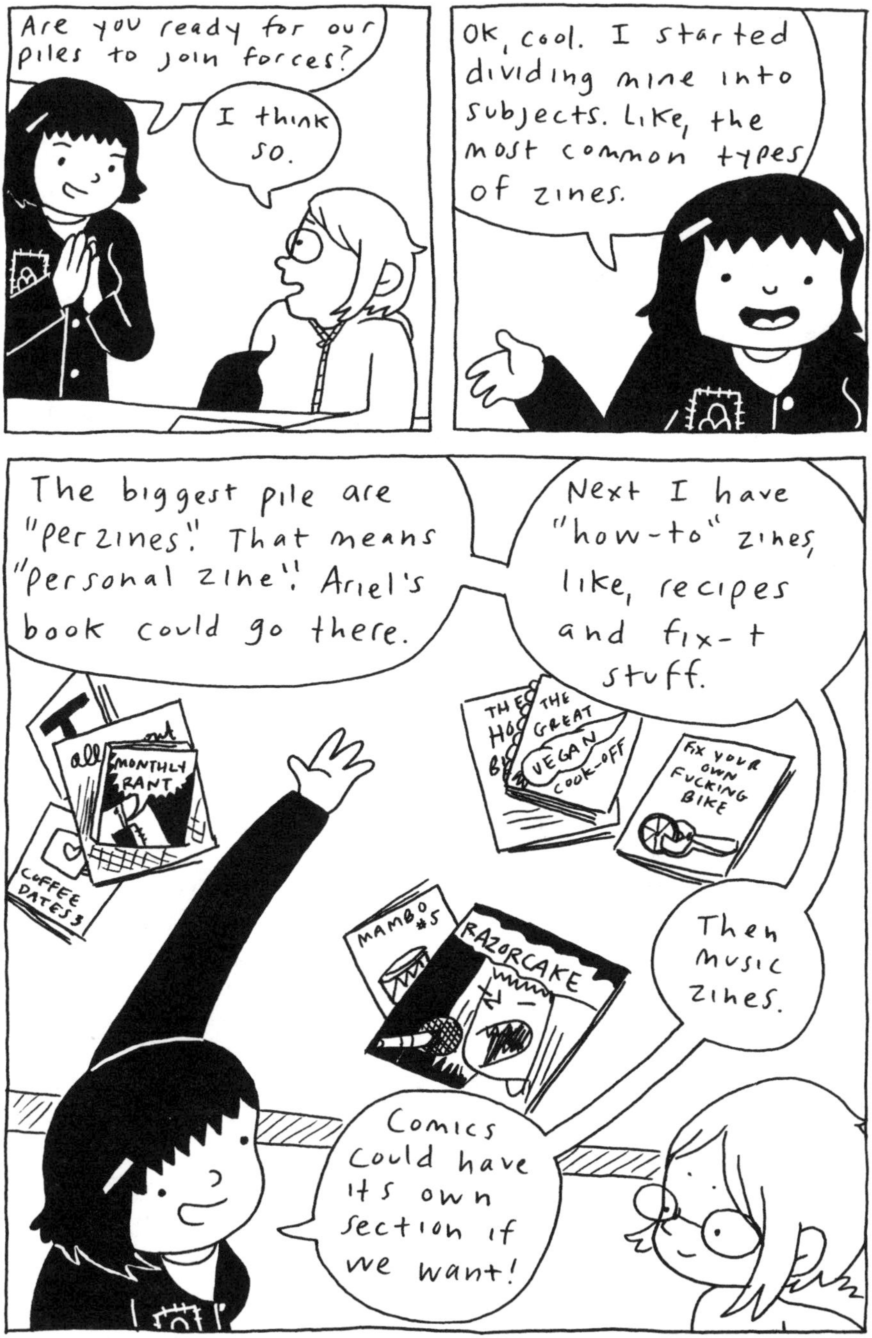
Are you ready for our piles to join forces?
I think so.
Ok, cool. I started dividing mine into subjects. Like, the most common types of zines.
The biggest pile are "perzines." That means "personal zine." Ariel's book could go there.
Next I have "how-to" zines, like, recipes and fix-t stuff.
MONTHLY RANT
COFFEE DATES 3
THE GREAT VEGAN COOK-OFF
FIX YOUR OWN FUCKING BIKE
Then music zines.
MAMBO #5
RAZORCAKE
Comics could have its own section if we want!

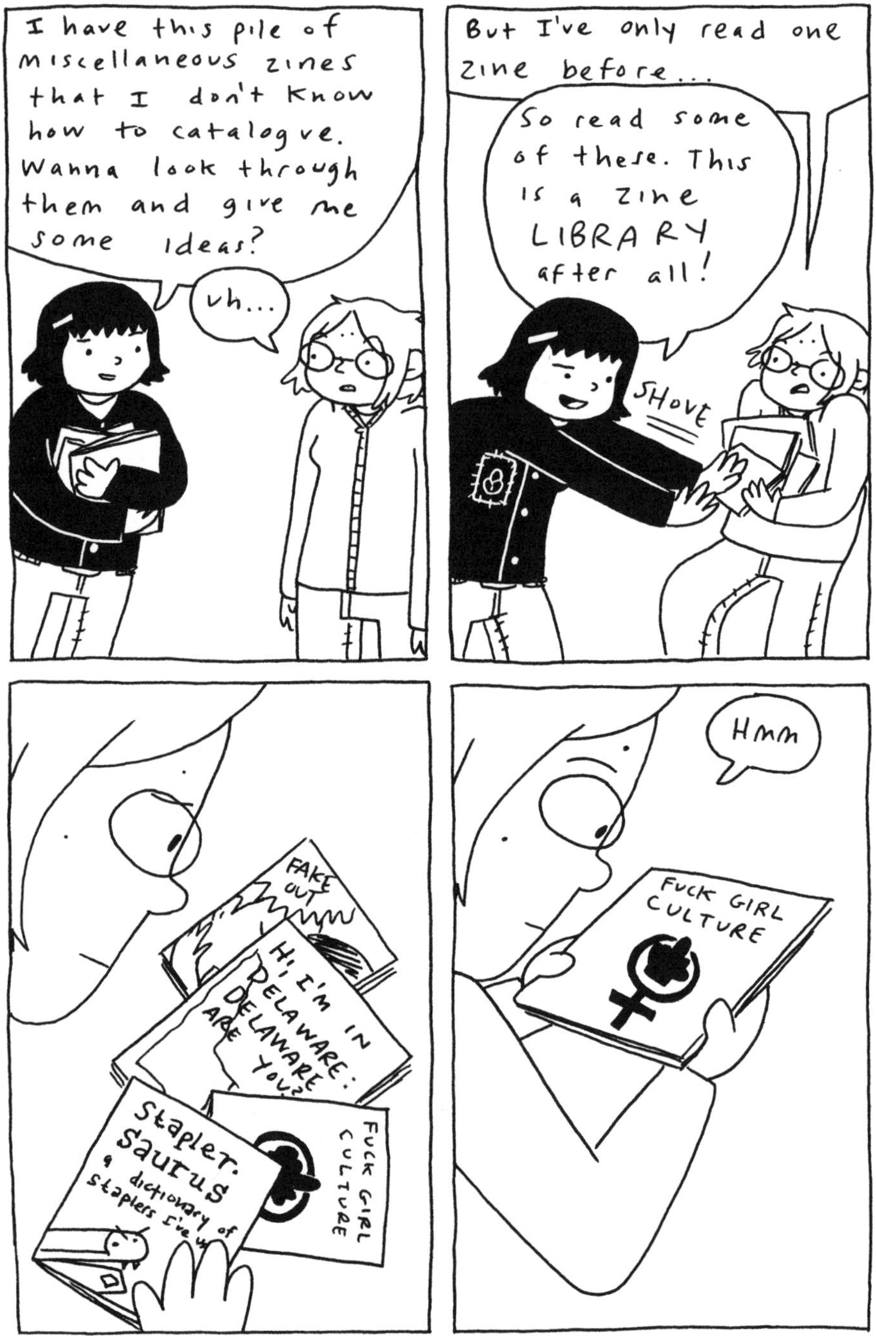

I have this pile of miscellaneous zines that I don't know how to catalogue. Wanna look through them and give me some ideas?
uh...
But I've only read one zine before...
So read some of these. This is a zine LIBRARY after all!
SHOVE
FAKE OUT
HI, I'M IN DELAWARE: DELAWARE ARE YOU?
Stapler-Saurus
a dictionary of staplers I've
FUCK GIRL CULTURE
Hmm
FUCK GIRL CULTURE

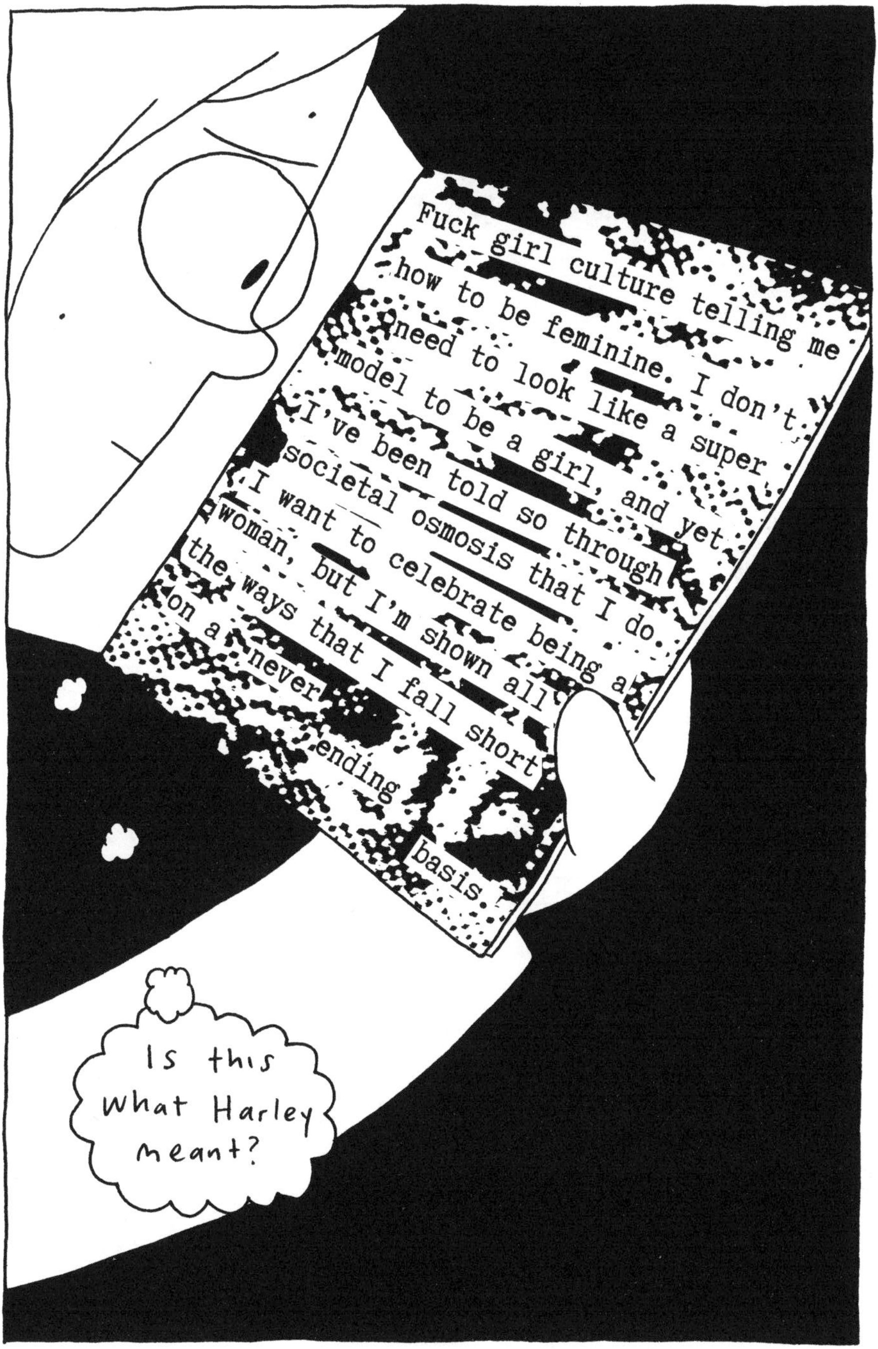
Fuck girl culture telling me
how to be feminine. I don't
need to look like a super
model to be a girl, and yet
I've been told so through
societal osmosis that I do.
I want to celebrate being a
woman, but I'm shown all
the ways that I fall short
on a never ending
basis.
Is this what Harley meant?

What a revelation I'd had at the hands of a preachy feminist perzine! I wasn't challenging the social norm, I was buying into it!

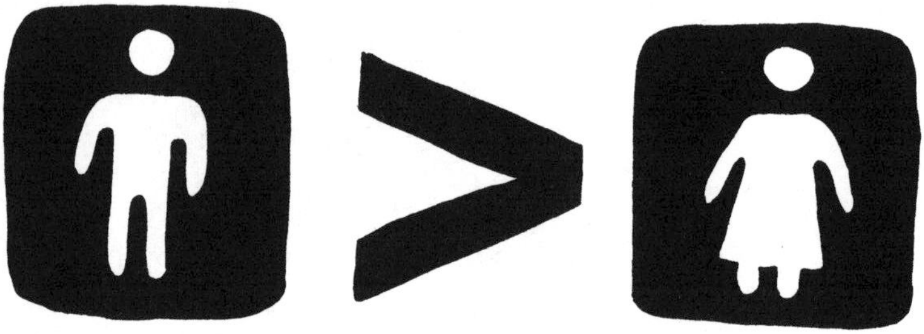

Because we are taught that boys are

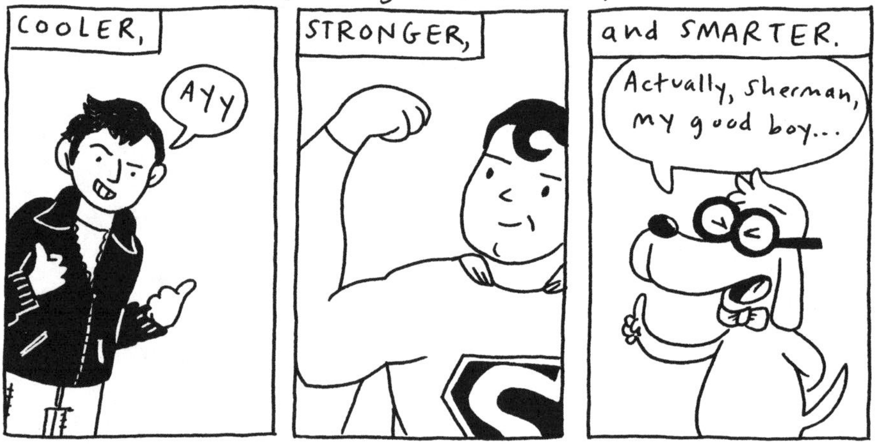
COOLER,
Ayy
STRONGER,
and SMARTER.
Actually, Sherman, my good boy...

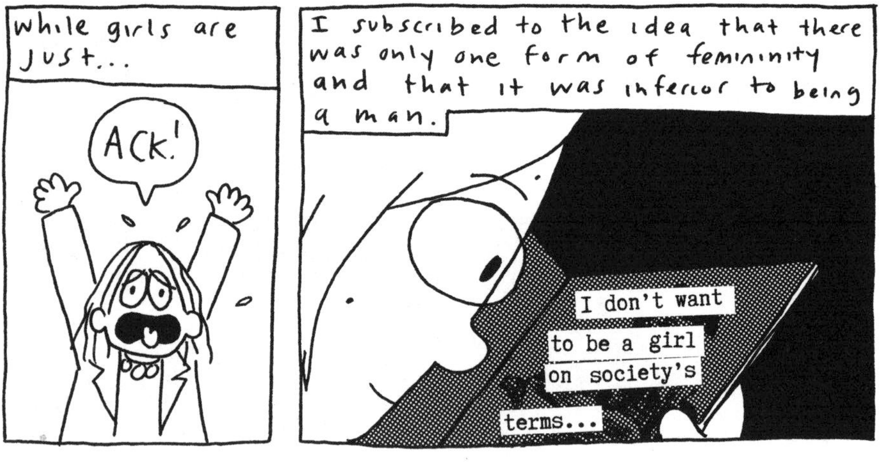
while girls are just...
ACK!
I subscribed to the idea that there was only one form of femininity and that it was inferior to being a man.
I don't want
to be a girl
on society's
terms...

"I want to be a girl on my own terms."

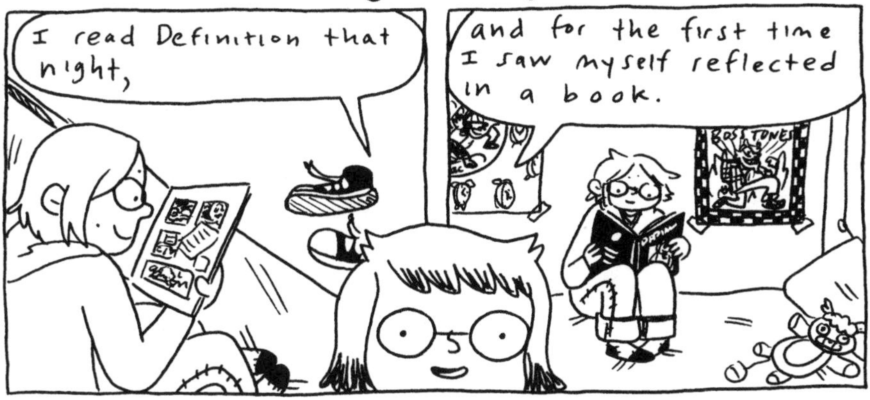
I read Definition that night,
and for the first time I saw myself reflected in a book.
BOSSTONES

I realized that even though the majority of my role models were men, a few women had worked their way in there, too.

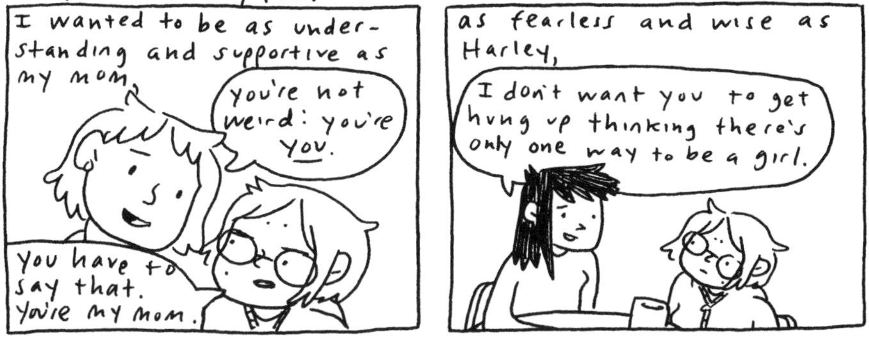
I wanted to be as understanding and supportive as my mom,
You're not weird: you're YOU.
You have to say that. You're my mom.
as fearless and wise as Harley,
I don't want you to get hung up thinking there's only one way to be a girl.

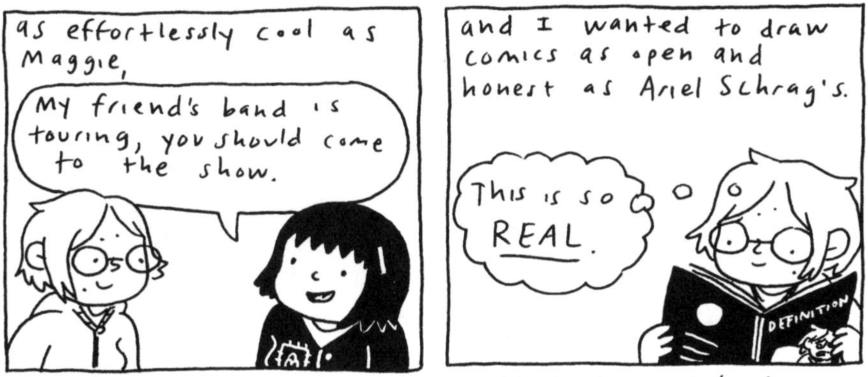
as effortlessly cool as Maggie,
My friend's band is touring, you should come to the show.
and I wanted to draw comics as open and honest as Ariel Schrag's.
This is so REAL.
DEFINITION

Could my problem have been that I was looking for validation in the wrong places all along?

I was spending more and more time helping out with the zine library and whatever other errands Warehouse 21 had.

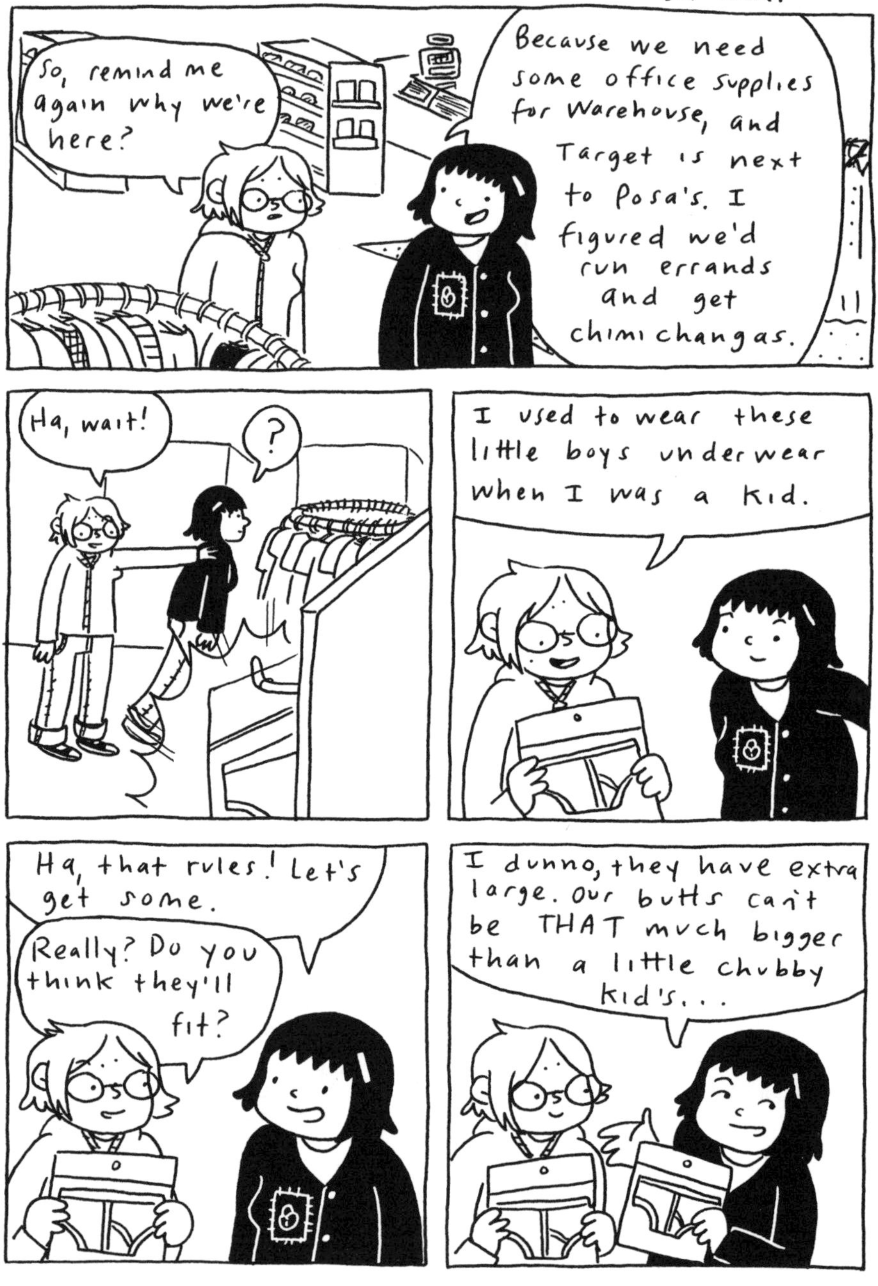
So, remind me again why we're here?
Because we need some office supplies for Warehouse, and Target is next to Posa's. I figured we'd run errands and get chimichangas.
Ha, wait!
?
I used to wear these little boys underwear when I was a kid.
Ha, that rules! Let's get some.
Really? Do you think they'll fit?
I dunno, they have extra large. Our butts can't be THAT much bigger than a little chubby kid's...

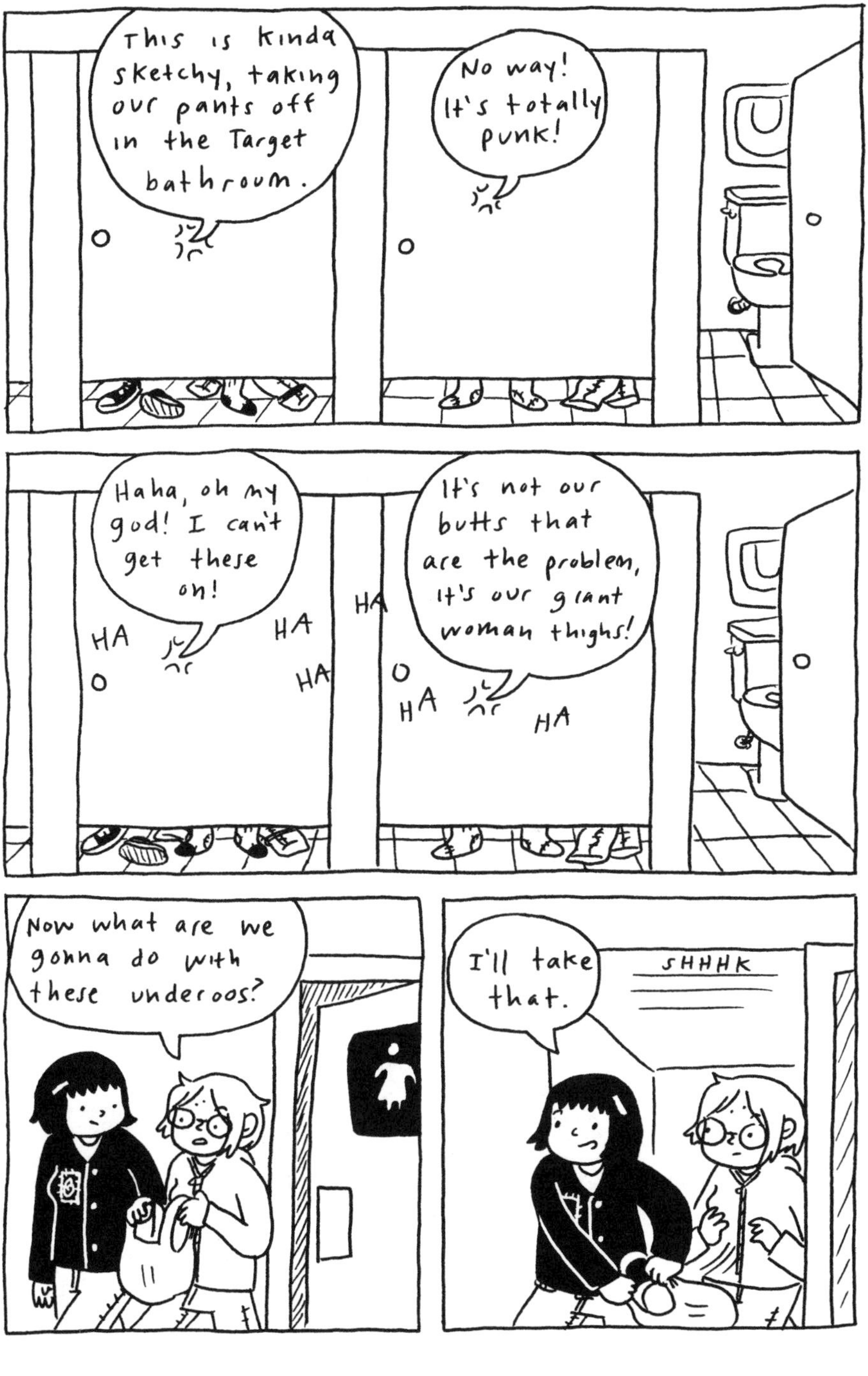
This is kinda sketchy, taking our pants off in the Target bathroom.
No way! It's totally punk!
Haha, oh my god! I can't get these on!
HA
HA
HA
HA
It's not our butts that are the problem, it's our giant woman thighs!
HA
HA
Now what are we gonna do with these underoos?
I'll take that.
SHHHK

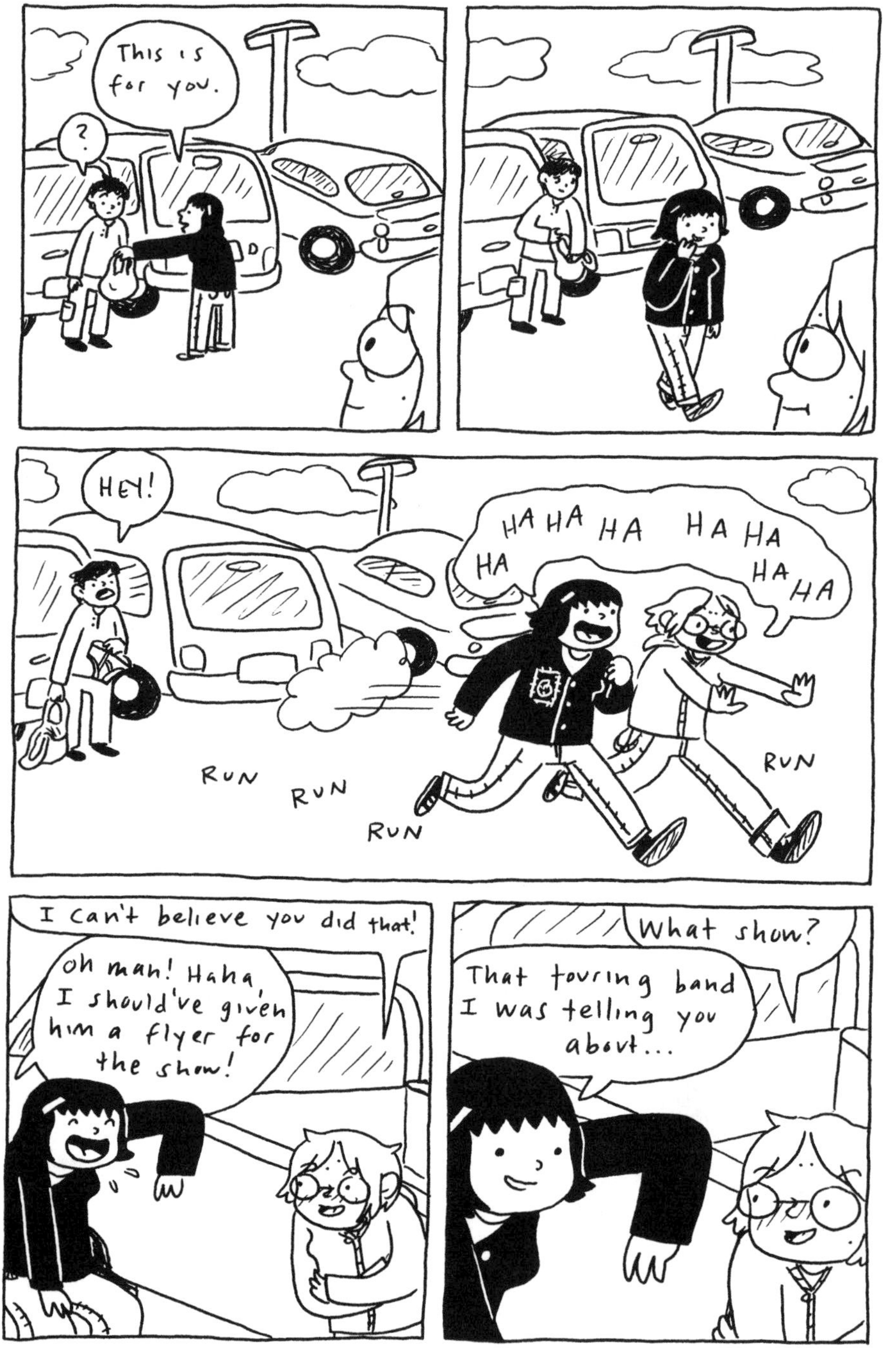
?
This is for you.
HEY!
HA HA HA HA HA HA HA HA HA HA
RUN
RUN
RUN
RUN
I can't believe you did that!
Oh man! Haha, I should've given him a flyer for the show!
What show?
That touring band I was telling you about...

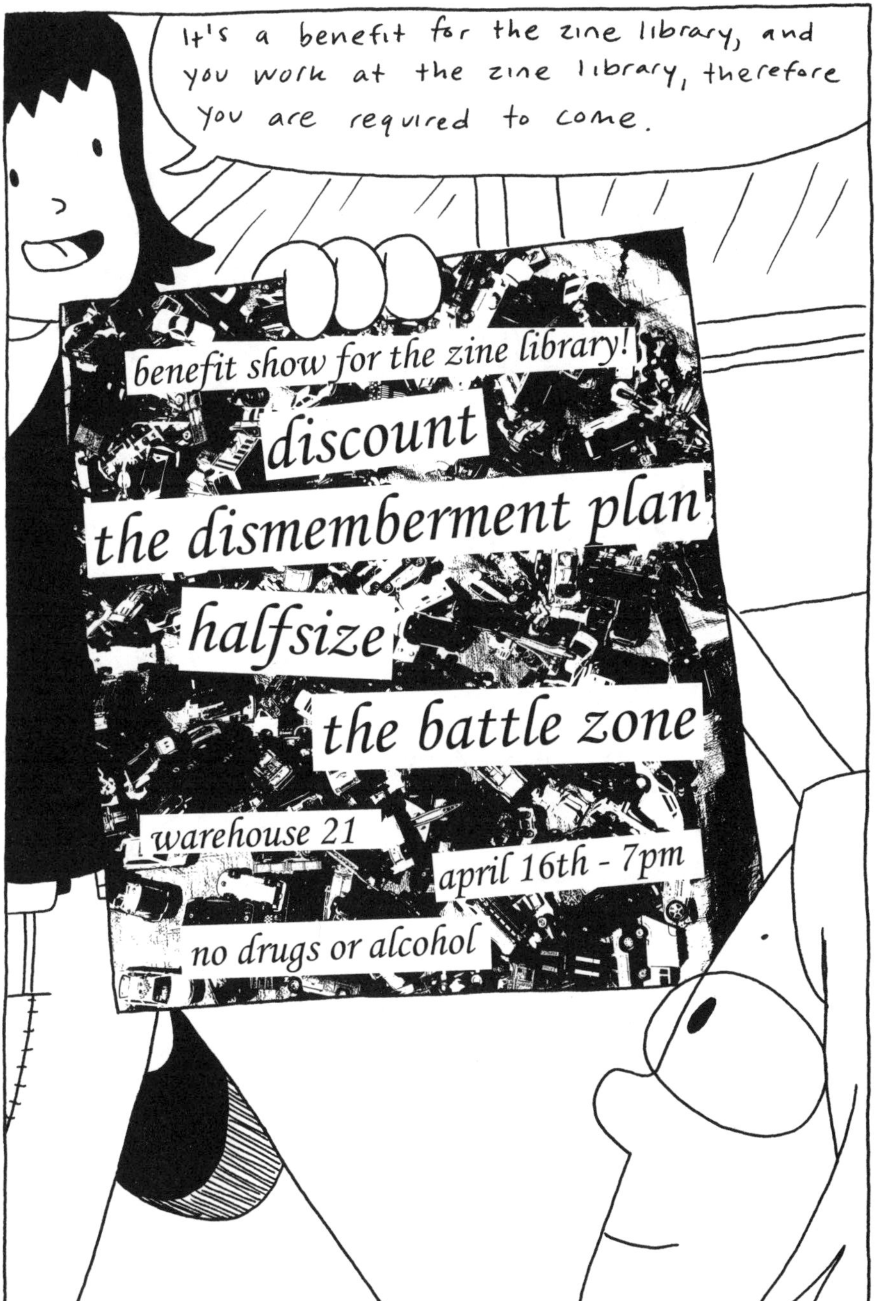
It's a benefit for the zine library, and you work at the zine library, therefore you are required to come.
benefit show for the zine library!
discount
the dismemberment plan
halfsize
the battle zone
warehouse 21
april 16th - 7pm
no drugs or alcohol

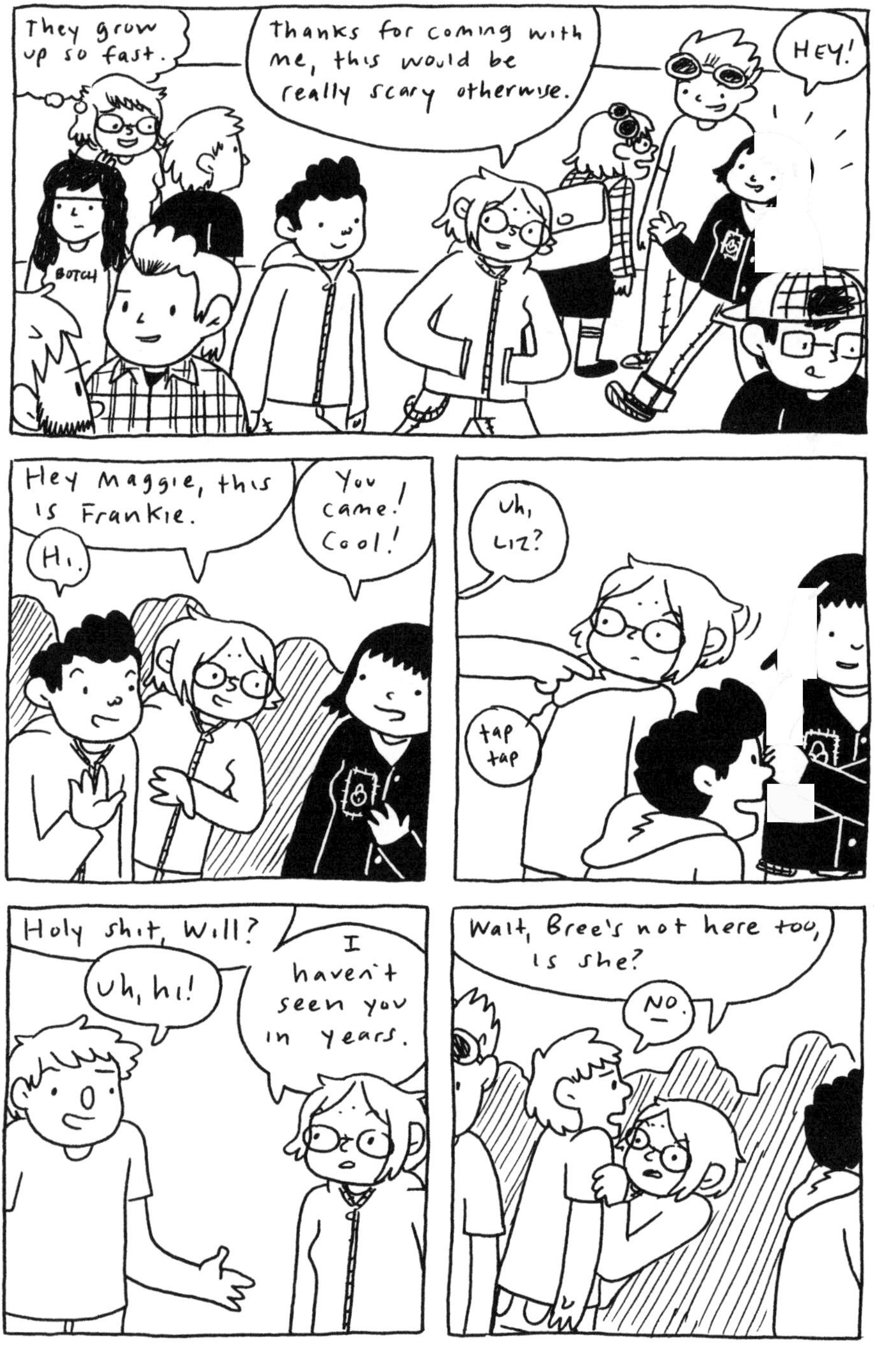
They grow up so fast.
Thanks for coming with me, this would be really scary otherwise.
HEY!
Hey Maggie, this is Frankie.
Hi.
You came! Cool!
Uh, Liz?
tap tap
Holy shit, Will?
Uh, hi!
I haven't seen you in years.
Wait, Bree's not here too, is she?
NO.

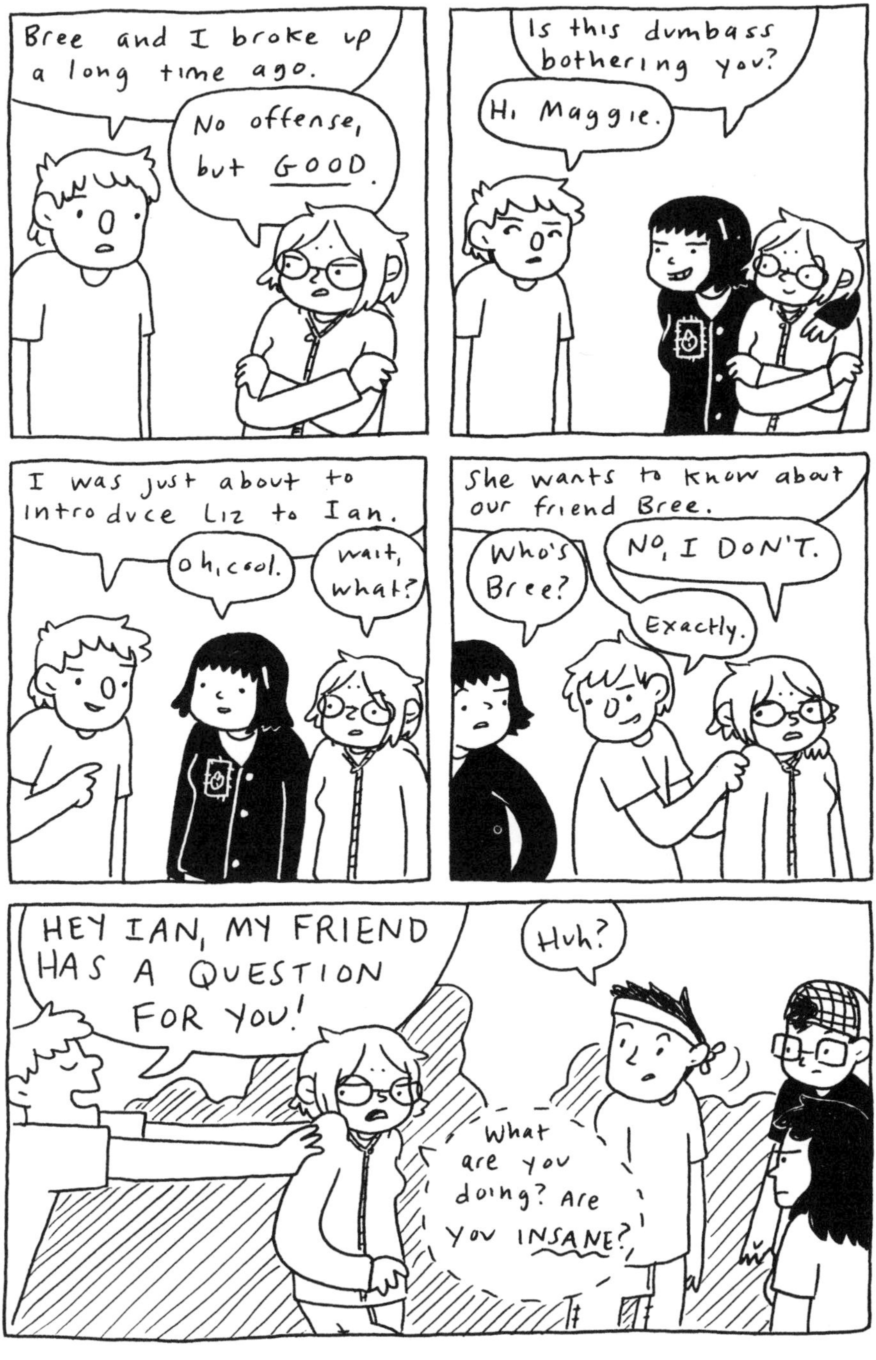
Bree and I broke up a long time ago.
No offense, but GOOD.
Is this dumbass bothering you?
Hi Maggie.
I was just about to introduce Liz to Ian.
Oh, cool.
wait, what?
She wants to know about our friend Bree.
Who's Bree?
No, I DON'T.
Exactly.
HEY IAN, MY FRIEND HAS A QUESTION FOR YOU!
Huh?
What are you doing? Are you INSANE?

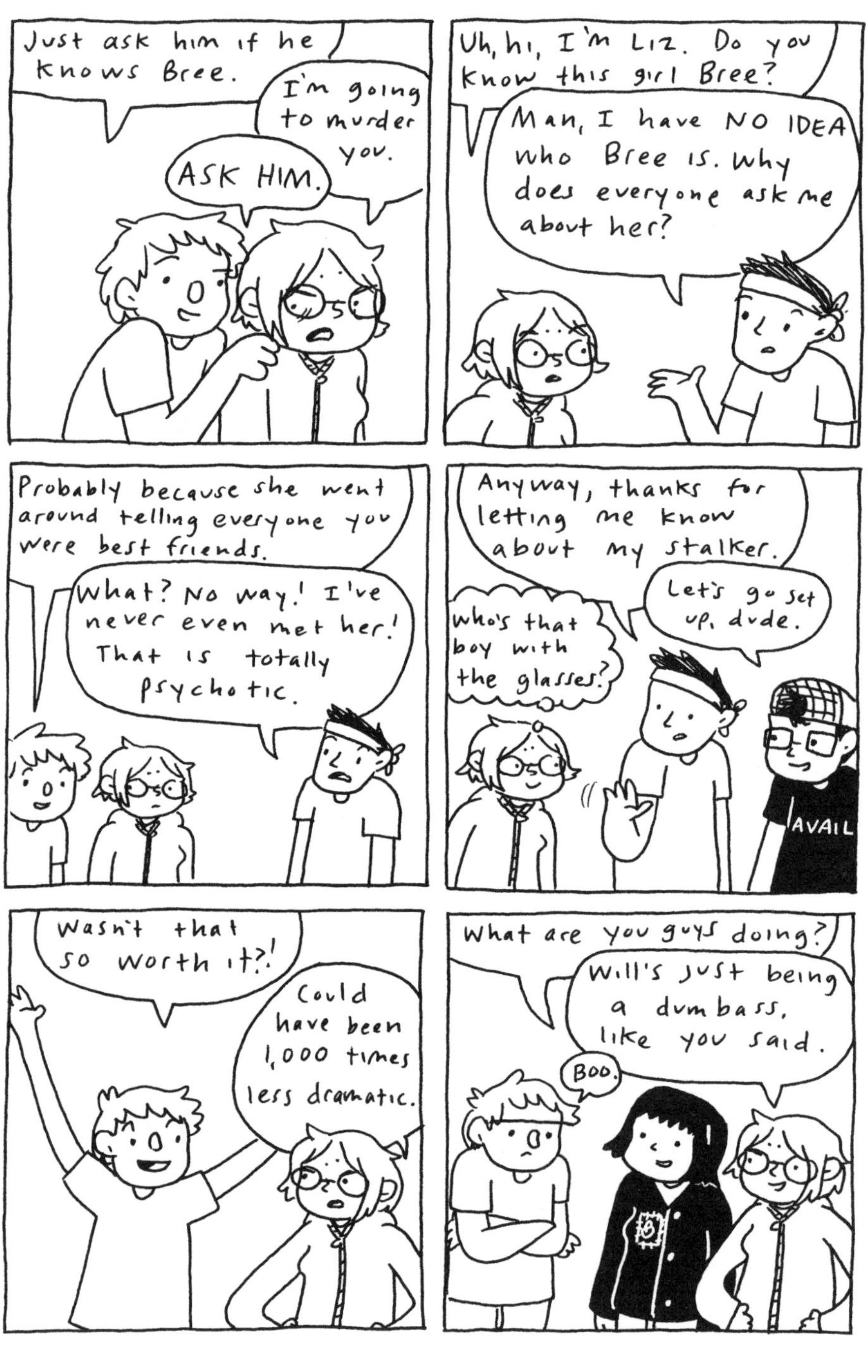
Just ask him if he knows Bree.
I'm going to murder you.
ASK HIM.
Uh, hi, I'm Liz. Do you know this girl Bree?
Man, I have NO IDEA who Bree is. Why does everyone ask me about her?
Probably because she went around telling everyone you were best friends.
What? No way! I've never even met her! That is totally psychotic.
Anyway, thanks for letting me know about my stalker.
Who's that boy with the glasses?
Let's go set up, dude.
AVAIL
Wasn't that so worth it?!
Could have been 1,000 times less dramatic.
What are you guys doing?
Will's just being a dumbass, like you said.
Boo.

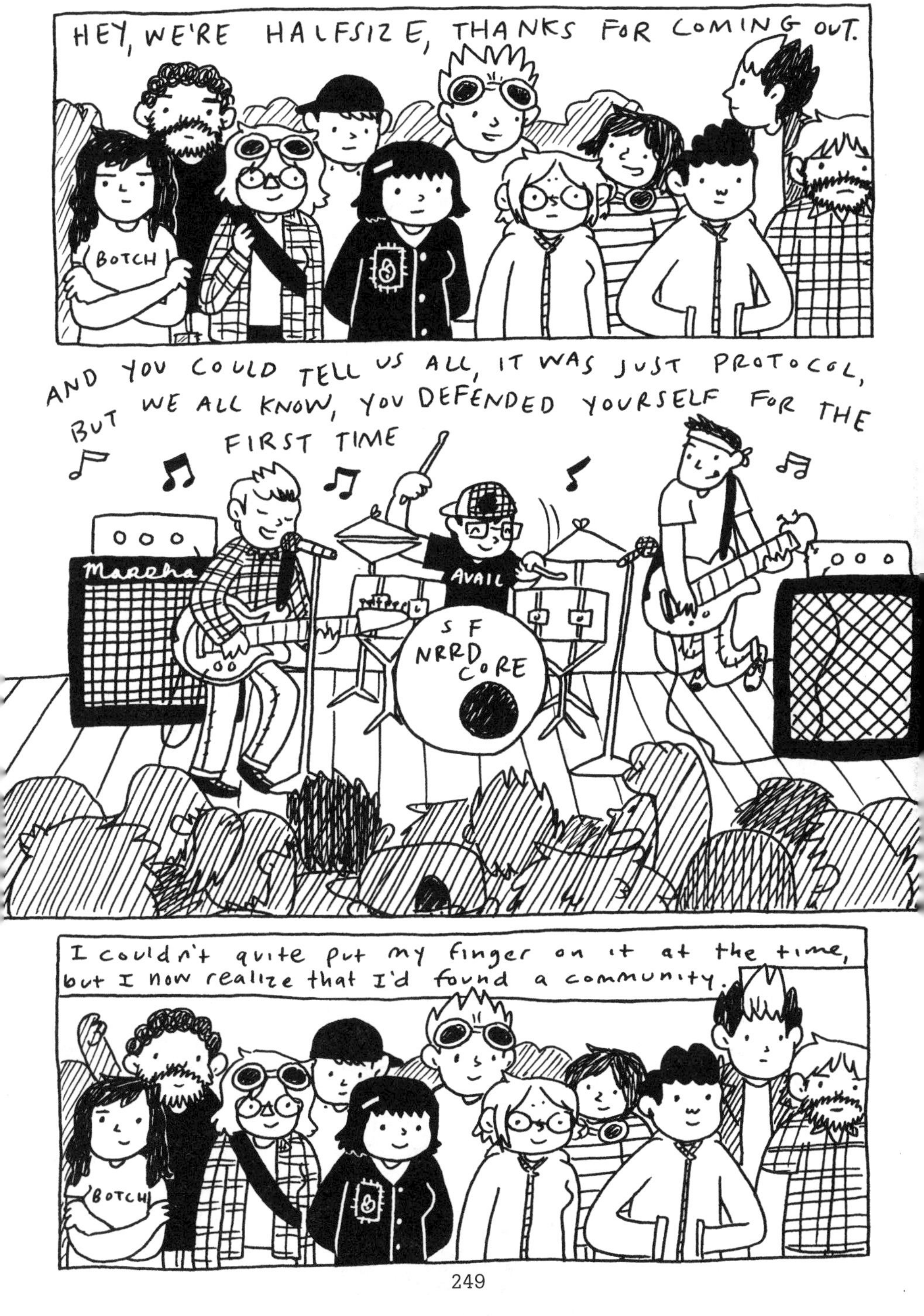
HEY, WE'RE HALFSIZE, THANKS FOR COMING OUT.
BOTCH
AND YOU COULD TELL US ALL, IT WAS JUST PROTOCOL, BUT WE ALL KNOW, YOU DEFENDED YOURSELF FOR THE FIRST TIME
Marsha
AVAIL
S F NRRD CORE
I couldn't quite put my finger on it at the time, but I now realize that I'd found a community.
BOTCH

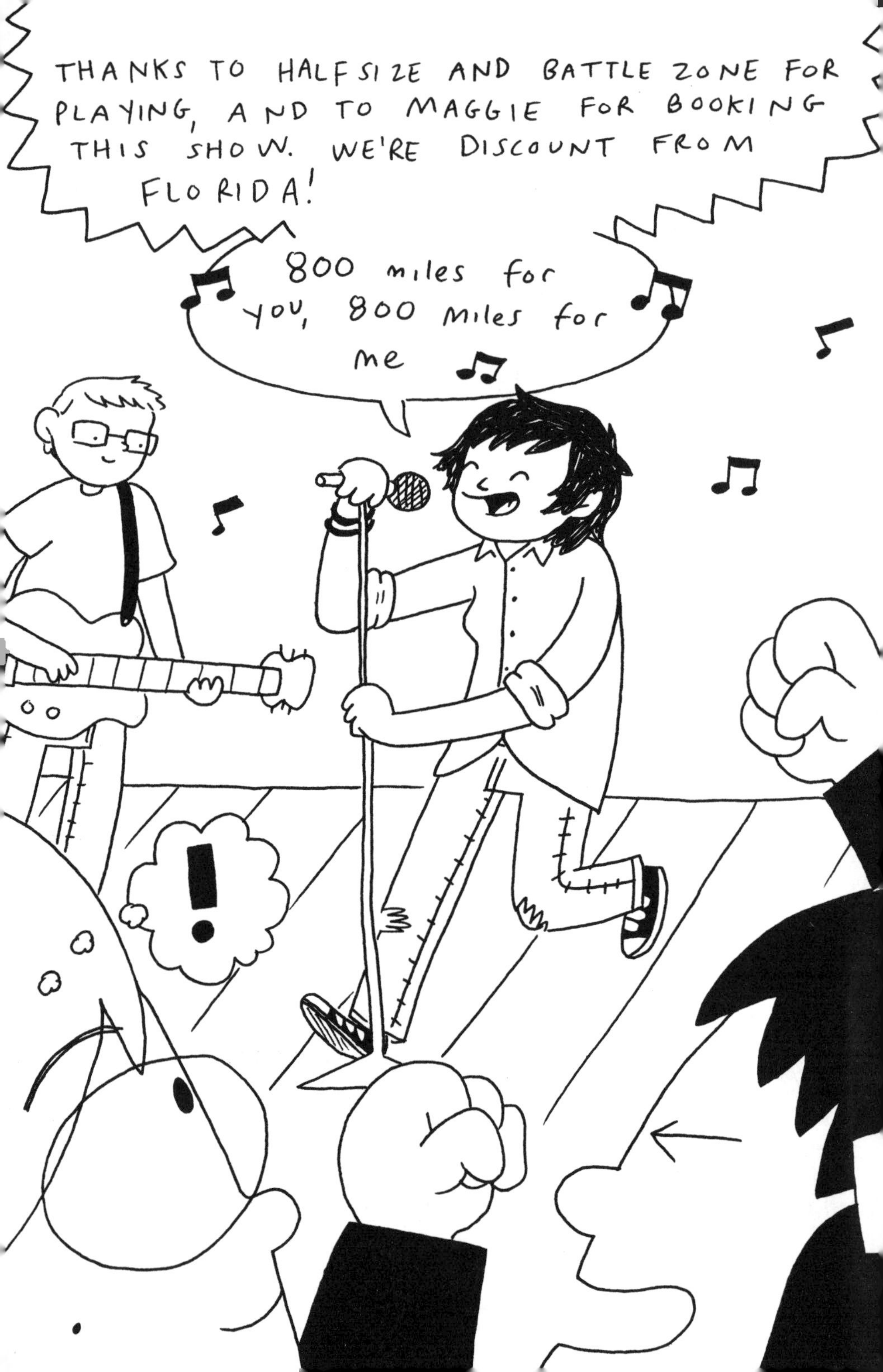
THANKS TO HALFSIZE AND BATTLE ZONE FOR PLAYING, AND TO MAGGIE FOR BOOKING THIS SHOW. WE'RE DISCOUNT FROM FLORIDA!
800 miles for you, 800 miles for me
!

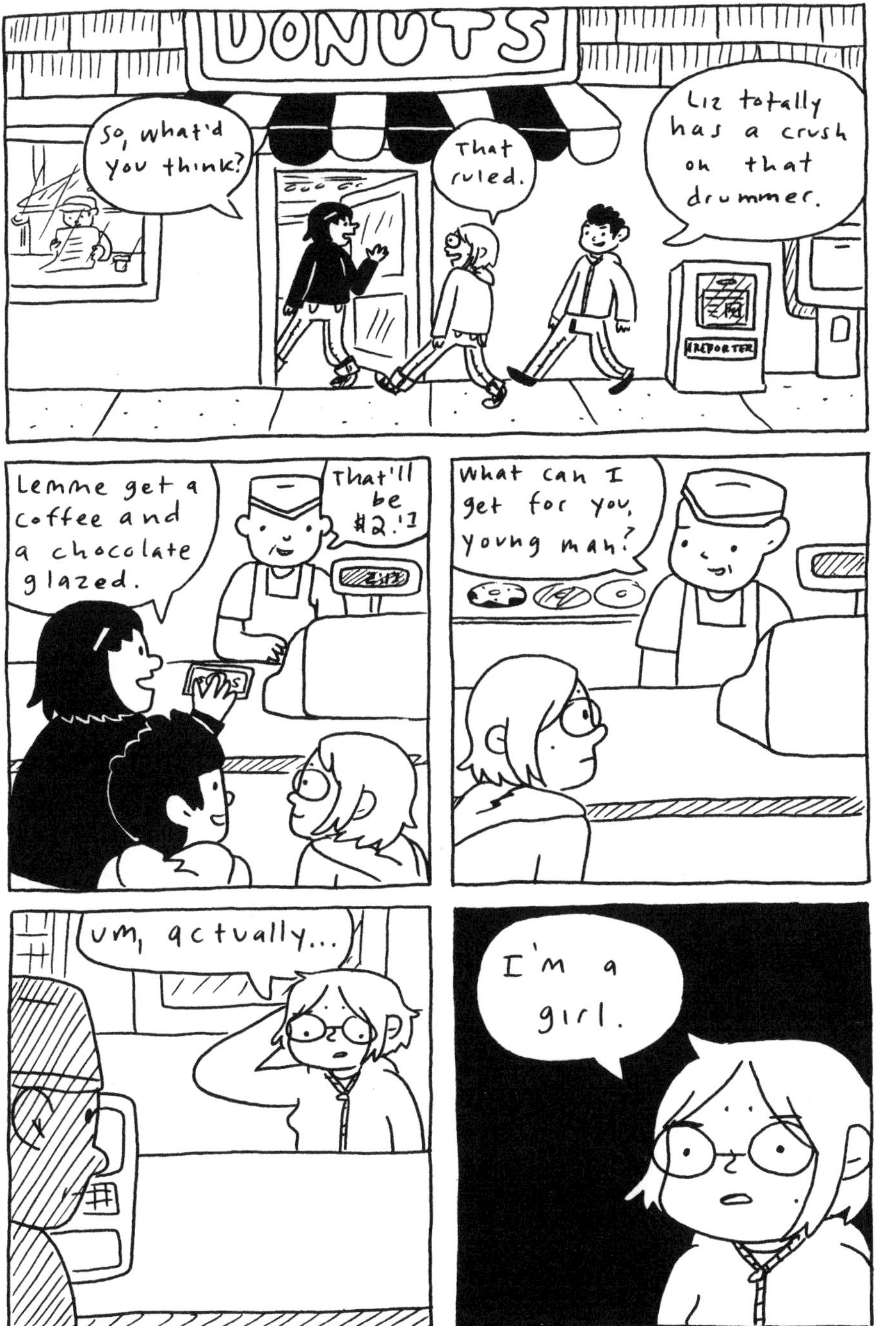
DONUTS
So, what'd you think?
That ruled.
Liz totally has a crush on that drummer.
REPORTER
Lemme get a coffee and a chocolate glazed.
That'll be $2.11
What can I get for you, young man?
um, actually...
I'm a girl.

EPILOGUE

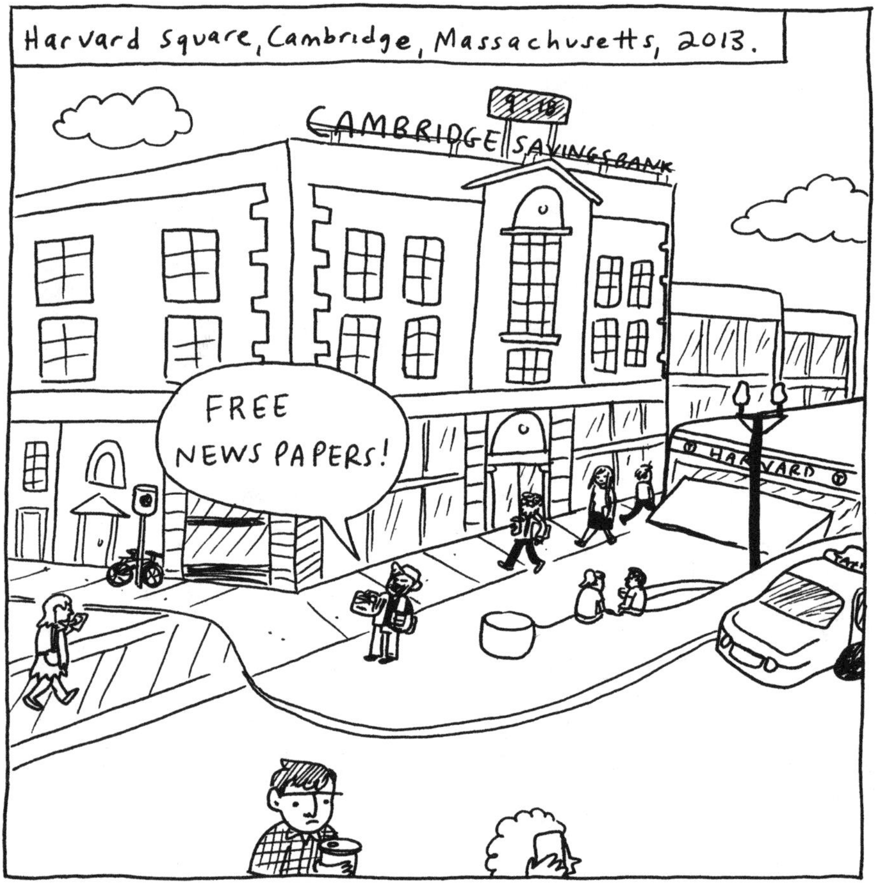
Harvard Square, Cambridge, Massachusetts, 2013.
CAMBRIDGE SAVINGS BANK
FREE NEWS PAPERS!
HARVARD

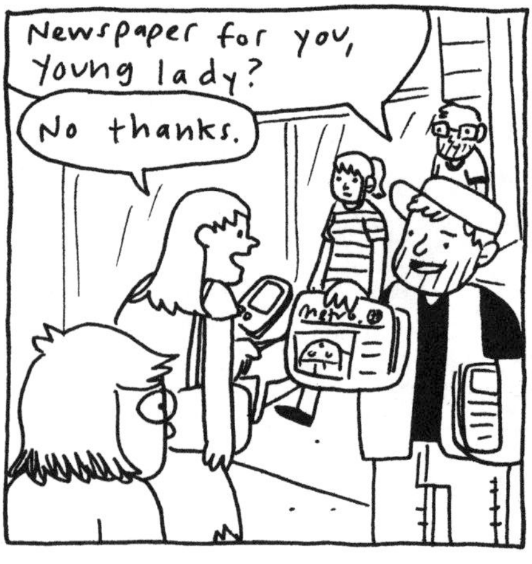
Newspaper for you, young lady?
No thanks.
metro

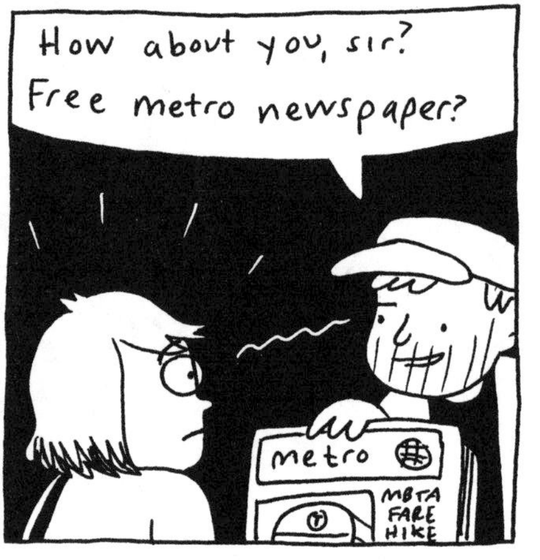
How about you, sir? Free metro newspaper?
metro
MBTA FARE HIKE

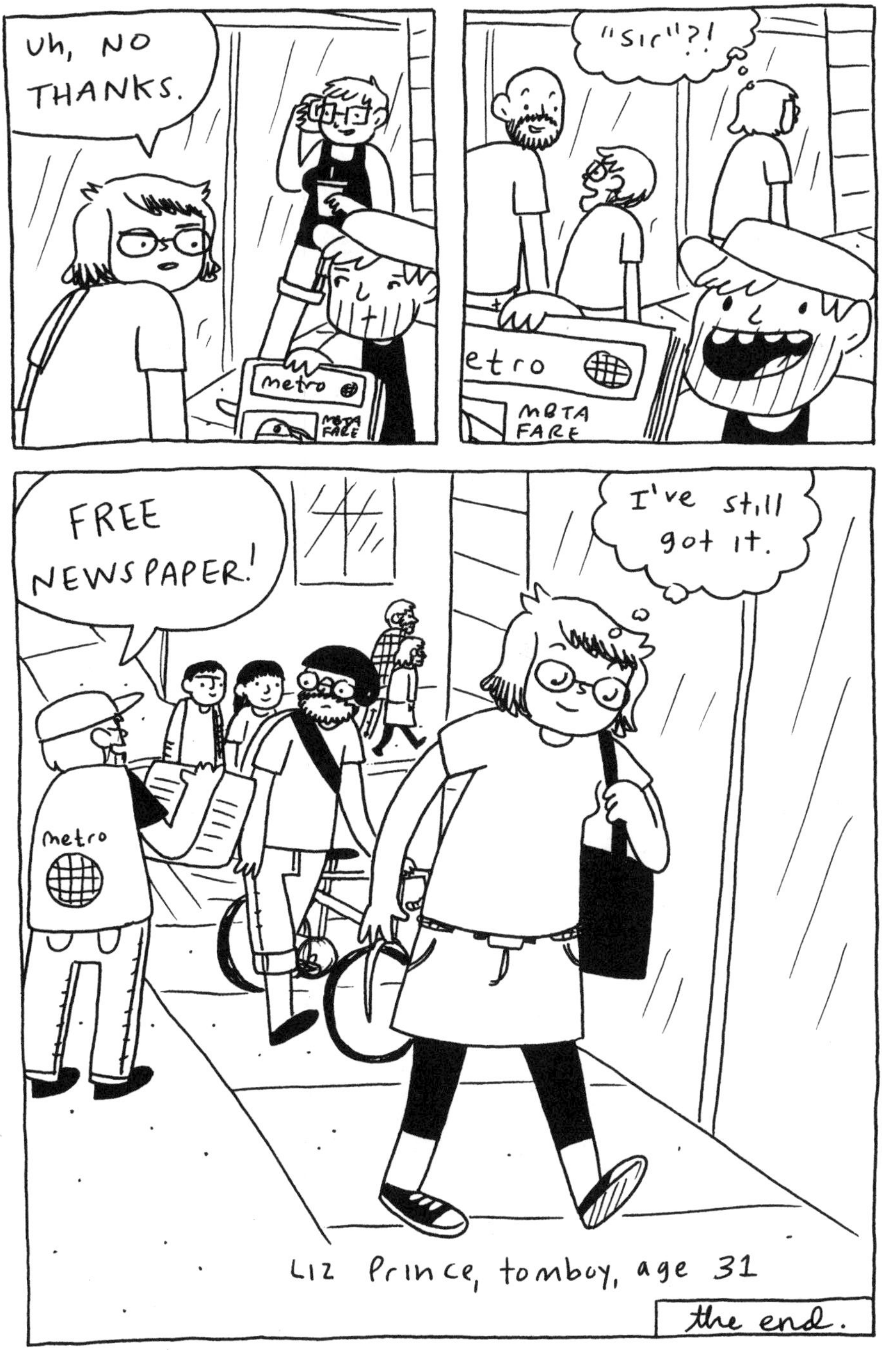
Uh, NO THANKS.
"SIR"?!
metro
MBTA FARE
FREE NEWSPAPER!
I've still got it.
metro
LIZ Prince, tomboy, age 31
the end.

ACKNOWLEDGMENTS

Thank you to my super special pals Jim Kettner, Tim Finn, Jordyn Bonds, Ramsey Beyer, and Joey Prince for reading early drafts of this story and helping strengthen it with their valuable input and eagle-eyed edits.

Much appreciation to my editor, Daniel Harmon, who nurtured my vision and endured my stubbornness: sorry if I put you through the wringer.

Endless gratitude to Kyle Folsom, who not only helped edit ALL drafts of this book, but who also designed the zine pages and show fliers therein. Thanks for being a patient sounding board.

And to my cats, Wolfman and Dracula, thanks for interrupting me every fifteen minutes for a cuddle break. I couldn't have maintained my sanity without you (and they can't read so they'll never even see this!).